JOHN MIRK'S *FESTIAL*

EARLY ENGLISH TEXT SOCIETY
O.S. 334
2009

God maker of alle thyng z // z // z // z // z // z // z //
be at oure begynnyng || z // z // z // z // z // z //
And zef vs alle hys blessyng z // z // z // z // z // z // z //
And bryng vs alle to a good endyng amen. z // z // z // z // z //
¶Y myne owne febul letture y fele how yt faruth by
othur that bene in the same degre that hauen charge of
soulus and bene holdyn to teche hore parischon of alle
the principale festus that cometh in the zere. schewyng
home what the seyntus soffreden and dedun for goddus
loue. so that thay schuldon haue the more deuocon in god
dus seyntys and wt the better wylle com to the chyrche.
to serue god. and pray to holy seyntys of her help. But
for mony excuson ham by defaute of lokus and symful
uys of letture ther in helpe of suche mene clerkus as i am
my selff. i haue drawe this tretu sewyng out of legenda
aurea wt more addyng to. so he that hathe lust to study
there in he schal fynde redy of alle the pnapule festus of the
zere a schort sermon nedful for hym to techym and othur
for to lerne and for this tretu speketh alle of festus. i wolle
and py that it be called a festial the wyche be gynnyth
the forme sonday of the aduent in worschip of god of al
le seyntus that ben wryten ther in. Explicit prefacio mayn
iler qui woatur festial. In dei nomine Amen.

JOHN MIRK'S *FESTIAL*

EDITED FROM BRITISH LIBRARY
MS COTTON CLAUDIUS A.II

BY

SUSAN POWELL

VOLUME I

Published for
THE EARLY ENGLISH TEXT SOCIETY
by the
OXFORD UNIVERSITY PRESS
2009

OXFORD
UNIVERSITY PRESS

Great Clarendon Street, Oxford OX2 6DP

Oxford University Press is a department of the University of Oxford.
It furthers the University's objective of excellence in research, scholarship,
and education by publishing worldwide in

Oxford New York

Auckland Cape Town Dar es Salaam Hong Kong Karachi
Kuala Lumpur Madrid Melbourne Mexico City Nairobi
New Delhi Shanghai Taipei Toronto

With offices in

Argentina Austria Brazil Chile Czech Republic France Greece
Guatemala Hungary Italy Japan Poland Portugal Singapore
South Korea Switzerland Thailand Turkey Ukraine Vietnam

Oxford is a registered trade mark of Oxford University Press
in the UK and in certain other countries

Published in the United States
by Oxford University Press Inc., New York

British Library Cataloguing in Publication Data

Data available

Library of Congress Cataloging in Publication Data

Data applied for

ISBN 978-0-19-957849-8

1 3 5 7 9 10 8 6 4 2

Typeset by Anne Joshua, Oxford
Printed in Great Britain
on acid-free paper by
The Cromwell Press Group, Trowbridge, Wiltshire

TO MY PARENTS
FOR THEIR LOVE AND SUPPORT

PREFACE

The *Festial* has been part of my life since my postgraduate research, when I brushed aside the wise advice of my supervisor, Ron Waldron, that I should look at the Vernon/Simeon lyrics and burrowed instead for something that nobody else had done. In truth, neither the *Festial* Revision which I edited for my London Ph.D., nor the present edition of the *Festial*, was an undertaking that 'nobody else had done'. In particular, I acknowledge the work of Theodor Erbe (1880–?1914), Rhodes Scholar at Merton College, Oxford, who produced Part I of his EETS edition in 1905, was actively working on Part II (which would have contained the Introduction and Notes) in 1908, but was killed in action in the German Artillery in the First World War.

Two collaborators must be acknowledged in this long-gestated work. Martyn F. Wakelin, whose death in 1988 was a sad loss to scholarship, was my first collaborator in a project to edit the Group B manuscripts; Alan J. Fletcher was my second collaborator in the present, larger project and organized a first draft of the manuscript transcription.

Very many colleagues and scholars have contributed to the present result. I am grateful to the Arts and Humanities Research Board (as it was then) for a Research Leave Award which enabled me (with matching leave from the University of Salford) to bring this project to near-completion. Formal acknowledgements must be made to the Marquess of Salisbury for permission to quote from MS Hatfield House Cecil Papers 280, to the Trustees of Dr Williams's Library for permission to quote from their MS Ancient 11, and to the British Library for permission to reproduce plates of MS Cotton Claudius A.II. For information on the etymology of Mirk, I am grateful to Professor Tom Schmidt and Dr Peter McClure. For their opinions on the manuscripts, I am indebted to Dr Ian Doyle (as to much more), Miss Pamela Robinson, Dr Michelle Brown, Dr Colin G. C. Tite; most recently, Professor Malcolm Parkes and Dr Keith Williamson have been immensely helpful in matters of hands and location respectively. For the translations of MS Havod 22 I am grateful to Professor John Hines and for opinions on its dialect and date to Dr Ian Hughes. Martyn Wakelin's widow, Diane, provided me with all Martyn's academic papers, for which I have been most grateful. Staff have been generous of their time at all the libraries where I have consulted manuscripts, perhaps most especially at the British Library, London.

Finally, I wish to thank Professors Anne Hudson and Derek Pearsall, whose wisdom and perseverance have, I think, been rewarded by a leaner and more coherent piece of work; Dr Bonnie J. Blackburn and Anne Joshua, the copy-editor and typesetter of these volumes; Dr Veronica O'Mara, who has shown unfailing commitment to the duties of both friendship and scholarship; and my husband, who has lived with the *Festial* in one incarnation or another for over forty years and is in the enviable position of knowing little more about it now than he did then.

S.P.

CONTENTS OF VOLUME I

LIST OF PLATES   xii

THE *FESTIAL* MANUSCRIPTS AND SIGLA   xiii

ABBREVIATIONS   xv

INTRODUCTION   xix
1. John Mirk: His Life and Works   xix
2. The Sermons of the *Festial*   xxviii
3. The Transmission of the *Festial* from Manuscript to Printed Book   xliii
4. The Relationship of the Manuscripts of the *Festial*   lix
5. The Scribal Production of MS Cotton Claudius A.II   lxxxiii
6. MS Cotton Claudius A.II as Base-Text   cx
BIBLIOGRAPHY   cxxviii

THE *FESTIAL*
Prayer   3
Prologue   3
1. Advent   3
2. St Andrew (30 November)   7
3. St Nicholas (6 December)   12
4. Conception of the Virgin (8 December)   17
5. St Thomas Apostle (21 December)   20
6. Nativity of Christ (25 December)   23
7. St Stephen (26 December)   28
8. St John Evangelist (27 December)   31
9. Holy Innocents (28 December)   35
10. St Thomas of Canterbury (29 December)   38
11. Circumcision of Christ (1 January)   44
12. Epiphany (6 January)   47
13. Conversion of St Paul (25 January)   51
14. Purification of the Virgin (2 February)   55
15. Septuagesima   60
16. Sexagesima   66
17. Quinquagesima   70
18. St Matthias (24 February)   75
19. 1 Lent   77

20. 2 Lent   81
21. 3 Lent   84
22. 4 Lent   88
23. Annunciation of the Virgin (25 March)   93
24. Passion Sunday   97
25. Palm Sunday   100
26. Tenebre   103
27. Good Friday   105
28. Maundy Thursday/Easter Eve   110
29. Easter Sunday   114
30. St George (23 April)   117
31. St Mark (25 April)   120
32. SS Philip and James (1 May)   123
33. Invention of the Cross (3 May)   126
34. 1 Lent (second sermon)   130
35. St John at the Latin Gate (6 May)   136
36. Rogation Days   138
37. Ascension Day   140
38. Eve of Pentecost   144
39. Pentecost   146
40. Trinity Sunday   150
41. Corpus Christi   154
42. St Barnabas (11 June)   160
43. St Winifred (21 June)   162
44. Nativity of St John Baptist (24 June)   166
45. SS Peter and Paul (29 June)   170
46. Life of Nero   174
47. Translation of St Thomas of Canterbury (7 July)   178
48. St Margaret (20 July)   181
49. St Mary Magdalene (22 July)   184
50. St James Apostle (25 July)   189
51. St Anne (26 July)   193
52. St Laurence (10 August)   195
53. Assumption of the Virgin (15 August)   200
54. Assumption of the Virgin (second sermon)   206
55. St Bartholomew (24 August)   213
56. St Alkmund (19 March)   218
57. Nativity of the Virgin (8 September)   221
58. Exaltation of the Cross (14 September)   225
59. Ember Days   228

60. St Matthew (21 September)   229
61. St Michael (29 September)   232
62. St Luke (18 October)   235
63. SS Simon and Jude (28 October)   237
64. All Saints (1 November)   239
65. All Souls (2 November)   241
66. St Martin (11 November)   244
67. St Katherine (25 November)   246
68. Dedication of a Church   249
Additional 1. Marriage sermon   252
Additional 2. Burial sermon   256
Additional 3. Burial notes   259
Additional 4. *Ave Maria*   261
Additional 5. Miracles of the Virgin   262
Additional 6. Paternoster sermon   262

[Sermons 50–68 and the six Additional Sermons are in Volume II]

LIST OF PLATES

MS Cotton Claudius A.II, f. 3^v (Hand A)   *Frontispiece*

1 MS Cotton Claudius A.II, f. 4^r (Hand B)   xc
2 MS Cotton Claudius A.II, f. 28^r (Hand C)   xcii
3 MS Cotton Claudius A.II, f. 40^r (Hand D)   xciv
4 MS Cotton Claudius A.II, f. 52^r (Hand D*)   xcvii
5 MS Cotton Claudius A.II, f. 122^v (Hand D/D*)   xcviii

THE *FESTIAL* MANUSCRIPTS AND SIGLA

α   London, BL MS Cotton Claudius A.II

GROUP A

A   London, BL MS Lansdowne 392
B   London, BL MS Harley 2403
C   London, BL MSS Harley 2420 and 2417 (originally a single manuscript)
D   Oxford, Bodleian Library MS Gough Ecclesiastical Topography 4
E   Oxford, Bodleian Library MS Douce 60
F   Oxford, Bodleian Library MS Douce 108
G   Oxford, Bodleian Library MS Hatton 96 (G(1), G(2), G(3) refer to the first, second, third occurrence of a particular sermon in G)
H   Cambridge, CUL MS Dd.10.50
I   Cambridge, Gonville and Caius College MS 168/89
J   London, Dr William's Library, London MS Ancient 11 (*olim* London, New College MS Z.c.19)
K   Southwell Minster Library MS 7

GROUP B

a   London, BL MS Harley 2371
b   London, BL MS Harley 2391
c   Oxford, Bodleian Library MS Rawlinson A.381
d   Oxford, Bodleian Library MS University College Oxford D.102
e   Leeds University Library, Brotherton Collection MS 502
f   Durham University Library MS Cosin V.III.5
g   Dublin, Trinity College MS 201
h   Hatfield House, Cecil Papers 280

THE REVISION

R1   London, BL MS Harley 2247
R2   London, BL MS Royal 18.B.XXV
R3   Dublin, Trinity College MS 428
R4   Gloucester Cathedral Library MS 22Add

THE RELATED MANUSCRIPTS

O   Oxford, Bodleian Library MS e Museo 180
Du   Durham, Durham University Library MS V.IV.3
Gl   Gloucester Cathedral Library MS 22 (*olim* 22, second binding)
L   Lincoln Cathedral Chapter Library MSS 50 and 51 (*olim* A.6.2
     and A.7.1)

OTHER MANUSCRIPTS CONTAINING *F* MATERIAL
(WITHOUT SIGLA)

Cambridge, CUL MS Ee.2.15
Cambridge, CUL MS Ff.2.38
Cambridge, CUL MS Nn.3.10
Cambridge, St John's College MS G.19
Cardiff, Public Library MS Havod 22
Lincoln, Cathedral Library MS 133
London, BL MS Arundel 279
London, BL MS Cotton Titus A.XXVI
London, BL MS Harley 1288
London, BL MS Harley 2250
London, BL MS Lansdowne 379
London, BL MS Royal 18.B.XXIII
Oxford, Bodleian Library MS Greaves 54
Oxford, Bodleian Library MS Bodley 123
Stonyhurst, College Library MS A.II.8 (St)
York, Borthwick Institute H.C.C.P. 1590/5

ABBREVIATIONS

Add	Additional sermon
add.	added
alt.	altered
AS	*Acta Sanctorum* [ed. J. Bollandus, G. Henschenius, et al.]; new edn. by J. Carnandet, 66 vols. (variously Paris, Rome, Brussels, 1863–1925)
AV	*The Bible: Authorized Version* (Oxford, 1954)
BL	British Library
canc.	cancelled
CUL	Cambridge University Library
dec.	*decorated*
Douay	*The Holy Bible translated from the Latin Vulgate diligently compared with the Hebrew, Greek, and other Editions in Divers Languages* (Old Testament 1609, New Testament 1582), new edn. (n.p.: Brepols, 1953)
EETS	Early English Text Society
Eng.	English
er.	erased
eras.	erasure
ex.	L. *extremum* ('end')
F	the *Festial*
FM	*Fasciculus Morum*
foll.	followed
Fr.	French
Gk.	Greek
GO	*Glossa Ordinaria* (*PL* 113–14: marginal gloss only)
GR	*Gesta Romanorum*
IMEP	*Index of Middle English Prose*
IMEV	Julia Boffey and A. S. G. Edwards, *A New Index of Middle English Verse* (London, 2005)
imp.	imperfect
in.	L. *initium* ('beginning')
IPP	*Instructions for Parish Priests*
JEH	*Journal of Ecclesiastical History*
L.	Latin
LA	*Legenda Aurea*

LALME	*A Linguistic Atlas of Late Mediaeval English*, ed. Angus McIntosh, M. L. Samuels, and M. Benskin, 4 vols. (Aberdeen, 1986)
LFC	*The Lay Folk's* Catechism, ed. T. F. Simmons and H. E. Nolloth, EETS os 118 (1901)
LFMB	*The Lay Folk's Mass Book*, ed. T. F. Simmons, EETS os 71 (1879)
lit.	literally
LP	Linguistic Profile
LSE	*Leeds Studies in English*
MÆ	*Medium Ævum*
ME	Middle English
MED	*Middle English Dictionary*, ed. Hans Kurath, S. M. Kuhn, and Robert E. Lewis (Ann Arbor, Mich., 1954–99)
med.	L. *medium* ('middle')
MedSt	*Medieval Studies*
MET	Middle English Texts
MLN	*Modern Language Notes*
MMBL	*Medieval Manuscripts in British Libraries*, ed. N. R. Ker, 5 vols. (vol. 4 with A. J. Piper, vol. 5 with I. C. Cunningham and A. G. Watson) (Oxford, 1969–2003)
MS	*Manuale Sacerdotis*
n	note (placed after a reference to indicate that there is an Explanatory Note, e.g. 'see 28/162–4n')
N&Q	*Notes and Queries*
NM	*Neuphilologische Mitteilungen*
no./nos.	(sermon) number(s)
NS	New Series
NT	New Testament
oblit.	obliterated
ODNB	*Oxford Dictionary of National Biography* (Oxford, 2004)
OE	Old English
OED	*The Oxford English Dictionary Online*
OF	Old French
OI	Old Icelandic
om.	omitted
ON	Old Norse
OT	Old Testament
PG	*Patrologiae Cursus Completus: Series Graeca*, ed. J.-P. Migne, 161 vols. (Paris, 1857–66)

PL	*Patrologiae Cursus Completus: Series Latina*, ed. J.-P. Migne, 221 vols. (Paris, 1844–64)
Pr	Prayer
prec.	preceded
Pro	Prologue
punct.	punctuated
QS	*Quattuor Sermones*
RCHM York	*An Inventory of the Historical Monuments in the City of York*, 5 vols., Royal Commission on Historical Monuments (London, 1962–81)
RDO	*Rationale Divinorum Officiorum* (*PL* 202 and see Bibliography: Douteil 1976)
rep.	repeated
RES	*Review of English Studies*
Rev.	the Revised *Festial* (R1–4)
s.	L. *saeculum* ('century')
sc.	L. *scilicet* ('understood', used when an ellipsis is expanded)
SEL	*The South English Legendary*, ed. Charlotte D'Evelyn and Anna J. Mill, 3 vols., EETS 235, 236, 244 (1956–9)
SENM&C	*The South English Nativity of Mary and Christ: ed. from MS BM Stowe 949*, ed. O. S. Pickering, MET 1 (Heidelberg, 1975)
SS	Saints
St	Saint
STC	*A Short-Title Catalogue of Books Printed in England, Scotland, and Ireland and of English Books Printed Abroad 1475–1640*, 2nd edn. rev. and enlarged, ed. W. A. Jackson, F. S. Ferguson, and K. L. Pantzer, 3 vols. (London, 1976–86)
sub	L. ('under', i.e. under the entry for)
TRHS	*Transactions of the Royal Historical Society*
trs.	transposed
VCH	Victoria History of the Counties of England
viz.	L. *videlicet* ('namely')
Vulgate	*Biblia Sacra Vulgatae Editionis Sixti Pont. Max. Iussu Recognita et Clementis VIII Auctoritate Edita*, ed. P. Michael Hetzenauer (Regensburg and Rome, 1914)
v./vv.	verse(s) (within a Bible chapter)
v.v.	vice versa

INTRODUCTION

1. JOHN MIRK: HIS LIFE AND WORKS

The *Festial* (*F*) was written, probably in the late 1380s, by John Mirk, canon and later prior of the Augustinian abbey of Lilleshall in Shropshire. Mirk conceived the collection as sixty-four sermons for the major feasts of the Church calendar, from Advent Sunday to the Dedication of a Church.[1] In addition to *F*, in what may be seen as a campaign to combat the ignorance of parish priests, perhaps particularly the unbeneficed clergy, Mirk wrote two manuals, one in the vernacular, known as the *Instructions for Parish Priests* (*IPP*), and another in Latin, the *Manuale Sacerdotis* (*MS*). The main source of *F*, as Mirk acknowledges in his Prologue, is the *Legenda Aurea* (*LA*) of Jacobus de Voragine, the source of numerous sermons and legendaries from its composition in late thirteenth-century Genoa throughout the European Middle Ages.[2]

The aim of *F* was to provide accessible preaching material for a typical poor parish, and it would appear to have been widely preached in such a context throughout the late Middle Ages and into the sixteenth century. It underwent an early recension (Group B) which resulted in not only textual variation and the omission of some sermons but also in a major reordering of the material into the service-book categories of *Temporale* and *Sanctorale*. This recension itself formed the basis of a major Revision (Rev.) of *F* some time after 1434, in which Mirk's sermons were comprehensively rewritten and intercalated with sermons from other sources in order to produce a more scholarly collection aimed at a more sophisticated audience. Rev. appears not to have attracted a wide circulation, and it was the recension, rather than the revision, which formed the basis for Caxton's first edition of 30 June 1483 (*STC* 17957). This, and subsequent editions and prints up to 1532, gave *F* a prominence unique amongst vernacular sermon collections before the Reformation. After 1532 its publication ceased altogether until the first volume of the scholarly edition by Theodor Erbe appeared in

---

[1] For this calculation, see §2.

[2] Ed. Graesse 1846, trans. Ryan 1993, ed. Maggioni 1998. Graesse is the basis for Ryan's translation and is used throughout this edition.

1905,[3] although there is evidence that the sermons continued to be read well into the sixteenth century (Powell 1994).

1.1. John Mirk, the Order of St Augustine of Hippo, and Lilleshall Abbey

The few known facts relating to the author of *F* are entirely dependent on internal references in manuscripts of his three works.[4] The consensus is that he was indeed John Mirk, although only the Latinized version of his name is recorded. The manuscript which forms the base-text of this edition, London, BL MS Cotton Claudius A.II (α), records the name *Iohanne[s] Mirkus/Myrcus* in the explicits to his two English works, *F* and *IPP*,[5] and three of the manuscripts of Mirk's Latin work *MS* similarly cite his name as *Mircus/Myrcus*.[6] It should, however, be noted that the variant *Marcus/Markus*[7] also occurs.[8]

If his name is a little uncertain, all the texts which record his domicile cite Lilleshall, an Austin canon house in Shropshire which had been settled from St Peter's Dorchester 1145–8 (Eyton 1854–60: viii. 210–27; Chibnall 1973: 70–80; Baugh & Cox 1988: 17–24). The ascription is again fullest in the two Cotton Claudius explicits, which refer to him as a canon regular of Lilleshall. In the prefatory dedication to *MS* Mirk refers to himself as prior of Lilleshall,[9] and it has been suggested that he wrote his two English pastoral works as canon, and his more advanced Latin manual as prior.[10]

Mirk himself refers to Lilleshall in two *F* sermons (see Glossary of

---

[3] Erbe's death in the First World War explains the absence of Part II (Introduction and Notes).

[4] For a brief biography, see Powell 2004; for a fuller discussion, see Powell 2006.

[5] See §5.1, Contents.

[6] MSS York Minster Library XVI.L.8 (*Mircus*, f. 11ʳ), Cambridge, Peterhouse 236 (*Myrcus*, f. 1ᵛ second booklet), and Oxford, Bodleian Library Bodley 632 (*Myrcus*, f. 98ᵛ).

[7] MSS Oxford, Bodleian Library Jesus College 1 (*Iohannem Marcus*, f. 129ᵛ) and Cambridge, Trinity College Library B.11.24 (*Iohannem Markus*, f. 93ʳ).

[8] The name *John Meyre* recorded in Southwell Minster Library MS VII, f. 171ᵛ (*explicit liber festiualis quod Iohannes meyre*) may be that of the scribe. The initials I. M. occur in Oxford, Bodleian Library MS Douce 108, p. 204 (*mary mircy Quod I. M.*).

[9] For example, Oxford, Bodleian Library MS Bodley 632, f. 68ʳ: *Amico suo karissimo domino B. uicario de A., Iohannes, dictus prior de Lylleshull, salutem in auctore salutis.* Of the ten manuscripts which include the *Prefacio*, only York Minster Library MS XVI.O.11 omits the *uicario . . . Lylleshull* reference.

[10] Fletcher 1987: 222. This is not inherently unlikely, but the references to Mirk as canon are later so cannot have the same status as Mirk's own reference to himself as prior in *MS*.

Proper Names *sub* Lylleshul(l)), but it is possible that his origins were not local. The name would appear to be a Scandinavian (most likely Danish) byname (*myrk(i)*), originally given to a dark-haired person. The evidence for the adjective *mirk(e)* ('dark') in *MED* and in place names indicates that it was common in Cumberland, Lancashire, Yorkshire, and the East Midlands but was spreading beyond those Danish-settled areas by the fourteenth century, although the relationship between adjective and byname is doubtful.[11] This offers some likelihood that Mirk's ancestry was Scandinavian, presumably from a more northerly or easterly part of England than Lilleshall. It would appear too that *IPP* originally utilized Northern rhymes alien to the dialect of Lilleshall (Kristensson 1974: 56–7).

It is tempting to link Mirk with his contemporary, Thomas Merk(e), bishop of Carlisle, d. 1409/10 (Davies 2004). Carlisle was the only cathedral served by Austin canons, who were, like those at Lilleshall, of the Arrouaisian order (Salter 1922: xi, xliv–xlv), and it is conceivable (but entirely speculative) that Mirk had spent time there. The references to his being canon and prior tend to encourage the assumption that he spent all his adult life at Lilleshall, but residence elsewhere at some stage in his career would provide one explanation for less westerly rhymes in *F* (see Appendix IV.5), as well as *IPP*. Merk himself was a Benedictine and was not appointed to Carlisle until 1397, when it may be assumed that our Mirk was already well established at Lilleshall, but, as a close associate of Richard II from the early 1390s, Bishop Merk, if a relative, may have had some influence in relation to Lilleshall, a quasi-royal foundation visited by the king in 1398 (Powell 2006: 175).

As for Mirk's own dates, it is now accepted that *F* belongs to the later 1380s,[12] with *IPP* possibly an earlier work and, as has been suggested above, *MS* perhaps later.[13] The explicits to *F* and *IPP* (*cuius anime propicietur deus*) seem to indicate that he was dead by at least the early fifteenth century (the likely date of the hand of the *F* explicit).[14] There is no record of his having been at either University,

---

[11] The name is not recorded in dictionaries of English surnames, but see Black (1946) for Scottish examples from the 16th to 20th cc.

[12] Powell 1982, Fletcher 1987: 218. The pre-2004 *DNB* dating of Mirk as '*fl.* ?1403' was based on the note of John Pits (1560–1616) in London, BL MS Harley 5306, f. 1ᵛ.

[13] Since references to Lollards are a contributory factor in the dating of *F*, it may be significant that *IPP* does not mention Lollards, whereas *MS* does (Fletcher 1987: 223 n. 8). For the Lollard references in *F*, see 40/27–47n, 41/106–9n. (Note: 'n' after a reference indicates an Explanatory Note.)   [14] See §5.2.1 Hand D below and §5 *passim*.

although it is possible that he at least attended lectures for some time.[15] Since Lilleshall was Arrouaisian, it was not under the jurisdiction of the Augustinian general chapters[16] and so was not required to keep a canon at University.[17] Only one canon, William of Longdon, is known to have been licensed, in 1400, to study at University for ten years (Chibnall 1973: 76), and the Austin canons had no college at Oxford until St Mary's was established in 1458, although by the mid-twelfth century the college of St George's in the Castle had close ties with the Austin canons of Oseney.[18]

A brief discussion of the order of Augustinian canons is relevant in order to place Mirk and his work in context. Austin, or black, canons appeared first in England in the eleventh century; their great period of expansion was the twelfth century (Dickinson 1950). 'A hybrid order of clerical monks' (Lawrence 1989: 163), they were usually in holy orders but lived a communal life. The Lateran Council of 1139 required all regular canons to follow the Rule of St Augustine of Hippo, but, in the case of Arrouaisian houses, the Rule was influenced by the Cistercian Rule.[19] Founded in imitation of the Apostles, the Austin canons were directed to be a missionary order by Lateran Councils of 1059 and 1063 (Postles 1993: 2). Although never many nor powerful, they became the largest religious institution in England, with 274 (admittedly small) houses (the Benedictines had 219), and so their presence was pervasive (Lawrence 1989: 167). They served churches and administered hospitals and were two or three

---

[15] See Evans 1992 for the variety of opportunities for study at Oxford, which is more likely than Cambridge to have been Mirk's University town, if he had one (p. 518). The absence of his name from Emden 1957–9, 1963 does not preclude University attendance, however, or even graduation, since Evans notes that Emden's data 'may well relate to only 15–25 per cent of the men who actually attended the university' (p. 519). For the prominence of regular clergy at Oxford before 1500, at least half of whom proceeded to a higher faculty in theology, or, less likely, canon law (for which Austin canons showed a particular interest), see Dobson 1992: 568–71.

[16] Indeed, canons seem to have occasionally transferred themselves to the Arrouaisians to escape visitations (Salter 1922: xxxvi).

[17] The 1339 Constitutions of Benedict XII (on which see McDonald 1986) required each house of twenty or more Austin canons to keep at least one scholar at University (although Lilleshall may well have been smaller). On this and the slowness of the canons to fulfil the obligation, see Dobson 1992: 539, 554, although Salter notes (1922: xxvi) that a chapter held at Newstead near Stamford in 1356 decreed that Benedict's constitutions should be observed.

[18] Barron 2002. On the Austin canons at Oxford, see Evans 1931 and Forde 1994. For a brief overview of the situation, see Dobson 1992: 554–5, 560, and for a full discussion, see Forde 1985: i. 55–108.

[19] Dickinson 1950: 77–8, 86–7, 181. For the Latin Rule, see pp. 273–9 (App. II).

times as likely to have a cure of souls as other regulars.[20] All this is endorsed by Mirk's own pastoral outreach, while his commitment to liturgy is specifically Arrouaisian.[21]

A bull of Innocent IV allowed an Arrouaisian canon to undertake the cure of souls in any parish church of the abbot's gift and for between two and four canons to present one of their number to the bishop or archdeacon to be licensed to exercise all the duties of a parish priest.[22] Lilleshall had been founded by Richard Belmeis, later bishop of London, on the endowments of the secular college of St Alkmund, Shrewsbury, of which he was dean (Chibnall 1973: 71), and the saint's first tomb had been at Lilleshall (56/117n). The fact that F includes a sermon for the feast of St Alkmund, and, even more, that the sermon refers to St Alkmund as *patron to þis chyrch* (56/2–3n, 138–40n), suggests that Mirk wrote the sermon to be preached at St Alkmund's (Fletcher 1987: 220–2). In conjunction with his statement that F was written out of fellow-feeling for *othur that bene in the same degre that hauen charge of soulus* (Pro/2–3, see Pro/2–5n), it seems at least possible that he himself had held parochial responsibility there, or was writing for those who held such responsibility.[23]

Little is known of Lilleshall during the years Mirk may have spent there.[24] Although it was a small community, because it had been founded on the revenue of St Alkmund's, which itself had been founded by Ethelflæd, queen of Mercia, it counted as a royal foundation (Chibnall 1973: 71–3). It was therefore favoured by, and had a a strong obligation towards, local gentry and even royalty. The bede-roll for the death in 1375 of Abbot Roger Norreys (Oxford, Bodleian Library MS Rolls Salop. 2) is extensive and suggests that Lilleshall had a significant presence in the monastic and lay communities. In 1398, perhaps when Mirk was prior, Richard II stayed at Lilleshall on his way to the Shrewsbury Parliament, and after the

---

[20] For these and other relevant details, see Hanna 2000: 27–9.

[21] Chibnall 1973: 76. Gervase, first abbot of Arrouaise (1121–47), had modelled the community on the stricter Cistercian customs (Lawrence 1989: 166).

[22] Chibnall 1973: 73, Dickinson 1950: 234–51. Roger Norreys, abbot of Lilleshall 1369–75, had himself served as vicar of North Molton in Devon (see 41/185n). For a useful note on canons and parish churches, see Spencer 1993: 384–5 n. 171.

[23] Powell 2006: 163–5. For a discussion of Fletcher's suggestion (1987: 222 and n. 27) that the MS dedication (in four manuscripts) to *Iohanni de S., uicario de A.* might be to John Sotton, vicar of St Alkmund's from 1414, see Powell 2009a: 114–15. For an extensive discussion of St Alkmund's, see Owen & Blakeway 1825: ii. 261–301.

[24] The abbey register (London, BL Add. MS 50121) is a random compilation with no relevant material.

Parliament John of Gaunt stayed there with a large company (Chibnall 1973: 76). The record of the visit was inserted, perhaps by Mirk himself (Powell 2006: 175–6), into a copy of the chronicle attributed to Peter of Ickham (Cambridge, Corpus Christi College MS 339(ii), f. 47^{r-v}). As prior he would have been responsible for such records and would have had a comprehensive knowledge of abbey property and local personnel.[25]

Almost nothing is known about the library at Lilleshall, apart from what can be gleaned from Mirk's sources.[26] If Mirk had studied at Oxford, it is likely that he would have brought books back with him.[27] Certainly, he had access to *LA* and (for *IPP* and *MS*) William of Pagula's *Oculus Sacerdotis*. As noted, Arrouaisian houses placed great emphasis on liturgy, and for *F* Mirk made much use of John Beleth's *Rationale Divinorum Officiorum* (*RDO*).[28] Apart from *LA*, he had access to other legends, particularly those relating to the local saints Alkmund and Winifred, and to the national saint, Thomas of Canterbury, who was accorded special status in Augustinian houses because of his stay at Merton Abbey (Dickinson 1950: 254 and 47/30–9n). Mirk's material sometimes bears comparison with *The South English Legendary* (*SEL*), although similar material may have been disseminated in various contexts (e.g. 47/56–71n, 79–108n). Lilleshall may have had one or more collections of exemplary *narrationes* and Marian legends, but (despite his frequent *I rede*, e.g. 16/77, 17/144, 19/110) Mirk may well have been working from memory for much of this sort of material. Other works to be expected in an Augustinian abbey and likely from references in *F* include the Vulgate Bible, the works of St Augustine, glosses and commentaries on the Scriptures, books on canon law, chronicles, *florilegia*, *pastoralia*, and various sermon collections.

In contrast with the Benedictines and other large and prestigious orders, Austin canons could not compete in scholarship (nor was it their duty to do so, given their pastoral outreach). At an earlier period than Mirk's, Richard of Bury in his *Philobiblon* (1342) represents the

---

[25] For circumstantial details of Lilleshall which may relate to earlier records of the Abbey, see 68/110–25n, 119n.

[26] There is no entry for Lilleshall in Webber & Watson 1998.

[27] The books of the Austin canon Richard Calne offer a representative collection (Parkes 1992: 423).

[28] The title *RDO* is used in this edition (as in *PL* 202), but the work is also known as *Summa de Ecclesiasticis Officiis* (ed. Douteil 1976).

complaint of the books of Austin canons: 'no materials at all are furnished us to commend the canons regular for their care and study of us, who though they bear their name and honour from their twofold rule, yet have neglected the notable clause of Augustine's rule, in which we are commended to his clergy in these words: "Let books be asked for each day at a given hour . . ."' (Thomas 1960: 183–4). Nevertheless, if Mirk's own library was perhaps limited, those of other houses, such as Leicester, St Mary Overie in Southwark, and Thurgarton, were more than respectable (Webber 1997; Webber & Watson 1998 *passim*), and the Augustinians produced several authors throughout the Middle Ages (Hanna 2000). Amongst the earlier Augustinians, Alexander Neckam was the most scholarly and Orrm the most determined, while the anonymous authors of the *Ancrene Wisse* and the *Northern Homily Cycle* demonstrate the characteristic pastoral and pedagogic aims of the Augustinians. In Mirk's own day, the Austin canon Philip Repingdon must have been a notable preacher, whose expositions of the Sunday gospels survive in eight manuscripts (Forde 1985). He became abbot at Leicester in 1394 and then Chancellor of the University at Oxford (1400) and Bishop of Lincoln (1404).[29] Another significant contemporary Latin sermon collection, the work of an anonymous Austin canon and doctor of canon law, survives in Hereford Cathedral Library MS O.iii.5 (Wenzel 2005: 159–65, 461–5). At Thurgarton in Nottinghamshire Walter Hilton produced *The Scale of Perfection*, which was widely disseminated in English and Latin (Sargent 1976), the *Siege of Jerusalem* was written at Bolton Abbey in Yorkshire (Hanna & Lawton 2003), and Henry Knighton wrote his chronicle at Leicester (Martin 1995). In this context of scholarly Austin canons, Mirk is perhaps to be seen less as a scholar than an unusually energetic and talented writer and preacher whose learning was entirely adequate but whose pedagogic and missionary endeavours were his great strength and interest.

1.2. The Three Works of John Mirk

Mirk wrote three works for parish priests: his sermon collection (F) and two pastoral manuals, one in English rhyming couplets (IPP)[30]

[29] For his concern to promote proper licensed preaching, see Spencer 1993: 180.

[30] The edition of Peacock 1902 has been superseded by Kristensson 1974, although neither discusses the text or sources, on which only Boyle 1955 and Foss 1989 offer some guidance.

and the other in Latin (*MS*).[31] The survival of sermons based on the epistle (no. 34) and gospel of the day (no. 54), as well as extra sermons for occasional use (Add1–6), suggests that Mirk's sermon output was not restricted to *F*, and the verse preface and conclusion to the Sentence of Excommunication may well be Mirk's own composition.[32]

IPP offers the priest guidance on his duties, particularly in relation to pastoral instruction (ll. 69–535), hearing confession (ll. 675–1698), the sacraments of baptism and confirmation (ll. 536–674), and the performance of the last rites (ll. 1699–1838). In the course of the work, Mirk deals with the Paternoster and Ave Maria (ll. 404–25), the Creed (ll. 426–53), the articles of the faith (ll. 454–525), the seven sacraments (ll. 526–35), the Ten Commandments (ll. 849–972), the seven deadly sins (ll. 973–1302), the seven deeds of mercy (ll. 1355–64), and the seven virtues as remedies for the seven deadly sins (ll. 1551–1624).

IPP therefore covers material which it had long been the duty of the priest to teach, but which had acquired greatest importance through the 1281 Lambeth Constitutions of Archbishop Pecham of Canterbury, and (more recently but for the other province) through the 1357 Injunctions of Archbishop Thoresby of York, the vernacular version of which is known today as *The Lay Folk's Catechism* (*LFC*).[33] It is extant in seven fifteenth-century manuscripts (Kristensson 1974: 13–22), three of which (αEF) also contain(ed) *F*. Only Oxford, Bodleian Library MS Greaves 57 contains just *IPP*: the other manuscripts are collections of material appropriate for priests, or, in the case of Cambridge University Library MS Ff.v.48, for layfolk. Dialect evidence suggests that there was originally a wide distribution across the Midlands (Kristensson 1974: 57–62).

IPP complements *F*. The latter supports the priest in his duty to preach by providing preachable matter, while the former supports him in his duty to teach by providing teachable matter. *F* itself contains little *pastoralia*,[34] although Mirk wrote at least one sermon

---

[31] Edited Girsch 1990 (on the inadequacies of Washburn 1974, see Girsch 1990: lxxx–lxxxiii). An edition and translation are in preparation by Girsch and Powell. For discussions, see Fletcher 1988, Powell 2009a.

[32] Kristensson 1974: 104–7. See §5.1 Contents.

[33] Ed. Simmons and Nolloth (1901). On *pastoralia* and their origins, see Gibbs & Lang 1934: 94–179, Haines 1971, Gillespie 1980, Boyle 1981, Spencer 1993: 196–227.

[34] The most extensive preaching on the tenets is in the Lenten sermons (see §2). For the provision of extra pastoral material in Rev. and in the *Quattuor Sermones* (*QS*) issued with *F* editions, see Powell 1991.

(Add6) specifically to provide preaching material on an essential tenet, the Paternoster. Some *F* manuscripts also include teaching material not properly part of the collection, either for the priest's own instruction (see 28/1–2n, 46/1n, 140–5n, Add3–4), or to preach to the people, but not as part of the *F* schedule (Add1–2).

One source for both *IPP* and *MS* was William of Pagula's *Oculus Sacerdotis* (1326–8), particularly (for *IPP*) *Pars Oculi* and *Dextera Pars*[35] and (for *MS*) *Sinistra Pars* on the seven sacraments.[36] *IPP* and *MS* are both pastoral manuals of advice and information, but the fact that *IPP* is in English verse and *MS* in Latin prose exemplifies the difference. *IPP* has the people always in mind, and its medium made it accessible to them as well as to their curate;[37] *MS* is directed only at the priest (seemingly, a specific priest, another John)[38] and, while its structure is a simple meander through the daily life of a typical priest, it nevertheless works at a significantly more advanced and intellectual level than *IPP*, in its emphasis on canon law, for example.[39] It survives in eleven complete or near-complete fifteenth-century manuscripts and two almost identical abridgements which reduce the work by three quarters.[40] Its distribution would appear to have been wide throughout the Midlands, with a particular concentration in the north-east, with a readership amongst the regular, as well as the secular, clergy. In almost every manuscript *MS* forms part of a compendium of pastoral or preaching material.

These two pastoral works written for the priest with a cure of souls, together with the sermons of *F*, which were written with the same recipient in mind (*in helpe of suche mene clerkus as I am myselff*, Pro/ 10), received their impetus from the parochial duties of the Augustinian order. The pedagogic purpose of all three is explicitly stated,[41]

---

[35] For comparison of each part (the first dealing with confessional practice and the second the moral and didactic section of the *Oculus*) with *IPP*, see Boyle 1955: 86 n. 1, 89 n. 2.

[36] See Fletcher 1988: 106, on whom Girsch 1990: xxi, xlii–xlvii is dependent. Boyle does not note specific dependence of *IPP* on *Sinistra Pars*, although the bulk of *IPP* deals with the sacrament of penance (Kristensson 1974: 108/675–163/1698), and Mirk also deals with baptism (96/536–101/642), confirmation (102/643–103/674), and extreme unction (163/1699–174/1912), after an introduction on the sacraments at 95/526–96/535.

[37] It is addressed to *þou preste curatoure* (Kristensson 1974: 68/11).

[38] See above, n. 23.   [39] See further Powell 2009a.

[40] Fletcher 1988, on whom Girsch 1990: lv–xviii is dependent.

[41] *IPP: lete other mo rede þys boke . . . / Hyt ys I-made hem to schowne / þat haue no bokes of here owne, / And oþer þat beth of mene lore, / þat wolde fayne conne more* (Kristensson 1974: 175/1920–6); *F: a schort sermon nedful for hym to techyn and othur for to lerne* (Pro/

and Mirk's purpose is clear in all three works: in a context where it is usual for the blind to lead the blind,[42] he provides vision for the *preste curatoure* who is *not grete clerk*.[43] In Mirk's own mind, at least, the three works constituted a full pastoral programme—the sermons for preaching and the manuals for constant reference—to be read often, not thrown into a corner but kept by the priest's side throughout his daily life.[44]

2. THE SERMONS OF THE *FESTIAL*

Mirk's pastoral and pedagogic aims characterize the whole of his sermon collection.[45] Its title derives from Mirk's own Prologue (*for this treti speketh alle of festis, I wolle and pray that it be called a Festial*, Pro/14–15), as well as from later incipits and explicits.[46] The priest will find in the work *of alle the principale festis of the ȝere a schort sermon nedful for hym to techyn and othur for to lerne* (Pro/12–14), that is, it was intended to provide a preaching programme sufficient to fulfil the requirements of the Church in a typical parish. Mirk's real concern for the needs of both the people and the priests responsible for their spiritual welfare is apparent throughout. His concern for the people shows in the care with which he explains Church custom and moral behaviour in the sermons; his concern for their priests is apparent in the non-preaching material, such as the Prologue, or Sermon 28, where he explains the significance of the *triduum* ritual so that the priest may not be

---

13–14); *MS: presentem libellum conscripsi scriptumque tibi karissime ad legendum et cum aliis communicandum transmisi* (Oxford, Bodleian Library MS Bodley 632, f. 68ʳ).

[42] *IPP: whenne þe blynde ledeth þe blynde, / In-to þe dyche þey fallen boo* (Kristensson 1974: 67/2–3); *MS: ipsi ceci duces cecorum facti* (Oxford, Bodleian Library MS Bodley 632, f. 69ʳ).

[43] Kristensson 1974: 68/11, 13. In *MS* Mirk's Latin medium allows him to be more outspoken than in the vernacular works, and he warns that the clergy's lack of discipline scandalises the Church. Care must be taken *medicinam correccionis eorum vulneribus apponere*, since, although the spirit may be willing, the flesh (in the shape of *nimia sciencie egestas*) is weak (Oxford, Bodleian Library, MS Bodley 632, f. 68ʳ).

[44] *IPP: Rede þys ofte, and so let oþer; / Huyde hyt not in hodymoke* (Kristensson 1974: 175/1918–19); *MS: libellum istum semel a te lectum in angulum camere non proicias . . . sed assidue illum legens, de manibus non dimittas* (Oxford, Bodleian Library MS Bodley 632, f. 68ᵛ).

[45] See further Powell 2006, Ford 2006. For an exhaustive bibliography, see Horner 2005: 4059–60, 4271–8.

[46] For the α explicit, see §5.1 Contents; for other manuscripts, see Appendix II *passim*.

left at a loss by the pert questions of his sometimes malicious parishioners (see 28/1–2n).

Ready-to-preach sermons such as *F* were not uncommon in the later Middle Ages. The title of one, *Dormi Secure*, advertises the peace of mind its possession would bring to the ill-prepared priest, and this and other such collections were the subject of later derision.[47] However, the problem facing the Church throughout the Middle Ages—the need to teach the people but the inadequacy of the available teachers—gave little reason to view ready-made English sermons cynically at the time. Mirk's sermons are tailored to the needs of both priests and people, and they demonstrate the sincerity of his claim that he wrote *F* as an aid to the poorly educated priest in his pastoral mission of preaching and teaching (Pro/8–14). It is significant that they are in English and give every sign of having been composed in English with oral delivery in mind.[48]

Any discussion of Mirk's preaching programme must take into account the fact that his original manuscript no longer exists. The base-text of the present edition preserves the fullest collection of Mirk's sermons, but some material is demonstrably extraneous to the original concept: the extra sermons for 1 Lent (no. 34) and the Assumption of the Virgin (no. 54), which are based on the epistle and the gospel of the day respectively; the material on Nero (no. 46); the sermons for a wedding and a burial (Add1–2); the sermon on the Paternoster (Add6); the material for Maundy Thursday and Easter Eve (no. 28); finally, the notes that make up Add3–5. Without this material (all of which is edited here), *F* offers itself as sixty-four sermons, beginning with Advent Sunday and ending with the feast of the Dedication of a Church.

The material edited here as Add1–6 is only found in some Group A manuscripts,[49] added after *F* proper.[50] The life of Nero (no. 46) is also restricted to Group A, where it is treated either as a long *narratio* to be added to the sermon for the feast-day of SS Peter and Paul or as

---

[47] For criticism of *Dormi Secure*, see Spencer 1993: 324 and n. 8, within a longer analysis of the post-Reformation reception of medieval sermons (pp. 321–34), including *F* (pp. 324–6).

[48] No Latin version is known and Latin quotations are rare (Sermon 34 is an exception), generally indicating scribal intervention (most markedly in K). Sermons preached in English were frequently written out in Latin, although by the later 14th c. English versions appear to have become more usual (Spencer 1993: 55–7).

[49] For Groups A/B, see §3.1.

[50] Except in C, where London, BL MS Harley 2417 (once conjoined with Harley 2420) begins imperfect in Add3 (see Appendix II.i.a).

part of that sermon itself (see 46/1n). All this was clearly part of Mirk's original oeuvre but, obviously extraneous to *F*, did not survive the transition to the recension (Group B). The material for Maundy Thursday and Easter Eve was originally intended (like no. 46) only as instruction for the priest, not to be preached to the people, but by the time of the Group B recension it had become a fully-fledged sermon, or two sermons in the case of Rev. manuscripts (see 28/1–2n).

Sermons 34 and 54 most likely have their origins outside *F* proper, not just because they are the only sermons wholly structured around the epistle and the gospel of the day, but also because they provide extra sermons for days already covered. It may be that they are survivors of larger collections of gospel and epistle sermons by Mirk, which, one might speculate, were perhaps suppressed after Arundel's 1409 Constitutions. Their greater length and greater sophistication distinguishes them from the run of *F* sermons.

Of the sixty-four sermons which make up *F* proper, nineteen are *Temporale* and forty-five *Sanctorale*.[51] Although Group B manuscripts (also C, which is Group A) arrange the sermons according to this service-book order,[52] Mirk himself arranged the sermons, more conveniently for the priest, in chronological order, beginning with Advent, the start of the Church year, and ending with the feast-day of St Katherine, the collection as a whole concluding with the Dedication of a Church (the date of which would depend on the church in which the sermon was preached). There are thirteen sermons for Sundays, ten of them (nos. 15–17, 19–22, 24–5, 29) providing a regular Sunday preaching programme throughout Lent from Septuagesima to Easter Day, the other three offering sermons for Advent 1, Pentecost, and Trinity Sunday (nos. 1, 39, 40). Sunday preaching would not, however, have been limited to these thirteen Sundays, since other *Temporale* feasts and many *Sanctorale* feasts would have had their sermons preached on the previous Sunday. Indeed, from the evidence of α (with the *caveat* that this may not accord with Mirk's original manuscript), it appears that the sermons for most saints' days were preached the Sunday before.[53] While this

---

[51] For an explanation of the terms, see Spencer 1993: 23–33.

[52] Rev. inserts sermons for the Christmas period (Nativity of Christ, St Stephen, St John Evangelist, the Holy Innocents, St Thomas of Canterbury, the Circumcision of Christ, and the Epiphany) into the *Temporale* section.

[53] The expression *such a day* at the start of Sermons 2–5, 13, 14, 18, 23, 30–3, 35, 42, 44, 45, 47–53, 55–8, 60–4, 66–8 indicates that the preacher, delivering his address on the Sunday, was to insert the name of the day in the following week on which the feast fell.

might seem to offer the likelihood of a regular Sunday preaching programme, the feasts of saints were not at regular intervals throughout the church year, and either more than one or none at all might occur within a single week, as in the case, for example, of St Nicholas and the Conception of the Virgin (6 and 8 December), or the long gap between SS Michael and Luke (29 September and 18 October). It appears that it was only at major feasts that the sermon was preached on the day itself. In the preaching programme represented by α, the sermon for St Mark's feast-day was clearly to be preached on the Sunday before the feast-day (*suche a day*, 31/3) but the parishioners are enjoined also to attend church on the feast-day itself (31/95–6). The feasts associated with Christmas (nos. 6–12), with Lent and Easter (nos. 26, 27, 29), and with the period thereafter (nos. 36, 37, 39–41, 65) were all of such importance that the sermon was delivered on the day itself (a Sunday anyway in the case of Easter Day, Pentecost, and Trinity Sunday). All the other Sunday feasts (nos. 1, 15–17, 19–22, 24, 25) naturally refer to *thys day*. Amongst the *Sanctorale*, apart from the Christmas saints (Stephen, John Evangelist, Holy Innocents, Thomas of Canterbury), who followed each other consecutively from 26 to 29 December and for each of whom the sermon was preached *þys day* (7/2, cf. 8/2, 9/2, 10/2), the only other sermon which was preached on the actual feast-day appears to have been, significantly, that for the important local saint, Winifred (no. 43). Interestingly, the second Assumption sermon found in some manuscripts was preached on the feast-day itself (54/3, 4, 5, 8, 10, 17, etc.), whereas the first (a genuine *F* sermon) was not (53/2). As noted above, Sermon 54 is eccentric in its use of the gospel of the day, and it is likely that it was originally written for a different context from that of *F*.

F, however, offered an impressive preaching programme at a time when regular preaching was not necessarily to be found in the parish church[54]—hence the popularity of the friars, who, with the priest's permission, often preached in church (Spencer 1993: 59–60). The sermons are not long, as Mirk himself notes (*a schort sermon*, Pro/13).

[54] For a similar programme (and similar material) in the perhaps contemporary *Speculum Sacerdotale* (ed. Weatherly 1936), see Spencer 1993: 369 n. 33; Horner 2005: 4060–1, 4278–9. There appears to have been a distinction between teaching (the duty of every priest) and preaching (less clearly the priest's duty). Quite apart from the priest's own disinclination and other reasons for infrequent preaching, the Blackfriars Council of 1382 had declared it erroneous that every priest and deacon had authority to preach (Spencer 1993: 51).

Medieval preachers sometimes prided themselves on the length of their sermons,[55] but Mirk's can only have taken between ten and twenty minutes, some being very brief and others lengthier.[56] He appears to be conscious of the need not to overstretch his listeners' patience, as when he assures them, before embarking on the Old Testament stories for the second and third Sundays in Lent, that he is truncating what might be much lengthier material (20/29–31, 21/53–4).

2.1. Legenda Aurea

The source of F sermons is almost always the *Legenda Aurea* of Jacobus de Voragine. Of the *Sanctorale*, only the sermons for the Conception of the Virgin, the Translation of St Thomas of Canterbury, and for Mirk's local saints, Winifred and Alkmund (nos. 4, 47, 43, 56) do not have parallels in Jacobus' work. For the *Temporale* feasts, *LA* usually, but not always, offers Mirk a basic text from which to construct his sermons; however, for the Lenten sermons he must generally look elsewhere, such as to the *Glossa Ordinaria* (*GO*), for example (see 17/103–32n, 19/28–34n, 20/89–101n). The reason is simple, that *LA* is self-evidently a legendary and includes very little *Temporale* material. Where Mirk, for example, provides sermons for all four Sundays in Lent, Jacobus offers only one cursory item (Graesse 1846: 151–3; Ryan 1993: i. 137–8; Maggioni 1998: i. 227–9), and for late-established feasts such as Trinity Sunday and Corpus Christi there is no material at all.

Mirk is selective of *LA* material, and his method appears to have been to read the legend and then to reproduce it, as concisely as he could, in his own words, truncating over-long details of narrative or explication.[57] Occasionally he will add a little new material from other sources (see e.g. 13/117–28n, 15/161–205n), but invariably *LA*, although rarely acknowledged beyond the Prologue,[58] is his sole source for a *Sanctorale* sermon. Jacobus scrupulously offers alternative accounts or authorities, and he attempts to direct his readers to

---

[55] Bridgettine sermons in Italy and Germany might last as long as an hour, or longer if delivered outside the church (Powell 2000: 252 n. 50).

[56] For example, the sermon for Septuagesima (no. 15), which begins the Lenten period, is exceptionally long (although it is exceeded in length by the non-F second sermon for the Assumption, no. 54), but that for Palm Sunday is very brief (see 25/4–5n).

[57] Rev. (especially R2) reinstates *LA* material omitted from Mirk's *Sanctorale* sermons, as does Group B (to a lesser extent).

[58] The number of references to *LA* increases towards the end of the collection (see Glossary of Proper Names).

the more reliable version. Sometimes he warns that material is likely to be, or actually is, apocryphal, but this does not prevent his dealing with it. Wherever possible, he assigns an authority to each statement he makes. Mirk, on the other hand, merely chooses one version, seemingly arbitrarily, and offers that without comment.

His handling of *LA* may be illustrated by a schematic comparison of his sermon for the Ascension (no. 37) with the *LA* material on which it is almost entirely based. The use of bold type in (A) below (a synopsis of the *LA* material on the Ascension, cf. Graesse 1846: 318–27; Ryan 1993: i. 291–8; Maggioni 1998: i. 480–92) identifies what use Mirk made of it. Mirk's own arrangement of that material in his Ascension Day sermon is shown in (B) below, with *LA* material in bold.

(A)
Seven questions are to be considered in relation to the Lord's ascension:

(1) Whence he ascended: **from the Mount of Olives**, i.e. the mount of three lights (explanation follows). **On the day of his ascension Christ appeared** twice **to his disciples**, once when **he appeared as they ate** (discussion of where they were) and, **having reproached them for their doubts, told them to go to the Mount of Olives**, and secondly **on the Mount when he ascended**. On that spot no pavement could remain intact when a church was later built, and **the impression of his feet can still be seen in that place** (Sulpicius and *GO*).

(2) Why he did not ascend immediately after the resurrection: **he waited forty days** for three reasons: (i) **to prove the resurrection of his body**, which was more difficult to prove than his passion (Pope Leo); (ii) to console the apostles; (iii) as a mystic sign. (Isa. 61: 2, *GO*, Isa. 54: 8).

(3) How he ascended: (i) powerfully (Isa. 63: 1, John 3: 13, *Historia Scholastica*, St Gregory); (ii) openly, **with the disciples watching** (Acts 1: 9, John 16: 5, *GO*); (iii) joyfully, **with the angels rejoicing** (Ps. 46: 6, St Augustine); (iv) **swiftly** (Ps. 18: 6, **Maimonides**, St Ambrose).

(4) With whom he ascended: **with a great host of men** (Ps. 68: 18) and angels (Isa. 63: 1: **the lower angels asked the higher, 'Who is this?'**, *GO*, Ps. 24: 8). The angels asked three

questions (Dionysius): (i) the higher angels asked amongst themselves: 'Who is he who comes from Edom?' (Isa. 63: 1, Christ's response); (ii) the higher angels asked Christ: 'Why is your clothing bloody?' (Isa. 63: 2). **Bede says Christ ascended with his wounds bleeding.** Christ's response (Isa. 63: 3); (iii) **the lower angels asked the higher angels: 'Who is the king of glory?' (Ps. 24: 8, the angels' response, St Augustine).**

(5)   By what merit he ascended: truth, meekness, justice (St Jerome).

(6)   Whither he ascended: above all the heavens (Eph. 4: 8–10). The heavens are material, rational, intellectual, and supersubstantial (each is discussed, with citations from Isa. 66: 1, Wisd., Dionysius, John Damascenus, Ecclus. 43: 1, Job 37: 18, Pss. 18: 7, 8: 2, S. of S. 2: 8, Pss. 103: 2, 17: 11, Mark 16: 19, St Bernard, Eph. 4: 10, Phil. 2: 8–9, St Augustine, Ps. 17: 11, Eph. 3: 19).

(7)   Why he ascended: for nine benefits: (i) the bringing down of divine love (John 16: 7); (ii) a greater knowledge of God (John 14: 28, St Augustine); (iii) the merit of faith (Pope Leo, St Augustine); (iv) **our security, so that he may be our advocate with God** (1 John 2: 1, **St Bernard**); (v) **our dignity, so that angels no longer allowed men to worship them** (Rev. 19: 10, *GO*, Pope Leo); (vi) the strengthening of our hope (Heb. 4: 14, 6: 18–19, Pope Leo); (vii) to show the way (Mic. 2: 13, St Augustine); (viii) to open the gate of heaven (liturgy); (ix) to prepare a place (John 14: 2, St Augustine).

(B)

37/1–11   Christ ascended this day. As a sign, the Paschal candle is taken from the choir.

37/12–28   **This is how he ascended: Christ appeared to his disciples today to assuage their doubts about his being flesh and blood. He told them to go to the Mount of Olives and there, with the disciples watching, he ascended, leaving the impress of his feet in the hard stone.** The olive tree is a symbol of mercy, showing that Christ is merciful. In his ascension **the rejoicing angels** made heavenly melody.

37/29–35 He rose swiftly, as Maimonides says. He took a great multitude of souls with him which he fetched from hell.

37/36–43 He rose with his wounds fresh and bleeding for five reasons (Bede).

37/44–54 He rose to bring security to mankind. Just as a lord has a lawyer that he trusts to speak for him before a judge, so we have Christ (St Bernard).

37/55–70 Man gained great dignity by the ascension, as shown by the fact that angels now worship man and no longer bar the gates of paradise (St Augustine).

37/71–90 Just as a worldly king has officers of different ranks, so has the heavenly king. Therefore the lower angels, seeing him rise with angels and the souls of men, and seeing the devils fly away through the air, asked the higher angels: 'Who is he . . . ?' The higher angels answered: 'This is the king of joy', etc. (based on St Augustine).

37/91–102 Those who were left after the ascension looked up and saw two angels who asked: 'Men of Galilee, why do you stand looking up to heaven? Just as you saw him ascend, so he will come at the Day of Judgment.' Therefore lift up your hearts to Christ and ask mercy and be saved.

37/103–31 A *narratio* relating to St Carpus demonstrates Christ's mercy.

It will be clear from the synopses above that Jacobus' method of construction, which is always highly schematic, with divisions and subdivisions, is ignored by Mirk, who simply lifts material as and when it interests him. At times he incorporates Jacobus' authorities but always provides many fewer than Jacobus and does not offer alternative or parallel interpretations. He often elides material, as at 37/71–90, which is based on parts of (A) 4 and 4 (iii). Most of the sermon is based on the Ascension material in *LA*, and the final *exemplum* is taken from the *LA* material on the Resurrection (see 37/103–31n). Of the material which is not directly from *LA*, that on the Paschal candle (37/1–11) is from Mirk's other most frequent non-biblical source, *RDO*, and the details after the ascension (37/91–102) are scriptural. Oil as a symbol of mercy is commonplace (37/22–3n), and the comparison of earthly and heavenly kings (37/71–90) is also common (cf. 36/46–60).

2.2. *Sanctorale* Sermons

The form and content of *F* sermons vary, depending on whether they deal with the legend of a saint or not. A saint's legend has a simple purpose: to present the saint in terms of her/his life, death (usually martyrdom), and posthumous miracles. Not all *Sanctorale* sermons deal with the whole life of a saint. There are two sermons for St John the Evangelist (nos. 8, 35), the first comprehensive and the second dealing with one key incident in his life,[59] and two for St Thomas of Canterbury (nos. 10, 47), both of which offer a complementary potted version of the saint's life, although the second relates to the translation of his body to its new shrine in Canterbury. There are several sermons which deal with different episodes in the life of Christ (Nativity, Circumcision, and Epiphany, nos. 6, 11, 12) and the Virgin (Conception, Purification, Annunciation, Nativity, and Assumption, nos. 4, 14, 23, 53, 54, 57).

In the *Sanctorale* sermons Mirk usually imposes a simple order which takes the form of a threefold division (generally relating to the life, death, and miracles), e.g. *þe qwhech day ȝe schul come to God and Holy Chyrch to see þi God and do worschep to þis holy seynt, specyaly for þre virtues þat he hadde. Won for he hadde gret holynes and was holy in lyuyng, þe secunde for gret myracules doyng, þe þrydde for gret passyon suffryng* (2/3–7). In most cases, the statement of the three principals involves a mnemonic end-rhyme, often -*yng*, although other end-rhymes are found (-*nes* 4/4–5, -*on* 7/21–3) and even the occasional full rhyme (*fey/way/day* 5/4–6, *schame/blame/hame* 9/8–9) (cf. Spencer 1993: 233). The source of the principals is generally to be found in *LA*. For example, *he ȝaf hym grace of virginite, and grace of kepyng hys modur fre, and grace of schewyng hys priuyte* (8/6–7) has its origin in three of the four privileges granted John according to Jacobus: *Secundum est carnis incorruptio . . . Tertium est secretorum revelatio . . . Quartum est matris Dei recommendatio* (Graesse 1846: 56; Ryan 1993: i. 50; Maggioni 1998: i. 87–8), and the three divisions of the Purification sermon *(in oure Lady puryfyng, in Symeones metyng and in candeles offryng,* 14/5–6) are based on the three names for the feast: *purificatio, hypopanti et candelaria* (Graesse 1846: 158; Ryan 1993: i. 143; Maggioni 1998: i. 238).

However, the major part of the collection does not maintain even this simple structuring of *Sanctorale* material. Of the saints' day

---

[59] The same *narratio* about St Edward the Confessor appears in both (see 8/120–9n).

sermons from St Matthias (no. 18) up to and including St Anne (no. 51), Mirk simply relates the legend in its three stages of life, death, and miracles. Thereafter, a threefold division occurs occasionally (nos. 52, 53, 55, 57, 60, 61, 62, 64, 65, 68). The reason for a block of less structured sermons in the middle of *F* (or, alternatively, from February to July) relates to some extent to the importance of the feast, in that nearly all the structured sermons are for feasts celebrated by a vigil and fasting, whereas the more cursory sermons were for lesser feasts.[60] The structured sermons are certainly more effective in the power of the threefold explications to foreground specific characteristics of the saint as a Christian model, e.g. *he was holy in lyvyng, he was meke in passyon suffering and perfytte in ensaumpul 3euing* (52/7–8).

2.3. *Temporale* Sermons

The majority of the sermons are saints' legends, which conform to a model, and the other sermons (set apart as *Temporale* in Group B and Rev. manuscripts, as too in C of the Group A manuscripts), though fewer in number, inevitably exhibit more difference.[61] They may be seen to fall into two types: those which deal with important feasts of the Church year such as Advent, Trinity Sunday, and Corpus Christi, and those which cohere as sermons in a Lenten programme from Septuagesima to Easter Day.

The general aim of a *Temporale* sermon is to explain the significance of the day and to offer scriptural, liturgical, and pastoral instruction, as appropriate.[62] Mirk's familiarity with scriptural text is strong but rarely referenced, since he is not writing in an academic context.[63] But for those sermons which have no model in *LA*, Mirk turns more frequently to his secondary source (also Jacobus' source for much of his material), John Beleth's *Rationale Divinorum*

---

[60] Sermons 45 and 50 are unstructured but refer to a vigil and fasting, as does Sermon 44 (which is based on a threefold division not of the saint's life).

[61] The imbalance of *Temporale* to *Sanctorale* is less in *F* than in *LA*, and Rev. balances the two areas even better by its inclusion of extra *Temporale* sermons (Powell 1991: 88–9).

[62] Insufficient recognition of Mirk's intensely pedagogic and pragmatic outlook (and inappropriate comparison with Latin academic sermons) may explain why Wenzel (2005: 58–65) finds in *F*'s mix of sermons, absence of themes, and emphasis on the meaning of a given occasion a 'peculiar kind of preaching' (p. 63).

[63] Sometimes it is only the supplying of the Vulgate text in K which alerts one to a scriptural origin for a statement (for example, K recognizes the allusion at 63/11n and adds from the same verse: *Gaudete quod nomina vestra scripta sunt in celis*). The K scribe easily translates Mirk's text into Vulgate Latin (see e.g. full collation of 24/17 *malys*, 31 *heven*, 63 *pus*, Appendix III.v). For a still useful discussion of pre-Wycliffite biblical study by the secular and regular clergy, see Deanesly 1920: 156–204.

Officiorum (*RDO*), a comprehensive account of Church services and ritual.[64] Lilleshall's emphasis on liturgy explains Mirk's use of *RDO* as a reference book, as well as his concern that the liturgy should be accurately performed and its significance understood by both priest and people. The *Sanctorale* sermons frequently begin with Beleth's rules on the fasting to be observed or otherwise (e.g. 32/5–6 n), and he is the source of the explanation of the complex ceremonies of Holy Week (nos. 26, 28) or the *minutiae* of hair-cutting and shaving on Maundy Thursday (see 28/42–4n).[65]

RDO, however, was simply the written authority for ritual with which Mirk, as a priest, would have been familiar, and his knowledge of the Sarum Use (the most common Use in England, as well as that adopted by the Austin canons) informs many of the *Temporale* sermons to a greater or lesser extent. To a lesser extent, each division of the Nativity of Christ sermon is punctuated by a brief exposition of the introit to each of the three masses of the day (see 6/73–4n, 122n, 155n). To a greater extent, in the Lenten sermons, where material in *LA* is cursory or non-existent and where ceremonial is less important than in Holy Week, the service-books nevertheless offer Mirk a source of material, perhaps a more immediate source than the Vulgate itself. In these cases, Mirk structures the sermon around the readings for the day or for the following week. The Old Testament lections were read only on the weekdays of Lent and some few other days (Dix 1945: 471). Mirk makes much of them in the sermons for Septuagesima, Sexagesima, Quinquagesima, and Lent 2–4 (nos. 15–17, 20–2), where he takes his listeners through the narratives of Adam and Eve, Noah, Abraham, Jacob, Joseph, and Moses. Where the lections themselves are not sufficiently full, Mirk turns to other scriptural or legendary sources, such as the *Vita Adae et Evae*, which is used (probably not at first-hand) to augment the Septuagesima sermon (see 15/161–205n). In almost every case these Lenten sermons touch too on the epistle and gospel of the day, and, in the sermons for Lent 1 and Palm Sunday (nos. 19, 25), the gospel narratives (the temptation of Christ and the entry into Jerusalem) provide the material out of which the sermon develops (although not with the presentation and explication of text which are characteristic of Sermons 34 and 54).

---

[64] The combination of *LA* and *RDO* is also used in *Speculum Sacerdotale* (Weatherly 1936: xxvii–xxxv; Horner 2005: 4060–1; Wenzel 2005: 61–3).

[65] There are thirteen references to Beleth by name in α (see Glossary of Proper Names), but Mirk's reliance on him is pervasive.

It is in these Lenten sermons that Mirk instructs his audience in some of the pastoral material which was taught during that period: the seven deadly sins (15/24–30), the seven deeds of mercy (16/46–56), the articles of the Creed (17/98–103), and, most fully developed, the Ten Commandments (22/41–76). The first of these sermons, in particular, is a *tour de force*. It is more formal and elaborate than others, as befits the position of Septuagesima as herald of the Lenten period. It signals the importance of the day, the first Sunday in the run-up to Lent, by a lengthy proheme (15/2–50), in which Mirk reminds the people of the sins of the previous year, *namely þe Crystonmas dayes* (15/7–8), admonishes them that Christ's love for mankind, revealed in his human life, should occasion great devotion (as it did in past days), and explains how the Church encourages concentration on worldly vanity and death in this period. The sermon proper then begins, with the three principals structured around the day's liturgy, using the office of the day (15/55–7) to introduce the first division of the sermon (capped with a *narratio*), the epistle (15/101–2), and the gospel (15/111–12) to introduce the second division, and the epistle again (15/154–6) to introduce the third division (both these divisions augmented from the week's Old Testament lections). The other Lenten sermons are more subdued, but the pastoral intent remains to the fore, with Mirk concentrating on the penitential aspects of the season: teaching the need to fast, to give alms, to recognize and avoid sin, and, in preparation for communion on Easter Day, to cleanse oneself through full confession.

It is in the addresses to his audience that Mirk's familiar tone and colloquial style are most apparent.[66] He is familiar with ordinary people, and rather weary of them, both the arrogant ones (28/3–11) and the self-righteous ones (21/138–43). He speaks to them forcefully and directly: *take hit in certeyne* (29/26–7), *I scharge ȝow heȝly in Goddus behalue* (29/72–3), *we amonysche ȝow . . . I amonyche ȝow . . . we amonech ȝow . . . I monas ȝow . . . I amonysche ȝow . . . I amonest ȝow* (34/5, 17, 38, 61, 149, 228), and warns them that he will help as far as he may (*I wil be redy to help in alle þat lythe in me myth gode wylle* 38/10–11) but that in the end he is a priest and the Church must be obeyed: *For ȝif I woste whyche weron*

---

[66] Mirk's own voice may be preserved in two frequent phrases: *more harme is* (see Glossary *sub* harm(e) *n.*) and *hoole asse fysche* (see Glossary *sub* hol(le) *adj.*). For his use of familiar proverbs, see 27/5–10n, 34/19–20n, 39/17–18n, 40/72n, 43/6–8n, 54/79–80n.

owte of scharite and vnschryuon, I moste be teching of holy wrytte wit a fulle mowthe say þus to hym in audiens of alle men: 'I ʒeue þe here not þi howsell bot þi dampnacion into euerlasting peyne til þou come to amendement' (29/75–9). The directness of tone is not incompatible with some rhetorical skill employed to shock (*For . . . neses*, 38/15–16), to inspire awe (*þus . . . heuen*, 37/87–90), or simply to hammer a point home (*To . . . nede*, 38/20–2).

In structure, the *Temporale* sermons do not conform to a pattern. Some (e.g. nos. 15, 16, 40, 41) have the rhyming divisions of the *Sanctorale* sermons; several others, while not exhibiting an overall structure, divide at least part of the sermon into three, such as the three reasons to fast and the three sins and their remedies in 1 Lent (no. 19), or the three reasons for darkness and the three reasons for silence at Tenebre (no. 26). The Advent sermon (no. 1) falls into the traditional two parts, dealing with the first and second comings of Christ. The Easter Day sermon (no. 29), which appears to be independent of any known source, is structured around the three contemporary names for the day, as is the sermon for the feast of the Circumcision (no. 11). The Lenten sermons (including the extra 1 Lent sermon, no. 34) are the most elaborate in structure, and those for Septuagesima and (perhaps) Sexagesima have a protheme to the main body of the material (15/3–50, 16/2–11).[67] Other sermons, however, are very simple, such as the sermon for the Eve of Pentecost (no. 38), based on the seven Gifts of the Holy Ghost.

2.4. *Narrationes* and *Exempla*

The simple structures and practical content of *F* sermons are appropriate, of course, to the preacher and audience which Mirk has in mind, and his sermons from outside the collection (nos. 34 and 54) show that he is capable of greater complexity in different contexts. However, even in more formal contexts (including *MS*), Mirk shows a propensity for *narrationes* to augment his text.[68] Stories are the distinguishing feature of the popular sermon of the Middle Ages, as identified by Chaucer's Pardoner:

> Thanne telle I hem ensamples many oon
> Of olde stories longe tyme agoon.

[67] On sermon form and structure, see Spencer 1993: 228–68.
[68] On exemplary material in sermons, see Owst 1926 (esp. Part III), 1966 (esp. ch. 4); Mosher 1911.

For lewed peple loven tales olde;
Swiche thynges kan they wel reporte and holde
(*The Canterbury Tales*, Pardoner's Prologue,
ll. 435–8)

They are an integral element of *F* and are essential to Mirk's pedagogical aims,[69] although several of his *narrationes* (such as the charcoal-burner's tale at 22/135–63 and Add1/92–121) tread a thin line between salaciousness and moral example. Even the unedifying life story of Nero is provided as an example of *honest talkyng* (46/2), and *to ʒeve prestes ensaumpul how þei schulde ocupye holy festes of þe ʒere* (140–1). In this context there may be more than chance in the fact that A. G. Dickens began his seminal work on the English Reformation by demonstrating the backwardness of the priesthood with a *narratio* from the commonplace book of an early sixteenth-century Austin canon (Dickens 1964: 1).

In some cases the *narrationes* of *F* overbalance the doctrinal content of the sermons, as, for example, in 4 Lent, where brief passages of instruction (22/87–95, 129–34) are intercalated with long and circumstantial *narrationes* of debatable spiritual benefit (22/96–128, 135–63).[70] Occasionally he introduces a *narratio* with no preamble at all, as when the third division of the Quinquagesima sermon (*studefaste beleue wythoute flotering*, 17/143) is quietly capped by a *narratio* about Robert Grosseteste's faith, or the sermon for the Assumption of the Virgin ends with three exemplary but otherwise undiscussed stories of the Virgin's readiness to help those in need (53/182–220). Sometimes there is a rudimentary introduction of the story, as in the *narratio* of the converted Jew in the sermon for the Nativity of the Virgin (*Wherefore I sette here þis ensaumpul*, 57/119), or, more fully, in the sermon for the Dedication of a Church (*þan to schewon ʒow how þat þe fende is dryuyn oute of chyrch be halowing, I telle ʒow þis ensaumpul*, 68/24–5).

While *narrationes* are common in *F*, actual *exempla* (exemplary comparisons) are rare.[71] Indeed, Mirk appears somewhat cautious in

---

[69] Wenzel's comment that *F*'s 'overabundance of narrative material would speak against actual delivery in this form' (2005: 64) seems totally to misunderstand these aims.

[70] The second *narratio* is omitted in most Group A manuscripts and in Rev. (see 22/135–63n).

[71] While the terms are often synonymous, the distinction is made in this edition between *narrationes* (used of stories) and *exempla* (used of similes and comparisons). For a similar distinction (but including the terms *figura* and *fabula*), see Owst 1966: 151–2. Mirk himself (like other sermonists) does not make this distinction, using *ensaumple* for both comparisons (e.g. 40/82, 84) and stories (e.g. 41/82, 118, 163). Scribal marginal annotations always use *narracio*.

using them, finding it necessary in the Trinity Sunday sermon to explain his motives before offering what is in fact an innocuous and useful *exemplum*: *But ȝette for many wyttes ben latte and heve to levyn þat þei mow note sene ne heryn, bot if þei be broght in be grete ensaumpul, perfore, þogh þis ensaumpul be not alle commendabul, ȝitte for þe more parte it may so lython his wytte so þat he may þe sonnar cum to beleve* (40/80–4n). His use of *exempla* is, in fact, rare, and in the Annunciation sermon he swiftly abandons even the simple and traditional comparison between the lily and the Virgin in favour of a didactic story of a converted Jew (23/88–110n).

Mirk's discomfort with allegory and interpretation may perhaps be explained partly by his evident awareness of the limitations of his audience rather than his own limitations, since in another context (see §2) he bases the sermon for the Assumption of the Virgin on Anselm's allegorization of the Virgin as a castle (see 54/31–4n). However, the moral of his stories is rarely developed in *F* itself. Even in his use of *Gesta Romanorum*, Mirk avoids the extensive moralizations and provides only the literal narrative (for example, at 15/65–96n, 24/38–49n, 102–21n, 25/58–72n). In the Tenebre sermon his interpretation of the story of the faithful lion is singularly inept (26/66–102n), as is his handling of the allegorization of the loaves and fishes at Lent 4 (22/87–95n). In Lent 2 (20/89–101n), the woman of Canaan and her daughter are interpreted as sinners who can only be saved by thorough confession and penance, a reading at variance with the text (and with *GO*), since the mother has shown great faith (as Christ himself says) and hardly deserves to be classed with the sinners. Where his source employs elaborate allegorization (as in Jacobus' interpretation of the candle in the Purification sermon), Mirk simplifies it (see 14/103–10n). Unlike Chaucer's duplicitous Friar, Mirk does not believe that *Glosynge is a glorious thyng, certeyn, / For lettre sleeth, so as we clerkes seyn* (*The Canterbury Tales*, Summoner's Tale, ll. 1793–4).

Mirk's emphasis is instead on what may be readily comprehended by his projected audience. This is the rationale of his defence (with the help of Beleth) of crosses and images of the saints in church (41/109–13). He was clearly aware of contemporary concern about images but endorses the Church's defence of them as *libri laicorum* (*lewed mennus bokys*, 41/113–14), using them as a pedagogic aid in, for example, the Epiphany sermon, where he offers an explanation as to why one magus is represented turning backwards and pointing to the star (12/46–54), and in the Annunciation sermon, where he explains the iconography of the lily pot (23/88–110).

Mirk's defence of images, *whatte-euer þeis Loleres seyne* (41/107), acknowledges the controversy surrounding a subject which he may well have thought would strike a chord in his audience (Ford 2006: 147). It is one of only two references in *F* to Lollards (Fletcher 1987; Powell 1990; Ford 2006: 143–50). The second is more explicit in its condemnation of them, linking them to earlier heretics, criticizing their *smethe wordys and plesyng to þe pepul* (40/32–3), and arguing that they seek the downfall of Christianity (see 40/27–47n). However, as to their teaching, the sermon is silent, and Mirk instead argues for unquestioning faith. Despite an effective *exemplum* of the Trinity (40/84–107), the subject is beyond the wit of man—how the Trinity works *we mow not despitoun bot saddely belevyn* (40/105–6), and the sermon ends with an eloquent example of the futility of theological speculation (40/132–47 n). Such reticence to engage with controversy is not surprising in a sermon *ad populum*. Mirk deals frankly with Lollards and transubstantiation in *MS*, where his audience is a fellow-priest,[72] but such discussion was not appropriate to an illiterate audience, or for semi-literate priests.[73] There is no evidence that Mirk wrote *F* to counter the growing Lollard movement among the people (although his sermons certainly offered a basis for such a counter-attack in their deliberate populism). In the next section, we look beyond Mirk and the late fourteenth century to the various incarnations of *F* in the fifteenth century, which may have offered more managed and more focused responses to the Lollard challenge.

3. THE TRANSMISSION OF THE *FESTIAL* FROM MANUSCRIPT TO PRINTED BOOK

There are extant today twenty-one perfect, or once perfect, texts of *F*,[74] contained in twenty-two manuscripts,[75] together with four

---

[72] Part IV, chs. 11–13 (cf. Oxford, Bodleian Library MS Bodley 632, ff. 90ᵛ–92ʳ).

[73] The rubric to Sermon 40 in IK warns of the dangers of careless talk on controversial subjects: *De festo sancte trinitatis sermo breuis ad parach[i]anos, sed caueat sacerdos dicens hu[n]c sermonem ne plus uel ultra aliter dicat quam hic in sequenti scribitur ne forte ducat audiente[s] in [e]rrorem* (I, p. 183, K (with minor omissions) f. 89ʳ).

[74] Cambridge, St John's College MS G.19 is a copy of a printed edition.

[75] C survives in two manuscripts, BL MSS Harley 2420 and 2417.

manuscripts of the revision (Rev.), two of which are complete. In addition, there are nineteen manuscripts (one in Welsh) with from one to twenty *F* sermons or extracts from *F* sermons.[76]

3.1 The Complete, or Once Complete, Manuscripts

Since the publication of Wakelin (1967), it has been accepted that the extant manuscripts of *F* fall into two groups, A and B.[77] These groups are characterized, in the first instance, by the arrangement and content of the collection:

From the order of the contents of *F*, the manuscripts can be classified, generally speaking, into two types: in Group A, commencing with Advent Sunday, the homilies are given for the sundays [*sic*] and feast-days as they occur through the Church year, together with homilies for various occasions, and these collections are usually prefaced by a prayer, and by a prologue of introductory matter; in Group B, the homilies are arranged *de temporibus et de sanctis*, i.e. the homilies for sundays [*sic*] and some of the major feasts are separated from those for saints' days, the latter being placed all together in the second half of the compilation . . . [T]he Group B manuscripts commence with Advent Sunday, and continue as far as Corpus Christi; they then recommence the liturgical year with S. Andrew (November 30th) . . . The Group B manuscripts omit the prayer and prologue with the exception of Durham University Library MS Cosin V.III.5, the homilies for S. Barnabas, S. Winifred, the homily on Nero, that for S. Alkmunde, and everything after the Dedication. [All] of them also omit the homily De Dominica Prima Quadragesime and the first one for the Assumption [as well as the material on Nero]. Finally, in all Group B manuscripts the homily for Good Friday and the explanation of the Maundy Thursday and Holy Saturday ceremonies are reversed. (Wakelin 1967: 93–4)

Wakelin has been quoted at length because (with the corrections and additions in square brackets) his analysis still holds good, although it should be noted too that BL MSS Harley 2420 and 2417 (C), although divided into *Temporale* and *Sanctorale* respectively, exhibit Group A texts, and that in Group B manuscripts the single sermon for SS Philip and James is divided into two separate sermons.

[76] For manuscripts and sigla, see above, p. xiii; for manuscript descriptions, see Appendix II.
[77] Horstmann had first drawn attention to a basic difference in the sermon arrangement of b (the only Group B manuscript known to him): 'Das Ms. verändert die Ordnung des *Festial* gänzlich, indem es das Temporale vorn zusammenstellt und darauf das Legendar folgen lässt' (1881: CXX).

In the course of his seminal article, Wakelin also demonstrated that 'the Group A manuscripts can mostly be localised in the west . . . On the other hand, the Group B manuscripts . . . seem to form two easterly groups' (p. 113). On the matter of textual variation between the two groups, he asserted, without demonstration,[78] that 'the texts themselves differ considerably from A to B' (1967: 13). Powell (1980: ii. 8–21; 1981: 25–7) pursued further the textual relationship of Groups A and B, and the relationship of manuscripts within Group B, in order to establish that Rev. was based on a Group B manuscript. Her findings corroborated Wakelin's suggestion that the Group A and B divisions extended beyond the arrangement and content of the sermon collection to textual affinities within each group. *F* manuscripts, therefore, 'display a bifurcated tradition, one recension stemming direct from Mirk's original *Festial*, and the other representing a later recension, showing a major change in the arrangement of the sermons and consistent, though generally minor, textual variation' (Powell 1981: 23).

3.1.1. Circulation and Reception of the Complete, or Once Complete, Manuscripts

Most of the manuscripts with complete, or once complete, *F* collections were prepared by or for priests. This is the case with ABC, which are textually close and show similarities in their careful rubrics and rubrication. Only C contains nothing besides *F*,[79] but it is a particularly careful piece of work, perhaps by a paid scribe who was responsible for dividing the sermons into *Temporale* and *Sanctorale*,[80] but perhaps by the priest himself, who moulded the work to his needs.[81]

Other manuscripts with no material other than *F* are DFHIJfg, but

---

[78] The subject had been touched on in his thesis (1960: i, pp. xvi–xvii), which provided an *en face* edition of all known manuscripts of the Pentecost sermon (ii. 603–20).

[79] This is likely always to have been the case, even though BL MS Harley 2417 (the second part of C) ends imperfect.

[80] Seemingly independent of the Group B division, since the *Temporale* includes the Christmas sermons from the Nativity of Christ to Epiphany, which Group B does not (although Rev. does).

[81] For example, *pat . . . itte* (38/51–5) is emended to suit a non-monastic context: *pat ys to forsake þe lust of þe flesh and þe vanyte of þe world and be gouerned by þe counsel of hooly wryt and of here curatus* (Harley 2420, f. 56ᵛ). Note too the unique rubric *sequitur informacio bona et neccessaria capellanis . . .* (Harley 2420, f. 47ᵛ) and the reference to *huius festiallis compilatorem* in the rubric at the end of the *Temporale* (Harley 2417, f. 9ᵛ). (See Appendix II.i.a, description of C (MS Harley 2417, Contents).)

it is more common to find related material in the manuscript. With a general *caveat* that the items currently making up these manuscripts may not always have been so placed together, several manuscripts contain *pastoralia* appropriate to a curate or parish priest: the Sentence of Excommunication (E(F)c), forms of confession (Eb), the articles of the faith (Bh), the Ten Commandments (Bbch), the seven deadly sins (bc and, in the form of Lavynham's *Litil Tretys*, E), the seven sacraments and five wits (h). The didactic material known as *Consilia Isidori* appears in a and c. Pastoral material is also found in G, which (like Ebh) contains English sermons other than *F*. *Narrationes* useful in sermon compilation are also found in *F* manuscripts—a has just one, but b has *narrationes* from the *Northern Homily Cycle*, as well as some Latin ones. K contains prose saints' legends, most of which are related to the *Gilte Legende*.

Some few manuscripts (AGbde) contain Latin material, such as Latin sermons (together with English in G) or sermon authorities (d). Liturgical material in the form of Latin/English Sequences in e predicates use by a priest, while commentaries, concordances, and lections are amongst the Latin material found in A, which might have been owned by a University-educated priest. EF were also prepared for priests, judging by the fact that they contain (contained in F's case) copies of *IPP*. Both offer shortened versions of *F* sermons arranged in thematic groups rather than chronologically or according to service-book arrangement, again presumably satisfying a market. The hand is easy and confident, suggesting a paid scribe who wrote for a market in customized versions of *F*. It is likely that they were the product of a one-man workshop in Northamptonshire (Doyle, personal communication).

Other manuscripts are likely to have been prepared professionally, such as H, most of which is in a very practised hand and has decorated initials for the Prayer, Prologue, and first sermon. These manuscripts may have lay connections. More professional and elaborate manuscripts are to be found in Group B than Group A manuscripts (the text itself is altogether more standard than Group A and may have circulated semi-officially). The hand of a is a very professional one, perhaps of a scribe in an ecclesiastical or government office, and the initials to sermons are well decorated in blue and red. The hand of c is also good and the manuscript is of parchment, carefully designed, with a particularly elaborate decorated initial and border for the first page of *F*. Its double columns indicate professional practice, and it may be a production handled by bookshop stationers. The scribe of g too shows a practised, professional hand (used to copying musical notation, according to Doyle, personal communication), and the manuscript is parchment, with rubrication and in double columns. Of all the manuscripts, however, it is f (with outer and inner bifolia of parchment) which has the most practised professional hand (a similar script to that of a, but less fancy). Moreover, it is the only manuscript to have a historiated initial, perhaps to be attributed to the same illustrator who prepared two works of Lydgate as a presentation gift to Henry VI or Edward IV. It is thus a very prestigious piece of work, and is textually unusual too, pivotal between Groups A and B (perhaps even the result of a collation of a Group A and B manuscript), although still predominantly Group B. It shows some modernization of lexis and the text is frequently rewritten (paraphrased, not revised). Its presence in a printer's shop is intriguing but not immediately explicable.

Other manuscripts of less good but still medium-quality work, which may have been written for pay, include I, which is rubricated and signed by its scribe, William Tybson, a secular priest or regular canon or monk. K is likely to be in the hand of the priest, monk, or canon (perhaps John Meyre) who was responsible for expanding the text considerably by adding Latin scriptural and legend citations, as well as appropriate Latin verse,[82] with rubricated Latin marginalia throughout. It appears that it was intended for preaching to a lay audience (see 24/124n). There is some indication that it might have been in the hands of friars in Oxford in the early sixteenth century. The hand of d is practised but not necessarily professional, and may be that of a priest for his own use. Early attempts at rubrication do not last throughout the *F* stint. Finally, h is an unpretentious hand, trying to produce a bookhand in a less current style than he is normally used to in order to produce a good effect (which he does not successfully achieve).

What we do not find in great number is the very ordinary production that a priest might scribble out and use himself. Presumably there were very many of these which disintegrated from over-use, well before any iconoclastic actions. One example of such a manuscript is b, which is inexpensive, without rubrication, and might

---

[82] For example, K adds at 16/136: *Coruum in diluuio Noe emittebat / Qui ingratus fuerat non reueniebat. / Columba post mittitur qui ramum ferebat / Oliue quo populus totus congaudebat* (f. 41^r). See further in full collations, Appendix III.

have been written by the priest himself (or by a cheap copyist). The hand of e is also amateur, unlike its textually close partner a. J is a clumsy piece of work, perhaps imitating a printed book, even, with initials left unrubricated. G is a compilation made over a number of years by one priest, but perhaps used later by another priest. F sermons are interspersed with Latin and English sermons from other sources, sermon extracts, and *pastoralia*. It was clearly intended for practical parochial use and contains insertions, additions, and marginalia. Sometimes the same F sermon is recopied later, but from a different copy-text.[83] It bears comparison with h, also prepared for use by a mid-fifteenth-century parish priest, with a mixture of sermons (F and otherwise) copied over a period of time, augmented later in the fifteenth century by further sermons, and with an inserted quire dating from the early sixteenth century (one sermon) and another of even later date (pastoral material).

With regard to the transmission of the manuscripts in time and place, some rethinking is necessary of Martyn Wakelin's argument that the Group A manuscripts 'can mostly be localized in the west', while the Group B manuscripts 'seem to form two easterly groups'.[84] From Lilleshall F will have circulated first along the Marches southwards, and several manuscripts are located in the central-west and south-west Midlands: Warwickshire ABG, Worcestershire C, Staffordshire D, Shropshire K, 'nineteen different kinds of west and central Midland English' G (McIntosh & Wakelin 1982: 445). Any further transmission will have been eastward (Wales being an obstacle to the English language westward), and other Group A manuscripts are more central and even central-east Midlands (Northamptonshire EF, Leicestershire/Derbyshire H, Nottinghamshire I, Leicestershire J).

The Group B manuscripts are much more tightly localized than the Group A manuscripts.[85] It is indicative of the wide transmission of Group A that it is almost always a Group A text which one finds when a few sermons or *narrationes* are transmitted in an anthology

---

[83] See Appendix III.v for a collation of the Passion Sunday sermon (no. 24) which includes two versions in G.

[84] Wakelin 1967: 113. Although the article was published before *LALME*, it was written in close correspondence with Professor Angus McIntosh. Some localizations are no longer sound (see below Appendix II, *passim*). In his map (1967: 103, rev. Beadle 1994: 81) Wakelin located all manuscripts known to him at the time (full, partial, and Rev.).

[85] The Anglo-Irish manuscript g may be an exception, although there appears to be no specific linguistic, only provenance, evidence for the dialect being Anglo-Irish (but see McIntosh & Samuels 1968).

manuscript. The Group B manuscripts are predominantly central Midlands (there are no west Midland texts). Three emanated from Leicestershire (cef), two from Nottinghamshire (bd), and one each from Rutland (a) and Northamptonshire (h). They are also much closer to each other textually than the Group A manuscripts. There appears to have been an attempt to standardize the *F* text and to circulate that version, at least within a narrow area of the central Midlands. There is no evidence that this circulation was orchestrated (which does not mean that it may not have been organized, if relatively informally, through parish priest networks).

3.2. The Partial Manuscripts

Numerous *F* sermons have found their way into other manuscript contexts, either intact, as whole sermons of the Group A or B tradition (sometimes revised and rewritten), or as extracts or *narrationes* taken from *F* sermons. The criterion for 'partial manuscripts' has been twenty or fewer full sermons, thus including CUL MSS Ee.2.15 (perhaps once complete but now only eight sermons, two imperfect) and Nn.3.10 (twenty sermons, much adapted), as well as more exiguous witnesses.

Dialect evidence in relation to the partial manuscripts reveals a far wider area of transmission than in the case of extant full manuscripts (see Beadle 1994: 81). For example, the dialect of *F* sermons in MS Harley 2250 is Cheshire, while that of MS Harley 1288 is Lincolnshire, and the sermons in MS Royal 18.B.XXIII were copied as far south as Berkshire. Nevertheless, it is of interest that 'the text only very seldom made its way north of the Humber, or south of the Thames valley'.[86]

Amongst the partial manuscripts, two have been mentioned already. The second booklet of MS CUL Nn.3.10, which contains twenty *F* sermons, is acephalous. What survives has been adapted, perhaps for a priest's specific needs, with sermons copied in groups and material omitted and added. It includes the Sentence of Excommunication and is bound with a manuscript copy of a print of the *Cordyal*.[87] MS CUL Ee.2.15, on the other hand, may once have

---

[86] Beadle 1994: 82. Beadle's further comment that there is 'no sign that it achieved any circulation in London' may well be true, although ownership and other evidence suggest that f was at some time in London.

[87] For particular insight into multiple-text manuscripts, including *F* manuscripts, see Doyle 1953.

been a full *F* collection, although *F* now consists of a booklet of only eight sermons from the *Sanctorale* section of a Group B text, imperfect at beginning and end, which has been bound with various verse items, including material by Chaucer and Lydgate, presumably for lay use.

Another CUL manuscript, MS Ff.2.38, contains only three *F* sermons (SS Mary Magdalene, Margaret, Thomas of Canterbury) which have been adapted to saints' legends, probably for lay devotional reading. The manuscript itself contains devotional material, *pastoralia*, and exemplary romances, including pieces from Chaucer and Gower. BL MS Cotton Titus A.XXVI is similar, though less elaborate, and contains verse and prose legends, lyrics, some Lydgate, and a single *F* sermon (St Mary Magdalene), which has been comprehensively rewritten and modernized.

However, occasional sermons occur most often in priests' manuscripts, such as MS Lincoln Cathedral Library 133. They are interspersed with other sermons in MSS Greaves 54 (which, apart from *F* material, includes English sermons and Latin *narrationes*), Royal 18.B.XXIII (three *F* sermons amongst many English sermons), and Arundel 279 (one imperfect *F* sermon amongst other English and Latin ones). The treatise most often found in these partial (sometimes very partial) *F* manuscripts for priests is the Latin pastoral manual *Speculum Christiani* (MSS Harley 1288 and 2250, Greaves 54, Lincoln 133). Other works include *Gesta Romanorum* (MS Bodley 123) and Lavynham's *Litil Tretys* (MS Harley 1288).

MS Harley 2250 also contains three *F* sermons (as well as *narrationes* and extracts) amongst various Latin and English material, including a verse life of Christ. Extracts from *F* sermons, sometimes just *narrationes*, are fairly common in manuscripts used by priests (and probably more exist than have so far been identified), such as MS Harley 1288 (which also contains Latin *narrationes* and Bozon's *Contes Moralisés*, as well as much material useful for a parish priest) and MS Lansdowne 379 (two *F* extracts amongst other English sermons and a part-print, part-manuscript text of the *Exornatorium Curatorum*).

Throughout this discussion *F* has been closely related to use by priests, as was Mirk's original intention, although perhaps some of the manuscripts assigned here to priests (particularly perhaps the more elaborate ones which have no obvious signs that they were prepared for lay use, e.g. c) were written for, or even in, different contexts: monasteries, friaries, colleges, cathedrals, for example. The provenance of not a single *F* manuscript can be certainly traced back to such places, although they were the source of many rescued post-Reformation (and later) manuscripts (Ker 1985, Humphreys 1986). William Tybson, who copied I, may have been a monk or regular/ secular canon, not necessarily a secular priest, as may have been the copyist of g (Thomas Norreys) or the compiler (John Meyre?) of K. The evidence does not, however, exist.

3.2.1. Four Related Manuscripts

Four related manuscripts qualify for separate discussion. MSS Bodleian Library e Museo 180 (O), Durham University Library Cosin V.IV.3 (Du), Gloucester Cathedral Library MS 22 (Gl) (*olim* 22, second binding), and Lincoln Cathedral Chapter Library 50 and 51 (L) are copies in the same hand of substantially the same collection of sermons (ed. Morrison forthcoming).

O appears to be the earliest of the four texts and is broadly a dominical collection (although it includes the Christmas feast-days and Ash Wednesday, as well as two Dedication sermons). Gl and L (which are textually close) contain, or originally contained, much the same sermons as O but with the addition in Gl (and presumably at one time in L, which has missing folios) of four Holy Week sermons (all from *F*): Tenebre, Maundy Thursday, Good Friday, Holy Saturday. Du now contains twelve sermons for Advent, Lent, and Passiontide.

The relationship of this collection with *F* is a complex one, as will only become fully apparent in the next section (§3.3). For the moment, attention will concentrate on the collection as a partial *F* manuscript. Gl provides fullest evidence of this, in that the four sermons for Holy Week are based on a Group B version of *F*. However, the compiler of the collection also used *F* in two other sermons, Passion Sunday and Ascension Day. Passion Sunday is also found in O and L. It follows the *F* sermon in a paraphrased and expanded text for about half the sermon (cf. 24/2–81) and thereafter continues differently; in Du a different sermon uses the *F narratio* of the talking statue (cf. 24/38–49). The Ascension Day sermon occurs in the same three manuscripts, again loosely following a paraphrased version of the text, omitting the final *narratio* (cf. 37/2–102). It may be that further sermons are minimally dependent on *F*, for example, the Circumcision sermon in the same three manuscripts includes details taken from the *F* sermon for the same day (cf. 11/77–102). In general, these sermons so comprehensively paraphrase and alter their sources by insertions and omissions that their exact relationship with *F* is hard to determine.[88] The compiler has comprehensively cannibalized several collections in order to create his own collection, which he then appears to have copied several times in different formats to sell on the market or to order.

3.3. The Revision of the *Festial*

Some time after 1434 (see 41/18–23 n), a Group B manuscript formed the basis for a substantial revision of *F* (Steckman 1937; Fletcher & Powell 1978, ed. Steckman 1934, partially ed. Powell 1980, 1981). Rev. is preserved most completely in two BL manuscripts, Harley 2247 (R1) and Royal 18.B.XXV (R2). Dublin, Trinity College MS 428 (R3) was presumably once complete (its text is closer to R1 than R2), while Gloucester Cathedral Library MS 22 Add. (R4), although seriously imperfect, may not have had the full complement of sermons. As it stands, R4 begins with the first four sermons of Advent, as in R1 and R2 (R3 is acephalous), then provides a Septuagesima sermon unconnected with Rev., followed by two more sermons, the first a cannibalization of two Rev. sermons, the second the remainder of one of these sermons (Powell 1981: 15).[89]

In Rev. the Group B arrangement into *Temporale* and *Sanctorale* was preserved, but the Christmas cycle (the Nativity of Christ to the Epiphany) was inserted into the *Temporale* after Advent and before Septuagesima. The single Advent sermon was divided into two (as in EF); the material on Maundy Thursday and Easter Eve (which in Mirk's original intentions was not to be preached but in the Group B manuscripts had been converted into a sermon) was divided into two sermons in their chronological order, separated by the sermon for Good Friday; the sermon for Corpus Christi was divided into two, the first half considerably augmented and updated (as it is in cd, see 41/18–23 n) by details of the extra indulgences of the Council of Basle of 1434. The Conception of the Virgin sermon was divided into two (R2) and the Annunciation sermon divided into three (R1); both Assumption of the Virgin sermons were included (although the first is not found in any Group B manuscript); a sermon was introduced for Relic Sunday. Some *Sanctorale* sermons were omitted, perhaps

---

[88] One awaits Morrison (forthcoming).

[89] For the relationship of the R4 sermons to R1 and R2, see Powell 1980: i. 16–34.

through an imperfect exemplar.[90] Otherwise the content of Rev. is as Group B. The sermons themselves were substantially rewritten from a renewed study of *LA*. This naturally affected the *Sanctorale* more than the *Temporale* of the collection,[91] but most sermons underwent some alteration in the form of rewriting the text, omitting material (particularly *narrationes* from the *Sanctorale*),[92] introducing Latin citations (mostly from the Vulgate), and adding material, largely from Mirk's original sources, *RDO*, *LA*, and the liturgy of the Church. Just a few sermons use other sources, such as *Fasciculus Morum* (*FM*) (Powell 1981: 123–4 (3/54–69), 129 (5/103–29)), Jacobus's dominical sermons (Powell 1981: 124–5 (3/103–31)), and the English version of Archbishop Thoresby's Injunctions of 1357 (see 22/47–76n).[93]

However, the most significant aspect of Rev. is the addition to the collection of at least one extra sermon (sometimes two, or even three in the case of Easter Day) for almost each day of the *Temporale*, resulting in twenty-six new sermons.[94] In the *Sanctorale*, there is only the new sermon for Relic Sunday and additional sermons each for All Saints' and All Souls' Days and a Burial (ed. Powell & Fletcher 1981).[95]

These new sermons are markedly different from Mirk's sermons. In construction they follow the 'modern', or academic, model;[96] they favour allegorical, rather than literal, explication of the text; they reject *narrationes*; and indeed are altogether more sophisticated (Blench 1964).[97] The source of ten of the new *Temporale* sermons

---

[90] The sermon for the Translation of St Thomas of Canterbury (7 July) is replaced by a sermon for Relic Sunday, which notes in its opening text that Relic Sunday is celebrated the first Sunday after the feast of the Translation (the norm in a diocese where the Sarum Use was followed but not in a major church which had its own relic day). The usual sermon to follow the Translation sermon is St Margaret, which is missing too. Similarly, the omission of SS Martin and Katherine at the end may not have been intentional.

[91] The *Sanctorale* sermons are more thoroughly revised in R2 than R1/3.

[92] Only three/four *narrationes* are removed from the *Temporale*: 22/135–63, 28/26–38, 41/163–84 (41/117–32 also om. R2).

[93] See further Fletcher & Powell 1978.

[94] R1 is taken as the norm here. For differences in the other manuscripts, see Appendix I.

[95] In addition, the original *F* sermons for All Saints' and All Souls' Days and a Burial (nos. 64, 65, Add2) are so thoroughly revised as to be practically new sermons.

[96] For a full discussion of sermon construction, see Spencer 1993: 228–68. The sermons ed. Grisdale (1939) are excellent examples of the 'modern' structure.

[97] Each of Blench's six chapters begins with pre-Reformation sermon material, in which R1 plays a prominent illustrative part. See too Spencer 1993: 311–16 and *passim*.

is closely related to a collection preserved imperfectly in CUL MS Gg.vi.16 (ff. 34^r–59^v), a preacher's commonplace book of the second quarter of the fifteenth century in the hand of a competent, practised scribe (Powell 1981: 32–9). This (perhaps already in its imperfect state) was transmitted independently in the sermon collection which has already been discussed (§3.2.1), that extant in ODuGlL. Eight sermons from this collection (Nativity of Christ, Circumcision, Sexagesima, Quinquagesima (two sermons), Ash Wednesday, 2 Lent, 3 Lent) are sermons added to Rev.^{98} The sources of these sermons include both the sermons and *distinctiones* of Jacobus de Voragine, as well as his *LA*, the *sermones dominicales* of Nicholas de Aquevilla, and *FM*.^{99} In addition, one sermon appears to be partly dependent on Alexander Carpenter's *Destructorium Viciorum*, completed in 1429 (Powell & Fletcher 1981).

The replication of sources in both *F* and the new sermons in Rev. suggests that one man was responsible for the whole reworking of the original Group B text. He was not a regular, like Mirk (see 39/5–21n),^{100} nor was he writing for an audience like Mirk's. The nature of his revision of *F* 'shows a careful academic and social upgrading of Mirk's text, which transforms a number of simple sermons aimed at a poor parish congregation into a larger and more erudite collection for a prosperous and educated audience' (Powell 1981: 32). This is revealed in several ways, apart from the rewriting, revision, and expansion of the collection itself: by the change of invocation to *Worshipfull frendes*; by the omission of criticism of the rich (Powell 1981: 29); by the use of Latin citation; (in R1) by the careful *ordinatio* of the text, with detailed marginal annotation. 'All these things point to an academic origin for the compiler himself, a man trained to acknowledge sources carefully, who had access to books more likely to be found in the environs of a university than a parish church' (Spencer 1993: 313–14).

While there is no evidence to link Rev. with either of the

---

^{98} Those from the Nativity of Christ to Ash Wednesday inclusive are not in Du (and Quinquagesima 1 is not in O), but Lent 2 and 3 are in all four manuscripts. For a transcription of all eight sermons, see Powell 1980: iii. 42–74. O was the base-text for Fletcher (1977), whose edition includes no *F*-related material.

^{99} The identification of BL Add. MS 21253 (Powell 1981: 33–4) as the sermons of Nicholas de Aquevilla post-dates Powell (1980, 1981) (see Spencer 1993: 481–2 n. 86).

^{100} For example, at 39/12–13, the reference to the monastic vow of poverty is altered in Rev. to almsgiving: *he þat hath wisdom and goode and woll parte with þe pore after Goddes preceptes of suche goodis as God hath sent hym he is holde a foule with sum men* (R1, f. 116^v).

Universities, it may be significant that the dialect of R1 (the best of the manuscripts) is Leicestershire, the centre for circulation of the Lollard sermon cycles. The unrevised *F* manuscripts do not offer evidence for the assertion that Mirk wrote *F* 'almost certainly to compete with the Lollard homily cycles' (Doyle 1989: 115), although the Group B recension, with its narrower circulation and closer textual affinities, is a not improbable candidate for that role. However, if anything were to compete with the Lollard sermons (on something like their own terms), the careful scholarship employed to prune and upgrade *F*, together with the immaculate presentation of R1,[101] makes Rev. an adequate competitor.[102] The scant survival of manuscripts,[103] and the fact that the printed editions are based on Group B, not Rev., manuscripts (Powell 2007: x–xi) suggests, however, that it never achieved that status, whatever its compiler's intentions.[104]

3.4. The Printed Editions

In the late fifteenth and early sixteenth centuries *F* was the sermon collection *par excellence*, thanks to the attention given it by the early printers (Powell 1997b). William Caxton first printed it in 1483 (*STC* 17957) and produced a second edition (*STC* 17959) in 1491, based on the 1486 edition usually attributed to Theodoric Rood (*STC* 17958)[105] (Powell 2007: x–xix). This led to a spate of ten more editions in the 1490s alone, produced by six different printers. Caxton's successor, Wynkyn de Worde, was himself responsible for nine editions, cornering the market by 1519 (*STC* 17973.5) and producing the last edition (*STC* 17975) in 1532, on the eve of the Reformation.

Whether deliberate or not (and there is no evidence that it was deliberate, although no other sermon collection was printed in England before the Reformation), *F* became the official source of sermon material for religious and lay consumption alike in the last fifty years of the Roman Catholic Church in England. The widespread

[101] On the care for *ordinatio* of the Lollard scribes, see Hudson 1989.

[102] The Wycliffite cycle (ed. Hudson and Gradon 1983–96) is much fuller than *F*, providing 294 sermons, including, for example, one on the gospel for each Sunday in the year and one for every day in Lent. For a brief but useful summary and bibliography of present evidence, see Somerset 2004: 200–1.

[103] Compared with thirty-one manuscripts which contain either all the Wycliffite cycle, or a self-contained part of it, and four which show adaptation outside Wycliffite circles.

[104] Although the distribution of the extant manuscripts (Leicestershire, Northampton-shire, Norfolk, Nottinghamshire) suggests a wider influence than appearances suggest.

[105] *Pace STC* 17959 ('reprints text of 17957').

transmission of its manuscripts was easily outmatched by the printed texts so that *F* became 'an early English best-seller'.[106] It seems to have been normally issued together with the *Quattuor Sermones* (*QS*) (*STC* 17957, ed. Blake 1975),[107] a large body of catechetical material presented in the rather makeshift form of four sermons, covering the Paternoster, Ave, Creed, Ten Commandments, two precepts of the New Testament, seven sacraments, seven deeds of mercy, seven virtues, seven deadly sins, five senses, nine pains of hell, and (very briefly) fourteen joys of heaven, together with material on the three elements of penance, contrition, confession, and satisfaction (Powell 1997a). *QS* is followed by the Sentence of Excommunication in English (Pickering, 1981),[108] with the pronouncement of excommunication in Latin, and the *Bedes on the Sonday*, the bidding prayers (Coxe 1840).

The sermons of *F* fulfilled the priest's preaching needs, while the *pastoralia* of *QS* answered his obligation to preach the pastoral tenets four times a year. The Sentence was also to be preached quarterly and the bidding prayers every Sunday after the gospel and offertory (Powell 1997a: 184–6), so that the combination of materials in a typical printed volume was a real *vade mecum* for the priest, who must have been seen as the main customer. However, at least by the time of his second edition (1491), Caxton had extended the market. First he updated *F* by adding three new sermons for feast-days which had recently acquired considerable lay popularity: the Visitation of the Virgin (2 July), the Transfiguration of our Lord (6 August), and the Holy Name of Jesus (7 August). Then he appended a quire of six in order to add a treatise aimed at both a lay and clerical market, the *Hamus Caritatis*, or hook of love. Its title (*A shorte exhortacyon ofte to be shewed to the peple . . .*) is designed to catch the eye of the priest (and indeed it takes the form of a short academic sermon, with theme, ante-theme, and division into two principals), but its content, which explains the practical application of the Ten Commandments of the Old Testament and two precepts of the New Testament in the lay household, is directed at the pious lay householder.[109]

---

[106] Marston 1972. In manuscript it is outnumbered by the *Mirror of the Blessed Life of Christ*, the circulation of which may have been helped by official endorsement (Doyle 1989: 115–16).

[107] *QS* was not, however, incorporated into an edition of *F* until Wolfgang Hopyl did so in 1495 (*STC* 17964); Wynkyn de Worde did not follow suit until 1508 (*STC* 17971).

[108] Amongst *F* manuscripts, the closest version to Caxton's Sentence is c (Pickering 1981: 236–7) and the closest version to Caxton's bidding prayers is G.

[109] The three sermons and *Hamus* are ed. in Powell 2007.

The ready market for printed versions of *F* has already been attested. The advent of printing did not, however, mean an end to the production of manuscripts, nor to the copying by hand of printed books (Blake 1989). St John's College Cambridge MS G.19 is a manuscript copy of *STC* 17966 (Rouen, 1499), copied by hand for the Sinclair family of Roslin.[110]

3.5. After the Reformation

After 23 October 1532, when Wynkyn de Worde printed *F* for the last time (*STC* 17975), it was not reprinted until the EETS edition (Erbe 1905). However, it continued to be read, as is clear from interventions and marginalia in extant manuscripts and prints, nor was its influence entirely at an end (Powell 1994).

The most extensive intervention in extant manuscripts is the cancellation and erasure of references to the Pope and to St Thomas of Canterbury, as directed in the Proclamations of Henry VIII.[111] Several manuscripts display clear evidence that the King's wishes were complied with (by removal of sermons 10 and 47, or scoring through, or erasure of the saint's name), and thus that the manuscripts were still in use, most likely by priests and parishes, after the Reformation (see manuscript descriptions, Appendix II *passim*). In other parts of the collection, the word *pope* is frequently erased, for example, in the Quinquagesima sermon (no. 17), where *pardon* is also erased in some manuscripts, or the Corpus Christi day sermon (no. 41), which also shows erasure in some manuscripts of *pardon* and *indulgence*. The complete manuscripts of Rev. (R1, R2) do not include sermons for the feast of the Translation of St Thomas, but in both manuscripts the single sermon for the saint remains intact, although references to the Pope are cancelled in R1.

Only a few manuscripts show clear evidence in their marginalia that they were read with care (rather than merely scribbled in) in the post-Reformation period. The reader of f was both familiar with, and hostile to, *F*, *LA*, and indeed Catholics in general, as some of his marginal comments attest: *the common fooles hold a man being ded goeth to purgatory . . . looke in All Sowles of Legenda Aurea* (f. 79ᵛ), *the catholick foles þat worship images think a dyvine poure to be in þem*

---

[110] The three new sermons are incorporated in their chronological position (a practice initiated by Wynkyn de Worde in 1493 (*STC* 17962)), followed by the *Hamus*.

[111] Hughes & Larkin 1964–9: i. 229–32 (no. 158), especially 231 (the Pope), 270–6 (no. 186), especially 276 (St Thomas Becket). Discussed Duffy 1992: 410–21.

(f. 139^r). R1 has extensive marginalia, in the scribe's own hand and other contemporary hands, but the few later comments of Dr John Covel (1638–1722) are curious, rather than condemnatory, as when he comments laconically alongside a *narratio* which presents the contrition of a rich man as so great that his tears soaked his bedclothes, bolster, and bed-straw: *Rich man had no Feather-beds* (f. 45^v). Other manuscripts may contain marginalia of the post-Reformation period, but they provide little, if any, evidence of engagement with *F*, except perhaps in the case of the Irish MS (g), which has pious sixteenth-century marginalia but no clear evidence that the Forster family, who owned the manuscript, had read the sermons.

There are, however, three cases which show that *F* was both used and even prized after the Reformation. One is the Welsh translation in Cardiff Public Library MS Havod 22; another is the single sermon preserved amongst the trial papers of York, Borthwick Institute H.C.C.P. 1590/5; the third is the single sermon in Stonyhurst College Library MS A.II.8.

MS Havod 22 appears to have been a priest's own compilation, located in north-east Wales, that is, not remote from Lilleshall itself, in the third quarter of the sixteenth century. The manuscript contains fifteen *Temporale* sermons from *F* (Advent to Pentecost) which appear to be a free translation and adaptation of a printed edition. The context is a fascinating collection of sermons, *pastoralia*, legends, scriptural translations, narratives, and even a dramatic rendering of the Passion, all in Welsh, dating from a period when such material would not have been copied in England.

The single sermon surviving amongst the High Commission Cause Papers at York relates to a case brought in 1589 against John Minet of East Drayton, Nottinghamshire by his fellow parishioners. Amongst the seven charges against Minet was his *takinge vpon him to preach in the church and for preachinge of false and erronius doctrine*. The preaching had taken the form of a sermon for the feast of St John the Baptist (no. 44), and the deposition includes a transcript of the offending sermon, which appears to be based on a post-1483 printed edition of *F* (O'Mara 1987b, Powell 1994: 14–16).

The third piece of evidence of sixteenth-century readership of *F* is an Elizabethan transcription (ed. de Smedt 1887) of the sermon for the feast of St Winifred (no. 43), now in a collection of material relating to the miracles of the saint in Stonyhurst College, near Blackburn. The sermon itself can only stem from a Group A manuscript (since only Group A contains the sermon for St Winifred), but that manuscript is now, it appears, lost (Girsch 1995). The sermon may have been copied from a full collection or may perhaps have survived as a single sermon in preaching use somewhere in Shropshire (Shrewsbury Cathedral, the former Benedictine abbey containing Winifred's shrine, is an attractive location for this speculation).

These three contexts in which *F* continued to be used after the Reformation appear to be rather different. In one case a priest in the Welsh marches, perhaps faced with a paucity of preaching or reading material, translated and adapted a printed edition which had reached him from England. In another, a licensed Reader in a Nottinghamshire village read out in the pulpit one of Mirk's sermons, probably from a printed edition, with (as it was proved, at least to the authorities' satisfaction) seditious, rather than pious, intent. In the third case, Stonyhurst College, a Jesuit public school in recusant Lancashire, preserved papers attesting the posthumous miracles at Holywell of St Winifred, a saint venerated in North Wales and the Marches, papers which included a later transcript of the *F* sermon for the saint. It is clear that *F* did not disappear immediately after the Reformation, despite efforts to dispose of it both physically and verbally.[112] However, before the end of the century, it had been entirely displaced from its once supreme position, along with those other collections and handbooks that had been so intrinsic a part of the library of the pre-Reformation parish priest and educated layperson.

4. THE RELATIONSHIP OF THE MANUSCRIPTS OF THE *FESTIAL*

As already noted (§3.1), *F* manuscripts can be divided into Groups A and B on the basis of the arrangement of their sermons, sermon content, dialect, and textual variation.

In establishing this basic grouping, Wakelin (1967) demonstrated that the arrangement into *Temporale* and *Sanctorale* was a feature of all Group B manuscripts (also C in Group A). The extra content of

---

[112] For post-Reformation criticism of medieval sermons, see Spencer 1993: 321–34, esp. 324–6, which deal specifically with criticism of *F*.

the Group A manuscripts confirmed Group A as the earlier group, that is, that Group B was a recension of Mirk's original collection. With the exception of the idiosyncratic manuscript f (which has the Prologue), no Group B manuscript contains the Prayer or the Prologue, which are demonstrably original to Mirk. Moreover, it is only Group A manuscripts (and not all) that have the sermons for SS Winifred and Alkmund (nos. 43, 56), saints local to Lilleshall. Some Group A manuscripts provide other sermons never found in Group B (e.g. nos. 34, 42) but which, together with material not originally intended for preaching (nos. 46, Add1–6), appear to be authentically Mirk's, if not all originally part of *F*. On the matter of non-preachable material, the details of Holy Week ritual offered in the Group A manuscripts, often with a clearly original rubric that the material is not to be preached (see 28/1–2n), appear in the Group B manuscripts as a normal sermon for Maundy Thursday/ Easter Eve, which is therefore found, not after the Good Friday sermon (as in Group A), but before it. In addition, several sermons in Group B manuscripts contain more material (often from *LA* or other legendary sources) than Group A manuscripts (see §4.4), evidence of the gradual accretion of Mirk's original text which in its fullest form is represented by Rev.

Wakelin's analysis of the dialects of the extant manuscripts served to confirm Group A as the earlier of the two groups, since its manuscripts were found to be predominantly western in origin, that is, nearer to Lilleshall than the Group B manuscripts. The argument was that Mirk's sermon collection moved into an area of transmission and distribution more central to the country than his isolated abbey near the Welsh marches.

As for textual variation between Groups A and B, that has been touched on already (§3.1) and demonstrated in print (Fletcher and Powell 1978: 75–6; Powell 1997c). For example, the following readings from the full collations demonstrate the distinctiveness of Group B readings:[113]

---

[113] Unless otherwise stated, examples may be verified in the full collations (Appendix III: Prayer, Prologue, Sermons 2, 14, 24, 34, 39, 56). All manuscripts have been collated informally in order to establish α's text, and (since the full collations supply minor variants but not many substantive cruxes), where necessary, discussion is based on material outside the full collations. Such discussion is signalled in the text above; where an Explanatory Note provides further details, the designation 'n' has been used after a reference.

(1) 2/90–1 *made men to take Androw and strype hym naked*] αacdefg, *mad men to take andrew and strypt hym nakyd* b, *made men to strype andrew nakyd* J; *made men to do androwe* (*to be* add. K) *naked* ABCDEFGHIK; *anon commawndyd that he schuld be don nakyd* h.

(2) 2/95–6 *art mad holy by þe presyous body of Cryst on þe hanget my mayster Ihesu Cryst*] α, *art* (*art*] *is* d] *made holy by the precious body* (*body*] *blode* cd) *of cryst that* (*that*] om. h) *on thee henge* (*henge*] *dyd hong* h) *my maister* (*maister*] *lorde* cd) *ihesu cryst* abcdegh, *art made holy by oure lorde ihesu crist* f; *my maystur* (*maystur*] *lorde* E) *ihesu crist* (*crist*] om. J) *dyed on* ABCDEF-GHIJK.

(3) 14/104 *a monnus owne selfe*] ABCGH, *a man hymselfe* DJ, *Amoncvs self* α, *manus self* I, *hit betokenyth his godhede ihyd in his manhede* K (EF absent); om. abcdefgh.

(4) 24/90 *strong*] αI, *prykkyng* AC, *prikked* EFK, *tyngynge* B, *stynkyng* D, *charpe* HJ (G(1) absent); om. G(2)abcdefgh.

(5) 39/30 *bot in hulkyng*] α, *but in hudlek* ABCDGK, *but in hidelles* EF, *bot in hedulys* I, *but yn hydnes* H, *but priuely* J; om. abcdefg (h absent).

Two more complex cruxes confirm the basic distinction between Groups A and B, but also serve to demonstrate the variation within Group A manuscripts (as do the above examples) and the idiosyncrasies of K and f:

(6) 14/33 *leue wel*] αabcdeg, *trowe ye right wele* f (h absent); *the* (*the*] om. I) *lawe wull* ABCGHIJ, *lawe ordeyneth a* (*a*] om. F) *remedy for to clanse hom* (*hom*] *hit* E, *him* F) *but þen 3e schull* (*ye* add. F) *know wele* (*wele*] om. E) DEF; *at þat tyme* K.

(7) 14/78–9 *þey hadden euore*] α, *they had euer* (*euer*] *euery* c) *the victorye* abcdegh, *it fortuned hem euer more to haue the victorie* f; *þey were euerous* BDFG, *they were errorus* J, *þay wer ebreus* I, *þey were so* (*so*] om. C) *euerows and my3ty* AC, *þey uyctues* H, *þey were chevalrous* K (E absent).

In addition, there is frequent major and minor variation in the Group B text, most notably three principal, extended passages (21/6–14n, 57/152–3n, 67/73–4n), one a rewriting of the text, the other two major additions to the text, which clearly demarcate the two Groups.

4.1. Group A as the Original Collection

The priority of Group A has been noted above in relation to the content of the collections in Group A manuscripts and their dialects. The fact that it is mainly Group A manuscripts which contain the Prayer (αABCDFHIf) and Prologue (αABCFHIKf) argues too for Group A as closer to Mirk's original manuscript. The Prologue in particular is demonstrably original to Mirk in that it refers in the first person to his purpose in compiling *F* and names his principal source and his preferred title for the collection.[114]

A number of cruxes will demonstrate the textual superiority of Group A. First, it may be demonstrated by comparison with Mirk's primary source, *LA*. The phrase *crebris ictibus pulsans* (referring to *ostium*) is correctly rendered (2/142) *bete vpon þe yate so harde* in B (A illegible) and (with minor variation) in the other Group A manuscripts; in Group B (except f) the reading is *bad open the gate so harde* (with variation in the adverbial phrase):

(8) *bete vpon þe yate so harde: bete*] BGHIJK, *did bete* EF, *bed* α, *put* D, *knokked* C; *vpon þe yate*] *þeron* K; *vpon*] BEFGIJ, *hopon* α, *on* C, *vp at* H, *open* D; *so*] BCDEFGHIK, om. J; *harde*] *fast* K, om. J.

bad open the gate so harde: bad . . . gate] abcdegh, *knokkid* f; *so*] *lowd and so grym* add. b; *harde*] *and so lowde* add. h, om. d.

Two further examples are taken from outside the full collations:

(9) The correct translation at 37/111 of *LA*'s *quaedam fornax immensa* is *a huge ovyn* (I, cf. *an hoged howuen* α, *an hoge on* D).[115] Those Group A manuscripts which are witnesses for this phrase accord with this reading: *a hoot ovyn* ABC, *a grete ovyn* J, *an ovyn* K. In Group B, as a result of a copy-text bearing features of both α and D, this is rendered *oon hangid* (abcefg, *one hang* d, h absent).

(10) At 45/87, *LA*'s *maximum canem* is correctly translated *a hoge doge* (I, cf. *an hoged dogge* α), with which other Group A witnesses

---

[114] At 29/81–3 the personal tone of the Group A text is lost by the replacement of *And . . . of* by: *ther was* (*ihappid ther was* f, *ffor I rede of* h). Also original to Mirk may be the (common) tag *(Amen) for charite*, found in most Group A manuscripts (e.g. A f. 23ʳ; D f. 10ᵛ (*Amen, amen, pur charyte*); E ff. 8ᵛ, 38ᵛ, 62aʳ, 66aʳ; F p. 92; G f. 264ᵛ) but in c only of the Group B manuscripts (*Amen per charite*, f. 59ᵛ).

[115] *MED* oven *n.* records *on* as a variant; *MED* huge *adj.* does not record *hoged* as a variant (only, once each, *hoge, hogge, hoger, howge*).

agree: *a dogge* BDHK, *a grete dogge* J. (C's reading *an honged dogge* is a misinterpretation of a reading such as α and may be compared with the transition from *an hoged howuen/ an hoge on* to *oon hangid* in the previous example.) In the Group B archetype, however, eyeskip from *teyhed*, 'tied' (l. 87) has resulted in *a tyed dogge* (ae, *a tydogg* bcf, *a band dog* d, *a dogg* h, g absent).[116]

The difficulty experienced by the scribe of the Group B exemplar is clearly the result of working with a different dialect, where *on* and *hoged* were not recognized (for a similar example, see 28/71–2n). Other misunderstandings of the copy-text which demonstrate the priority of Group A can be cited from the full collations. In α's reading *þus is a man browght into plithe to be lorne* (39/115–16), variation within Group A is unusually minimal:

(11) *is*] *many* add. J; *a*] *many* H; *into*] *in* BDGHJ; *be*] *lost and* add. I; *lorne*] *lost* HJK.

Although the Group B *Ur*-text appears to have rendered this satisfactorily, in that two manuscripts are broadly correct (*þus a man in plite to be lorne* c, *thus is a man in poynt to be lost* f), the probable loss of the preposition in the exemplar to abeg has resulted in the interpretation of *plit(h)e* (*MED* **plight** *n.* 'danger') as past participle of *plighten* (*MED v.* 'to pledge'): *thus is a manne plight to be [l]orn*, 'thus is a man pledged to be lost' (a, emended). Variants are:

þus] *þis* d; *is*] om. c, *makes* d; *browght into plithe*] om. d; *browght*] om. abcefg; *into*] *in* cf, om. abeg; *plithe*] *point* f, *lyke* b; *be*] om. b; *lorne*] *loste* f, *born* ae.

The scribe of the Group B exemplar has sometimes had difficulty in reading his copy-text, most evident in the rendering of proper names in Group B, as at 28/26n *Rycharde* (left blank),[117] 38/88 *Remys* (*Iames*).[118]

Lacunae and single word/phrase omissions (sometimes the result of eyeskip in the exemplar) are common to Group B manuscripts, as at 24/55 *on . . . metton*.[119] Outside the full collations, the following examples may be given of omissions in Group B:

---

[116] See further 24/71n, 33/78n, 50/164n, 52/145–50n, 66/66n.

[117] The name also caused confusion in Group A MSS (e.g. *rycary* CI, *sycany* B), and F replaces *in þe lyue of Seynt Rycharde* (28/26) by *that there was an holy man.*

[118] See 38/87–99n (f agrees with Group A).

[119] f makes sense of the exemplar (Appendix III.v, 24/55 *on . . . on*).

(12) 25/30–1 *rythe* . . . *processioun*, 36–7 *and* . . . *worlde* (36–7 *in*[2] . . .
worlde om. E); 26/89–90 *whan* . . . *so* (also om. FGHJ); 27/25–6
and . . . *reuerens* (also om. H), 26–7 *hade* . . . *and*, 76n *in Trenis*
(also om. H: a difficult reading only correctly rendered in
αABCD); 38/38–9 *þat* . . . *oþur*.[120]

There are many cases of lexical variation throughout the manuscripts, the inevitable result of copying in different parts of the
country at different periods of time.[121] On the principle of *difficilior
lectio*, the original lexeme is very rarely found in a Group B manuscript. At 65/76, the term *potagur* from Gk ποδαγρος, cf. *LA dolore
pedum* (Graesse 1846: 731; Maggioni 1998: ii. 1117), is recorded in all
Group A witnesses except J (*gowty*). The Group B text replaces *was
potagur* by the more ponderous: *had such an euell that no thinge might
keele him*.[122] Further examples of *difficilior lectio* include:

(13) 6/77n *heþen* (αD), 143n *barm* (αD); 8/97n *lure* (α); 9/72 *styked*
(αABCEFHIJ, *slogh* DK and Group B), 83n *onfax* (α); 14/132n
bout (α); 22/91n *drogh* (α, *drawht* I); 26/89 *rerde* αBK;[123] 32/
46n *seser* (αACD), 78n *disparpulled* (αACK); 41/46 *myngyng*
(αI, *mengyng* I, cf. *mynnyng* DE, *memnyng* F);[124] 46/58n *tayte*
(αC); 49/28n *boyste* (αDI); 51/22n *tysyng* (α), 56n *conveyon*
(αI).

In some cases, a word is replaced in Group B because it is regional
and/or archaic, as at 6/6–7, where this is clearly the reason for the
loss of rhyme in the third of the rhyming principals (*for* . . . *tylle* in
(most) Group A manuscripts) from *hym tylle* (the syntax disordered
for the sake of the rhyme) to *to hym* in Group B manuscripts.[125]
Another type of evidence of Group A's priority is the occasional
survival of a rhyming conclusion to a sermon in Group A, but never
in Group B manuscripts (see, for example, 1/141–5n, 26/64–5n).

---

[120] In general (see 38/39n), the Group B text accommodates these lacunae.

[121] Some lexemes show regular variation between (most) Group A and all Group B
manuscripts, e.g. 7/4 *forme* (α only, otherwise *first*, see too 40/12n), 8/42 *folwed*
(αBCDEFK, *baptyst* HJ, *cristoned* AI and Group B); 11/20 *paynemus* (α and Group A,
sarasenes Group B). For the problem of *Astur* ('Easter'), see 29/7n.

[122] *an euell*] *in his feet* f; *that*] *was so colde þat* add. c, *he cowde gete* add. f; *thinge*] *þat* add.
f; *might*] *cowe* f; *him*] *it* cdf.

[123] *Rore* DFHIJabegh, *roring* cdf, *he cried and roryd* G, ACE absent.

[124] *MED* **mingen** *v.* 3 to remember. The other manuscripts have *myndyng* (*MED*
minden *v.* 1a to remember), cf. *mynd hauyng* H.

[125] Discussed Appendix IV.5.

These rhymes (Long 1955) are likely to be original, given Mirk's propensity for end-rhyming in his sermon principals. In general, Group A conclusions are fuller than Group B (see e.g. Appendix III.iii 2/176 *hure soules*, III.iv 14/184 *aftur*, III.v 24/128–9 *haue . . . Amen*, III.vii 39/147 *vnbrente*).[126]

(14) In the sermon for St Thomas of India, α and Group A manuscripts provide concluding verse (5/111–12, *þus . . . day*), originally in the form of a quatrain rhyming on *fay*, *way*, *day*, *ay*, but with several minor variants and the rhymes variously realized. Only DI have the fourth rhyme on *ay*, which was perhaps also in K's exemplar, since K's reading (*that ys to sey to euerlastyng ioy to the which et cetera*) appears to paraphrase a copy-text such as D (*that ys þe ioy þat lestyth ay*).

(15) Manuscripts αG and Group B end at 40/147, but the Group A manuscripts (apart from J, which provides a conventional ending) continue to announce the coming feast of Corpus Christi, followed by a rhymed conclusion only preserved in D: *And praye we now alle to the Holy Trynyte / That we may so worschip here yn erthe yn vnyte / That we may come ynto hys mageste / Where he ys veraye Gode yn persons thre. Amen.*

Finally, one may note the final *narratio* (witnessed by αBCD GIKbcdfh) in the final *F* sermon (no. 68). Here a clear continuum can be traced from αI, which preserve the original text best (see 68/119–20n), through the other Group A manuscripts, which name the priest (see 68/119n), to the Group B text and Rev., which omit most details and for whom the location in Lilleshall is meaningless (see 68/113n).

4.2. Relationships within Groups A and B

An explanation of the relationships within the two Groups is essential to a proper understanding of not just the transmission of *F* but the complexity of the chosen base-text of this edition (see §5, §6). Although some groups of manuscripts (ABC, abeg) play a lesser and some a greater (DI, cd) role in establishing the text of α, because of different Hands and exemplars the base-text variably relates to both Group A and Group B and to a range of manuscripts within (in particular) Group A.

---

[126] This is less true of the later sermons, where Group B provides fuller conclusions.

Wakelin (1967) had little to say on the matter of relationships within the two Groups, noting only (p. 113) the close relationship between a and e. Manuscript e had formed the base-text for Wakelin (1960), where the focus was on the Group B manuscripts, whose text, he noted, was 'completely different from that of [Group A], but they all agree closely with one another' (i. xvi–vii).[127] Similarly, although Wakelin (1967: 116–18) provided tables of contents for a typical Group A manuscript (α) and a typical Group B manuscript (a), the matter of internal differences of content within each group was not explored.

The discussion above (§4, §4.1), although not so designed, has already revealed relationships within the two Groups which will be established below: AC (examples 4, 7, 13 (32/46, 78)), DI (example 14), EF (examples 4, 5, 6, 8), HJ (example 4), ae (example 11), cd (example 2), and the eccentricity of K (examples 6, 7, 8) and f (examples 6, 7). It has also demonstrated that α variously agrees with Group A (examples 3, 4, 5, 9, 10, 11, 14) and Group B (examples 1, 2, 6). In the narrow cruxes at 4, 9, and 10, α agrees with I, DI, I respectively. In the superior readings at 13, α's presence is the most consistent.

In two cases, α's reading appears to be pivotal between the Group A and the Group B text. At example 7, α's use of the rare lexeme *euore* ('victory') is reflected in the Group B reading *they had euer* (*euer] euery* c) *the victorye*, whereas the Group A manuscripts appear to have agreed in an exemplar where the adjective *euerous* ('victorious') was the norm (see further 14/78–80 n).

At example 8 (where α unemended reads: *bed hopon þe ȝate so harde*), an exemplar prior to αD has interpreted the correct *vpon* as 'open', i.e. 'beat open the gate so hard' (*put open þe ȝeate so hard* D). In α the original form *bet* ('beat', from *MED* beten *v.*(1), with recorded past tense *bet*) has been reinterpreted (despite the incongruous adverbial phrase *so harde*) as *bed* ('bade', from *MED* bidden *v.*, with recorded past tense *bed*), with excrescent *h-* in *hopon* ('open'). A reading like that of α has then influenced the Group B manuscripts except for f: *bad open the gate so harde* (*so harde] and so lowde* add. h, *so*

---

[127] To corroborate the statement, he provided a collation for the Pentecost sermon of all the manuscripts known to him (ii. 603–20, Appendix Ib). In this collation, odd-numbered pages give the text of α with variant readings from Group A manuscripts, and even-numbered pages the text of e with variant readings from Group B (see Wakelin 1960: ii. 594 for an explanation of the sigla).

lowd and so grym b; *harde*] *om.* d). In particular the closeness of d's reading (*bad hopyn*) to α is notable.

As a final conjecture, it may be that α's corrupt reading *Amoncvs self* (example 3) is the explanation for the phrase's omission in Group B.[128]

4.3. Relationships within Group A

As noted above (§4), only Group A has sermons 34, 42, 43, 46, 56, Add1–6. The sermon for St Winifred (no. 43) occurs in αABCDIK, that for St Alkmund (no. 56) in αDI. αDEFG are the only manuscripts to offer a second sermon for 1 Lent (no. 34). The sermon for St Barnabas (no. 42) is omitted from EFG and the material on Nero (no. 46) from EFGJ (and A, which is defective here). Only αABCDIK provide, variously, all or some of the Additional sermons.[129] In summary, only αD contain all this material, demonstrably original to Mirk; of the other manuscripts, I contains next most.

The Prayer and Prologue offer clear evidence of textual relationships within Group A. ABCFHI have Prayer and Prologue, but D has only the Prayer and K only the Prologue.[130] Since f is the only Group B manuscript to contain either Prayer or Prologue (it has both), it will be considered here too. There are two versions of the Prayer: Prayer i, which is likely to be original and is found in αDFI, and Prayer ii in ABCHf (see Appendix III.i and Explanatory Notes to Prayer). Within Prayer ii ABC agree closely (B offers one minor variant), while Hf are less closely related (on f's general idiosyncracies, see §4.5.2). In Prayer i the grouping of αDFI confirms the relationship of αDI suggested by the contents of those manuscripts (on F's eccentricity, see §4.3.2), and the grouping of ABC in Prayer ii is confirmed by a major crux in the Prologue (Pro/10–11 n), a crux in which variant readings unite ABCK and HIf respectively.

Taken together, the evidence of Prayer and Prologue suggests several interrelated groupings within Group A: ABC have the same Prayer, and ABCK have the same reading at Pro/10–11 (K has no Prayer). AC are closer than B (Pro/3 **holdyn**, 7 **Goddus**), and K has

---

[128] Occasional reference will continue to be made in this chapter to α, where appropriate, but the fullest discussion will be reserved until after the make-up of the manuscript has been discussed in §5.

[129] The evidence for Add1-6 is compromised by the fact that several manuscripts are atelous.

[130] E is eccentric in arrangement and does not have either, but both are present in F. J is acephalous.

several readings which distance it from the ABC group (Pro/2
lettrure, 9 **letture,** 11 **more addyng to**).[131] Hf are linked to ABC
in that they have the same Prayer, but they have a different Prologue.
I's closeness to αDF rather than ABCHf in the Prayer is compromised by its closeness to Hf in the Prologue's major crux, although in
other, minor variants it stands apart from Hf (Pro/6 **loue,** 11 **more
addyng to, so he**). The best text of the Prologue is that provided by
α (Pro/10–11n).

While the Prayer and Prologue offer helpful preliminary evidence,
they are not found in all Group A manuscripts. The particular
relationship of EF, for example, is not apparent because E has
neither Prayer nor Prologue. D's close relationship to α, which is
apparent throughout *F* and which is suggested by its having Prayer i,
cannot be demonstrated at this stage beyond the grouping with FI,
because D has no Prologue. The complexity of G, which has an
unusual arrangement of *F* sermons from different sources, at first
interspersed with other sermons, means that it has no formal
beginning and so omits the Prayer and Prologue. J cannot be used
as a witness, as it is acephalous. Most important of all, the fact that α
has been copied in different hands, seemingly at different times and
from different exemplars, and that the Prayer and Prologue represent
the only work of Hand A, obscures any conclusions that might be
drawn from them about α's relationship to the other manuscripts.
Nevertheless, these initial groupings are useful and are confirmed by
the textual evidence of the sermons themselves.

4.3.1. The Relationship of ABC

ABC do indeed form a group (as demonstrated by example 9 at §4.1
above). Mostly the agreements are minor, sometimes unique, as the
full collations demonstrate:

> 2/58 **Androw;** 14/148 **offred;** 24/9 **nolde,** 12 **so fowle,** 52
> **schal,** 128–9 **haue** . . . **Amen;** 39/15 **oute,** 136 **hadde makyd**

but generally in agreement with various other Group A manuscripts:

> 2/101 **kutte,** 166 **Lucyfer;** 14/6 **Symeones,** 33 **leue wel;** 24/6
> **asentud,** 67 **displesuth,** 82 **be ryche;** 39/30 **hulkyng.**

---

[131] Lemmata in bold direct the reader to the full collations in Appendix III; lemmata in
italics either refer to material not in the full collations or to material in the full collations
presented differently from the Appendix lemmata.

Although AB at times agree:

> 2/60 þat² . . . and; 14/118 hys **lyght**; 24/42 **3ode**; 39/12 **forsake**, 25 **loued**, 29 **herte**,

or BC at times agree:

> 2/2 **day**; 14/87 **ys now**; 24/60 **þoo**, 97–8 be⁴ . . . **blode**; 39/33 **infere**, 42 **wysest and**, 45 **not**,

it is the two manuscripts AC which are overall closest within the ABC group:[132]

> 2/46–7 **so** . . . **modur**; 14/7 **gode men**, 35 **touchyng** . . . **mon**, 42–3 **þe** . . . **fulfulled**; 24/45 **miston**, 57 **bak**, 120 **of** . . . **and**; 39/46 **schaffet**, 49 **alle**, 92 **nesche²**, 102 **standyng**, 103 **most**, 123 **mon**.[133]

In the most extended example (outside the full collations), the Group A text has an elaborate conclusion (17/152), prefaced in AC by a note on Ash Wednesday, which incorporates part of the next sermon, the first Sunday in Lent (cf. 19/12–17):

> Also, surrus, on Venusday nexte cumyng þat is called Askewennysday 3e schalle cum to churche hoolly and take askus at þe prestus honde and beyre forthe in iowre hertus þat he sayth to yow when he leyth askus on iowre heydus, for þen he saythe þus: 'Mon, þenke on þou arte butt askus and into askus schalte turne a3eyne.' þat day also 3e schull bygynne too faste 3owre lenton, as Goddus chyldryn owen to do, and cum and schryue iowe and cla[n]se the howse of iowre conceynce, for þat day and iijᵉ dayes folowyng ben called the clansyng dayes.[134]

AC then continue with the sermon ending proper, which, with variants, is the version in the other Group A manuscripts.

Lacunae in AC, such as 24/27 **wyth** . . . **mowthe**, 108–9 **so** . . . **alle**, and shared readings in AC, such as 14/167 **were goyng**; 24/16 **heven**, 33 **gulte**, 43 **þat** . . . **on**, 83 **recchyþ** . . . **and**, sometimes reveal greater distance from the other Group A manuscripts than B, and B frequently agrees with the other Group A manuscripts rather than with AC:[135]

[132] As demonstrated at §4 and §4.1 above in examples (4) 24/90 *strong*, (7) 14/78–9 *þey hadden euore*, (13) 32/78n *disparpulled*.   [133] See too 8/35n, 12/104–5n.

[134] A, ff. 39ᵛ–40ʳ. The text of this passage in C is badly damaged, but its presence is discernible (MS Harley 2420, f. 31ʳ).

[135] However, AC were not copied directly from B. At 10/34–45 (*He . . . seluer*), ll. 34–45 are omitted in B and ll. 34–41 (*He . . . sokur*) in AC.

2/35 **dampnet** (BDEFGIK), 72 **on** vs (BDEFGHK), 116
schaffly (BDI); 14/49–50 **fro** . . . **deth** (BDHI), 50 **of hure
chyld** (BDEFGIJK), 79 **hadden euore** (BDFG); 24/112 **tomar-
ryd** (BDEFG(1)G(2)HIJK), 120 **of** . . . **and** (BDEFG(1)-
G(2)HIJK); 39/30 **opynly** (BDEFGHIK).

Outside the full collations, at 35/2–3, B follows the other manuscripts, while AC agree in an alternative reading (*the which is nott
hooly day but þere as þe place is of hym*), and at 26/64–5n, AC end the
sermon early with a rhyming conclusion.[136]

C very occasionally stands apart from A and all the other manuscripts in a unique addition (39/147n), or omission (35/42–78n),
which sometimes indicates a parochial interest,[137] or in a textual
variant (for example, 24/59 **behynden hym**). C could not, therefore,
have been copied by A. The evidence of lacunae (2/59 **helpe**; 14/
20–1 **offryng** . . . **hure**; 24/24–5 **And** . . . **heven**; 39/41–4 **beforyn**
. . . **beforen**) and variants (for example, 24/87 **for**), shows too that C
could not have been copied from A.

4.3.2. The Relationship of EF

The grouping αDFI suggested by the text of the Prayer (§4.3) is
complicated by the eccentricities of F, which will be considered next,
together with E. The relationships of manuscripts in Group A are
throughout distant enough for it to be clear that several intermediate
manuscripts have been lost. EF, on the other hand, immediately stand
out as distinctive. Both manuscripts shorten the original text,
although E shortens more than F, sometimes exclusively (see
Explanatory Notes to Sermons 4, 8, 14, 15, 17, 18, 23, 26, 33, etc.),
but F sometimes omits more than E (see Explanatory Notes to
Sermon 39).

EF are in the same hand and may have had the same copy-text, as
suggested by shared lacunae:

2/49 **to** . . . **and**; 14/7–8 **þat** . . . **Lady**, 30–1 **þerfore** . . . **mon**,
41–2 **For** . . . **law**; 24/73 **My**[1] . . . **ȝow**, 108–9 **toke** . . . **alle**; 39/
59–60 **and** . . . **vndir**.

They very frequently agree in variant readings:

---

[136] However, B itself is further from the original reading at 65/56–7n (where it
substitutes *cyte* for *heyre*).

[137] For example, 19/130, where C adds: *Now þis wyke also ben þe ymbrydayus as ȝe
knowen wel.*

2/42 **By** ... ylost; 14/2 **Suche**, 21 **offren** ... **a³**; 24/12 **hym²**, 63 **Ieremye**, 128–9 **haue** ... **Amen**; 39/18 **os**,

or in (sometimes distinctive) variant lexemes not witnessed by other manuscripts:

2/85 **do**; 14/32 **cowpul**, 34 **coupul**; 24/6 **wykkyd**, 96 **me¹**; 39/ 27 **mased**, 30 **hulkyng**.

Sometimes the readings are erroneous, as at 24/54, 55 **Ioab** (also G(2)), or (outside the full collations) 23/87 (*ascencion* for *annunciacion*, corrected above the line in E) and 35/24 (*childe* for *derlyng*). Neither manuscript was copied directly from the other. F was not copied from E, since E has lacunae not in F:

2/149 **and** ... **fote**; 24/7–8 **abowton** ... **weron**, 57 **smotte** ... **and**; 39/5–6 **bot** ... **wytte**, 7–8 **haue** ... **fewe**.

This is corroborated by 2/176 **hure soules** (where E has truncated the sermon conclusion), by 24/44–6 **so** ... **And** (where F's reading may be the result of a more intelligent handling of a shared lacuna in the copytext), and by 14/53–163 **Heo** ... *Item*, 39/38 **of²** ... **tonges²**, **os** ... **fyre**, 55–6 **of²** ... **is**, **of²** ... **new**, where lacunae in E are longer than in F. F was not copied by E: for example, at 14/87–115 **now** ... **þat**, F may have missed a page in his copy-text; at 14/126–63 **I** ... *Item*, F omits a *narratio*; at 24/35–7 **For** ... **allegate**, there is a lacuna in F; at 39/71 **þe forme**, E's misinterpretation of the reading *to þe forme* (*to enforme* E) is closer to the original than F's reading *to tel*.[138]

4.3.3. The Relationship of DEF

In terms of comparison with other manuscripts, EF may appear to be unhelpful. Their selectiveness and idiosyncratic grouping of sermons mean that they do not provide a witness for every sermon in the collection, nor do they always replicate each other's sermons. Nevertheless, they are important for their textual relationship with D, the manuscript generally closest to α. DEF often share minor variants (for example, 39/16 **wyse**, 18 **ʒeven to**, 21 **alle aboute**), but they occasionally agree in substantive variants:

14/33 **leue wel**] *lawe ordeyneth a* (*a*] om. F) *remedy for to clanse hom* (*hom*] *hit* E, *him* F) *but þen ʒe schull* (*ye* rep. F) *know wele*

---

[138] Compare (outside the full collations), 12/17, where F's misinterpretation of the reading *by aunsetrye* (*by assent* F) is closer to the original than E's *speke*.

(*wele*] om. EF) DEF, 40 **mekud**] *made* DEFK, 51–2 **Holy Chyrche**] *god* DEF; 24/12–13 he . . . **deuel** (αDEFG(2)HJ), 67 **displesuth** (αDEFG(1)H); 39/9 to **haue²**] *aftyr* DEFIK, 18 **ʒeven to**] *yn* DEF, 61–2 **holde out**] *halowet* DEF.

Because of the complexity of the *F* transmission, it is impossible to posit direct relationships. For example, at times E agrees with D (2/99–100 þey . . . **iustyse**) and at times F agrees with D (2/55 **dede**, 87 **wold haue hadde**; 24/38 **Herby** . . . **ensaumpul**).

4.3.4. *The G Sermons*

It is also evident that DEF have a relationship with the two main exemplars of G. (These are the only manuscripts apart from α which contain Sermon 34, the extra 1 Lent sermon; unlike α, it occurs directly after the other 1 Lent sermon, no. 19.)

The problem of G is more complex than that of EF. G is a manuscript whose compiler added to his collection over a period of time, and McIntosh & Wakelin (1982) were able to distinguish five different hands and eleven different languages in the *F* sermons. The longest stints are in languages 2 and 5, and it is these stints only which are considered here. Language 5 is a *Temporale* run from Advent to Tenebre, written by Hand A over most of ff. 209^v–245^v (excluding ff. 209^v–212^v and 244^r–245^v in language 2,[139] and ff. 213^r–217^v, which are *Sanctorale* sermons in Hand C and language 15). These sermons (G(1)) mostly recur in Language 2 (G(2)), which occurs, largely in Hand D, throughout most of ff. 262^r–305^r, a run of sermons from Advent to Pentecost in *Temporale* order.[140]

Of the sermons fully collated for this edition, no. 24 (Appendix III.v) provides examples of both G(1) (ff. 240^r–242^v) and G(2) (ff. 290^r–292^r). Both stints are copied from Group A manuscripts. The exemplars of G(1) and G(2) were not, however, the same, and the two languages correspond to two separate exemplars. G(1) is most

---

[139] McIntosh & Wakelin appear to be wrong in citing f. 244^v instead of 244^r. These ff. cover sermons for Advent (the same text as the Advent sermon at ff. 262^r–264^v, which is also Language 2) and Tenebre.

[140] The end of this stint (the last part of the Ascension sermon and the whole of Pentecost) is completed by Hands E and A (see manuscript description, Appendix II.i.a, G). The Pentecost sermon in Hand A appears to be copied from a different exemplar from the other sermons in this run, with G closest here to ABC rather than the D(EF) group (see Appendix III.vii *passim*). The sermon for Rogation Days also occurs twice in G in the same hands and, according to McIntosh & Wakelin, the same languages, *viz.* Hand A, Language 5 ff. 92^v–93^v, Hand D, Language 2 ff. 299^r–300^r. Here too Hand A's stint is closest to C.

commonly close to ABC(I)K and G(2) to DEFHJ, as in the cruxes at 24/12–13 he . . . deuel, 81 luyte . . . wordys, 82 be ryche, where the Group A relationships are ABCG(1)(I)K and αDEFG(2)HJ. In particular, G(2) appears to have a close relationship with EF and may be close to the exemplar of EF: 24/39 cyte, 54, 55 loab, 77–8 tresoure . . . ʒow, 83 here . . . is, 108–9 toke . . . alle. Not surprisingly, the two groupings are not without contamination, so that both G(1) and G(2) agree, for example, with DHI at 24/82 weltheful; G(1) agrees with DEFHIJK at 24/120–1 and sweryng; G(2) agrees with ABCIJK at 24/67 displesuth. Inevitably, G(1) and G(2) have their own idiosyncrasies: G(1) at 24/86–94 Wherefore . . . þat, or at 24/107 weron so wonte and 24/107–8 be . . . woundys (at both of which its reading is shared with K), and G(2) at 24/55–6 sayde . . . bot, 66 tretuth, 71 heron. G(2) in particular appears to make several errors, e.g. 24/10 spare, 33–4 defendeth . . . and[1], 86 persoun, 88 wepe.

G(2) only is represented in sermon 34 (also in αDEF), where it is more individual than the other manuscripts, adding, omitting and substituting words and phrases, and paraphrasing the text at times (for example, 34/7 pistul, 16 monyche, 30 and . . . helde, 125–6 þow . . . vs). G's interventions can be explained as deliberate and scribal, given G's general coherence with DEF in this sermon (see §6.1.2), and it is the least corrupt of all the manuscripts at l. 129 (see 34/129 n).

4.3.5. The Relationship of HIJK

In HIJK (as in DEFG), although broad agreements are fairly clear-cut, the permutations of agreement are such as to suggest that a limited number of manuscripts was copied and inter-copied, with the inevitable creation of numerous interrelationships, often (but not always) of a minor and non-substantive nature. Typical of their relationship is the fact that they all omit *myth scowreges* at 17/134 but read variously *scouryd and betun* (H), *skorget* (I), *scorgyd and betynn* (J), *scornyd and scorgyd* (K).

HIJK form an overall group but rarely in isolation from the other manuscripts (for minor evidence of their agreement in readings not found in the other Group A manuscripts, see 39/78 of[2], 138 þereof). In this broad and loose group, I and K are variable, often independent, partners, as will be demonstrated. The Prayer did not offer clear evidence on the relationships within HIJK, given that JK have no

Prayer and those in HI are Prayer ii and i respectively. Moreover, the Prologue is not found in J, and, although in the major crux at Pro/10 HI agree, elsewhere H/IK is also evident (Pro/3 holdyn, 4 that cometh, 6 loue), and each manuscript also has minor idiosyncratic Prologue readings of its own.

The absence of Prayer and Prologue in J serves to obscure the clear relationship of HJ. They are the only Group A manuscripts not to have the sermon for St Winifred, no. 43 (apart from EFG, where the omission is explicable in terms of the idiosyncrasies of the manuscripts). They frequently have shared readings:

2/44 longe, 99 ham[1], 127 ȝoure; 14/4–5 oure . . . Cryst, 66–7 of chyld, 82 chyualous, euorus; 24/50 trew, 58 fareth; 39/40 frytyng, 51 berste, 73–4n[141]

or lacunae:

2/25–6 put . . . he; 14/30 þe forme womon, 69–71 into . . . both, 70–1 and[1] . . . both, 76 and hegh reuerence, 86 was, 86–7 February . . . Romans, þe[1] . . . now; 24/59 bot . . . hym[2], 115 answerud . . . and[1]; 39/7 haue wysdom, 34 and comforde, 94 he . . . warme,

and in one sermon they offer a markedly rewritten version of a *narratio* (see 22/135–63 n). The lemmata at 14/37 byddeth and 38 wyst . . . was suggest a lacuna in a shared copytext, which HJ make good in different ways, H by retaining the omission, J by conjectural emendation. HJ are not, therefore, sister manuscripts, and each frequently has an idiosyncratic reading of its own:

H: 2/27 entysyng, 138 scho gentyly; 14/27 sende, 28 al þe dayes, 127–8 þe[2] . . . in; 24/54 Ioab, 89 suffer, 106 schyrus; 39/93 hye hertys, 93–4 ȝeveth . . . meke

J: 2/88 studfastly ȝeynstod, 124 noryschet; 14/112 be at one, 128 hureself, 179 leue þe soule; 24/48 worsed, 48–9 his . . . brokon, 59 tonge; 39/86 hym, 113 boyleth.

Lacunae in J demonstrate that H was not copied from J (2/96–8 Y[1] . . . þe, 144–6 and . . . for; 24/25–6 þan . . . þan, 39–40 stolne . . . hadde[1]),[142] and lacunae in H demonstrate that it was not copied by J

---

[141] See too (outside the full collations) 12/104–5n.
[142] J truncates Sermons 3 and 8 (see Explanatory Notes).

(14/37 **byddeth**, 38 **wyst** . . . **was**; 24/82 **sadde**). Indeed, J is sometimes eccentric (for example, 24/48 **worsed**, 59 **tonge**, 66 **tretuth**, 81 **haue**), especially later in the manuscript (perhaps explicable by a different exemplar for H after f. 126^r, where Hand D takes over from Hand C in H).[143]

As noted above, the situation is akin to that already outlined for DEFG: HIJK form a loose group, but multiple copying, with the loss of intervening manuscripts, means that lines of descent are no longer clearly traceable. HJ are close, but there are also groupings (though less significant) of HI/JK:

2/125 **castyte**, 149–51 **n**; 14/34 **coupul**, 49–50 **fro** . . . **deth**, 73 **Holy Chyrche**; 24/74 **opon**, 82 **weltheful**; 39/48 **loue**, 123–4 **and lyven wele**.

HK occasionally agree (2/5 **he**^{2} . . . **lyuyng**, 99–100 **þey** . . . **iustyse**, 176 **hure soules**; 14/147–8 **to þe prest**; 39/68 **worlde** (also AB)), as do IJ (2/57 **feet** (also G); 24/102 **þe**^{1} . . . **Romaynus**), besides permutations such as HJK, IJK, HIK, and HIJ. It is noteworthy, however, that of the four manuscripts I is most frequently the outsider in these groupings.

Each of the manuscripts HIJK has its own idiosyncratic readings, and some of those of H and J have been demonstrated above. Idiosyncratic readings of I are found at 2/114 **welleth**, 124 **chyrslych**, **wele**; 14/9 **wyrchyng**, 46 **caht**; 24/93 **tackyd**, 111 **cladde**; 39/51 **hardon**, but it is K, in particular, that displays most variation:

2/117 **plente**, 124 **noryschet**, 142 **harde**, **halle**; 14/20 **come**, 21 **rych**; 24/8 **weron lettyd**, 48 **worsed**, 52–3 **þilk** . . . **For** (also G(1)),[144] 97–8 **be myne blode**; 39/8 **many**, 51 **berste**.

Indeed, K stands out as a manuscript whose scribe is more than a copyist. K is notable for its Latin insertions, which are largely from *LA* or from Scripture, but which sometimes show use of additional Latin legends of the saints (see Nevanlinna 1993 for Sermon 67, ed. from K).[145] K is a late and sophisticated production. Lexis is often modernized:

---

[143] For examples of substantive divergence, see 54/28n, 57/120–53n, 68/8–15n, 57n.

[144] G(1)K are particularly close, e.g. 24/31 **foule**, 48 **may**, 52–3 **þilk** . . . **For**, 65 **to**, 107–8 **be** . . . **woundys**, 128–9 **haue** . . . **Amen**.

[145] Other manuscripts occasionally provide Latin citations, for example, at 37/91–7 **þus** . . . **dede**, where GIJ (as well as K) supply parts of the Vulgate text.

2/117 **plente**, 124 **noryschet**, 142 **harde, halle;** 24/112 **lappe;** 39/59 **wytteth,** 69 to **wytyn,** 73 **rewlyd,** 129 **rydel,** 131 **colver.**

The readings are always strong, though not always original. The scribe is also a reviser, who pays close attention to the text (2/149n **A** . . . **fote;** 14/17–19 **and** . . . **temple)**,with a real concern to elucidate it properly (14/35 **touchyng** . . . **mon,** 104 **and²** . . . **self;** 24/108 **toke,** 110 **iusterye,** 118 **awne;** 39/111–12 **greuyth** . . . **herte,** 115 **enmye,** 144–5 **alle** . . . **made**) and to expand it judiciously by new study of *LA* (see e.g. 14/17–19n, 103–4n).

4.3.6. The Relationship of DI

None of the groupings discussed above is discrete, and there is frequent cross-fertilization across the groups (see Appendix III *passim*). It was noted above (§4.3.5), without comment, that, of the group HIJK, I is most frequently the outsider. Where I stands apart from HJK, it is most commonly in agreement with αD(EF), as already noted in Prayer i (αDFI):

> 2/19 **sewed** αDEFI, 21 **when** . . . **heuen** αDEFI, 46–7 **so** . . . **modur** αDEFI, 122 **scryfte** αDI, 132 **hure²** αDEFIK, 165 **hyt** α(D)EFI, 167 **alle** αDI; 14/79 **rotton** α(D)(FI) (E absent); 24/67 **displesuth** αDEFG(1)H; 39/7 **techeres** αDEFI, 57–8 **for** . . . **felowes** αDI, 97 **and²** αDI (F absent),

or with DEF:

> 2/101 **kutte**] *knot* DEFI, 134 **sayde scho** om. DEFI; 39/68 **worlde**] *then hit ys* add. DEFI.[146]

It is clear that there are good grounds for excluding EF from further discussion in relation to α, since (despite its textual closeness to D) its text has been deliberately and extensively edited. K too has undergone rewriting. D is a manuscript crucial to the *F* transmission and was wisely chosen by Erbe (1905) as the base-text of his edition. Next to α, it is the fullest manuscript of *F*, and it is in one hand, in a dialect (Staffordshire) close to Mirk's own. Likewise, I is a complete manuscript in one hand and a good dialect (north-east Nottinghamshire),

---

[146] DI sometimes share unique readings: 2/131 **hee** (where only DI have an erroneous feminine personal pronoun); 14/53 **þe** . . . **Anne** *symones and anne aȝeyncomyng* DI; 39/56 **new** *now* DI, 111 **betwene** *bytwyx* DI, 125 **eure** *ay* DI.

which offers the next fullest number of sermons.[147] Only αDI have sermons for both the local saints, Winifred and Alkmund (nos. 43 and 56), with the more obscure St Alkmund only in αDI. Evidence for the relationship is consolidated by the fact that extra material added to the Group B text is consistently found in α and next most often in DI. This will be discussed next.

4.4. The Transition to the Group B Text

At some point soon after the circulation of *F* commenced, a process of augmentation of the sermons began. This augmentation, which takes the form of extra *narrationes* or additional comments, is always found in the Group B manuscripts. Very commonly it takes the form of additional use of *LA* and so represents a stage towards the comprehensive revision of the *F Sanctorale* which is characteristic of Rev. (particularly R2).

The most significant augmentation is the addition to the sermons for the Nativity of the Virgin and St Katherine of extra legendary material about, respectively, the Virgin's marriage and the shrine of St Katherine (57/152–3n and 67/73–4n).[148] In addition, Group B sometimes condenses, omits, expands, or embellishes sermons, in a way more fundamental than the numerous examples of minor variation which characterize the Group; the most significant example is the rewriting of the introduction to the sermon for 3 Lent (21/6–14 n).[149]

However, it is important to note that augmentation of Mirk's original text up to and including Sermon 33 (but most marked in Sermons 3–8) is also found consistently in α and variably in Group A manuscripts. The augmentation takes the form of extra *narrationes* or additional comments. After α (which always includes the material), DI have the extra material most often. It is thus always found in α and the Group B text, but of the Group A manuscripts in α alone in Sermons 3–5 (see 3/101–3n, 149–91n;[150] 4/90n;[151] 5/78–96n[152]), in αDI at 5/113–17n, in αDHIJK at 6/59–61n, in αBCDFHIK at

---

[147] The last sermon in I is Add3.
[148] For other additions (mostly from *LA* and all also found in α and sometimes Group A manuscripts), see 3/101–3n, 149–91n; 4/90n; 5/78–96n, 113–17n; 6/59–61n; 7/107–31n; 8/120–9n; 16/128–30n; 22/135–63n; 26/64–5n; 33/126–7n.
[149] Other significant alterations in Group B are noted in the Explanatory Notes, e.g. 22/110–11n, 135–63n; 44/20–4n, and headnotes to nos. 31, 32, 36, 54, 55, 57–9, 61, 65–8.
[150] Group A omits 3/102–27, 149–91.   [151] Group A omits 4/91–112.
[152] Group A omits 5/68–70 (*pat . . . he*), 78–96.

7/107–31n, in αABCDHIJ at 8/120–9n, in αDG(1)HIJ at 16/128–30n, in αDG(2)I at 22/135–63n,[153] in αBDFGHIJK at 26/66–102 (see 26/64–5n), and in αDHIJK at 33/126–7n. (At 5/78–96 it is so incompletely incorporated into *F* that it is still in its original Latin.) After Sermon 33, such additions are confined to the Group B text, for example, in Sermons 57 and 67 as noted above.

The fact that all the texts except E (which often omits material) demonstrate augmentation at one time or another suggests a process of accretion towards the fuller Group B text, a process in which α, and next αDI, are prominent in their closeness to Group B. The sole appearance of α in conjunction with Group B in Sermons 3–5 suggests the particular closeness of the text of α to Group B in the early sermons of the collection. The fact that, next to α, DI are constants in all the examples of augmentation tends to confirm the particular relationship of αDI noted above. The lack of prominence of E(F) and, to some extent, G can be explained by the vagaries of those manuscripts, but the fact that ABC and HJ also show closeness to the Group B text at times reveals the complex degree of inter-copying of the manuscripts.[154]

4.5. Relationships within Group B

As noted already (§4, §4.1, §4.4), Group B is a recension of Group A, whose manuscripts display numerous minor, and some major, variant readings, omissions, and additions. The relationships within Group B are simpler than those of Group A (as the examples at 4 and 4.1 have already demonstrated),[155] for which there may be a number of (not mutually exclusive) explanations: that the recension circulated in fewer copies, that it was more narrowly localized, and/or that it was copied more strictly.

4.5.1. The Relationship of abeg

Amongst the Group B manuscripts, abeg are closely related (although g is not a witness for the full collection). For example:

2/4 þre, 11 And when Seynt, 18 and kalled ham, 92 and[2] . . . of (see 2/92–3n), 124–5 þat . . . floure, 128 to[2] . . . sokur; 14/4

---

[153] HJ offer a different version of these lines, and the Group B text a different version again.

[154] This last point needs to be stated, since in general, as has been noted above, it is the sub-group αD(EF)(G)IK which shows the greatest textual affiliation with Group B.

[155] For a minor, but telling, example, see 25/68n.

melody, 20 þat day, to þe temple, 30 dude, 41–2 to . . . law, 58 lyued, 111 charyte, 144 goyng; 24/55 Amasa¹, 92 harmes, 96 vmbreydust, 103–4 Botte . . . comynge, 110 iusterye; 39/ 12 a, 28 þratte, 75 wyl . . . hur, 97 lustus.

Within this grouping, ae are sister manuscripts:

2/85 do . . . ys, 150 yfere, 157–8 for . . . heuene; 14/21 a payre, 59 grant; 24/82 weltheful, 99 foule, 104 kowthe swere; 39/16 of¹, 25 haddyn, 32 30dyn, 49 þat day, 51 demyd,

with frequently thoughtless readings (39/116 lorne] *born*, 127 pope] *poete*), as in the mistaking of *his* in *oure Lady, his modur* (28/55–6) as the genitive of possession (*oure ladies moodir*), or the rendering of the Group B phrase *with oyntmentes* (cf. *oynementys* 28/157) as *without mendis*.

Despite their closeness, neither was copied directly from the other. For example, a was not copied from e, since e reads *a new(b canc.)ill* for a's *an euell* (39/74 A); e was not copied from a, since a reads *neede* for e's *dede* (39/47–8 drede . . . penaunce).[156] Inevitably, given the eccentricities of ae, the abeg group does not always cohere, and occasionally, anyway, g differs from abe (39/5 schul, 12 man).

4.5.2. The Relationship of cdfh

The group cdfh may broadly be considered in contradistinction to the group abeg (2/124 þat . . . of; 14/30 dude, 173 wold euer; 24/73 bowed),[157] although evidence for the grouping of all eight manuscripts is compromised by the vagaries of fh.

Physically the most elaborate of the manuscripts (it is approached only by c), and the only one with a historiated initial, f has interesting associations and may have been prepared for an important client. Features of f certainly suggest that its exemplar was revised for a less provincial and more sophisticated audience, in that it shows frequent lexical variation, some of which indicates modernization:

---

[156] *Dede* is closer to the correct reading *drede*. It is more likely that e precedes a than that a precedes e. At 24/11 the majority reading is *tellys*: ae read *saith*, but e also has *tellis* (canc.).

[157] Outside the full collations, the arresting simile at 26/81 (*as¹ . . . spaynell*) is omitted completely in cdh and replaced by *and thankid him* in abeg (*as yeving him thankyngis* f).

2/20 **stegh**, 66 **see-warth**, 104 **rewthe**; 14/12 **purgacyon**, 19
temple, 30 **womon**, 47 **sklandur**, 82 **chyualous**; 24/6 **asentud**,
32 **grownded**, 33 **gulte**, 59 **tonge**, 83 **recchyþ**; 39/4 **prechyng**,
9 **travelyth**, 19 **wel**[2].

and it paraphrases often:

Pro/6–8 **in** . . . **But**; 2/27–8 **on** . . . **he**[1], 35–6 **þanne** . . . **hym**,
56–7 **to**[1] . . . **sone**, 57 **in** . . . **and**[1], 59 **to**[1] . . . **hym**; 14/12
purgacyon, 54–5 **but** . . . **God**[1], 78–80 **þey** . . . **but**, 83 **praying**
. . . **wold**, 104–5 **a**[2] . . . **soule**, 134 **þan hure þoght**, 157
bytwysse ham too; 24/12–13 **a** . . . **hym**[1], 54 **þat envyed**, 55
on[1] . . . **on**[2], 57 **in** . . . **hym**; 39/13 **bene**, 24 **sorowful** . . .
hertys, 26 **pore**, 53 **þeis men**.[158]

The status of f within Group B is not as secure as the other
manuscripts. In the three major cruxes and other Group B additions
and revisions, its affiliation is to Group B. Overall, textually, it is
clearly a Group B text:

2/90–1 **take** . . . **hym**[1]; 14/2–3 **Wherfore** . . . **3ou**, 37–8 **þe**[2] . . .
þyng, 73 **of** . . . **Chyrche**; 24/4 **and þe Sarsynnes**, 12 **fowle**, 22
whyl . . . **erthe**; 39/7–8 **more harm is**, 29 **here herte**, 30 **bot in
hulkyng**.

However, that affiliation to Group B is not constant, and at times it
accords closely with Group A:

2/122–3 **þan** . . . **þus**, 142 **bet** (see 2/142 n); 14/178 **sayden þe
fendus**, 181 **soule**; 24/55 **on**[1] . . . **on**[2], **on**[1] . . . **metton** (where f is
the only Group B manuscript to preserve the verb *met*), 67
displesuth; 39/124 **fede**.

Of the Group A manuscripts, although there are occasional other
affiliations, it appears to agree most commonly with the HIJK
group.[159] This grouping strengthens the evidence of the Prayer and

---

[158] See too 2/149n. For a particularly elaborate example (outside the full collations),
cf. 6/166–72 *scho*[1] . . . *hure*, which f paraphrases: *and he knowinge her gilti wolde sende her
into the payne of helle, for ther she supposinge was tormenting was ordeyned for suche as she was.
And yet at the last she bithought vpon the passion of Crist and wist wele that she hadde be an
vnknde* [sic] *wreche vnto him.* Occasionally f provides small extra detail, such as the
(erroneous) assertion at 14/56 **þys Anne**, 57 **anoþur** . . . **wedded**.

[159] HJf 14/125 **by**; Hf 39/8 **travayle**, 12 **forsake**, 14 **bringyth**, 34 **grete**, 89 **alle**; Jf 2/
122 **scryfte**, 14/150 **offren**; If 14/32 **cowpul**, 39/51 **berste**; Kf 14/38 **þus**, 132 **fest**, 24/
44 **sone**, 52 **discuron** (IKf), 92 **karolus** (ABCKf).

Prologue, where, as noted, Prayer ii is found in ABCHf and HIf agree in the major Prologue crux.[160]

Manuscript f perhaps represents an offshoot of an early stage of the continuum of Group A to Group B, a stage at which the Prayer and Prologue were still in place, but the sermons had been rearranged into *Temporale* and *Sanctorale*. This might explain its insecure place within Group B. On the other hand, given the careful preparation of the manuscript, further study might reveal collation between a Group A and B manuscript (for example, at 14/12 **purgacyon**, f offers a doublet based, although perhaps by chance, on both Group A and B variants).

Manuscript h, like f, is an independent piece of work. Like f (but less consistently), h paraphrases (14/57–60 **wedded . . . dyed**, 113– 14 **þys . . . elles**) and has idiosyncratic readings (14/36 **foure**, 41 **company**).[161]. Notably, however, the scribe/reviser of h selects and adapts the text, omitting (14/15–35 **þe . . . mon**; 24/102–29 *Narracio* . . . **Amen**), reducing (2/21–64 **And . . . lyuyng**; 14/ 89–90 **womon . . . doyng**),[162] or inserting material:

> 2/86–91 **maked . . . hym**[1], 91 **blod**, 176 **pepul**; 14/46 **lawe**, 96 **Sone**, 127 **heo ȝaf**, 127–8 **saue . . . hureself**, 138 **þan**, 145 **dekenes**, 145–6 **beren . . . begonnon**; 24/26–61 **in . . . hertus**, 82–3 **alle . . . in**, 83 **here**.

The most extensive alteration of his material is the amalgamation and revision of the sermons for Septuagesima and Sexagesima.[163] In the case of the St George and Pentecost sermons (see Explanatory Notes to Sermons 30 and 39), he takes only the beginning from *F* and continues with a different sermon (which breaks off, for Pentecost, at the foot of the page). He may well have been a parish priest, copying and adapting the collection for his own use, as when, at the end of his revised Sexagesima sermon, he adds: *In ista ebdomada dicendum est de decem preceptis vel de septem peccatis mortalis vel de confessione ad placytum* (f. 25[r]).[164]

---

[160] The blank at 14/66 **processyon** may be the result of the f scribe having been faced with a reading such as H's inexplicable *passyon*.

[161] At 13/35 α's *freþon . . . mowþe* becomes *fare as he were wode with hymselfe and fome at the moyth.*   [162] Perhaps the original intention at 14/5–6n.

[163] He often edits his material, omitting, for example, 3/176–91 (*þer . . . cetera*) and commenting instead on St Nicholas's compassion and his miracles, and replacing 6/75–92 *and . . . synne* by *and if we wyll kepe vs his chylderyn and he woll bryng vs to his pes that neuer schall haue ende Amen et cetera* (f. 9[r]).

[164] At 17/28 he suggests introducing an extra *narratio: Exemplum þerof I rede that þer was*

As noted above, cdfh descend from the same exemplar, although examples of agreement between all of cdfh are compromised by the intrusions into fh.[165] The best texts of the cdfh group are, therefore, cd, which include the extra indulgences decreed by the Council of Basle (41/18–23n) and are therefore important as the manuscripts closest to Rev. and to the first (1483) edition of *F* (Powell 2007: x–xi).[166] cd sometimes agree in readings eccentric from all other manuscripts, e.g. 2/39 **bad**, 40 **God**; 14/106 **monhed**; 39/82 **hate**, or in lacunae, e.g. 24/75–7 **and . . . ʒeftus**; 39/9 **wytte and**, 87 **For . . . fyre²**; they sometimes agree with Group A rather than with other Group B manuscripts, e.g. 2/75 **partees**, 134 **be wel holpon**; 14/4 **melody** (cdf), 16 **holden** (cdf), 35 **conseyt**, 58 **lyued** (cdf); 39/43 **son**, 77 **fyre²**, 94 **hem²**; and they sometimes agree with another member of Group A, rather than with α, e.g. 14/46 **caht** (see 14/45–7n); 24/102 **þe¹ . . . Romaynus** (where they agree with IJ). However, they do not agree invariably:

> 2/20 **stegh**, 106 **doun**; 14/26 **turne**, 30 **vexud**, 32 **cowpul**, 34 **coupul**, 125 **tende**; 24/43 **discure**, 52 **discuron**, 73 **clyppon**, 93 **grete**; 39/24 **loste**, 27–8 **and þratte**,

and neither was copied from the other, as individual lacunae demonstrate: d was not copied by c (2/113–14 **out . . . tombe**, 129 **þat² . . . þat³**; 24/34 **and ben**; 39/139 **he² . . . hole**), nor was c copied by d (2/156–7 **þeras . . . þe**; 14/52–3 **oure . . . of²**, **oure . . . of¹** (where the longer eyeskip is in d); 24/63–4 **Whatte . . . me**; 39/137 **so clerkelyk**).

4.6. Summary

The discussion above has been necessary in order to place the complex text of α within the context of the extant complete manuscripts. A clear relationship exists within the groups ABC, AC, DI, EF, HJ, ae, abeg, cd, while wider groupings variably embrace, for example, HIJK and cdfh. However, the degree of inter-copying means that, especially within Group A, there is such overlap that

---

a *vycius woman al here lyffe and hit apperyd þat S. Austin schuld cum to preche in þat same cyte per þis woman was, cetera* (f. 26ʳ).

[165] cdf agree to the exclusion of h (2/11 **Ion**, 87 **hadde**; 14/4 **melody**), or (more commonly, since f paraphrases more than h) cdh to the exclusion of f (2/5 **and . . . lyuyng**, 18 **hure**, 145–6 **Dame . . . now**; 14/41–2 **For . . . law**, 43–4 **ryght . . . Sone** (ch), 83 **ʒerne**, 161 **masse**; 24/89 **suffer, wreþe**; 39/4 **Crystes**).

[166] f omits this material; Sermon 41 is not in h.

the group ABC may agree with members of the HIJK group at times. Of the group ABC, B appears to be the earliest member which then branched into an exemplar prior to AC. EF are good texts which often agree with DI, for example, but which have been considerably (and to some extent differently) abbreviated and truncated. K is related to this group as well as to HIJ. HJ agree most closely within the broad group HIJK. Amongst the Group B manuscripts, groupings are more clear-cut, and abeg and cdfh, while not consistent, are broadly secure groupings. In general terms, α is closest to DI among the Group A manuscripts and to cd among the Group B manuscripts. However, α's affiliations depend on the different hands and exemplars of the manuscript, a complex issue which will be discussed next (§5, §6).

5. THE SCRIBAL PRODUCTION OF MS COTTON CLAUDIUS A.II

Among the several reasons for choosing London, BL MS Cotton Claudius A.II (α) as the base-text, the most weighty may be the fact that it appears to offer a carefully assembled 'collected edition' of Mirk's vernacular works. The interest of this has been felt to outweigh the fact that α is to some extent an uneven text, compromised by a piecemeal assemblage of the text, perhaps from different periods, certainly by different scribes using different exemplars which themselves may well have been copied from other different exemplars. The case for choosing α as base-text will be presented in §6; the task now is to explain the nature of the manuscript.

5.1. Manuscript Description

DESCRIPTIONS: Planta 1802: i. 188;[167] Horstmann 1881: cxiii–vii; Wakelin 1967: 94–5, 116–17; Kristensson 1974: 13–15.

CONTENTS:

I. [*Festial*], ff. 3ᵛ–125ᵛ, preceded (f. 3ʳ) by contents list (see Hands, Dates, and Languages below)

> f. 125ᵛ *Explicit tractus qui dicitur ffestial: Per fratrem Iohannem mir/ kus compositus canonicum regularem monasterii de lulshull./ cuius anime propicietur deus. Amen.*

---

[167] Apparently copied from the 1696 catalogue of Thomas Smith (Tite 1984: 37ᵃ).

II. *De magna sentencia pronuncianda hoc modo* [Sentence], ff. 125^v–128^r (f. 128^v blank)

III. *Propter presbiterum parochialem instruendum* [*IPP*], ff. 129^r–154^v

f. 154^v *Explicit tractatus qui dicitur pars oculi de latino in angli/ cum translatus per fratrem Iohannem myrcus canonicum regu/ larem monasterij de lylleshul cuius anime propicietur deus. Amen.*

IV. *Hec sunt festa ab omnibus operibus/ tenenda per constitucionem Ricardi Arundelis/ Cantuariensis archiepiscopi videlicet* [*festa ferianda*] ff. 154va–155ra

V. [English prose notes on the early popes],[168] ff. 155^v–156^r

PHYSICAL APPEARANCE:

Collation. Two booklets: vi + 1 + 1–5^{12}, 6^6, 7–10^{12}, 11^{10} + 1; 1–3^8, 4^4 + vi, i.e. i–iv modern flyleaves, v–vi old flyleaves (ff. 1–2), singleton (f. 3), five quires of 12 (ff. 4–15, 16–27, 28–39, 40–51, 52–63), one quire of 6 (ff. 64–9), four quires of 12 (ff. 70–81, 82–93, 94–105, 106–17), one quire of 10 (ff. 118–27), singleton (f. 128);[169] three quires of 8 with signatures (ff. 129–36,[170] 137–44, 145–52), one quire of 4 (ff. 153–6), vii–viii old endleaves (ff. 157–8), ix–xii modern endleaves.

Material. Four modern card leaves at beginning and end (i–iv, ix–xii), two parchment leaves within them at beginning and end (ff. 1–2, 157–8, once part of a large noted gradual (s. xiv/xv), trimmed right and bottom),[171] 154 parchment ff. The parchment in quires 7–9 was holed before the scribe began to write (e.g. ff. 72, 84, 99); at one point it has been mended (f. 93).[172] There is some damage, perhaps by damp (upper part of ff. 94^v–95^r, 95^v, 100^r, 101$^{r–v}$, 105^r).

Numeration. Original foliation 1–155 in ink in the upper right corner, omitting all front flyleaves and numbering first endleaf 155. Later cancelled in pencil and renumbered 1–158 (to include original fly- and endleaves) in pencil in the upper and lower right-hand corners of each folio (*recto*).

---

[168] Incipit: *Gregory the tenthe pope ordyned þat men schulde pay here types to here modure chyrche and not were hem lykyd as thie myȝt do byfore* . . . , explicit: *herby may men witte þat all popes haue nod* [sic] *be goode men þouȝ þie were clepud holyest fadures in here lyues* (f. 156^r).

[169] Signatures, some cropped, are discernible in quires 4, 6,7, 9, 10.

[170] Ff. 132–3 a bifolium made up of two separate folios with pasted stubs.

[171] The front flyleaves (which should be taken in the order 2^r, 1^v, 2^v, 1^r) are from the Mass for the Dead (cf. Dickinson 1861–3: 860*–79*), and the endleaves (which should be taken in the order 157^r, 158^v, 157^v, 158^r) from the Kyriale (cf. Dickinson 1861–3: 928*–34*).

[172] See apparatus to 49/155–9, 50/30–3.

Size. Page size approx. 240 × 165 mm., with a writing space (for I and II) of 180–205 × 130 mm. (depending on the stint). I and II are framed, with 26–42 lines to a page according to the stint; III is framed, with 37–40 lines to the page.

Decoration. For I and II, see the individual hands in §5.2.1 below. III has red initials within a brown ink decorated square, rhymes (and groups of rhymes) linked with brackets. Other rubrication is largely red, with blue used occasionally, e.g. for paraphs ff. 139^r, 146^r and for the initial of *Ihesu* through 4 lines (f. 132^v).[173]

Marginalia and Annotation. Contemporary (perhaps in the same hand as f. 3^v) insertion with red paraph in top margin f. 4^r: *Assit principio sancta maria meo*. Contemporary pointing hands f. 15^{r-v}, but others on ff. 15^v, 16^{r-v}, 17^v, 64^v, 67^{r-v}, 68^v, 69^r, 70^v, 75^r, 79^{r-v} in a later hand ('the long hand'). Frequent contemporary marginal *nota* with rubricated paraph mark (often cropped) and occasional *Narracio* (e.g. ff. 13^r, 22^r); occasional *Narracio* (e.g. ff. 13^r, 65^r, *Narracio bona* 67^v) and marks of annotation (e.g. ff. 27^r, 29^r, 70^r, 81^r) in 'the long hand'. A contemporary rubricated drawing of a little dog perhaps looking at a sleeping cat, bottom margin f. 58^r; another (also rubricated) of a bird like a cockatoo, f. 100^r. Letters of the alphabet practised in blank space, f. 155rb and *gloryus Iosus kep you from/ all euell thynkh and al com/peyne from pens of hels amen* (partly repeated below the alphabet). In a s. xv hand *liber Thome [blank] Capellani*,[174] top f. 156^v; thereafter pen trials: *liber Thome* (four times), *Thomas balon*, *Thomas ballon*, *Robert walkar*, *lyber home*, *lyber Thome*, and three doodles on *Robert*; *in my deyr son* and doodles of *d*, *l*, *ly*, and *be the lord god thow/ shalle pray hyme dayly/ to halpe the*, probably in the same hand (early s. xvi in.); upside down, also in the same hand, *Robertt walkar aw thys boke*, *Robert Jhon willam thomas*, *Necoles sander*.

Binding. Leather binding (s. xix), the Cotton coat of arms impressed in gold leaf on front and back covers. Three sets of information recorded on spine, separated by cording covers: *FESTIAL./ IN OLD ENGLISH./ ETC./ BY/ JOHN MIRK./ CANON OF LYLLESHUL, MUS. BRIT./ BIBL. COTTON.*, and *CLAUDIUS A II*.

---

[173] See further Kristensson 1974: 14.

[174] The surname has been removed and only *-son* can clearly be read under ultraviolet light. The further doodles might suggest a variant of *Bal(l)on*, but this is not confirmed by the dimly discernible outline of letters before *-son*, and the top flourishes of the first letter suggest *V*, not *B*.

HANDS, DATES, AND LANGUAGES:

Contents list (probably copied from Cotton's 1621 catalogue, London, BL MS Harley 6018, no. 79)[175] and pressmark (f. 3^r) in 'the stylized hand' of an anonymous employee of Cotton (Tite 2003: 248 (Annex 3a), 255 (Annex 5a), cf. 21 (Fig. 4.b.)).[176] I (*F*) and II (Sentence) in four hands of s. xiv *ex.* to xv^1 (see the individual hands at §5.2.1 below); III (*IPP*) in Anglicana formata s. xv^1; IV (*festa ferianda*) s. xv^1 in a good textura in coloured inks; Item V (notes on popes) s. xiv/xv in a current hand.[177] For the languages of *F*, see the individual hands at §5.2.1 below. The language of *IPP* is Shropshire (*LALME*: i. 105, iii. 424–5 (LP52)).

HISTORY:

The manuscript (or, at least, the second booklet) was owned in the fifteenth century by a chaplain (*Thomas -son*) and then in the early sixteenth century by *Robert Walkar*. It passed into the possession of Henry Savile of Banke (1568–1617), when it was certainly in (or acquired) its present form (two booklets).[178] From Savile it had passed by 1621 (the start-date of his early catalogue) into the ownership of Sir Robert Cotton (1571–1631) (Tite 2003: 121), and thence into the hands of his son, Sir Thomas (1594–1662), and his grandson, Sir John (1621–1702). At the latter's death the Cotton library became national property, belatedly in accordance with Sir Robert's wishes, and in 1753 it became a foundation collection of the British Museum Library. In 1973 the greater part of the Cotton collections, including MS Cotton Claudius A.II., passed into the care of the newly formed British Library.

[175] This was itself dependent on Savile's catalogue, cf. London, BL MS Add. 35213, f. 19^r: *Festa excerpta et collecta de Legenda aurea cum additis multis. per fratrem Johannem Myrcum Canonicum regularem monasterij de hilleshull* [sic]. *Anglice. Item de magna sententia. prosa. Angl. Item liber qui dicitur (pars oculi) translatus de latino in Anglicos rhythmicos. per predictum myrcum.* The same hand has recorded in the margin: *Item propter presbyterum parochialem instruendum Anglicanis metris.* The α contents list is the fairer copy and so was most likely copied from it (not *v.v.*) (Tite, personal communication).

[176] The hand was used for prestigious manuscripts, such as Lindisfarne and the Utrecht Psalter (Tite, personal communication).

[177] However, given that it occurs after s. xv^1 hands, it is presumably an old-fashioned hand.

[178] This is not apparent from Watson (1969: 36 [90]), where the absence of his usual [*etc.*] implies that only *F* was recorded by Savile, but see n. 175 above.

5.2. The *Festial*/Sentence Booklet

As indicated above, the manuscript is made up of two separate booklets, ff. 3–128 containing *F* and the Sentence of Excommunication (ed. Peacock 1902: 60–7)[179] (Items I and II), and ff. 129–56 containing *IPP* (ed. Peacock 1902, Kristensson 1974), a list of *festa ferianda*, and added notes on early popes (Items III–V). Discussion here focuses on the first booklet (the manuscript as a whole is considered from §5.3 below).

5.2.1. The Hands, Dates, and Languages of the *Festial*/*Sentence* Booklet

There is evidence of correction throughout the booklet, most noticeably in Hands A–C (where caret marks regularly indicate omissions later supplied) but continuing into Hand D (f. 42^r). Erasure and rewriting are usual throughout the manuscript. Differences of rubrication within the stints show that it took place at the end of each stint, rather than after the completion of the whole task, although the decoration of initials, which appears to be in the same hand throughout, is likely to have taken place after the whole booklet had been assembled into quires.[180] Each hand has prepared his pages by framing (see further in the individual hands below). The pages have been cropped, with some loss, for example, of part of the marginal rubric f. 66^v.

In terms of date, the datings of previous scholars have not taken the different hands into sufficient account,[181] and new opinions are advanced here. So too in terms of dialects. The *LALME* analysis of α (1986: i. 105, using the previous foliation, emended here within square brackets) was based on the assumption that there were three s. xv^2 hands: Hand A f. [3]^v (also Hand A in this edition), Hand B ff. [4]^r–[39]^v (Hands B and C in this edition),[182] Hand C ff. [40]^r–[128]^r (Hand D in this edition). The *LALME* analysis was of ff. [3]^v, [4]^r–[15]^r (i.e. no analysis of this edition's Hand C), [40]^r–[48]^r (i.e. no

---

[179] Peacock (1868) prints the Sentence from E (see 1902: xii), as does Kristensson 1974: 104/1–107/90.

[180] All hands show the same type of (post-1380) red pen flourishing of initials. Some extra rubrication may have taken place at the end, since the blue ink of f. 4^r (the first f. of *F*) has smudged f. 3^v (the singleton Prayer and Prologue).

[181] For example, the manuscript is dated *c*.1420 (Horstmann 1881: cxiii), 1425–50 (Wakelin 1967: 94; Kristensson 1974: 14).

[182] *LALME* i. 105 suggests a possible change of hand at f. [28]^r and inserted a question mark before f. [39]^v.

analysis of this edition's D*), and all three hands were placed in Staffordshire, 'probably' in the case of Hand A (*LALME* i. 105).[183] For the present edition a new analysis has been made of all four hands, including the insertion (D*) in Hand D's stint (ff. 52^r–69^v, 122^v–128^r),[184] and the *LALME* fit-technique (Benskin 1991a, Williamson 2000) has been applied anew to the new analysis.[185]

Graphical and phonological features common to all three main hands (B, C, D/D*) are the frequent confusion of ⟨e⟩/⟨o⟩, e.g. *scheppe* ('shop') 3/130, *templo* ('temple') 4/48, *know* ('knew') 10/85; transposition of *-th*, e.g. *comeht* 1/89, *syngeht* 9/10; ⟨gh⟩ for ⟨th⟩, e.g. *wrogh* ('wrathful') 3/134, *mogh* ('mouth') 5/41; ⟨k⟩, e.g. *kalleth* ('calls') 6/71; ⟨ng⟩ for ⟨nn⟩, e.g. *sungeth* ('sins') 9/23; ⟨sc⟩ for ⟨sch⟩, e.g. *scryfte* ('shrift') 2/122; ⟨sc⟩ for ⟨s⟩, e.g. *sclepyng* 9/94; excrescent ⟨t⟩/⟨d⟩, e.g. *ynoght* ('enough') 3/37; excrescent *h-*, e.g. *howt* ('out') 10/113. Graphical errors in all three main hands are the omission of nasal contraction marks (e.g. *fydeth* 6/117, *couersyon* 13/3, *brennyg* 37/116), the transposition of letters (e.g. *senyt* 2/8, *flowen* 12/118, *sewen* 21/79), and minim error (e.g. *sechem* 5/29, *whem* 14/165, *bene* 34/31).

HAND A (see frontispiece)

Hand: very careful example of Textura semi-quadrata; *Date*: s. xv^I; *Language*: North Somerset/South Gloucestershire (Williamson, personal communication).

The Prayer and Prologue were added later on a ruled singleton (f. 3^v). They are written in red, with blue for the decorated three-line-deep initial *G* of the Prayer and for the one-line-deep initial *B* of the Prologue. The four lines of verse of the Prayer are decorated to the end of each line in blue and red. There is one scribal omission (*fore*) noted by a red caret and corrected in red. Item IV (ff. 154va–155ra) appears also to be in Hand A.

---

[183] Horstmann (1881: cxiii) identified three hands for the main body of the text (foliation updated in square brackets): up to f. [27]^v, ff. [28]^r–[39]^v, [40]^r–[125]^v. Wakelin (1967: 95) identified f. [3]^v as Hand A, ff. [4]^r–[39]^v as Hand B, and the rest of the *Festial* as Hand C, an opinion which influenced the analysis of the language in *LALME*.

[184] See Appendix IV for the Linguistic Profile (LP), compiled from f. 3^v (Hand A), ff. 12^r–19^v (Hand B), 30^r–37^v (Hand C), 95^r–102^v Hand D, 57^r–64^v, 95^r–102^v (D*). Where an item was not recorded in the sample, the text was scanned.

[185] By Dr Keith Williamson of the University of Edinburgh, using the most recent (2008) version of the computer fitting program (Williamson 2000).

HAND B (Plate 1)

Hand: mixed (Anglicana/early Secretary); *Date*: s. xv¹ (Doyle, personal communication);[186] *Language*: South Central Staffordshire (Williamson, personal communication), Staffordshire (*LALME* i. 105).

The first two quires of 12 (ff. 4–15, 16–27) (Sermons 1/1–10/165) are written by the same hand, although the hand of the second quire writes larger, with a broader nib.[187] There are 26–31 lines to the page, with a written space of approx. 180 mm. × 125 mm. The work has been subjected to careful scrutiny by a supervisor, and caret marks (some with red ink) indicate frequent omissions which have been supplied in the original hand, e.g. the last lines of f. 5ʳ. There is also evidence of erasure and correction. There is intelligent rubrication, with alternate red and blue paraph marks, which, like the caret marks, become less frequent in the course of the two quires, e.g. twelve paraph marks f. 5ʳ, two f. 26ᵛ, one f. 27ᵛ. *Assit principio sancta maria meo* has been written in the top margin f. 4ʳ in a contemporary hand with a decorated red paraph.[188] The first sermon (f. 4ʳ) has a red and blue initial *T* through six lines within a decorated red square. Thereafter a blue initial in a red decorated square marks the beginning of each sermon, for example, sermon 2 (f. 6ʳ: also f. 6ᵛ within the sermon, cf. f. 4ᵛ within the Advent sermon), Sermon 3 (f. 8ᵛ). Sermon 6 has two rubricated pointing hands either side of the title (f. 15ʳ).

Sermon 1 has no title, and the titles of the following sermons are crammed into the body of the text, sometimes occupying the last line of the previous sermon (e.g. f. 6ʳ), occasionally with a one-line gap (e.g. f. 15ʳ). The scribe is responsible for frequent marginal annotation, e.g. *narracio* (cropped with blue paraph f. 13ʳ, with red paraph f. 20ʳ), and both quires have catchwords: a rubricated pointing hand and red paraph f. 15ᵛ (*ffor aȝeyn*) and a red paraph f. 27ᵛ (*þus in ierusalem*). The sermon conclusions are truncated throughout this stint, ending abruptly without the conventional sermon ending (e.g. *yfound et cetera* f. 11ᵛ, *concepcyon of me* f. 13ʳ).

Distinctive graphical features of this hand are elisions of weak

---

[186] Perhaps earlier: Parkes (personal communication) suggests s. xiv *ex.*/xv *in.* by comparison with Parkes 1969: Pl. 9.

[187] *LALME* notes 'a change in language at f. [15] and the script has also altered in character by f. [18]'.

[188] For the same prayer in other manuscripts of Mirk's works, see description of E (Appendix II.i.a).

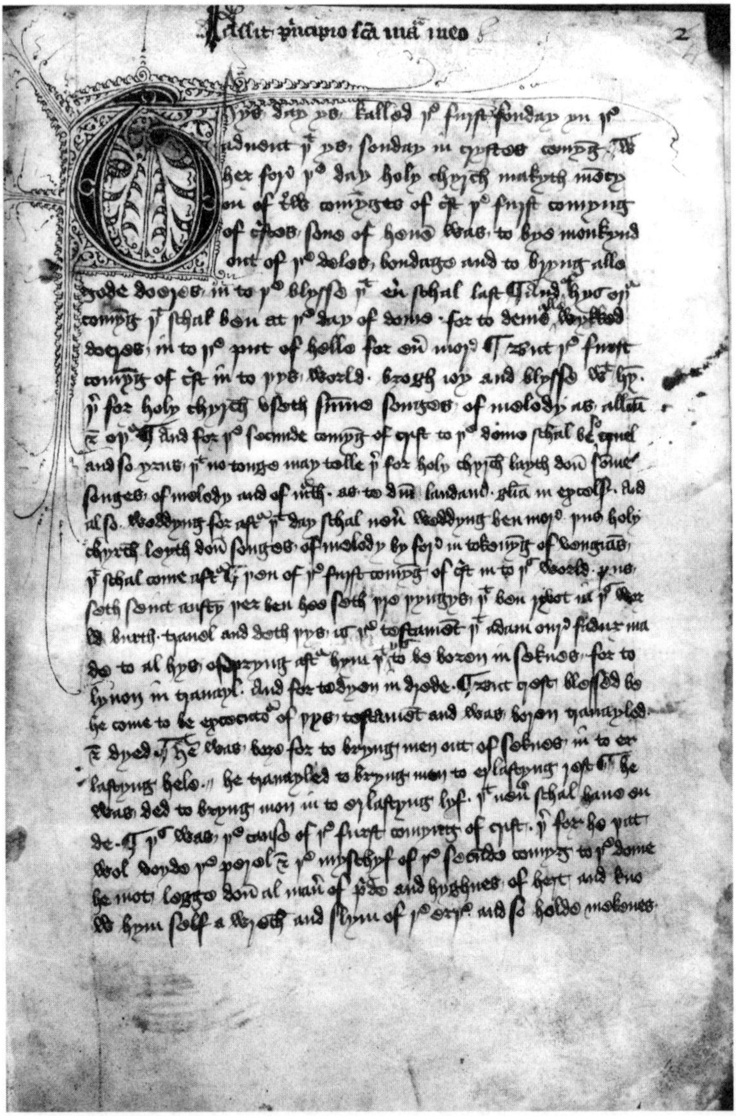

PLATE 1. MS Cotton Claudius A.II, f. 4^r (Hand B)
Reproduced by permission of the British Library

stressed words, e.g. *hacussed* ('have kissed') 3/51, *strangulym* ('strangled him') 3/154, *adarknes* ('a darkness') 4/76; *þus* (with *us* contraction) used variously for 'thus', 'this', and 'these' (see Glossary *sub* þus *dem. adj.*). A distinctive occasional phonological feature is the voicing and devoicing of plosives, e.g. *grede* for *grete* 1/52, *3ont* for *3ond* 2/12, *amonk* for *among* 2/22. The feminine third person singular personal pronoun is *heo* (as Hand C), with occasional *hoo* (4/41), *hoe* (7/105); the third person plural is occasionally *heo* (e.g. 2/76) but normally *þey*.

HAND C (Plate 2)
Hand: mixed (Anglicana/early Secretary); *Date*: xv[1];[189] *Language*: North Staffordshire (Williamson, personal communication), not analysed *LALME*.

 The third quire of 12 (ff. 28–39) (sermons 10/165–15/159) is in a larger and rougher hand than Hand B, perhaps a little later but with similar characteristics, although more slapdash and amateur. Hand C increases the lines to the page as he proceeds, perhaps because of the need to fit the text of his exemplar into his quire (e.g. 30 ll. f. 28[r], 42 ll. f. 38[v]). In general he has more lines to the page than Hand B, with a correspondingly larger written space, 185–95 mm. × 135 mm. Material at the bottom of f. 32[v] is written in small in the last two lines, as if the scribe had left something out and had to fit it all in later (but it is neither the end of a quire nor a change of hand). The corrections are less often marked by caret marks than in Hand B.[190] Some of the less significant omissions and mistakes have been marked and corrected, and there is evidence of erasure and rewriting, but in general the oddities and errors of this scribe remain.[191]

 There is less, and less careful, rubrication than for Hand B's stint, nor does it alternate red and blue (e.g. no rubrication ff. 28[r], 29[v], two blue and three red paraphs f. 29[r], six red paraphs f. 30[r]). Blue is used only at the beginning of the quire (ff. 28[v], 29[r]) and in the usual blue initial in a red decorated square to begin Sermons 11 and 15 (ff. 28[v], 37[v]). The title of Sermon 14 is in red, and there is some touching of capitals with red ink, e.g. ff. 34[r], 35[r]. Traces of red ink from f. 34[r] on f. 33[v] suggest that the quire was folded soon after rubrication. The

[189] Perhaps earlier: s. xv *in*. (Parkes, personal communication).
[190] The cross which marks an omission f. 31[r] (see Apparatus for 12/68) is distinctive to this quire.
[191] They are only emended in this edition where understanding would be seriously impaired.

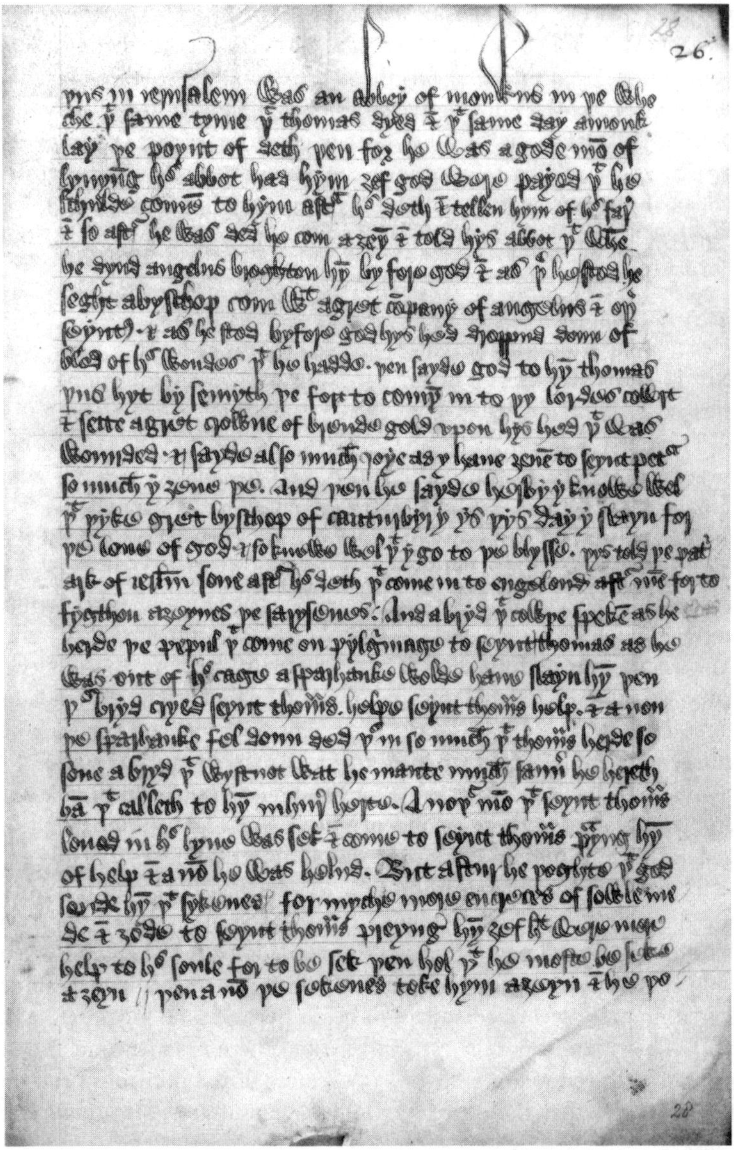

PLATE 2. MS Cotton Claudius A.II, f. 28ʳ (Hand C)
Reproduced by permission of the British Library

titles to the sermons are set out on a separate line from the rest of the text. The conclusions of the sermons are occasionally more expansive than those of Hand B, e.g. *to þat hylsse god bryng vs et cetera* f. 30^r, *dwelle wyth hym for euer amen* f. 35^r. There are some contemporary marginal rubrics, e.g. ff. 35^r, 38^v. There is no catchword f.39^v. The characteristics of the language are much the same as those of Hand B. A distinctive graphical feature (cf. Hand B) is *þ^s* ('thus', 'this', 'these'), and a notable orthographical feature is ⟨ch⟩ for ⟨c⟩, e.g. *challed* ('called') 11/75, *challeth* ('calls') 12/3, *chause* ('cause') 14/29, and ⟨th⟩ for ⟨t⟩, e.g. *thechyng* ('teaching') 12/65, 13/17. Other such features also found in Hand D/D* are ⟨w⟩/⟨v⟩ variation, e.g. *ewe* ('Eve') 11/53, *dewowt* ('devout') 14/126, *vayes* ('ways') 12/6, *veren* ('were') 14/119; *h*- deletion, e.g. *ast* ('hast') 12/111, and excrescent *h*, e.g. *hensampul* ('example') 15/56). The feminine third person singular personal pronoun is *heo* (as Hand B); the third person plural is on one occasion *heo* (13/115) but normally *þey* (also 13/115).

Hand C is remarkable for his inaccurate copying: single letters are omitted, e.g. *crst* (for *cryst*) 11/47, 54, 56, 67, 68, 102; *fowed* (for *folwed*) 13/64, *wyntryng* (for *wyn turnyng*) 12/145; single letters are added, e.g. *lorld* 12/83; single letters are misinterpreted, e.g. *loly* (for *holy*) 12/77, *sveles* (for *skeles*) 13/10, *wrastebyng* (for *wrastelyng*) 14/159, especially ⟨f⟩/⟨s⟩ confusion, e.g. *desendyng* (for *defendyng*) 13/11, 75, *stodon* (for *fondon* with nasal contraction mark omitted) 13/31, *sendes* for *fendes* 13/113, etc.; letters are transposed, e.g. *for* (for *fro*) 14/11, *braforth* (for *bar forth*) 14/158; words are mistaken, e.g. *wyne* (for *when*) 12/150; words are omitted, e.g. *at* 12/102, *make* 12/106; words are repeated, e.g. *for* 14/21, *and* 14/145; more frequently than other hands, nasal contractions are omitted, e.g. *couersyon* (for *conuersyon*) 13/3, and falsely expanded, e.g. *aʒanyn* (for *aʒayn*) 12/41, *rybandy* (for *rybaudy*) 15/30.

HAND D (Plates 3, 5)

Hand: Anglicana formata; *Date*: s. xiv/xv; *Language*: border of East Central Staffordshire and West Central Derbyshire (Williamson, personal communication), Staffordshire (*LALME* i. 105).

The rest of *F* and the Sentence (ff. 40^r–128^r) are in Hand D (for D*, see below). Hand D writes in a small Anglicana formata (but with short ⟨r⟩), appearing to date from the late fourteenth or early fifteenth century. The written space ranges from 185 to 200 mm. × 130 mm., with between 38 and 41 lines to a page, and the small, neat hand

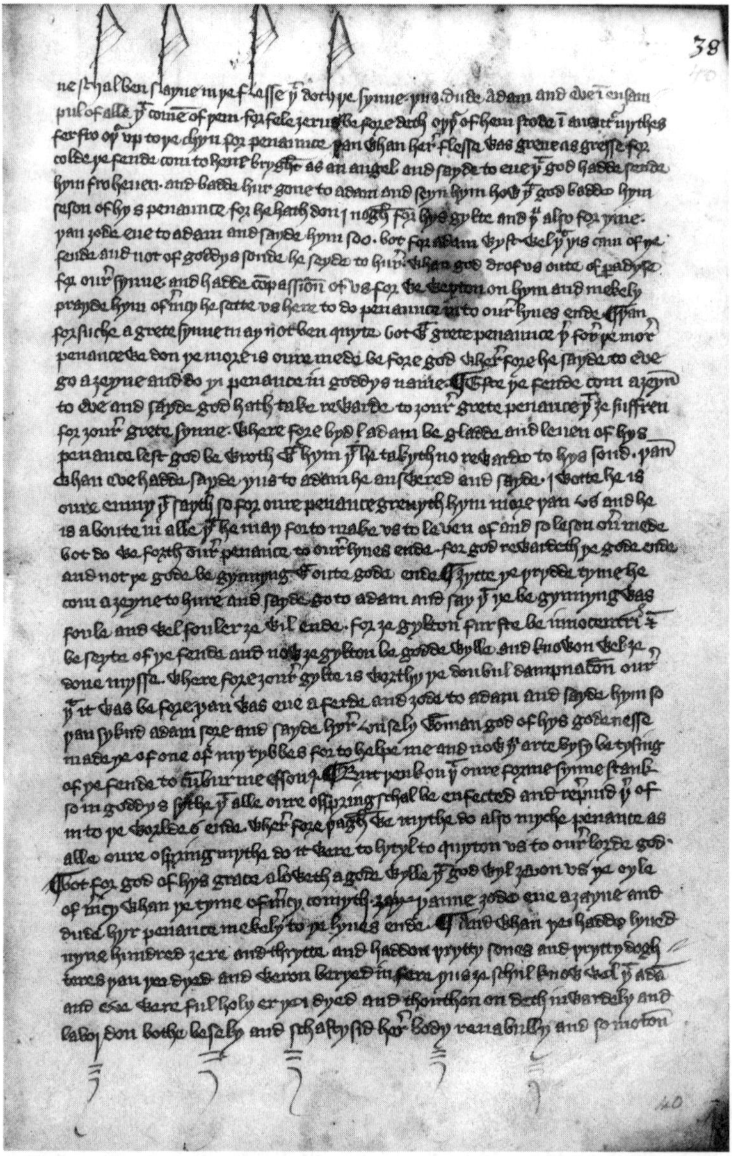

PLATE 3. MS Cotton Claudius A.II, f. 40ʳ (Hand D)
Reproduced by permission of the British Library

becomes increasingly cramped as the scribe proceeds in his stint. There are few caret marks in this stint, but there appear to be several erasures with writing over (see apparatus *passim*). Marginal annotation, often partially lost by cropping, occurs fairly frequently, e.g. *nota* with blue paraph f. 44ʳ, *nota* in red f. 70ʳ, *nota* with red paraph f. 107ʳ. Catchwords occur (usually within a decorative surround) at the end of each quire (ff. 51ᵛ, 81ᵛ, 93ᵛ, 105ᵛ, 117ᵛ). Initials are decorated in the usual manner (except f. 70ᵛ, where the red surround is missing), and paraph marks are rubricated red and blue, varying from none (ff. 51ʳ, 105ʳ) to as many as ten (f. 72ᵛ). The titles of sermons now appear in false textura but continue to occupy the last line of the previous sermon (f. 40ᵛ), or the first line of the commencing sermon (f. 84ʳ), or both (f. 91ᵛ).

Certain features are distinctive to this Hand (and to D*) and separate it from Hands B and C: -*ce* (for -*se*), e.g. *houce* 21/65, 147, *falce* 22/70, *horce* 22/72; ⟨sch⟩ for ⟨ch⟩, e.g. *schylderon* 15/213, *schylde* 15/218; ⟨w⟩ in *wyche* 16/4, 45, etc. (frequent from f. 40ᵛ but previously recorded only at ff. 3ᵛ and 9ᵛ). Consonants are often doubled, e.g. *godde* 16/15; *os* appears alongside *as* from f. 40ᵛ, e.g. 16/10, 69; -*re* is more common than -*er*, e.g. *oure* ('over') 15/190, 17/5, *eure* ('ever') 15/223, 17/38, *neure* ('never') 23/19, 28. Graphically/ phonologically distinctive is -*the* for -*ght*, e.g. *mythe* ('might') 15/197, cf. *nythe* 17/36 (but *nyght* 17/38), *sythe* 18/86 (but *syght* 18/88), *rythe* (19/32, 104), *knythe* (19/110), *þowthe* (19/117). Northern features are also more frequent in Hand D/D* than the other hands (see Items 44 and 47 in the LP, Appendix IV.1), e.g. *qwan* ('when') 36/57, *qwyt(h)e* ('white') 44/94, 48/87, *askus* ('ashes') 19/14, 16 (Jordan 1974: §182); *haly-day* 22/59, 61 (§44);[192] *salte* ('shalt') (22/51), *sal* ('shall') 16/95, cf. *sul* 16/69 (§183 Remark 2 and map p. 171). Notably, the feminine third person singular personal pronoun is not *heo* (as Hands B/C) but *scheo* (15/214, 215, 216, etc., *sche* 16/157, etc.), although occasional forms such as *hoo* 43/71, 72, *ho* 47/11 suggest an *h*- exemplar, especially given the confusion over *h*- forms at, for example, 43/71–3n, 63/50n. Graphically, unlike the previous hands, this hand effectively does not differentiate between ⟨þ⟩ and ⟨y⟩.

A few features are unique to Hand D: *sch*- for *sc*- (*schore* 16/7, *Schariote* 18/12, *schare* 49/103 (*MED* scarre *n.* 2); -*th(e)* for the weak

---

[192] In particular, *haly* is frequent in Hand D/D* (see Glossary *sub* **haly-day, haly-watur/whatyr**).

past tense singular inflexion (*schewyth* 16/30, *commawndeth* 50/66–7, *scheweth* 52/14, *ordeyneth* 52/16, *commaundeth* 52/102, 108, 156), cf. the present tenses *louid* 17/82, and for the past participle (*comfordeth* 18/80, *spenduth* 52/95, *glorifyeth* 53/125).[193] At 68/74 *commaundeth* is the catchword at the bottom of f. 117[v] but f. 118[r] begins *commaundud* (the past tense is intended).[194]

HAND D* (Plates 4, 5)
Hand and Date: as Hand D. Language: combination of results, reflecting Hands C and D (Williamson, personal communication), Staffordshire (*LALME* i. 105).

Sandwiched within Hand D's stint are two quires, ff. 52[r]–63[v] (Sermons 23/116–32/15), 64[r]–69[v] (Sermons 32/16–33/86, 34), which, written in a looser, more variable, and less cramped style and in a different ink, are superficially different from the surrounding hand (Plate 4). These quires also display some notable differences in language and in the treatment of the text. The same linguistic features may be observed in the final *F* sermon (Add6) and the Sentence, ff. 122[v]–128[r] (Plate 5). The hand is the same but the material was added at a later date, and, it appears, from a different exemplar (see further §5.2.3 below).

As already noted, the language of D* shares many features with the rest of Hand D and can be assumed to reflect Hand D's own scribal habits:[195] doubled consonants, e.g. *hytte* ('it') 25/58 (*hitte* Add6/149), *botte* ('but') 25/4, Add6/50, *schalle* Add6/66, 69, *sellerres* 25/47, *missedoerres* 26/15, *neyteburres* Add6/36; -*ce*, most often in *houce* (29/11, 13, 16, etc.) or *howce* (29/18, 19, etc.); *sch-* for *ch-*, e.g. *schylde* (32/111, 34/217, with plurals at 27/72, 80, 28/93, 30/10, Add6/20, etc.), and occasionally *ch-* for *sch-*, e.g. *chyppe* 26/87, *chryuen* 29/74; -*ythe*, e.g. *rythe* 34/63, *mythe* 25/63, 26/90, *sythe* 24/110, 29/91, Add6/69, *thouthe* 26/70, *nythe* Add6/160; -*re* for -*er* (rarer than in the rest of Hand D), e.g. *oure* ('over') 24/103, 25/64, 26/25, 27/31, 32, *owre* 33/45, *owrecomeþ* Add6/192; *eure* ('ever') 23/140, 25/35, 27/154. *Os* remains common (29/2, 11, 17, 30/7, 13, 35, Add6/10,

---

[193] See too 68/30n.

[194] It is perhaps more likely that the catchword represents the scribe's usual form, whereas *commaundud* shows his return to his exemplar. The -*the*/-*d* confusion may relate to north(-west) Midland devoicing of unaccented /d/ > /t/ (Jordan 1974: §200, Remark 1) (for initial *th-* for *t-*, cf. *thechyng* ('teaching') 12/65, 13/17 in Hand C; for final -*t* for -*th*, see D* below).

[195] Several of these features, such as doubled consonants, occur much more frequently in D*.

¶The secunde ioy was on cristenmesse day whan sche was delyuered
of hur sonne & outen any payne of hur body. ffor ry[gh]t as sche was
conseyued hym & outen luste of flesse. ry[gh]t so sche was delyuered
of hur sonne & outen payne of flesse. ¶ The pryde ioy was on estur
day whan hur sonne rose fro me deth to lyue. & com to hur & cussud hur. & makud hur more ioyful of hys vpryste. þan sche was
sory before of his deth. ¶ The furþe ioy was whanne sche se[gh]e hy[m]
steyou vp in to heuen on holy þursday. in þe same flesse & blode þt he
tole of hur body. ¶ The fyfte ioy was in hur assumpcion when sche
& hur sonne comen. & grete multitude of angellus and seyntu[s]
& fecchur in to heuen. & krowned hur quene of heuen. & empryse of
helle. & lady of alle þe worlde. ¶ Þy[en] alle þt ben in heuen schul euer
do hur reuerence & worchep. And y wille þt ben in helle schul be buyn
to hur bysshyng. & y wille þt bene in erþe schul done hur seruyce & gretyng. ¶ Þese ben þe fyue ioyes þt sche hadde of hur swete sonne
Ihu. ¶ þan schul [g]e knowe wel þt he schal neuer fele þe sorowes of helle
þt schul deuo[u]tly uche day gretyn hur & þese v. ioyes in erþe ¶ ffor to
be of an holy maydon þt was deuoute in oure lady seruice. & uche a day
grette hur & hur v. ioyes. þan hir felle þt sche was seke & þan sche
sawe deel þt sche schulde be dede sche syed wou[n]der sore. & makyd
grete mone, for enchason þt sche schulde soone wydur sche schulde gone
aftur hur deþe. ¶ Þen com oure lady to hur & sayde why arte þi so so
ry þi haþ makys me so ofte ioy, greting me & þa v. ioyes þt i hadde
of my sonne. where fore know wel þt þt schalte go wyth me to þe ioy
þt euer schal laste. ¶ Narracio. ¶ I redde also of seynte hylberde þat
was negh dede on þe quynasy. whan hys throte was so grete þt
sche lon þt he mythe unneþe drawen breþe. oure lady come to hym
& sayde. hylberte my seruaunte hit þere enely done þt þin throte schulde
lenger suffur þis penaunce. þt haþ so ofte glad[d]ud me & my v. ioyes.
& par & tok oute hur swete pappe. & mylkyd on hys throte. & so sone
hur þay. & anone þt wyth he was hole as[s]a ffysshe. & þankud oure lady
he[r]thly. & taute alle other to do so þe same. And at hys ende he hadde
blysse of heuen. to whiche blysse god bryng vs alle to amen.

Dominica in passione d[omi]ni. Sermo ad parochianos hoc mod[um].

Gode men & wymmen. þis day is callyd in holy chirche sonday
in þe passion. ffor enchason þt oure lorde ihu criste be gan his
passion þis day. þe iewes & þe sarsynnes hadde sthyche enuye
to hym. for enchason þt hir olde hem her vy[ce]us & repreuid here wyckud
lyuyng þt þis day weron fully asettud for to done hym to deþe.
Oft be fore þei weron abowton for to haue slayne hym. bot ay

PLATE 4. MS Cotton Claudius A.II, f. 52ʳ (Hand D*)
Reproduced by permission of the British Library

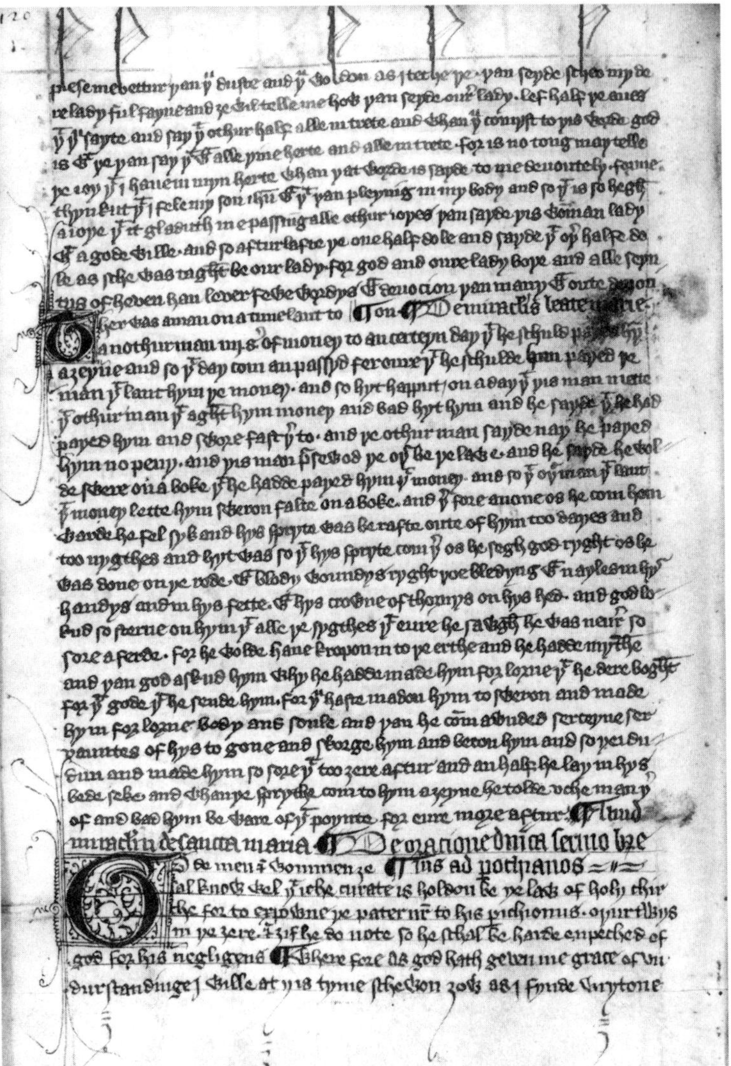

PLATE 5. MS Cotton Claudius A.II, f. 122ᵛ (Hand D/D*)
Reproduced by permission of the British Library

22), and *myche* is also found (29/85, 115, 33/25, 35, 80, Add6/188, 207). The feminine third person singular personal pronoun is still *scheo*, but there are no *h-* forms, although in the third person plural pronoun several such forms survive, e.g. *heo* 28/159, 29/99, 32/79; *he* 32/11. There appear to be more frequent northern dialect features in the inserted quires of D*, e.g. *qwyle* ('while') 26/55, *qwelle* ('wheel') 30/58; *knaw* 32/8, *awte* 31/96, *awne* 24/118, 27/90, 29/28, 32/7; *haly-day* 28/25, *blady* 34/160, *clathus* 25/63; *mykul* 25/71, 34/100. A few northern morphological features appear in Add6: *-se* for the third person present singular in *fo[s]turse*, l. 195 and for the plural in *trespaces*, l. 120.

Peculiar to D* are two features. The common spelling *wit* ('with') is not found in the manuscript before f. 53^r (24/79) and then not until ff. 60^v–69^v (e.g. 30/14, 21, 30, 32, etc.), followed by ff. 123^r–125^v (Add6/22, 24, 54, 56, etc.).[196] Likewise, initial, medial, and final *ff*, especially *off* ('of'), occurs only in the D* quires (*offt* 24/7, *ffyffty* 26/14, *off* 27/34, 35, *peroff* 27/56, 89, etc.) and then not until f. 124^r and Add6 (*ffor* ll. 3, 15, 16, *luff* 53, 80, 82, *mysschecheff* 85, etc., cf. Jordan 1974: §157 Remark 2). Their presence in D* alone would appear to confirm a different exemplar for D* from D.[197] Only *wit* can perhaps be localized, most common in Norfolk, but also found in the north Midlands (West Riding of Yorkshire, Lancashire, Lincolnshire, Staffordshire, etc.).[198]

The computer analysis of the languages of the Hands (noted in the headword to each Hand above and based on the LP, Appendix IV.1) places Hands B and C in Staffordshire. Hand B is more firmly located in the south (very approximately within a ten-mile radius of a point between Lichfield and Stafford) and Hand C in the north (approximately within a ten-mile radius of Leek). Hand D is thus confirmed as the less westerly hand, more firmly located in Derbyshire than Staffordshire, west of Derby itself. D* shows features of both Hands C and D, suggesting that the exemplar was close to the language of Hand C (Leek district). Hand A is, however, very different, seemingly written in a language best located within a fifteen-mile radius of Bristol. (For a full discussion, see Appendix IV.)

[196] The spelling *wyt* occurs rarely in Hands C, D/D* (e.g. ff. 39^v, 60^r, 73^{r-v}).

[197] This exemplar perhaps did not feature the *-th(e)* inflexions and use of *sch-* for *sc-* mentioned above (since these features are found in D but not D*). However, the *wit* spelling may be related to the ⟨th⟩/⟨t⟩ variation suggested above as an explanation for *-th(e)* inflexions, and so may not be entirely alien to D, even if unique to D*.

[198] *LALME* iv. 288 (item 258 WITHOUT).

5.2.2. The Construction of the Festial/*Sentence Booklet*

To summarize, four hands can be identified in the *F*/Sentence booklet: Hand A f. 3^v; Hand B ff. 4^r–27^v; Hand C ff. 28^r–39^v; Hand D ff. 40^r–128^r. Hand A provides only the Prayer and Prologue on a singleton (but also ff. 154va–155ra in the second booklet). Of the other Hands, Hands B and C work in discrete quires (1–2^{12} and 3^{12} respectively). Hand D completes the rest of the booklet, largely in quires of 12 (4^{12}, 7–10^{12}), but with the insertion of two quires (5^{12}, 6^6, ff. 52^r–69^v) and the addition of the Paternoster sermon and the Sentence which follows it to the final quire, which has a singleton appended (11^{10} + 1, ff. 122^v–125^v Add6, 125^v–128^r Sentence). In comparison with other *F* manuscripts, the date is early. Hand D is earlier than the other Hands (but see Parkes's opinion of Hand B at nn. 186 and 189 above) but may be an older scribe writing in an old-fashioned hand. In terms of language and graphology, similarities between Hands B and C and differences between Hands B/C and D/D* have already suggested two different origins for B/C and D/D* (see too Appendix IV.2).

In terms of the construction of the booklet, Hand D's stint begins with a lacuna because of a faulty transition from the previous hand (which supplied no catchword at f. 39^v). Hand C ends *so þat by sclappnes of penans þe*, and Hand D begins mid-word *ne schal ben slayne in þe flesse þat doth þe synne*, omitting *lyking of syn-* (see emended text 15/159–60). No such faulty transition occurs between Hands B and C (which are also coherent in language), and it seems that *F* was assembled from two discrete units, three quires of Hands B/C and the acephalous *F* of Hand D, which had been augmented by two inserted quires of *F* sermons and the addition of a final sermon and the Sentence at the end of the manuscript (D*). This assemblage took place during the medieval period (see §5.1 above, History).[199] Discussion will now concentrate on the bulk of the manuscript, in order to elucidate the nature and purpose of the insertion of D*.

5.2.3. The Insertion of D into Hand D's Stint*

In several ways the quires of D* (ff. 52^r–63^v, 64^r–69^v, sermons 23/116–33/86, 34) and the addition of Add6 and Sentence (ff. 122^v–128^r) accord with other codicological aspects of Hand D: crowded

---

[199] This needs to be stressed, as an explanation for the two diverse parts of the *F* booklet might suggest an antiquarian's patching together of two faulty manuscripts.

titles in false textura, occasional marginal annotation, decoration, and rubrication. However, distinctive characteristics of these quires are: more frequent rubrication, textura for Latin quotations (e.g. ff. 66^v, 67^v, 68^v), and frequent, intelligent pointing. The written space ranges from 205 to 215 mm. × 140 mm., with between 35 and 40 lines to a page, and the quires of this stint have been ruled in lead point and favour repeated double horizontals to the edge of the page (Hand D's stint uses brown crayon and simple single frame lines). The scribe of D* favours crossed tironian *et* (Hand D uses *and*), is more calligraphic and flamboyant in the decorative cadels above the top line, and uses a more prominent and differently formed false textura for the sermon titles. In addition, (originally marginal) *narracio* is included in the body of the text.[200] Sermon rubrics are fuller, e.g. *De dominica in Ramis palmarum. Sermo breuis ad Per-ochianos vestros* (25/1–2), *Sermo iste debet dici ad tenebras post matutinas dictas priusquam detur disciplina. Perachianis suis hoc modo incipietur* (26/1–2);[201] likewise, sermon conclusions are fuller, e.g. *to wyche blysse god bryng vs alle to amen* (23/149–50), *haue þe blisse þat he bowte ʒow to amen* (24/128–9), *haue þe blysse þat euer schal laste amen* (25/82). (For the especially full conclusion to the Passion Sunday sermon, see 24/122–9.) All these features point to later additions from a different exemplar.[202]

This is confirmed by more detailed study of D*. In the first of the two inserted quires, the sermon for St George (no. 30) ends f. 62^v: *(sub)scripsit addeley* ('Addeley signed (his name *sc.*)') (see 30/102n and §5.5 below). The wording suggests that this was copied from the scribe's exemplar, as does the appearance of the lines in the text, sandwiched between the end of the sermon and the rubric of the next, and copied in the same textura script as that rubric.[203] No such inscription occurs anywhere else in the manuscript.

The second inserted quire, ff. 64^r–69^v, comprises only six ff., which, within a booklet predominantly of 12s, further suggests an

---

[200] All fifteen occurrences occur in D* (ff. 52^r, 53^v, 54^v, 55^v, 57^r, 57^v, 58^r, 61^r, 62^r, 63^r, 64^v, 67^v, 68^v, 69^r, 125^r).

[201] The phrase *hoc modo* begins with the D* stint and occurs in eight of the eleven sermon titles (24, 26, 27, 28, 31, 32, 33, 34), as well as in the title of the Sentence (see §5.1 above); elsewhere it occurs only twice, both times in Hand D (Sermons 36, 54).

[202] The suggestion that D* is a different hand from D (perhaps even a hand deliberately imitating D) has been dismissed by both Parkes and Doyle but is an intriguing suggestion of Dr Michelle Brown (personal communications).

[203] Had it been an original signature, the usual form would have been *Quod Addeley*, and the inscription would have been given more prominence.

insertion. At f. 66^v the scribe finished copying Sermon 33 (*þus gode men as holy chirche makuþ mynde þis day þe holy crosse was fowndon*, 33/ 85–6) and began a new sermon (*Hic incipit aliud sermo scilicet dominica prima quadragesime ut supra. Hoc modo*, 34/1–2).[204] What is interesting here is that, in the first place, Sermon 33 (the Invention of the Cross) is not complete at this point (despite the valedictory nature of the final sentence),[205] and, in the second place, the new Sermon 34 is indeed *aliud sermo . . . ut supra*, i.e. another sermon for the first Sunday in Lent, as above. The previous 1 Lent sermon (no. 19) had been included earlier in the manuscript at ff. 45^r–46^r, in its correct chronological position, after St Matthias and before 2 Lent. The new 1 Lent sermon was therefore inserted out of place (no. 34).[206] In the other manuscripts which have this sermon (DEFG, see full collation, Appendix III.vi), its position is always after the first sermon for 1 Lent (no. 19). Moreover, Sermon 34 is one of only two instances in the whole collection where two sermons are provided for the same day (the others are nos. 53 and 54), and it is the only sermon in the collection to be based on the epistle of the day (Sermon 54 is similarly unusual in being based on the gospel of the day). The scribe copied Sermon 34 (a long sermon) from f. 66^v to the end of his quire of 6, f. 69^v. It fits exactly into this space, and he ends with a flourish: *In nomine patris et filij et spiritus sancti amen*. Such an ending is unique in the manuscript and indicates clearly that this was a stint which he had completed separately from the main body of the work. Indeed, the first new D* quire begins with a faulty transition, suggesting either that he did not have immediate access to the previous quire or that he wished to mark off the new material by starting his new stint at a discrete unit, the beginning of the second of the five joys of the Virgin, rather than mid-sentence: the catchword f. 51^v was *conseyved*, but f. 52^r begins instead by repeating the last line and a half of f. 51^v (f. 51^v *þe secunde ioy was on cristenmesday whan sche was delyuered of hure sone wythoute any peyne of hure body ryght os scheo [conseyved*

---

[204] *Hic . . . sermo* canc. (see apparatus).

[205] Although not complete, it ends at a discrete stage. The first part of Sermon 33 (33/1–86) in the second of the D* quires (ff. 65^v–66^v) deals with the finding of the Cross; the second part (33/87–136) provides two *narrationes* to the Invention sermon (f. 70$^{r–v}$) at the start of the next quire. Sermon 34 intervenes. There may have been precedent in D's copytext for this division, since it also occurs in F: EF both end at 33/86, but F continues with 33/87, again at a later point (after Sermon 38).

[206] It is inserted between the (truncated) sermon for the Invention of the Cross (3 May) and that for St John at the Latin Gate (6 May).

catchword] | f. 52^r *þe secunde ioy was on cristenmesse day whan scheo was delyuered of hur sone wythowten any payne of hur body. ffor rythe os scheo* [*was* canc.] *conseyued hym*) (23/114–16).

It will be helpful for the discussion to turn at this point to the additions made at the end of the manuscript (Add6 and the Sentence). α is one of only a small number of Group A manuscripts which contain what are here called Add1–6, not originally part of *F* (see §2).[207] Hand D's text becomes increasingly corrupt as the collection draws to a close, with numerous minor omissions (see, for example, Explanatory Notes to Add1). The likelihood that the copy-text was damaged at the point where Hand D paused in his stint (f. 122^v, Pl. 5) is perhaps confirmed by the 'groups of words which indicate the amount of text retained in the scribe's memory when transferring his attention from the exemplar to his copy', the 'numerous misalignments', and the 'differences in the density of the ink on this page' (Parkes, personal communication). It is also supported by textual evidence. Near the bottom of f. 122^v the scribe finishes the *narratio* edited here as Add5 and announces a second *narratio*: *Aliud miraculum de sancta maria*, the rubric crammed into the end of one line and the first half of the next. It may be assumed that he paused there, perhaps because the *aliud miraculum* was unreadable, or perhaps because he realized that the *narratio* which he had just finished copying (headed *De miraculis beate Marie*) was not a miracle of the Virgin (nor perhaps was the one he was about to copy).[208] At some later stage, Hand D added a final sermon (Add6) and the Sentence of Excommunication.[209] The material has all the spelling and palaeographical characteristics of the two quires at ff. 52–69 and clearly used the same D* exemplar.

If we consider the point at which the D* material was added, the most likely explanation is that the whole D* intervention took place at the end of the scribe's copying of *F*. The scribe had access to new material (including Sermons 34 and Add6), added Add6 to the

---

[207] Manuscripts are vulnerable at beginning and end, but it is likely that the material was only ever in Group A manuscripts: only αBK contain all six items; I has Add1-3, C Add 3–6, AD Add6. The Sentence appears to be a conflation of EF (or a similar text) with an unknown text (Pickering 1981: 230–1).

[208] Or he may not have realized it. Parkes (personal communication) suggests that the Paternoster rubric (Add6/1) is in a different hand.

[209] It is likely that he had always planned to include this, or similar, material, since he had embarked on a quire of 10 at f. 118. In the end, he needed an extra side and added a singleton at the end of the manuscript.

incomplete manuscript, and replaced an earlier quire with material from the new exemplar, including Sermon 34. The new material in fact occupied more than the previous quire of 12, and the scribe had to include a quire of 6 as well. There are problems with this suggestion. It was noted above that at f. 66^v (in the second quire of D*) the scribe finished copying Sermon 33 at an incomplete (but discrete) stage and began Sermon 34 (with which he finishes the D* stint and the second quire). Sermon 33 was then completed at the beginning of the following quire.[210] If the new quires were inserted at the end of the scribal copying (i.e. at the same time as the scribe was completing the collection with Add6 and the Sentence), it would have to be pure chance that the discrete second part of the Invention sermon began exactly at the top of f. 70^r in his original stint. Moreover, it was noted above that there is a faulty transition at the start of the D* stint. If the D* scribe were handling the whole process of preparing the F text, there could be no reason for his allowing this weak transition, unless he did not have access to the previous quire (which he himself had copied).

There is no satisfactory solution to this conundrum. The suggestion that D* might be a different hand from D (perhaps even a hand deliberately imitating D) would explain much but has been dismissed by both Parkes and Doyle. The possibility that the D* stint was prepared away from the rest of the manuscript would provide an explanation for its peculiarities but would involve too much conjecture. Nevertheless, the matter of stints may be of some relevance and will be suggested below (§5.4) as a possible explanation for the other faulty transition in the manuscripts, between the B/C and D/ D* quires.

5.3. The *Instructions for Parish Priests/Festa Ferianda* Booklet

The main text of the second booklet is Mirk's other vernacular work, *IPP*, copied by the most professional hand of the manuscript in a Shropshire dialect.[211] It is followed by a short Latin list of feast-days (Appendix V), arranged by month, written in blue and

---

[210] An overseer (perhaps) adds in red textura in the cropped left margin of f. 66^v: [*Cau*]*ias*(?), in the bottom margin of f. 66^v: *Residuum huius istorie post tria folia quere*, and in the top margin of f. 70^r: *Cauias antea*.

[211] Located precisely at Lilleshall in *LALME* ii. 384, but perhaps without specific justification.

red and seemingly, by the similarities of decorative technique, by Hand A.[212]

This list purports to give feasts and vigils of feasts to be observed by cessation from labour (*festa ferianda*), as decreed by Richard [*sic*] Arundel, Archbishop of Canterbury, but in fact not by [Thomas] Arundel (1396–7, 1399–1414) but by Simon Islip (1349–66) in 1362 (Johnson 1850–1: ii. 425–7).[213] The list agrees with that of Islip, apart from omitting the feast of Corpus Christi, placing the Dedication feast in January,[214] and adding the feasts of St Augustine of Canterbury (May), St Winifred (June), St Anne (July), All Souls and St Katherine (November), and, on the last line, at the end of the December details, the feasts of *Sancti Cedde episcopi* and St George.[215]

These saints, Chad and George, are last in the list, still highly decorated and still part of the same piece of work, but in December, whereas their feast days were 2 March and 23 April respectively. It seems likely that the names had been added to the bottom of the scribe's copy-text and he copied them from there. Their addition may therefore relate merely to date, since the 1416 consitutions of Archbishop Henry Chichele ordered St George's day to be celebrated with cessation of labour (Johnson 1850–1: ii. 476–7) and reaffirmed the celebration of SS David, Winifred, and Chad previously affirmed in the 1398 constitutions of Roger Walden (Johnson 1850–1: ii. 454–5).[216]

However, apart from the post-1416 date for the list, the addition of SS Chad and George (but the omission of David) may reflect particular local veneration. St Chad's closest association was with Lichfield, where he had served as the first bishop of the Mercians (669–72) and where he had (since 1148) been buried in the cathedral

---

[212] The following (mildly Wycliffite) notes on the popes (see §5.1 Contents and n. 168) cannot have been intended as part of the original assemblage.

[213] Discussed Cheney 1961: 133.

[214] Perhaps relating to an original date of dedication, as in the list for the Austin priory at Barnwell, near Cambridge (Cheney 1961: 141 n. 1).

[215] Some differences indicate feasts upgraded since Islip, e.g. St Anne 1383, but such lists are notoriously variable in content (see Cheney 1961; Harvey 1972). They also vary according to diocese: none of those in Cheney is for Coventry and Lichfield. For 13th-c. Sarum/Lichfield calendars, see Morgan 2001. A calendar of Mirk's period survives in Acton Burnell Missal (Birkenhead, Shrewsbury Diocesan Curial Office) (Nigel Morgan, personal communication).

[216] The text of α has been variably updated to encompass post-Mirk legislation, e.g. the rubric to the sermon for St George allows for later legislation (see 30/1–2n), whereas the sermon for St Winifred does not (see 43/2–3n). For another variable attempt to modify the original text, see 56/2–3n.

(Kettle & Johnson 1970: 140). However, St Winifred's position in the list (in the month of June) indicates a significance beyond mere dating and links the list with Shropshire, rather than Staffordshire.[217] Walden's constitutions, like Chichele's, had ordered her feast to be celebrated 3 November, the day of her death (*AS* 1867: November i. 736), whereas local veneration had focused around 21 June, when her head had been miraculously restored to its body.[218] The St Winifred sermon is placed chronologically in June in the *F* manuscripts closest to Mirk's intentions, which order the sermons chronologically (Group A).

5.4. The Assembly of the Booklets

The manuscript as a whole suggests a carefully assembled collection of Mirk's two vernacular works: in one booklet, a collection of ready-to-preach sermons for the Church year, to which was added as much material of Mirk's as was perhaps available at the time; in a second booklet, Mirk's rhyming manual, covering all the duties and problems encountered by a parish priest. The first booklet was made up of two separate sets of quires, the bulk of the booklet in a hand trained in the late fourteenth century and the first three quires in later (or younger) and more amateur hands. At the end of this booklet, an explicit (f. 125^v) was added to identify *F* with John Mirk of Lilleshall, followed by the Sentence of Excommunication which the priest was required to deliver several times a year as a warning to his parishioners.[219] At this stage the two booklets must have been brought together. At the end of the second booklet (f. 154^v), an explicit was written which matches in appearance and text the explicit in the first booklet (see §5.1 Contents). This closely matches the hand of the *F* explicit (f. 125^v), the scribe responsible for the rubric at f. 122^v.[220]

The *IPP* explicit (at the end of the second booklet) was followed by

[217] The 1241 statutes of Hugh Patshull, bishop of Lichfield, list the double feasts celebrated at the cathedral and include Chad but not Winifred, nor is her feast-day mentioned in any of his details of observances (Dugdale 1846: 1241; Kettle & Johnson 1970: 145–6).

[218] The date varies (see the discussion in *AS* 1867: November i. 696–9).

[219] Twice or thrice according to the version of the Sentence in E (Kristensson 1974: 104/2), four times (on the Sunday after the feast of St Michael, Mid-Lent Sunday, Trinity Sunday, and the Sunday after the Purification) in the version in α (Peacock 1902: 60). On the significance of the Sentence in the context of *F*, see Powell 1991: 92. Amongst *F* manuscripts, it is found in E(F)c.

[220] See n. 208 above.

a list of *festa ferianda* (ff. 154va–155ra), and *F* itself (at the start of the first booklet) was provided with a Prayer and Prologue, both in the same good textura hand (Hand A). The initials of Prayer and Prologue appear to be decorated to match f. 4^r and it seems likely that *assit principio sancta maria meo* (f. 4^r) was added in the top margin of the first *F* sermon at this stage. All this must have happened soon after the completion of the first booklet, since the *verso* of f. 3 (Prayer and Prologue, Hand A) and the *recto* of f. 128 (the last page of the first booklet, Hand D*), both singletons, are similarly pricked, line-framed, and line-ruled, suggesting that they were prepared at the same time.

However, if Hand D oversaw (to some extent, at least) the final stages of the manuscript as a whole, or at least was present (as the similarities of ff. 3 and 128 would seem to suggest), what had happened to his first three quires? As noted above (§5.2.2), Hand D begins his stint at 15/160 mid-word (-*ne*) and with a faulty transition from the previous quire (Hand C). This indicates clearly that, first, he had finished the previous quire with the first half of the word (*syn*-) but that quire (and the two previous ones) was now unavailable, and, secondly, that neither he nor Hand C was trying to match the other's work. This can only suggest, either, that they were working in different locations, or perhaps that, in a context where much copying went on (some of it in stints),[221] Hand D's first three completed quires had been misbound with other quires and he was forced to make up the manuscript with the three quires of Hands B and C.

To return to the assembly of the manuscript. As noted, Hand A would seem to have played a crucial role in this. The *festa ferianda* are in Latin (Appendix V), but the language of the Prayer and Prologue is English. As a further turn of the screw, it has been located somewhere in the area of north Somerset and south Gloucestershire (Appendix IV.3).[222] However, the evidence of the *festa ferianda* discussed above (§5.3) has made clear that we need not suppose a south-western location for the manuscript assembly, only a south-western exemplar (interesting in itself, since *F* is not otherwise recorded in that area).[223]

---

[221] For the likelihood that the scribes of α were working in stints from a variety of different exemplars, see §6, particularly §6.1 and §6.3 (see too n. 238). The lack of evidence of stint-work in copying *F* is perhaps testimony to the efficient destruction of monastic and cathedral libraries.

[222] Too far north to link with Robert Norreys (see §1.1, n. 22).

[223] It may be significant that the Prologue has one example (*myselff*, Pro/10) of the *-ff* feature peculiar to D*.

The question remains, whether the focus for the assembly of the manuscript was Staffordshire (first booklet) or Shropshire (second booklet), and in what sort of context.[224] The list at the end of the second booklet is clearly linked to Shropshire by its inclusion of St Winifred as a *festum feriandum* within June (that is, outside the Canterbury legislation).[225] There is ample evidence of the importance of the saint to the economy of Shrewsbury in the Middle Ages and beyond (Sutton 2005, esp. 113–18). Her veneration centred on the Benedictine monastery, where she had been translated in 1138 (Chibnall 1973: 33, citing Owen & Blakeway 1825: ii. 33–42), but the whole town was the focus of an annual midsummer fair, which had taken place since at least Henry II's reign (1154–89) and which was extended in 1227 right up to 28 June, the vigil of St Peter (Chibnall 1973: 31, 34–5).[226] St Alkmund's, Shrewsbury was a royal foundation in the patronage of Lilleshall (see §1.1 above and Powell 2006: 163–4), and its connection with the manuscript is very likely, since at least one *F* sermon was written for St Alkmund's (see §1.1).[227] However, the list's addition of SS Chad and George, if more than merely contingent on new legislation,[228] might suggest a connection with the important church of St Chad, the oldest of the churches in Shrewsbury, with its own college of canons (Gaydon 1973: 114–19; Somerset 1994: ii. 363); the town also had a hospital of St George (Gaydon 1973: 105). Shrewsbury was a considerable town, whose Benedictine monastery and two colleges of canons (St Mary's was the second) had important associations, not just in the region but nationally.[229]

Both St Chad's and St Mary's claimed royal foundation (as did St Alkmund's and Lilleshall itself) and both had strong connections with

---

[224] The rubric at 26/1–2n suggests an important church where the disciplines were administered.

[225] Its attribution to Richard (not Thomas) Arundel can be explained by the fact that Richard Fitzalan III, fourth earl of Arundel (1346–97) and one of the 'appellants', had been a more significant local (and probably national) figure than his brother, Thomas, Archbishop of Canterbury (*ODNB sub* Fitzalan, Richard (III)).

[226] This Abbey fair of St Peter may have begun early enough to encompass St Winifred's feast-day, although a fair specific to the saint was granted to the town only after 1586 (Somerset 1994: ii. 371). For the establishment of a fraternity of St Winifred, see Sutton 2005: 115–18.

[227] Only in α does the rubric to this sermon specifically associate him with Shrewsbury (56/1), although his burial place after Lilleshall was in Derby.

[228] If so, David has not been added.

[229] For the monastery's associations with royalty and nobility (as well as local gentry), see Chibnall 1973: 34–5; for the appointment of king's clerks to prebendaries at St Chad's and St Mary's, see Gaydon 1973: 115–16, 120–1.

Lichfield Cathedral (which cannot be discounted for the Chad addition). As the seat of the bishop of the diocese of Coventry and Lichfield, it was the ecclesiastical headquarters for Shropshire and Staffordshire and of considerable regional and national importance (Kettle & Johnson 1970: 140–98; Lepine 1995: 16, 198). A connection with Lichfield Cathedral would also explain the fact that the flyleaves of the manuscript (taken from the Mass for the Dead in a noted gradual) include rubrics for a dead bishop,[230] suggesting that the gradual is likely to have been in use in a cathedral. The decoration and assembly of the manuscript, as well as the context of its (at least partial) copying in quires, could also be more firmly located in Lichfield Cathedral than anywhere else, given the importance of Lichfield's library at the time, and canons of St Chad's frequently held office at Lichfield.[231]

5.5. The Later History of the Manuscript

The earliest ownership name in the manuscript is that of the chaplain *Thomas -son* (f. 156^v), perhaps chaplain to a secular canon, since clerics often served this role (Lepine 1995: 126), or perhaps a chantry chaplain.[232] Thereafter the manuscript may have had Cambridge connections, in that *Robert Walkar* (f. 156^v) might be one of the several Robert Walkers at the University in the sixteenth century (Venn & Venn 1922–7: iv. 318),[233] as might *Necoles sander* (f. 156^v) (Venn & Venn 1922–7: iv. 14). A further University connection is entirely speculative, but, in relation to the copying of D* from an exemplar signed by *addeley* (§5.2.3 above), Ralph Adderley is recorded to have graduated B.Th. (but 'probably of Oxford'); he was, moreover, an Austin canon, prior of the house at Newark, Surrey around the year 1445 (Emden 1957–9: i. 14).[234] (The movement of

---

[230] *Quandocumque adest presens corpus et in omnibus missis pro/ episcopis defunctis dicitur . . .*, *ad caput corporis . . . vel episcopi defuncti/ si adest*, f. 2^r, ll. 5–6, 8–9. See n. 171 above.

[231] Between 1331 and 1350 at least seven canons, and between 1405 and 1460 at least ten, held prebendaries at Lichfield ('or other office in the diocese') (Gaydon 1973: 116). As a (later) indication of the interconnections, Adam Grafton held at various times and amongst other titles the position of vicar of St Alkmund's, canon-prebendary of St Chad's, prebendary of the Wellington stall at Lichfield Cathedral, and dean of St Mary's (*c*.1509–13) (Owen & Blakeway 1825: ii. 277, 327–8; cf. Gaydon 1973: 121, Sutton 2005: 117, 121–6).

[232] By 1468 the chantry of Jesus and St Anne at Lichfield Cathedral was supported by annual payments from Lilleshall itself (Kettle & Johnson 1970: 165).

[233] An earlier Robert Walker of Eton and King's, Cambridge was associated with Uttoxeter, fifteen miles north of Lichfield, forty miles east of Shrewsbury (Emden 1963: 611).

[234] For the Christian name Robert, not Ralph, see Cox 1905: 105.

Mirk's manuscripts around Austin canon houses might explain the oddness of a Bristol provenance for the Prayer and Prologue added to the first booklet.)

However, the problems of the manuscript must remain partly unresolved. Were the facts not against it (see §5.1 History), one might assume that the assembly of the manuscript is so devious that one of the later collectors, Savile or Cotton, had a hand in its production. It is certainly the work of someone with the mentality of a collector, someone who went to great efforts to assemble a remarkably full manuscript of Mirk's vernacular writings, certainly the fullest that survives today.

6. MS COTTON CLAUDIUS A.II AS BASE-TEXT

§5 has described the different hands and languages in the complex production of the base-text of this edition, in which different exemplars were an implicit, and sometimes explicit (D*), factor. This final section will consider how far α's affiliations to other *F* manuscripts relate to the different hands working on the text. Given the restricted number of the collations (and the complexity of the transmission, even if all manuscripts were fully collated),[235] all that can be offered here is a snapshot of the relationships of six sermons in three hands and of the Prayer and Prologue in a fourth hand. The section will conclude with a defence of α as base-text and an explanation of editorial procedure in relation to the problems of the different hands and languages.

6.1. The Textual Affiliations of MS Cotton Claudius A.II

The discussion at §4 above offered a comprehensible, even neat, picture of the relationships of the *F* manuscripts and started to suggest relationships (DEFIcd) which might be crucial to α. It must be stressed, however, that the particular relationships discernible amongst the manuscripts are not invariable. The numerous inter-relationships are the result of intensive inter-copying, to varying, largely unknowable, extents, complicated by different exemplars copied to different extents (and perhaps then recopied, again to different extents). Hence, although groupings can be discovered,

---

[235] They have all been collated informally by the editor.

such as AC, EF, ae, cd, and (variably) HJ (in none of which can be discerned direct copying one from the other), no clear stemmatic relationships are demonstrable, the process of transmission having been, most likely, a matter of localized multiple copying from a limited number of texts, or even parts of texts, rather than the serial copying of one manuscript after the other.[236]

When α is brought into the picture, the discussion becomes more complex by reason of the complexities of the manuscript itself. The full collations (Appendix III) have been chosen in order to demonstrate the text of each Hand: Hand A Prayer and Prologue, Hand B sermon 2, Hand C sermon 14, Hand D sermons 39 and 56 (D* sermons 24 and 34).[237] Whereas conclusions suggested below may well apply beyond the individual sermon collated, they must be treated warily in the light of the complexities of copying and the clear loss of a large number of *F* manuscripts.

6.1.1. Hand D (Sermons 39 and 56 Fully Collated, Appendix III.vii, viii)

Building on the discussion at §5 above, which stressed the role of Hand D in the *F* booklet as a whole, discussion will begin with that hand. Hand D is responsible for copying the major part of the text (ff. 40^r–128^r) (15/159–Add6/239) and his hand is in appearance the earliest of the manuscript. Within his stint occur the insertion and addition (D*), which will be considered separately at §6.1.2 below.

As noted already (§4, §4.4), significant differences of material serve to confirm the Group A/B division of *F* manuscripts. Those in which α and Group A are in agreement against Group B occur all within Hand D's stint, confirming that Hand D is following a Group A exemplar. The most significant paraphrase occurs at 21/6–14n, and the most significant additions at 57/152–3n and 67/73–4n, that is, both before and after the insertion of D*, suggesting that Hand D remains a Group A text throughout his stint.[238] (For other significant differences in the Group B text only, see §4.4 and n. 149.)

---

[236] Rather than a stemma, a wave-diagram, such as used by Trask (1996: 186, Fig. 7.8) in place of the traditional Indo-European family tree, would better demonstrate relationships, although the high degree of overlapping would make such a diagram hard to read.

[237] Lemmata in bold direct the reader to the full collations in Appendix III; lemmata in italics either refer to material not in the full collations or to material in the full collations presented differently from the Appendix lemmata. References to the Explanatory Notes are followed by 'n'.

[238] However, the fact that augmentation of the Group B text (§4.4) can be parallelled in

Sermon 39 occurs after the D* insertion and was fully collated. Excluding α, the basic division between Groups A and B may be demonstrated by some simple cruxes:

1. 39/30 (30–1n) *but in (in]* om. J) *hudlek (hudlek] hidelles* EF, *hedulys* I, *hydnes* H, *preuely* J) ABCDEFGHIJK; om. abcdefg (h absent)

2. 39/61–2n *þe holy goste schuld be (be]* om. J) *halde (halde] held* BH, *hilde* G, *hold* I, *helde* J, *halowet* DEF, om. K) *owte (owte]* om. DEFJK) ABCDEFGHIJK; *the holi goost shulde (be* add. bcdefg) geue abcdefg (h absent)

3. 39/107n *sowrenesse (sowrenesse] sorones* H, *sorowe* J, *euyll wyll* G) *and (and] or* DK) *moystur (moystur] mayster* J) *of males* ABCDE-GHIJK (F absent); *sorynesse (sorynesse] sorenes* d) *of (of] or* f) *malice* abcdefg (h absent)

As usual, the Group A text offers much more variation than Group B, but α's affiliations (although sometimes idiosyncratic) are with Group A:

1. *bot in hulkyng*
2. *þe Holy Gost schulde ben holde oute*
3. *sowrenes and m[i]scheues of malys*

In one crux, however, α is in agreement with Group B: *heretykys woldyn han brent alle þat þis holy man made and hadde made* (unemended text, cf. 39/144–5n):

heretykys woldon han brende (woldon . . . brende] branyd H, *þe bokes of* add. D) *þis (þis] þe* BCGJ) *holy monnus makyng (makyng] werkys* J) ABCDGHIJ *heretyckys wold haue brend þat he expownyd* K (EF absent)

an heritique wold haue brent all that this holy manne had made (had made] om. f, *had]* om. dg) abcdefg (h absent)

The plural subject agrees with Group A but the predicate with Group B, while the original reading *made and hadde made* appears to be an amalgam of the Group B readings *had made* (abce) and *made* (dg).

α (and sometimes other Group A manuscripts) before Sermon 33 but not afterwards may be related to a change of exemplar for Hand D after the D* stint at ff. 52^r–69^v (D begins again at 33/87, f. 70^r). There may have been other changes of exemplar. For example, it may be evidence of a change of exemplar that references to *LA* do not occur in the sermons until the very end of the manuscript (58/78, 64/55, 65/22, 48, 64, 74, 68/25).

Such mixed relationships within the Groups are sometimes apparent, as at 39/56, where GH agree with Group B in omitting the gloss of *must* (þat . . . wyne), or 39/74, where the best reading (*A tong*, without the adjective, see 39/73–4n) may be preserved by αDIdf, suggesting a pivotal group of manuscripts both close to Mirk's original text and close to the breaking away of the recension:

> *A (A] wykked* add. ABCEFGK, *euell* add. abcg, *new(b canc.)ill* add. e, *angels* add. HJ) *tong is fyred (fyred] fret* I, *kyndylid* d) αABCDEFGHIJabcdefg (h absent)

The relationship of αDI here confirms suggestions made earlier (§4.3.6) about that relationship and is further demonstrable in Sermon 39, e.g. 39/57–8 for . . . felowes (αDI), 97 and² (αDI). In order to test the relationship, the St Alkmund sermon (no. 56) was fully collated. It survives in only three manuscripts (αDI), was written by Mirk for St Alkmund's church, Shrewsbury (see §1.1 above), and contains several specific and local references (see Explanatory Notes to Sermon 56 *passim*). However, in terms of text, when the three manuscripts are scrutinized, their relationship is clearly attenuated, suggesting, firstly, that several more manuscripts once contained this sermon and, secondly, that the relationship of αDI is so marked in the presence of more witnesses largely because of the loss of many other manuscripts.

In Sermon 56 no two manuscripts of αDI demonstrate a particular closeness. At times αI agree (e.g. 21 sum . . . anothyr, 34 parich, 39–40 sokuruth . . . and¹, 51 in² . . . how, 54–5 proude and, 67 man . . . cursyd, 95 defense . . . of, 99 hylte),²³⁹ at times αD (e.g. 16 tokyn, and trode it, 17 cristen men, þei, 35 mayn swyng, 67 and¹ . . . and², 69 refylud, 133 reneyned),²⁴⁰ at times DI (e.g. 8 dew, 22 to defende, 27 stylle, 29 anyþing, 51 werkys, 55 prowde, 68 hem, 86 Goddys). All three variously exhibit omissions, with the most substantial lacuna in α, emended from DI (see 56/117–21n).

D would appear to offer the best text, since αI offer, separately, unique readings more often than D. D is the only manuscript to preserve all three references to St Alkmund as *patron of þys chyrche* (see §1.1); α alters only the first reference, whereas I alters them all (56/2–3, 42, 140). I also appears more remote than αD from the local colour of the text (see 56/117n). However, in another sermon where local colour is crucial to originality, Mirk's final sermon, no. 68

---

²³⁹ See 56/78n.   ²⁴⁰ See too 56/34n, 34–5n, 117n.

(Dedication of a church), it is αI alone which preserve the information that Sir Thomas Wodewarde had previously been parish priest at Ruckley, a very local and circumstantial reference lost in all the other manuscripts (see 68/119–20n).

6.1.2. Hand D* (Sermons 24 and 34 Fully Collated, Appendix III.v, vi)

The text of the insertion at ff. 52^r–63^v (23/116–32/15), 64^r–69^v (32/16–33/86, 34), and the addition at ff. 122^v–128^r (Add6, Sentence) is a stint different in several ways from the rest of Hand D (see §5.2.3), but its exemplar was still a Group A manuscript (see e.g. 24/71n). This is apparent from the fact that it includes Sermon 34 (found only in Group A manuscripts DEFG). Indeed, of extant manuscripts, DEFG appear to be crucial to the D* material. For example, as noted above (§5.2.3), *narracio* is (unusually for the manuscript) included in the body of the text in the D* stint, a feature whose origins may be in a text like G (where the same happens) or like DEF, where *narracio* is set out mid-line.

In particular, EF show the closest relationship to α in this stint (although the closeness is compromised by their selective truncation of the F text)[241]. F shares with α the division of Sermon 33 into two parts.[242] The Sentence added by D* at the end of F is a conflation of the EF Sentence with another text (Pickering 1981: 230–1). The explicit of *IPP* in E is notably similar to that in α.[243] Furthermore, one might hazard the guess that it was from an EF exemplar that *assit principio sancta maria meo* was added to the top margin of the first F sermon (f. 4^r), since E(F) also have (had, in the case of F) that phrase (see §5.1, §5.2.1 Hand B above and manuscript description, Appendix II.i.a, E). Finally, F is the only manuscript to include what may be an internal reference to Mirk indicative of early copying from the *Ur*-text: *mary mircy Quod I. M.* (p. 204).

---

[241] For example, the attempt to associate DEFG with D* may appear compromised by the fact that EFG omit Add6, but they are such unusual manuscripts that this fact need not detract from the argument. Moreover, Add6 is only found in ABCDK and was clearly not part of the original F collection, while the problem of loss at the end of the manuscripts is an additional factor.

[242] See n. 205 below.

[243] Compare α (f. 154va) (§5.1 Contents) with E (ff. 188^v–189^r): *Explicit tractus qui dicitur pars oculi de latino in anglicum/ [translatus per fratrem Iohannem Mirk Canonicum Regularem Monasterij de Lilleshull cujus] anime propicietur deus Amen* (material in square brackets in Douce's hand below damaged original). The *IPP* explicit may have dictated the form of the F explicit.

In terms of textual relationships with the other *F* manuscripts, the relationships are complex, indicative of several layers of exemplars, but the grouping of DEFG(I) appears to hold (see 24/4n (αG(1)IK), 52n (αG(2)), 67n (αDEFG(1)Hf), 81–2n (αDEFG(2)), 90n (αI), 93n (αFHJ) and 24/87 **waymentacion** (αD), 96 **me**[I] (αI).[244] The most difficult crux occurs at 24/94–6. Christ speaks from the cross: *And ouer þis, þat greues me moste: þou settyst notte be my passione þat I sufferud for þe, bot* (24/94–5), after which the Group B text provides the reading: *with thy horrible swering (swering] swerynges* b) *thou reyuest (reyuest] vmbraydes* dfh, *vpbraydis* c) *me.* Group A manuscripts are predictably more complex, best viewed in distinct groups:

1. *by thi (thi] þe* I) *orribulle owthes alday (alday]* om. C, *þow* add. CK] *vmbredyste me (þerof* add. C, *of my passioun* add. K) ABCG(1)IK

2. *by my passioun horribly þou swerest alday vmbraydest me* EF

3. *by me þou swerist oryble (ely* canc.) *and all day vnbraydist me* G(2)

4. *by me horribile sweryst and all way (and all way]* all day J) *umbraydyst me* HJ

5. *by me horrybull swerus all day vmbraydys me* D

Here G(2)HJD are closely related (HJ omit *þou*, D omits *þou* and *and*), while α is a corrupt version of D (*be þe orybull swerus alle day vmbreydust me*, emended at 24/96).

In order to assess the relationship of α to DEFG, a full collation was prepared for Sermon 34, which is witnessed only by αDEFG (Appendix III.vi). All the manuscripts have occasional best readings (e.g. α 34/129 **he doth**, E 76 **wedde**, F (see 34/208n), G 127 **vndampnud**), and at one crux, all are variously corrupt (see 34/129n). Even with so few manuscripts, relationships are complex.[245]

---

[244] The fuller sermon rubrics of D* bring I into the grouping at 26/1–2n, 28/1–2n, where αI agree in the fullest rubric of all the manuscripts (but only α has the informative rubric at 30/1–2n).

[245] For example, αD agree at 34/40–1 **but . . . grace** (where EFG have a lacuna) and 64 **Anselme**; αE agree at l. 77 **But, þis kny3te**. EF share lacunae (perhaps deliberate omissions), at, for example, ll. 28–32 and 40–1, E's lacunae becoming more frequent as the text proceeds (for example, 34/134–7 **So . . . purgatory**), with frequent paraphrase and abbreviation of the text from l. 199 on. EF generally agree, but differ at ll. 34 **byggon**, 66 **for . . . his**, 75 **bote, myche gode**; DEF share lacunae, for example, at l. 37 **þus . . . pore**; DG are close at ll. 158 **lythe þerinne**, 171–2 **makon . . . hym**[1]; FG are close at ll. 106–7 **so . . and**; DF and EG have different variants at l. 34 **byggon**.

However, DEFG form a coherent group (apart from α) in numerous minor, but substantive, variants (e.g. 45 **3elduth**, 53 **takon**, 57 **do**, 121 **schryue**, 145–6 **þat heluth**), within which EFG are closest (see e.g. 122–3n). (For further details of G in this sermon, see §4.3.4.) In Sermon 34, therefore, α is eccentric, very frequently in fifty unique minor variants (e.g. 34/8 **Goddus**, 112 **a boy**), substantive variants (34/45 **3elduth**, 53 **takon**, 57 **do**, 121 **schryue**), and errors (34/52 **for two causes**, 129 **hauynge**, 166–9n, 208n). Nevertheless, α is the least defective text compared with DEFG's various lacunae, and shares more readings with D (fourteen) than with any other manuscript, including one demonstrably superior reading (34/64–5n).

6.1.3. Hand B (Sermon 2 Fully Collated, Appendix III.iii)

Hand B supplies ff. 4^r–15^v, 16^r–27^v (1/1–10/165). In an article published at an earlier stage of research into the relationships of the manuscripts (Powell 1997c), it was argued that α was the pivotal text between Groups A and B: Wakelin's assumption that α was an unproblematic Group A text was based on his choosing for full collation only the Pentecost sermon (no. 39), which does not reveal substantial affiliation with Group B. In contrast to Sermon 39, Sermons 1 and 2 offered several examples of α's agreement with Group B in major cruxes, while still being fundamentally a Group A text.[246] It was argued that α offered a unique text, pivotal between Groups A and B. However, full study and collation of all the manuscripts in relation to Hands B, C, D/D* revealed over time that the evidence of α's uniquely close relationship to the Group B text was most demonstrable only in the early part of Hand B's stint. As Wakelin had surmised, α was a standard Group A manuscript in Sermon 39 (Hand D); it was not a standard Group A manuscript, however, in Sermons 1 and 2 (Hand B).

Major cruxes in Hand B's stint confirm α's important role in relation to the Group B text. Since these have been demonstrated in Powell (1997c: 173–7), only one simple example will be offered here, from 1/29–30, where α agrees with Group B:

he þat wol voyde þe perel and þe myschyf (perel and þe myschyf] om.

---

[246] For agreement with Group A, see 2/149–51n (αABCEFG), 154n (αABCG); for agreement with Group B, see 2/90–1n, 94–6n, 165–6n (see too 6/6–7n, 9/9n, discussed in Appendix IV.5).

h, *and þe myschyf* om. bcd] *of (of]* om. h) *þe secunde comyng (of crist* add. h) *to þe dome (to þe dome]* om. bcdh) αbcdh (aeg absent)

he þat (he þat] ʒef ʒe H, *if we* f) *walle schape (walle schape] schapith* G) *þe (þe] this* H, *the perel of the* add. f) *doome þat he (he] ye* H) *woll (woll] schall* K) *cum too in (in]* at DGHKf) *his (his] þe* DHKf) *seconde cumynge* ABCDGHKf (EFJ absent).[247]

The pivotal relationship of α to both Groups may be demonstrated by an example cited at §4.1 (example 8), where there is a broad division between *bete vpon þe yate so harde* (Group A) and *bad open the gate so harde* (Group B). Here α reads: *bed hopon þe ʒate so harde* (emended at 2/142), a Group A reading (but with voiced final *-t* in *bed* and excrescent *h-* in *hopon*) which appears then to have influenced the Group B text (the superior reading of Group A is confirmed by *LA* (see 2/142n), as well as by the survival of the inappropriate *so harde* in the Group B reading).

However, the close relationship to the Group B text and the occasionally pivotal status of α become less apparent as the stint proceeds and are certainly less evident by the second quire of Hand B (which begins at 6/34). Since a change of language is discernible at Sermon 6 (see §5.2.1 Hand B, n. 187), this appears to relate to a different exemplar from that used for the previous sermons. The unusual sermon introductions at 7/2, 8/2 may relate to this change of exemplar.[248] Moreover, it is prior to Sermon 6 (in Sermons 3–5) that the cases occur where α is the sole manuscript to agree with Group B in adding extra material (§4.4). Thereafter other Group A manuscripts share the content with α. In the final sermon of this stint, for example, α and a group made up variably of DEFI(K) (especially DI) are prominent in agreement with Group B, e.g. *bad . . . and*[1] at 10/66–7 (αDI), *myddel* at 10/81 (αDEFI) where the Group A reading is *commyn (meene* K), *þrytty* at 10/89 (αD) where the other manuscripts agree with *LA* in *xiij*, *demot* at 10/113 (αEFI) where the other manuscripts read *dampned* (but *iuged* f), the distinctive (and original) oath of 10/135–6 (αDI), and the lexeme *sparreden* (αDI) at 10/139.

The Hand B text therefore differs markedly from that of D/D* in offering frequent Group B readings, which, because of change(s) of exemplar, become less frequent in the course of the two-quire stint. The instances where Hand B's text provides unique evidence of a

---

[247] *for ʒe þat hope for to come to þat dome þat he wyll come to at hys secound comyng* I.

[248] Note too that a full conclusion is provided only at 1/141–5n.

relationship to Group B (with no such evidence in Group A manuscripts) indicate that the later change(s) of exemplar were to more commonly circulating texts which also influenced some Group A manuscripts.

6.1.4. Hand C (Sermon 14 Fully Collated, Appendix III.iv)

In Hand C, ff. 28^r–39^v (10/165–15/159), α is predominantly a Group A text but with demonstrable affiliations with Group B, e.g. 14/33n, 45–7n, 167 **were goyng** (where only α and Group B omit references to *hell/gate*). There is still evidence of α's pivotal role, as at 14/78–80n and 103–4n. At 14/79 **hadden euore** and **euore**, a reading such as α's *hadden euore* has been responsible for the Group B misunderstanding of *euore* to mean 'ever', and at 14/104 **and**[2] . . . **self** it must be some such erroneous reading as α's *Amoncvs self* which has caused the Group B exemplar to omit the phrase altogether. Only α has the rare noun *euore* at 14/79,[249] only αD read *euer* at 14/80, and only DFI have *euorus* at 14/82, suggesting that Group B broke away at an early stage from a pivotal text such as α(DFI) At 14/127 **heo 3af**, the Group B readings may represent attempts to make sense of a text like α, where the crucial word *3af* has been omitted.

As with Hand B, DEFGI(K) (variously) continue to agree with α in sharing Group B readings, e.g 14/2 **Suche** (αI), 6 **Symeones** (αDEFI), 12n **purgacyon** (αEFI), 106 **brende** (αI), 142–3n (αDGIK). Occasionally, α is excluded from the manuscripts closest to Group B, e.g. 14/82–3 **Wherefore . . . batel**, 100 **wente**, 123–4 **So . . . lyght**, 129 **an honest womon**. At 14/129 the Group B reading stems from a type represented here by D and (more closely) I (but see 129 **an** for I's original reading *vnhonest*). The closeness of α to DI is demonstrable in Hand C (as in Hand B) in contradistinction to Group B readings, as well as in agreement with them, e.g. 14/22n (αI), 82n (αDFI). Of extant manuscripts, given that EF and K respectively are too individual to be regularly comparable, αDI are demonstrably the closest Group A texts to the Group B textual tradition.

6.1.5. Hand A (Prayer and Prologue Fully Collated, Appendix III.i, ii)

The single side written by Hand A (f. 3^v) was added on a singleton, after the *F* booklet had been assembled, in a language remote from

---

[249] Although most Group A manuscripts (not H(IJ)K) have the adjective *euerous*.

that of the other hands (see §5.2.1, Hand A),[250] but it represents an excellent text of the Prayer (αABCDFHIf) and Prologue (αABCF HIKf). Prayer i, which is found only in αDFI, is likely to be original, while a significant crux in the Prologue (Pro/10–11n) reveals α's reading as authoritative and those of ABCK and HIf as more remote (F condenses the reading). (For a discussion of relationships within the Prayer and Prologue, see §4.3.)

6.2. The Relationship of the Text of Hands B and C to Group B

The discussion above has treated Group B as if it were a single text without complexity, noting affiliation to 'Group B'.[251] However, while the Group B text is notably stable in comparison with the very variable Group A text, it has already been demonstrated (§4.5, §4.5.1, §4.5.2) that there are groupings within the text. Group B manuscripts sometimes (but variably) split over a Group A or B reading, while still remaining Group B manuscripts. The explanation seems to lie in the pivotal nature of certain manuscripts: just as αD(EF)I(K) may be seen as on the cusp of the transmission to the Group B text, so cd(fh) may be seen as on the cusp of the transmission from the Group A text, that is, they are Group B texts with affiliations to (variably) αD(EF)I(K).[252]

In the full collations which include Group B (i.e. not Sermons 34 and 56), when α agrees with Group B, it is more commonly with cdfh (although f can be eccentric and h absent) than with abeg,[253] e.g. 2/4 þre, 11 walkyng, And when Seynt, 18 and kalled ham; 14/16 holden; 24/55 Amasa[1], 92 harmes, 94 walus, 96 vmbreydust, 102 rede; 39/97 lustus. Of cdfh, α is closest to cd(h) (see 2/92–3n) and closer to cd than to fh, e.g. 2/5 holynes; 24/71 schal; 39/43 son, 45 gon, 94 hem[2]. It is generally closer to c rather than d, e.g. 14/39 so, 156 wyth strenþe; 24/63 fadurres, 94 walus; 39/25 lafte, 106 brennyn. However, for αd agreement see, for example, 14/152 sende; 39/51n demyd, 107n sowrenes (where d's reading *sorenes* is arguably closer to α than the other Group B manuscripts,

---

[250] Hand A is also responsible for the Latin *festa ferianda* (see §5.4).

[251] Where 'Group B' has been referred to above, it has meant all or the majority of Group B manuscripts (the eccentric texts f and h are frequently different).

[252] And so closer to Mirk's original text than other Group B manuscripts (for this argument, see 6.1.4 above). For c's preservation of a tag possibly original to Mirk, see 4.1, n. 114.

[253] In the following examples, other Group A manuscripts agree variably with α.

which have *sorynesse*).[254] It is clear that, although cd are overall the closest Group B manuscripts to α, closer manuscripts once existed but are no longer extant.[255]

6.3. The Best Text?

The discussion above has demonstrated that the two parts of the *F* booklet (Hands B and C; Hand D/D*) were dependent on Group A exemplars, but that the exemplars of Hands B and C (particularly the early part of Hand B's stint) were substantially influenced by Group B readings. Given that Group A is closer to Mirk's original text, the major part of *F* may therefore be considered more authoritative than that of the first three quires (Hands B/C). The added Prayer and Prologue (Hand A) are of supreme authority amongst the extant manuscripts. The role of α in relation to a pivotal group of both Group A and Group B texts (DEFGIKcdfh), posited in §4 above, has been confirmed, despite the different hands and different exemplars at work in, and the complex interrelationships of, the other manuscripts. The Group A texts of this pivotal group are closer than the Group B texts to Mirk's original text, as they are too (again variably) in the chronological arrangement of sermons and the content of the *F* collection. The Group B texts of this pivotal group are closer than the Group A texts to Rev. and to the printed editions of 1483 and later (on which, see §3.3, §3.4). These manuscripts therefore may be seen as the fulcrum to the *F* transmission, authoritative in terms of *F* in its past and future incarnations.

Of them all, it is α which has been chosen as the base-text of this edition. It is the earliest of the extant manuscripts (certainly for the main hand). It is the only manuscript to affirm Mirk's authorship of both *F* and *IPP* in detailed explicits. It has (with D) the earliest form of the Prayer, and provides the most authoritative version of the Prologue (D absent), both clearly by Mirk himself. It has more sermons and sermon material than any other manuscript: with D it is the only manuscript to have the sermons for Mirk's local saints Winifred and Alkmund (nos. 43 and 56) and the second sermon for 1 Lent (no. 34), and with K it is the only manuscript to contain all the material edited here as Additional sermons. Where manuscripts vary in the amount of material they include for some sermons, α has more of that material than any other Group A manuscript (see §4.4 above).

---

[254] See 19/48n for an original reading preserved only in d.

[255] The exemplar from which Rev. developed was also a cd-type manuscript.

It preserves (in the first part of Hand B, at least) the most pivotal exemplar to the Group B text of all the Group A manuscripts. Despite the complications of the mixed language of the *F* text, the three main hands can all be located in Staffordshire, the neighbouring county to Mirk's county of Shropshire. (The text of the second booklet of the manuscript, with which *F* is paired, came from Shropshire itself, perhaps even from Lilleshall.) The α lexis is authentic, archaic in comparison with the modernized lexis of Group B (and most Group A manuscripts)[256] and often offering the *difficilior lectio*, the more difficult reading which is a sign of authenticity (e.g. 14/78–80n, 31/17n, 27–8n, 39/107n, 46/18–19n, 53/188n, 61/84–6n). It was assessed by Horstmann, who first brought *F* to light after its post-Reformation obscurity, as the oldest and best manuscript (1881: cxii). Horstmann was not unaware of its problems,[257] but it is a much more complex manuscript than he (or others, including the present editor at one time) was aware. Nevertheless, with all its problems and frustrations, in its mixed exemplars and languages it offers a much more accurate picture of the nature of the *F* transmission than an anodyne text such as that edited by Erbe.[258] It is as a collected edition, assembled from various sources in order to preserve as much of Mirk's vernacular writings as possible, that it is offered as the base-text to this edition.

6.4. Editorial Policy and Procedure

Given the problems of the different Hands, particularly the idiosyncrasies of Hand C (see §5.2.1, Hand C), and the different exemplars (discussed above at §6.1, §6.2), an editorial policy is needed which can be reasonably consistent across all Hands. The policy is, therefore, to restrict intervention in the base-text to those cases where omission or error is evident and confirmed by the other manuscripts,

---

[256] Only α is a constant in the archaic lexemes (in all three hands) cited at §4.1 (example 13). Grammatically, αD use archaic genitive constructions at 11/53 (*owre allur modur*) and 13/43 (*allor clerest*) and the archaic past participle *icore* in the lyric at 54/197.

[257] 'Der Text ist nicht so correct, wie man nach dem Alter des Ms. vermuthen sollte; er bedarf sehr der Verbesserung durch andere MSS und steht dem Originale keineswegs immer am nächsten; auch fehlen öfter Wörter und Sätze', i.e. the text is not as correct as one might expect from the age of the manuscript; it needs a lot of correction from other manuscripts and is in no way always closest to the original; words and sentences are more often (than one might expect *sc.*) missing too (1881: cxiii).

[258] Although D is more complex than one might assume from Erbe's edition, in which he inexplicably omitted most variants from his apparatus.

as in the case of the lacunae at 1/68–9n or 55/165–8n and the misreadings of the exemplar at 38/77 (*be his myght* for *he is myche*) or 38/84 (*be rehersyd* for *he rehersyth*). Where there is a lacuna in α, that lacuna has been emended unless the text has been adapted to accommodate the lacuna (e.g. 30/7n). Where α is alone in a unique reading (good or bad), that unique reading is retained, unless so defective or erroneous as to impede sense (e.g. 14/103–4n).

Where emendation is needed, it is based on a comparison of all available full manuscripts (Groups A and B), and the reading most consistent with α's text is preferred (bearing in mind that α's text variably offers Group A and Group B readings while remaining essentially a Group A text). Given the different Hands and exemplars, any attempt to return α to an *Ur*-text closest to Mirk's original would be fundamentally misguided, as well as involving constant and major intervention. It is stressed, however, that this is not a diplomatic edition but a critical edition, and superior readings consistent with the α text are preferred (e.g. 1/141–5n).

Where there is a clear error in terms of transposition of letters or words, minim error, nasal contractions omitted or erroneously added or expanded, confusion in writing the characters ⟨f⟩ and ⟨s⟩, and ⟨c⟩ and ⟨t⟩, these have normally been emended. The matter of variation between the similarly formed characters ⟨e⟩ and ⟨o⟩ is more complex. Such variation is common in the three main hands and is clearly erroneous in readings such as *deserto* and *multitudo* in English text (2/9, 17/66), but the question of graphical error or linguistic variant is harder to answer in other cases.[259] *MED* has frequently recorded variant readings which may well have been considered acceptable by scribe and reader at the time. Such cases have therefore only been emended where there is reasonable certainty that the manuscript spelling is actually erroneous. As a general rule, *MED* has frequently been the arbiter of decisions, so that, where a variant is recorded in *MED*, it has not normally been emended, e.g. *mensengger* 2/171 (*MED* messager *n.* with variants *mensenger*, *mensingere*, *mansonger*).

---

[259] Linguistic variation occurs in words descended from OE *eo* (Jordan 1974: §§65–80, 84–6, 105), e.g. 10/27 *schert* ('short', from OE *sceort*), 10/72, 86 *knowen* 3 pa. pl. ('knew', from OE *cnēowon*), but it clearly encouraged confusion, e.g. 10/180 *knewe* (imp. sg.).

6.4.1. Explanatory Notes

The Explanatory Notes provide commentary on and explication of the edited text, including, where necessary, comments explanatory of the manuscript text itself.

A headnote gives brief details of the source of the sermon, followed by details of lacunae and significant differences in the witnesses (details of which are supplied in Appendix I). Since *F* is dependent on *LA*, and *LA* itself dependent on *RDO*, the Notes refer normally to the source in *LA*, with references to Graesse's Latin edition (1846),[260] and provide details of *RDO* (with references to *PL* and Douteil (1976)) only when it appears to have been used independently by Mirk (e.g. 68/78–125n), or is especially interesting (e.g. 26/47–6on).

All the manuscripts have been informally collated for this edition, and emendation and discussion are based on a consideration of all witnesses. Minor emendations are not discussed in the Notes, since they are invariably confirmed by the majority, if not all, of the manuscripts (e.g. *closyd* 44/77, where all manuscripts confirm the emendation to *clopyd*; *com* 60/33, where all manuscripts confirm the omission in α). All lengthy emendations and cruxes, together with any conjectural emendations, are discussed when there is some doubt about the original reading and/or when different readings in different manuscripts are of interest in terms of emendation or manuscript relationships.[261]

Editorial procedure in relation to emendation from Group A or B has been outlined above (§6.4). Where emendation is from Group A, it is generally from D and then I, the Group A manuscripts closest to α textually; where emendation is from Group B, it is generally from c and then d, the Group B manuscripts closest to α textually. If there are reasons for emendation using other manuscripts, those reasons are explained. Where a Group A/B reading is cited, the citation is from the first of the sigla for that group, i.e. A/a (or, if either is imperfect, B/b, etc.), unless otherwise noted. If considered necessary, variants are recorded fully, but the phrase 'with minor variants' is also used to indicate that other variants exist but not of so substantive a kind as to alter the general thrust of the citation, e.g. 2/90–1n, 14/33n.[262]

---

[260] Reference to Maggioni's edition (1998) and Ryan's English translation of Graesse (1993) are supplied in the headnote only.

[261] Such discussion is fuller in the case of sermons fully collated in Appendix III.

[262] In these cases, a full collation is supplied in Appendix III.

6.4.2. *Collations (Appendix III)*

Full collations are provided for at least one sermon in each hand (selected as far as possible to demonstrate all the manuscripts of that sermon), *viz.* Hand A (Prayer and Prologue), Hand B (Sermon 2), Hand C (Sermon 14), Hand D (Sermon 39). In addition, a sermon from the two inserted quires (D*) has been collated (Sermon 24), and two further sermons have been fully collated in order to demonstrate relationships between those manuscripts (DEFGI) particularly close to α, i.e. Sermons 34 (Hand D*, witnessed by αDEFG) and 56 (Hand D, witnessed by αDI).

Only substantive variants are recorded in the full collations. Where the text is the same but word order varies, those differences of word order are considered non-substantive and are not noted. An entry such as *12 fynde] þere* add. *AC* indicates that *þere* is added after *fynde* in A and also occurs in C (although C might in fact read *þere fynde* rather than *fynde þere*, since minor transpositions of text are not noted). Orthographic variants are ignored, even where they indicate dialect variation.[263] Morphological variants are noted when substantive (e.g. singular/plural, present/past tense) but not when merely orthographic and/or dialectal. Strong and weak variants are not normally distinguished, e.g. *holpe/helped, reysed/rysen, steyd/stye, awoke/awaked, queynt/quenched, low3/loughed*, etc., nor are aphetic variants, e.g. *(a)mende, (at)tempted, (com)pleyneth, (de)faute, (for)-lorne.* The following variants are not generally noted: *a/an; er (þan/ þat), how (þat), so (þat), till (þat), why (þat); like (to); in/on/upon; to/for/for to/*zero infinitive; *to/vnto; tyll/to; þat/þe whiche*, etc.; *þer(as)/where (as/ þat)*, etc. No distinction is made between numerals (e.g. *xxx*) and the written form of numbers (e.g. *þrytte*). Pointing of the manuscripts is ignored, as are cancellations unless of special interest. Marginal and interlinear additions are noted thus: *2/26 by]* `bi´ c. Contemporary marginalia are recorded but not details of rubrication or decoration. Entries record variants in the order closest to the lemma and/or to the previous variant, otherwise generally observing the order αABCDEFGHIJKabcdefgh.

---

[263] An exception has been made where the scribe has been confused by his copy-text's use of *he* for the feminine singular personal pronoun (see Appendix IV.5); in these cases, the collation records all variants of the pronoun, e.g. 14/43, 154.

6.4.3. *Apparatus*

The apparatus at the foot of the text therefore records only the base text (α), in terms of both original readings and manuscript details such as erasures, cancellations, marginalia, and decoration. Marginalia are in the scribe's hand unless otherwise noted (e.g. 'in the long hand'). Marginal and interlinear additions to the text which are not included in the edited text are noted in the apparatus by the same convention as in the collations.

6.4.4. *The Base-Text and Editorial Practice*

Editorial practice follows EETS guidelines. The text is printed with modern punctuation (even when this disagrees with the manuscript pointing, e.g. *heven. Hyt fel* is edited as *heven, hyt fel* 44/131). Word-division is normalized to current practice, and elisions in Hand B (e.g. *hacussed* 3/51, *aderthe* 3/58) have been separated, unless separation would involve emendation, e.g. *strangulym* ('strangled him') 3/154. Capitalization is modern but minimal (e.g. *God, Crist, Holy Gost, (Holy) Trinite, Seynt Andrewe, Kyng Charles, Lylleshull*). Periphrastic terms for God, Christ, and the Virgin Mary (other than *Fader, Sone, Lorde, Lady*) are not normally capitalized. The manuscript forms of ⟨i⟩/⟨j⟩ and ⟨u⟩/⟨v⟩ have been preserved. Where ⟨y⟩ represents ⟨þ⟩ (commonly in Hands D/E), it is transcribed ⟨þ⟩. However, where ⟨3⟩ represents ⟨þ⟩ (or, even more rarely, where ⟨þ⟩ represents ⟨3⟩), the grapheme is retained and the form noted in the Glossary (see Glossary *passim*, e.g. *sub* 3an(ne), þendur). Initial *ff-* is transcribed as *F*, according to the convention that *ff-* indicates a capital letter (most commonly in *ffor* in all hands). However, in the stint of D* the use of *ff* is a distinctive feature of the hand (initially, medially, and finally) and is only by chance at times indicative of a capital letter (see §5.2.1, Hand D*). The spelling has therefore been preserved as a distinctive feature of the hand.[264]

Abbreviations (including the ampersand and Tironian *et*) are silently expanded.[265] The contraction *ihu* is transcribed *Ihesu*; the less common *ihc* is transcribed *Ihesus*. Latin text is printed in italics.

---

[264] However, editorial punctuation means that *ff-* must sometimes be capitalized, in which case its occurrence has been noted in the apparatus, e.g. 23/143 *Fylberte*] *ffylberte*.

[265] Where the plural is not contracted, *-es* is the most frequent form in all hands (see Appendix IV.1, item 56), and contractions have been so expanded throughout the text. When uncontracted, *myth* is the most common form in all hands and has been used for the silent expansion.

In Hand B the form *þus* (with the contraction mark for *us*) and in Hand C *þys* (with superscript *s*) are frequently used to mean 'this', 'these' or 'thus'. In all such cases the abbreviation is expanded as it stands (*þus* and *þys* respectively) and the occurrences noted in the Glossary *sub* þis, þys *adv.* and *dem. adj.*, þus *dem. adj.* and *dem. pron.* Emendation of the base-text is indicated in square brackets and the original reading recorded in the apparatus. Omission of words or letters in the base-text is, in line with EETS practice, recorded only in the apparatus. Marginal and interlinear additions to the text are noted by the same convention as in the collations and apparatus: *ther`fore´* (Pro/9).

Punctuation has been designed to ease the comprehension of what is often syntactically difficult or confusing. In particular, the following syntactic features have been felt to require careful and frequent editorial punctuation:

1. Ellipsis of subject pronoun. This can be simple, as in the frequent *and so did* at the end of a sentence, e.g. *he badde vche man pray to God to reyson hyr aȝeyne to lyve, and so dydde* 43/55–6, *ȝef he wolde plyghte hure trowþe for te wedde hure, heo wolde helpon hym out of dystresse, and so deden* 10/7–9 (where the change to the plural form *deden* indicates an elliptical subject 'they'). Many examples are, however, more complex: *he commaunded þe dragon for to gone into a wyldurnesse þere he schul neuer greue man ne beste, and so ȝode forthe and was neuer seyne aftur* 32/28–31, where *ȝode* and *was neuer seyne* are not dependent on the subject of the previous verb (*commaunded*) but refer to the object of that verb, *þe dragon*. Or *þerefore wykkud men of þat cite tokon hym and dedon hym on a crosse, as Cryste was, and so pynud hym to þe dethe, and so ȝode to Cryste his maystur for to dwellon with hym in þe ioy þat neuer schal haue ende* 32/35–8, where the verb *pynud* is dependent on *wykkud men of þat cite* but the verb *ȝode* is dependent on an unexpressed subject (St Philip) and refers back to *hym* (*dedon hym . . . pynud hym*).

2. Ellipsis, combined with lack of concord between subject and verb, e.g. *þei eton here schone and her botus for hongur, and þe fadur rafte þe mete owte off þe sonus hande, and tokon hit owte off his mowþe, and þe sone off þe fadur, þe husbonde off þe wyffe, and þe wyffe off þe husbande* 32/106–9, where the change from the past singular *rafte* (dependent on *þe fadur*) to past plural *tokon* indicates that the subject is no longer only *þe fadur* but includes *þe sone . . . þe husbande*.

3. Change of tense, which has sometimes been editorially accom-

modated by assuming a change from *oratio obliqua* to *recta*, e.g. *þen com þer a voys to on of ham . . . and bede hym go erly on þe morwe . . . and make hym byschop þat he fond þere: 'and ys kalled Nycholas'* 3/23–6. At other times emendation has been thought preferable, e.g. *And so þey token hym and sacred hym byschop* 3/33 (emended from *taken*).

4. Complex sentences, e.g. *þan for þis Decius sawgh þat þe emperoure dude hym so grete reuerens and worschep, and þoght in his herte it was for fer of hym and þoght he wolde ben emperoure hymself, þenkyng þat he were myche more worthy þan he was, wherefore in þe nyght aftyr, as þe emperoure lay in hys bedde slepyng, þis knyght Decius ʒode to hym and slowe hym and so toke hys oste wyth hym to Rome* 52/63–9.

In all such cases, careful and frequent modern punctuation has been used to explicate the text, while the Explanatory Notes explain and/ or translate the more difficult passages.

BIBLIOGRAPHY

Abbot, T. K. (1900) (ed.), *Catalogue of the Manuscripts in the Library of Trinity College, Dublin* (Dublin).

Aston, Margaret (2003), 'Lollards and the Cross', in Fiona Somerset, Jill C. Havens, and Derrick G. Pitard (eds.), *Lollards and their Influence in Late Medieval England* (Woodbridge), 99–113.

Baer, Barbara (2004), *A Heritage of Holy Wood: The Legend of the True Cross in Text and Image*, trans. Lee Preedy (Leiden and Boston, Mass.).

Bannister, H. M. (1903), 'The Introduction of the Cult of St Anne into the West', *English Historical Review*, 18: 107–12.

Barber, Richard, and Barker, Judith (1989), *Tournaments: Jousts, Chivalry and Pageants in the Middle Ages* (Woodbridge).

Baring-Gould, S. (1872–98), *The Lives of the Saints*, 12 vols. (London).

Barron, John (2002), 'The Augustinian Canons and the University of Oxford: The Lost College of St George', in Caroline Barron and Jenny Stratford (eds.), *The Church and Learning in Late Medieval Society: Studies in Honour of Professor R. B. Dobson*, Harlaxton Medieval Studies, 11 (Donington), 228–54.

Barron, W. R. J., and Burgess, Glyn S. (2002) (eds.), *Voyage of St Brendan* (Exeter).

Baugh, G. C., and Cox, D. C. (1988, 1982), *Monastic Shropshire*, Shropshire Victoria County History Booklet 2 (Shrewsbury).

Beadle, Richard (1994), 'Middle English Texts and their Transmission, 1350–1500: Some Geographical Criteria', in Margaret Laing and Keith Williamson (eds.), *Speaking in our Tongues: Medieval Dialectology and Related Disciplines* (Cambridge).

Benskin, Michael (1982), 'The Letters ⟨þ⟩ and ⟨y⟩ in Later Middle English, and Some Related Matters', *Journal of the Society of Archivists*, 7: 13–30.

—— (1991a), 'The "Fit"-technique Explained', in Felicity Riddy (ed.), *Regionalism in Late Medieval Manuscripts and Texts* (Cambridge, 1991), 9–26.

—— (1991b), 'In Reply to Dr Burton', *LSE* NS 22: 209–62.

Binski, Paul (1996), *Medieval Death: Ritual and Representation* (London).

Black, G. F. (1946), *Surnames of Scotland* (New York).

Blake, N. F. (1972) (ed.), *Middle English Religious Literature* (London).

—— (1975) (ed.), *Quattuor Sermones*, MET 2 (Heidelberg).

—— (1989), 'Manuscript to Print', in Jeremy Griffiths and Derek Pearsall (eds.), *Book Production and Publishing in Britain 1375–1475* (Cambridge), 403–32.

Blench, J. W. (1964), *Preaching in England in the Late Fifteenth and Sixteenth Centuries: A Study of English Sermons 1450–c .1600* (Oxford).

Bloomfield, Morton W. (1952), *The Seven Deadly Sins: An Introduction to the History of a Religious Concept, with Special Reference to Mediaeval English Literature* (East Lansing, Mich.).

Blume, C., and Dreves, G. M. (1886–1922) (eds.), *Analecta Hymnica Medii Aevi*, 55 vols. (Leipzig).

Boase, T. S. R. (1972), *Death in the Middle Ages* (London).

Boffey, Julia, and Edwards, A. S. G. (1997) (eds.), *The Works of Geoffrey Chaucer and 'The Kingis Quair': Facsimile of Bodleian Library, Oxford, MS Arch. Selden. B .24*, with an Appendix by B. C. Barker-Benfield (Cambridge).

[Botfield, B.] (1838) (ed.), *Catalogi Veteres Librorum Ecclesiae Cathedralis Dunelm*, Surtees Society, 7 (London).

Boyle, Leonard E. (1955), 'The *Oculus Sacerdotis* and Some Other Works of William of Pagula', *TRHS* 5th series, 5: 81–110.

—— (1981), *Pastoral Care, Clerical Education and Canon Law* (London).

Brandeis, A. (1901) (ed.), *Jacob's Well*, EETS os 115.

Braswell, L. (1987) (ed.), *The Index of Middle English Prose. Handlist IV: A Handlist of Manuscripts Containing Middle English Prose in the Douce Collection, Bodleian Library Oxford* (Cambridge).

Brewer, D. S. (1954), 'Observations on a Fifteenth-Century Manuscript', *Anglia*, 72: 390–9.

Bühler, Curt F. (1960), *The Fifteenth-Century Book: The Scribes, the Printers, the Decorators* (Philadelphia).

Burgess, Clive (1988), '"A fond thing vainly invented": An Essay on Purgatory and Pious Motive in Later Medieval England', in S. J. Wright (ed.), *Parish, Church and People: Local Studies in Lay Religion 1350–1750* (London), 56–84.

Burton, Tom (1991), 'On the Current State of Middle English Dialectology', *LSE* NS 22: 167–208.

Cappelli, A. (1929), *Dizionario di abbreviature latine ed italiane*, 6th edn. (Milan).

Chambers, J. K., and Trudgill, Peter (1998), *Dialectology* (Cambridge).

Chazelle, Celia M. (1990), 'Pictures, Books and the Illiterate: Pope Gregory I's Letters to Serenus of Marseilles', *Word and Image*, 6: 139.

Cheetham, Francis (2003), *Alabaster Images of Medieval England* (Woodbridge).

Cheney, C. R. (1961), 'Rules for the Observance of Feast-Days in Medieval England', *Bulletin of the Institute of Historical Research*, 34: 117–47.

Chibnall, Marjorie M. (1973), 'The Abbey of Shrewsbury', 'The Abbey of Lilleshall', in A. T. Gaydon (ed.), *A History of Shropshire*, VCH (London), ii. 30–8, 70–80.

Clark, Anne L. (1999), 'Holy Woman or Unworthy Vessel: The Representations of Elisabeth of Schönau', in Catherine M. Mooney (ed.), *Gendered Voices: Medieval Saints and their Interpreters* (Philadelphia), 35–51.

Colgrave, Bertram (1956) (ed. and trans.), *Felix's Life of St Guthlac* (Cambridge).

—— and Mynors, R. A. B. (1981) (eds.), *Bede's Ecclesiastical History of the English People* (Oxford).

Colledge, E., and Bazire, J. (1957) (eds.), *The Chastising of God's Children and the Treatise of Perfection of the Sons of God* (Oxford).

Cooper, Tim (1999), *The Last Generation of English Catholic Clergy* (Woodbridge).

Cox, J. C. (1905), 'The Priory of Newark', in H. E. Malden (ed.), *A History of the County of Surrey*, VCH (London), ii. 102–5.

Coxe, H. O. (1840), *Forms of Bidding Prayer, with Introduction and Notes* (Oxford).

—— (1852) (ed.), *Catalogus Codicum MSS qui in Collegiis Aulisque Universitatis hodie adservantur*, 2 vols. (Oxford).

Crane, T. F. (1890) (ed.), *Exempla or Illustrative Stories from the Sermones Vulgares of Jacques de Vitry*, Publications of the Folklore Society, 26 (London).

—— (1911), 'Miracles of the Virgin', *Romanic Review* 2: 235–79.

Cressy, David (1989), *Bonfires and Bells: National Memory and the Protestant Calendar in Elizabethan and Stuart England* (London).

Cronin, Jr., Grover (1942), 'John Mirk on Bonfires, Elephants and Dragons', *Modern Language Notes*, 57: 113–16.

Dalton, O. M. (1967, repr. from 1927) (trans.), *The History of the Franks by Gregory of Tours*, 2 vols. (Oxford).

Daniell, C. (1997), *Death and Burial in Medieval England 1066–1550* (London and New York).

Darlington, Reginald R. (1928) (ed.), *The Vita Wulfstani of William of Malmesbury, to which are Added the Extant Abridgments of This Work and the Miracles and Translation of St. Wulfstan*, Camden Series 40 (London).

Davies, R. G. (2004), 'Merk [Merke], Thomas', in *ODNB*.

Davis, Norman (1970) (ed.), *Non-Cycle Plays and Fragments*, EETS ss 1.

Deacon, Malcolm (1980), *Philip Doddridge of Northampton* (Northampton).

Deanesly, Margaret (1920), *The Lollard Bible and other Medieval Biblical Versions* (Cambridge).

Dent, R. W. (1984), *Proverbial Language in English Drama Exclusive of Shakespeare, 1495–1616: An Index* (Berkeley and Los Angeles).

D'Evelyn, Charlotte (1935) (ed.), *Peter Idley's Instructions to his Son*, Modern Language Association Monograph Series, 6 (Boston and London).

Dickens, A. G. (1959) (ed.), *Tudor Treatises*, Yorkshire Archaeological Society Record Series 125 [Leeds].

—— (1964), *The English Reformation* (London).

—— (1982) (ed.), 'The Writers of Tudor Yorkshire', in A. G. Dickens, *Reformation Studies* (London), 217–44.

Dickinson, F. W. (1861–3) (ed.), *Missale ad Usum Insignis et Praeclarae Ecclesiae Sarum* (Burntisland).

Dickinson, J. C. (1950), *The Origins of the Austin Canons and their Introduction into England* (London).

Dix, Gregory (1945), *The Shape of the Liturgy*, 2nd edn. (Westminster).

Dobson, R. B. (1992), 'The Religious Orders 1370–1540', in J. I. Catto and Ralph Evans (eds.), *The History of the University of Oxford*: ii: *Late Medieval Oxford* (Oxford), 539–79.

Douteil, Herbert (1976) (ed.), *Iohannis Beleth Summa de Ecclesiasticis Officiis*, 2 vols., Corpus Christianorum, Continuatio Mediaevalis, XLI, XLIA (Turnhout).

Doyle, A. I. (1953), 'A Survey of the Origins and Circulation of Theological Writings in English in the 14th, 15th, and early 16th Centuries, with Special Consideration of the Part of the Clergy Therein', 2 vols. (Ph.D. thesis, Cambridge).

—— (1989), 'Publication by Members of the Religious Orders', in Jeremy Griffiths and Derek Pearsall (eds.), *Book Production and Publishing in Britain 1375–1475* (Cambridge), 109–23.

Duffy, Eamon (1992), *The Stripping of the Altars: Traditional Religion in England c.1400–c.1580* (New Haven and London).

—— (2001), *The Voices of Morebath: Reformation and Rebellion in an English Village* (New Haven and London).

Dugdale, Sir William (1846, 1693) (ed. John Cayley, Henry Ellis, and the Revd Bulkeley Bandinel), *Monasticon Anglicanum*, 2nd edn. (London).

Edden, Valerie (2000) (ed.), *The Index of Middle English Prose. Handlist XV: Manuscripts in Midland Libraries* (Cambridge).

Elliott, J. K. (1993) (ed.), *The Apocryphal New Testament: A Collection of Apocryphal Christian Literature in an English Translation* (Oxford).

[Ellis, Henry, and Douce, Francis] (1812–19) (eds.), *A Catalogue of the Lansdowne Manuscripts in the British Museum with Indexes of Persons, Places and Matters*, 2 vols. (London).

Emden, A. B. (1957–9), *A Biographical Register of the University of Oxford to A.D. 1500*, 3 vols. (Oxford).

—— (1963), *A Biographical Register of the University of Cambridge to 1500* (Cambridge).

—— (1974), *A Biographical Register of the University of Oxford A.D. 1501 to 1540* (Oxford).

Emerson, R. K. (1981), *Antichrist in the Middle Ages: A Study of Medieval Apocalypticism, Art, and Literature* (Manchester).

Erbe, Th. (1905) (ed.), *Mirk's Festial: A Collection of Homilies, by Johannes Mirkus (John Mirk)*, Part I, EETS ES 96.

Evans, Evangeline (1931), 'St Mary's College in Oxford for Austin Canons', *North Oxfordshire Archaeological Society*, 76: 367–91.

[Evans, J. Gwenogvryn] (1902) (ed.), *Report on Manuscripts in the Welsh Language*, ii/1, Historical Manuscripts Commission Command Papers C. 8829 (London).

Evans, Joan, and Serjeantson, Mary S. (eds.) (1933), *English Medieval Lapidaries*, EETS 190.

Evans, T. A. R. (1992), 'The Number, Origins and Careers of Scholars', in J. I. Catto and Ralph Evans (eds.), *The History of the University of Oxford*, ii: *Late Medieval Oxford* (Oxford), 485–538.

Eyton, R. W. (1854–60), *Antiquities of Shropshire*, 12 vols. (London).

Feasey, H. J. (1897), *Ancient English Holy Week Ceremonial* (London).

Feldman, Louis H. (2000) (trans. and commentary), *Judean Antiquities 1–4*, vol. 3 of Steve Mason (ed.), *Flavius Josephus: Translation and Commentary*, 10 vols. (Leiden, Boston, and Cologne).

Fletcher, Alan J. (1977) (ed.), 'A Critical Edition of Selected Sermons from an Unpublished Fifteenth-Century *De Tempore* Sermon Cycle' (B.Litt. thesis, Oxford).

—— (1978), '"I sing of a maiden": A Fifteenth-Century Sermon Reminiscence', *N&Q* NS 25: 107–8.

—— (1980), 'Unnoticed Sermons from John Mirk's *Festial*', *Speculum*, 55: 514–22.

—— (1987), 'John Mirk and the Lollards', *MÆ* 56: 217–24.

—— (1988), 'The Manuscripts of John Mirk's *Manuale Sacerdotis*', *LSE* NS 19: 105–39.

—— (1991), '"The Unity of the State exists in the Agreement of the Minds": A Fifteenth-Century Sermon on the Three Estates', *LSE* NS 22: 103–37.

—— (1998), *Preaching, Politics and Poetry in Late-Medieval England* (Dublin).

—— and Powell, S. (1978), 'The Origins of a Fifteenth-Century Sermon Collection: MSS Harley 2247 and Royal 18 B XXV', *LSE* NS 10: 74–96.

Ford, Judy Anne (2006), *John Mirk's Festial: Orthodoxy, Lollardy and the Common People in Fourteenth-Century England* (Cambridge).

Forde, Simon (1985), 'Writings of a Reformer: A Look at Sermon Studies and Bible Studies through Repingdon's *Sermones super evangelia dominicalia*', 2 vols. (Ph.D. thesis, Birmingham).

—— (1994), 'The Educational Organization of the Augustinian Canons in

England and Wales, and their University Life at Oxford, 1325–1448',
History of Universities, 13: 21–60.

[Forshall, J.] (1840) (ed.), *Catalogue of Manuscripts in the British Museum*, NS
i (3 parts in 1 vol.) (London).

Foss, David B. (1989), 'John Mirk's *Instructions for Parish Priests*', in W. J.
Sheils and Diana Wood (eds.), *The Ministry, Clerical and Lay*, Studies in
Church History, 26 (Oxford), 131–40.

Foster, F. A. (1926), *A Stanzaic Life of Christ*, EETS 166.

French, Katherine L. (2001), *The People of the Parish: Community Life in a
Late Medieval English Diocese* (Philadelphia).

Furnivall, F. J. (1867) (ed.), *Hymns to the Virgin and Christ and Other
Religious Poems*, EETS OS 24.

Gameson, Richard (2007) (ed.), *Treasures of Durham University Library*
(Durham).

Gaydon, A. T. (1973), 'The Hospital of St George, Shrewsbury', 'The
College of St Chad, Shrewsbury', 'The College of St Mary, Shrewsbury',
in A. T. Gaydon (ed.), *A History of Shropshire*, VCH (London), ii. 105,
114–19, 119–23.

Gelling, Margaret (for 1984–5, 1985–6) (ed.), *The Place-Names of Shropshire*, Part 1 of 3 parts, English Place Name Society 52/53.

Gibbs, M., and Lang, J. (1934), *Bishops and Reform 1215–1272* (Oxford).

Gilchrist, Roberta, and Sloane, Barney (2005), *Requiem: The Medieval
Monastic Cemetery in Britain* (London).

Gillespie, V. (1980), '*Doctrina* and *Praedicacio*: The Design and Function of
Some Pastoral Manuals', *LSE* NS 11: 36–50.

Girsch, James Martin (1990) (ed.), 'An Edition with Commentary of John
Mirk's *Manuale Sacerdotis*' (Ph.D. thesis, University of Toronto).

—— (1995), 'An Elizabethan Manuscript of Mirk's *Festial* Sermon on St
Winifred and Observations on the "Shrewsbury Manuscript"', *NM* 96:
265–9.

Le Goff, Jacques (1984), *The Birth of Purgatory*, trans. Arthur Goldhammer
(Chicago).

Görlach, Manfred (1972), *The South English Legendary, Gilte Legende and
Golden Legend*, Braunschweiger Anglistische Arbeiten, 3 (Braunschweig).

—— (1974), *The Textual Tradition of the South English Legendary*, Leeds
Texts and Monographs, NS 6 (Leeds).

Graesse, Th. (1846) (ed.), *Jacobi a Voragine Legenda Aurea vulgo Historia
Lombardica Dicta* (Dresden and Leipzig).

Gray, Douglas (1972), *Themes and Images in the Medieval English Religious
Lyric* (London and Boston).

Greene, R. L. (1977) (ed.), *The Early English Carols*, 2nd edn. (Oxford).

Greenway, George (1961) (trans. and ed.), *The Life and Death of Thomas
Becket, Chancellor of England and Archbishop of Canterbury, Based on the*

Account of William Fitzstephen, his Clerk, with Additions from Other Contemporary Sources (London).

Grisdale, D. M. (1939) (ed.), *Three Middle English Sermons from the Worcester Chapter Manuscript F. 10*, Leeds School of English Language Texts and Monographs, 5 (Kendal).

Grosjean, P. (1940), 'De Codice Hagiographico Gothano', 'Codicis Gothani Appendix', *Analecta Bollandiana*, 58: 90–103, 177–204.

Haines, R. M. (1971), 'Education in English Ecclesiastical Legislation of the Later Middle Ages', in A. K. McHardy (ed.), *Superior Spirituality versus Popular Piety in Late-Medieval England*, Studies in Church History, 7 (Oxford), 161–75.

Hamer, Richard, and Russell, Vida (2000) (eds.), *Supplementary Lives in Some Manuscripts of the Gilte Legende*, EETS 315.

Hampson, R. T. (1841), *Medii Aevi Kalendarium*, 2 vols. (London).

Hanna (III), Ralph (1984) (ed.), *The Index of Middle English Prose. Handlist I: A Handlist of Manuscripts containing Middle English Prose in the Henry E. Huntington Library* (Cambridge).

—— (2000), 'Augustinian Canons and Middle English Literature', in A. S. G. Edwards, Vincent Gillespie, and Ralph Hanna (eds.), *The English Medieval Book: Studies in Memory of Jeremy Griffiths*, BL Studies in the History of the Book (London), 27–42.

—— and Lawton, David (2003) (eds.), *The Siege of Jerusalem*, EETS 320.

Harbus, Antonina (2002), *Helena of Britain in Medieval Legend* (Cambridge).

Harvey, Barbara (1972), 'Work and *Festa Ferianda* in Medieval England', *JEH* 23: 289–308.

Hearne, Thomas (1810) (ed.), *The Works of Thomas Hearne*, 4 vols. (London).

Heist, W. W. (1952), *The Fifteen Signs before Doomsday* (East Lansing, Mich.).

Hennig, J. (1948), 'The Meaning of All the Saints', *MedSt* 10: 147–61.

Herrtage, S. J. H. (1879) (ed.), *Early English Versions of the Gesta Romanorum*, EETS ES 33.

Hill, R. (1962) (ed.), *Gesta Francorum et aliorum Hierosolomitanorum* (London).

Holmstedt, G. (1933) (ed.), *Speculum Christiani*, EETS 182.

Horner, FSC, Patrick J. (2005), '2. Later Middle English Sermons and Homilies', in Peter G. Beidler (ed.), *A Manual of the Writings in Middle English 1050–1500*, xi: 4057–167, 4271–310 (New Haven).

Horstmann, C. (1880), 'Prosalegenden', *Anglia*, 3: 293–360.

—— (1881) (ed.), *Altenglische Legenden*, 2nd edn. (Heilbronn).

—— (1896), *Yorkshire Writers*, 2 vols. (London).

—— (1901), *Nova legenda Anglie*, 2 vols. (Oxford).

Hudson, Anne (1989), 'Lollard Book Production', in Jeremy Griffiths and

Derek Pearsall (eds.), *Book Production and Publishing in Britain 1375–1475* (Cambridge), 125–42.

—— and Gradon, Pamela (1983–96) (eds.), *English Wycliffite Sermons*, 5 vols. (Oxford).

Hughes, P. L., and Larkin, J. F. (1964–9) (eds.), *Tudor Royal Proclamations*, 3 vols. (New Haven and London).

Humphreys, K. W. (1986), 'The Loss of Books in Sixteenth-Century England', *Libri*, 36: 249–58.

Hunt, R. W. (1953) (ed.), vol. 1 of *Summary Catalogue of Western Manuscripts in the Bodleian Library at Oxford*, 7 vols., 1895–1953 (Oxford).

Hussey, Maurice (1958), 'The Petitions of the Paternoster in Mediaeval English Literature', *Medium Ævum*, 27: 8–16.

Ingram, R. W. (1981) (ed.), *Records of Early English Drama: Coventry* (Manchester).

James, M. R. (1907–14) (ed.), *A Descriptive Catalogue of the Manuscripts in the Library of Gonville and Caius College*, 2 vols. and supplement (Cambridge).

—— (1913), *A Descriptive Catalogue of the Manuscripts in the Library of St John's College, Cambridge* (Cambridge).

Jansen, Katherine Ludwig (2000), *The Making of the Magdalen: Preaching and Popular Devotion in the Later Middle Ages* (Princeton).

Jeffrey, David Lyle (1988) (trans. and ed.), *The Law of Love: English Spirituality in the Age of Wyclif* (Grand Rapids, Mich.).

Jenkins, Jacqueline, and Lewis, Katherine J. (2003) (ed.), *St Katherine of Alexandria: Texts and Contexts in Western Medieval Europe* (Turnhout).

Johnson, J. (1850–1, 1720) (ed.), *A Collection of All the Ecclesiastical Laws, Canons, Answers, or Rescripts . . . of the Church of England . . . Translated into English with Explanatory Notes*, 2nd edn. by John Baron, 2 vols. (Oxford).

Jolliffe, P. S. (1974), *A Check-list of Middle English Prose Writings of Spiritual Guidance*, Subsidia Mediaevalia, 2 (Toronto).

Jones, Gwenan T. (1939), *A Study of Three Welsh Religious Plays* (Bala).

Jordan, R. (1974), *Handbook of Middle English Grammar: Phonology*, trans. and rev. Eugene Joseph Crook (The Hague and Paris).

Joynes, Andrew (2001) (ed.), *Medieval Ghost Stories: An Anthology of Miracles, Marvels and Prodigies* (Woodbridge).

Kane, George, and Donaldson, E. Talbot (1975) (eds.), *Piers Plowman: The B Version* (London).

Keene, Derek, Burns, Arthur, and Saint, Andrew (2004) (eds.), *St Paul's: The Cathedral Church of London 604–2004* (New Haven and London).

Kengen, J. H. L. ([1979]) (ed.), *Memoriale Credencium: A Late Middle English Manual of Theology for Lay People Edited from Bodley MS Tanner 201* ([Nijmegen]).

Ker, N. R. (1985), 'The Migration of Manuscripts from the English Medieval Libraries', in A. G. Watson (ed.), *Books, Collectors and Libraries: Studies in the Medieval Heritage* (London and Ronceverte), 459–69.

Kettle, Ann J., and Johnson, D. A. (1970) (ed.), 'The Cathedral of Lichfield', in M. W. Greenslade (ed.), *A History of the County of Stafford*, VCH (London), iii. 140–99.

Klausner, David N. (2005) (ed.), *Records of Early English Drama: Wales* (London and Toronto).

Knight, Ione Kemp (1967) (ed.), *Wimbledon's Sermon Redde Rationem Villicationis Tue: A Middle English Sermon of the Fourteenth Century*, Duquesne Studies, Philological Series, 9 (Pittsburgh, Pa.).

Kohlenberger III, John R. (1997) (ed.), *The Parallel Apocrypha* (New York and Oxford).

Kristensson, G. (1974) (ed.), *John Mirk's Instructions for Parish Priests*, Lund Studies in English, 49 (Lund).

Kurvinen, Auvo (1960), 'The Life of St Catharine of Alexandria in Middle English Prose' (D.Phil. thesis, University of Oxford).

Lavery, Simon (1984), 'The Source of the St Brendan Story in the *South English Legendary*', *LSE* NS 15: 21–32.

Lawrence, C. H. (1989, 1984), *Medieval Monasticism: Forms of Religious Life in Western Europe in the Middle Ages* (London and New York).

Leclercq, J., and Rochais, H. (1957–74) (eds.), *Bernard of Clairvaux: Opera*, 7 vols. (Rome).

Legg, J. Wickham (1890 for 1889), 'On an Inventory of the Vestry in Westminster Abbey Taken in 1388', *Archaeologia*, 52: 195–286.

—— (1916) (ed.), *The Sarum Missal Edited from Three Early Manuscripts* (Oxford).

Lepine, David (1995), *A Brotherhood of Canons Serving God: English Secular Cathedrals in the Later Middle Ages* (Woodbridge).

—— and Orme, Nicholas (2003) (eds.), *Death and Memory in Medieval Exeter* (Exeter).

Letts, Malcolm (1947), 'Prester John: A Fourteenth-Century Manuscript at Cambridge', *TRHS* 4th ser. 29: 19–26.

—— (1949), *Sir John Mandeville: The Man and his Book* (London).

Lewis, Henry (1921), 'Darnau o'r Efengylau', *Y Cymmrodor*, 31: 193–216.

—— (1925) (ed.), 'Darn o'r Ffestifal (*Liber Festialis*) allan o Lawysgrif Havod 22, TD. 80–195, gyda Rhagymadrodd a Nodiadau', *Supplement* to *The Transactions of the Honourable Society of Cymmrodorion*, 1923–4 (London).

Lewis, Katherine J. (2000), *The Cult of St Katherine of Alexandria in Late Medieval England* (Woodbridge).

Lewis, R. E., Blake, N. F, and Edwards, A. S. G. (1985) (eds.), *Index of Printed Middle English Prose* (New York, London).

Lindsay, Philip (1934), *King Henry V* (London).

Lindsay, W. M. (1911) (ed.), *Etymologiarum sive originum libri XX*, 2 vols. (Oxford).

Long, Mary McDonald (1955), 'Undetected Verse in Mirk's *Festial*', *MLN* 70: 13–15.

[Luard, J. R., Mayor, J. E. B., Bradshaw, Henry, et al.] (1856–67), *Catalogue of the Manuscripts Preserved in the Library of the University of Cambridge*, 5 vols. (Cambridge).

Luibhéid, C. (1987) (trans.), *Pseudo-Dionysius: The Complete Works* (New York).

Lumby, J. R. (1865–86) (ed.), *Polychronicon Ranulphi Higden, Monachi Cestrensis; together with the English Translation of John of Trevisa and of an Unknown Writer in the 15th Century*, 9 vols. (vols. 1–2 by C. Babington), Rolls Series, 41 (London).

Lumiansky, R. M., and Mills, David (1974) (eds.), *The Chester Mystery Cycle*, EETS ss 3.

Lyall, R. J. (1989), 'Books and Book Owners in Fifteenth-Century Scotland', in Jeremy Griffiths and Derek Pearsall (eds.), *Book Production and Publishing in Britain 1375–1475* (Cambridge), 239–56.

McCarthy, Conor (2005), *Marriage in Medieval England: Law, Literature and Practice* (Woodbridge).

McDonald, Peter (1986), 'The Papacy and Monastic Observance in Late Medieval England: The *Benedictina* in England', *Journal of Religious History* 14, 117–32.

McIntosh, Angus, and Samuels, M. L. (1968), 'Prolegomena to a Study of Mediæval Anglo-Irish', *MÆ* 37: 1–9.

—— and Wakelin, M. F. (1982), 'John Mirk's *Festial* and Bodleian MS Hatton 96', *NM* 83: 443–50

McKitterick, David (1986), *Cambridge University Library: A History: The Eighteenth and Nineteenth Centuries* (Cambridge).

Macray, W. D. (1862), *Catalogi Codicum Manuscriptorum Bibliothecae Bodleianae*, Part 5, Fascicule 1 (Oxford).

McSparran, F. and Robinson, P. R. (1979) (ed.) *Cambridge University Library Ff.2.38* (London).

Madan, Falconer (1895) (ed.), vol. 3 of *A Summary Catalogue of Western Manuscripts in the Bodleian Library at Oxford*, 7 vols., 1895–1953 (Oxford).

—— (1897) (ed.), vol. 4 of *A Summary Catalogue of Western Manuscripts in the Bodleian Library at Oxford*, 7 vols., 1895–1953 (Oxford).

—— and Craster, H. H. E. (1922) (eds.), vol. 2, Part I of *A Summary*

Catalogue of Western Manuscripts in the Bodleian Library at Oxford, 7 vols., 1895–1953 (Oxford).

——— Craster, H. H. E, and Denholm-Young, N. (1937) (eds.), vol 2., Part II of *A Summary Catalogue of Western Manuscripts in the Bodleian Library at Oxford*, 7 vols., 1895–1953 (Oxford).

Maggioni, Giovanni Paolo (1998) (ed.), *Iacopo da Varazze: Legenda Aurea*, 2 vols. (Florence).

Manly, John M., and Rickert, E. (1940), *The Text of the Canterbury Tales*, 8 vols. (Chicago).

Marks, Richard, and Williamson, Paul (2003) (eds.), *Gothic Art for England 1400–1547* (London).

Marshall, P. (1995), 'The Rood of Boxley, the Blood of Hailes, and the Defence of the Henrician Church', *JEH* 46: 689–96.

Marston, T. E. (1972), 'An Early English Best-Seller', *Yale University Library Gazette*, 46: 86–8.

Martin, G. H. (1995) (ed.), *Knighton's Chronicle 1337–1396* (Oxford).

Marx, William (2003) (ed.), *An English Chronicle 1377–1461: A New Edition* (Woodbridge).

Masson, Georgina (1965), *The Companion Guide to Rome* (London).

Millett, Bella (1982) (ed.), *Hali Meiðhad*, EETS 284.

Morgan, Nigel (2001), 'The Introduction of the Sarum Calendar into the Dioceses of England in the Thirteenth Century', in Michael Prestwich, Richard Britnell, and Robin Frame (eds.), *Thirteenth-Century England VIII: Proceedings of the Durham Conference, 1999* (Woodbridge), 179–206.

Morris, Richard (1863) (ed.), *The Pricke of Conscience* (Berlin).

——— (1871) (ed.), *Legends of the Holy Rood*, EETS os 46.

Morrison, Stephen (forthcoming) (ed.), *A Late Fifteenth-Century Dominical Sermon Cycle*, 2 vols., EETS 337, 338.

Mosher, J. A. (1911), *The Exemplum in the Early Religious and Didactic Literature of England* (New York).

Murray, Hilda M. R. (1911) (ed.), *The Middle English Poem, Erth vpon Erthe, Printed from Twenty-Four Manuscripts*, EETS os 141.

Murray, Jacqueline (2001) (ed.), *Love, Marriage, and Family in the Middle Ages*, Readings in Medieval Civilizations and Cultures, 7 (Peterborough, Ont.).

Nelson, Venetia (1981) (ed.), *Myroure to Lewde Men and Wymmen*, MET 14 (Heidelberg).

Nevanlinna, Saara (1972) (ed.), *The Northern Homily Cycle: The Expanded Version in MSS Harley 4916 and Cotton Tiberius E vii*, Part I, Mémoires de la Société Néophilologique de Helsinki, 38 (Helsinki).

——— (1993) (ed.), 'The Sermon on the Day of St. Katherine in John Mirk's *Festial* in Southwell Minster MS 7', in R. Hiltunen et al. (eds.), *English*

Far and Wide: A Festschrift for Inna Koskenniemi, Annuales Universitatis Turkuensis B: 197 (Helsinki), 183–94.

—— and Taavitsainen, Irma (1993) (eds.), *St. Katherine of Alexandria: The Late Middle English Prose Legend in Southwell Minster MS 7* (Cambridge).

Nichols, Ann Eljenholm (1994), *Seeable Signs: The Iconography of the Seven Sacraments 1350–1544* (Woodbridge).

Nixon, Virginia (2005), *Mary's Mother: Saint Anne in Late Medieval Europe* (University Park, Pa.).

Ogilvie-Thomson, S. J. (1991) (ed.), *The Index of Middle English Prose. Handlist VIII: Manuscripts Containing Middle English Prose in Oxford College Libraries* (Cambridge).

O'Mara, Veronica, M. (1980) (ed.), 'An Edition of Selected Marian Sermons from Trinity College Dublin MS. 428' (MA thesis, University College, Dublin).

—— (1987a), 'A Study of Unedited Late Middle English Sermons that Occur Singly or in Small Groups, with an Edition of Selected Sermons' (Ph.D. thesis, University of Leeds).

—— (1987b), 'A Middle English Sermon Preached by a Sixteenth-Century "Athiest": A Preliminary Account', *N&Q* 323: 183–5.

—— (1988), 'A Checklist of Unedited Late Middle English Sermons that Occur Singly or in Small Groups', *LSE* NS 19: 141–66.

—— (1992), 'From Print to Manuscript: The *Golden Legend* and British Library Lansdowne MS 379', *LSE* NS 23: 81–104.

—— (1997), 'Manuscript and Print: The Relationship between "The Revelation of the Hundred Pater Nosters" and *The Seven Sheddings of the Blood of Jesus Christ*', *Ephemerides Liturgicae*, 111: 1–14.

—— and Paul, Suzanne (2007), *A Repertorium of Middle English Prose Sermons*, Sermo: Studies on Patristic, Medieval, and Reformation Sermons and Preaching, 4 vols. (Turnhout)

Oosterwijk, Sophie (2005), 'Food for worms—Food for Thought: The Appearance and Interpretation of the "Verminous" Cadaver in Britain and Europe', *Journal of the Church Monuments Society*, 20: 40–80.

Oppenheimer, Francis (1953), *The Legend of the Sainte Ampoulle* (London).

Orme, Nicholas (2004), 'The Dead Beneath our Feet', *History Today*, 54: 19–25.

O'Rourke, Jason (2003), 'English and Latin Texts in Welsh Contexts: Reflections of a Multilingual Society in National Library of Wales MS Peniarth 12', *Yearbook of English Studies*, 33: 53–63.

Owen, H., and Blakeway, J. B. (1825), *A History of Shrewsbury*, 2 vols. (London).

Owst, G. R. (1926), *Preaching in Medieval England: An Introduction to Sermon Manuscripts of the Period c. 1350–1450* (Cambridge).

—— (1966, 1933), *Literature and Pulpit in Medieval England* (Oxford).

Page, W. (1905), 'Collegiate Church of All Saints, Derby', in W. Page (ed.), *A History of Derbyshire*, VCH (London), ii. 87–92.

Parkes, M. B. (1969), *English Cursive Book Hands 1250–1500* (Oxford).

—— (1992), 'The Provision of Books', in J. I. Catto and Ralph Evans (ed.), *The History of the University of Oxford*, ii: *Late Medieval Oxford* (Oxford), 407–83.

Peacock, E. (1902, 1868) (ed., rev. F. J. Furnivall), *Instructions for Parish Priests*, EETS os 31.

Peterson, Clifford J. (1974), '*Pearl* and St Erkenwald: Some Evidence for Authorship', 'The *Pearl* Poet and John Massey of Cotton, Cheshire', *RES* NS 25: 49–53, 257–66

—— (1975), 'Hoccleve, "Maister Massy", and the *Pearl* Poet: Two Notes', *RES* NS 26: 129–43

—— (1977), 'Hoccleve, the Old Hall Manuscript, Cotton Nero A.X., and the *Pearl* Poet, *RES* NS 28: 49–56.

Pfaff, R. W. (1970), *New Liturgical Feasts in Later Medieval England* (Oxford).

Pickering, O. S. (1981 for 1980 and 1981), 'Notes on the Sentence of Cursing in Middle English: Or, a Case for the *Index of Middle English Prose*', *LSE* NS 12: 229–44.

—— (2004), 'Saints' Lives', in A. S. G. Edwards (ed.), *A Companion to Middle English Prose* (Cambridge), 249–70.

—— and Powell, S. (1989) (eds.), *The Index of Middle English Prose. Handlist VI: Manuscripts containing Middle English Prose in Yorkshire Libraries and Archives* (Cambridge).

—— —— (2005), 'A Neglected Copy of John Mirk's Mary Magdalene Sermon', *Medieval Sermon Studies* 49: 59–68.

[Planta, Joseph] (1802) (ed.), *A Catalogue of the Manuscripts in the Cottonian Library, Deposited in the British Museum. Printed by Command of His Majesty King George III &c. &c. &c. in Pursuance of an Address of the House of Commons of Great Britain*, 2 vols. (London).

Postles, D. (1993), 'The Austin Canons in English Towns, c1100–1350', *Bulletin of the Institute of Historical Research*, 66: 1–20.

Powell, Susan (1980) (ed.), 'A Critical Edition of the *Temporale* Sermons of MSS Harley 2247 and Royal 18 B XXV', 3 vols. (Ph.D. thesis, London).

—— (1981) (ed.), *The Advent and Nativity Sermons from a Fifteenth-Century Revision of John Mirk's Festial*, MET 13 (Heidelberg).

—— (1982), 'A New Dating of John Mirk's *Festial*', *N&Q* NS 29: 487–9.

—— (1990), 'Lombards and Lollards: Late Mediaeval Bogeymen?', *MÆ* 59: 133–9.

—— (1991), 'John Mirk's *Festial* and the Pastoral Programme', *LSE* NS 22: 85–102.

—— (1994), 'The Medieval Church in the Sixteenth Century: The Post-

Reformation History of a Fourteenth-Century Sermon Collection', University of Salford, European Studies Research Institute Working Papers in Literary and Cultural Studies, 2.

—— (1997a), 'Why *Quattuor Sermones?*', in V. J. Scattergood and Julia Boffey (eds.), *Texts and their Contexts: Papers from the Early Book Society* (Dublin), 181–95.

—— (1997b), 'What Caxton did to the *Festial*', *Journal of the Early Book Society*, 1: 48–77.

—— (1997c), 'Prolegomena to a New Edition of the *Festial*', *Manuscripta*, 41: 171–84.

—— (2000), 'Preaching at Syon Abbey', *LSE* NS 31: 229–67.

—— (2003), 'St George of England: An Edition of the Sermon for St George's Day from Mirk's *Festial*', *The Ricardian*, 13: 371–83.

—— (2004), 'Mirk, John', in *ODNB*.

—— (2006), 'John Mirk's *Festial*: the Priest and his Parish', in Clive Burgess and Eamon Duffy (eds.), *The Parish in Late Medieval England*, Harlaxton Medieval Studies, 14 (Donington), 160–76.

—— (2007) (ed.), *Three Sermons for Nova Festa, together with the Hamus Caritatis*, MET 37 (Heidelberg).

—— (2009a), 'John to John: The *Manuale Sacerdotis* and the Daily Life of a Parish Priest', in Julia Boffey and Virginia Davis (eds.), *Recording Medieval Lives*, Harlaxton Medieval Studies, 17 (Donington), 112–29.

—— (2009b), 'John Audelay and John Mirk: Comparisons and Contrasts', in Susanna Fein (ed.), *'My Wyl and My Wrytyng': Essays on John the Blind Audelay* (Kalamazoo, Mich.), 86–111.

—— (forthcoming 1), '"For ho is quene of cortaysye": The Assumption of the Virgin in *Pearl* and the *Festial*', in David Matthews (ed.), *In Strange Countries: Essays in Memory of J. J. Anderson* (Manchester).

—— (forthcoming 2), 'The Nativity of the Virgin and St Katherine: Additions to John Mirk's *Festial*', *LSE* NS 42 (2011).

—— and Fletcher, Alan J. (1981 for 1980 and 1981), '"In Die Sepulture seu Trigintali": The Late Medieval Funeral and Memorial Sermon', *LSE* NS 12: 195–228.

Preest, D. (2002) (trans.), *Deeds of the Bishops of England (Gesta Pontificum Anglorum)* (Woodbridge).

Procter, Francis, and Wordsworth, C. (1879–86) (eds.), *Breviarium ad Usum Insignis Ecclesiae Sarum*, 3 vols. (Cambridge).

Quinn, E. C. (1962), *The Quest of Seth for the Oil of Mercy* (Chicago).

Rand Schmidt, Kari Anne (2001) (ed.), *The Index of Middle English Prose. Handlist XVII: Manuscripts in the Library of Gonville and Caius College, Cambridge* (Cambridge).

Raymo, Robert R. (1968), 'Works of Religious and Philosophical Instruction', in vol. 7 of Wells, J. E. (1916, 1919–51) (ed.), *Manual of the*

Writings in Middle English 1050–1500 and Supplements 1–9, rev. Burke Severs, J. and Albert E. Hartung (1967–2005) (New Haven).

Réau, L. (1955–9), *Iconographie de l'art chrétien*, 6 vols. in 3 (Paris).

Riches, Samantha (2000), *St George: Hero, Martyr and Myth* (Stroud).

Riley-Smith, Jonathan (1986), *The First Crusade and the Ideal of Crusading* (London).

Robbins, Rossell Hope (1963–4), 'Good Gossips Reunited', *British Museum Quarterly*, 27: 12–14.

—— (1970), 'Signs of Death in Middle English', *MedSt* 32: 282–98.

Roberts, Phyllis B. (1992), *Thomas Becket in the Medieval Latin Preaching Tradition: An Inventory of Sermons about St Thomas Becket* (The Hague).

Robertson, James Craigie (1875–85) (ed.), *Materials for the History of Thomas Becket, Archbishop of Canterbury*, 7 vols. (vol. 7 by J. B. Sheppard), Rolls Series, 67 (London).

Ross, W. O. (1960) (ed.), *Middle English Sermons Edited from British Museum MS. Royal 18 B. xxiii*, EETS 209

Rossi, Pietro (1981) (ed.), *Commentarius in Posteriorum Analyticorum libros* (Florence).

Rubin, Miri (1991), *Corpus Christi: The Eucharist in Late Medieval Culture* (Cambridge).

Ryan, W. G. (1993) (trans.), *Golden Legend: Readings on the Saints*, 2 vols. (Princeton).

[Salisbury, Robert Cecil, Roberts, Richard Arthur, Salisbury, Edward, and Giuseppi, M. S.] (1915) (eds.), *Calendar of the Manuscripts of the Most Honourable the Marquis of Salisbury: Preserved at Hatfield House, Hertfordshire*, 13, Historical Manuscripts Commission Series, 9 (London).

Salter, H. E. (1922) (ed.), *Chapters of the Augustinian Canons*, Canterbury and York series, 29 (London).

Sandred, K. I. (1971) (ed.), *A Middle English Version of the Gesta Romanorum Edited from Gloucester Cathedral Manuscript 22*, Studia Anglistica Upsaliensia, 8 (Uppsala).

Sargent, M. (1976), 'The Transmission by the English Carthusians of Some Late Medieval Spiritual Writings', *JEH* 27: 225–40.

Saul, Nigel (2002), *Death, Art, and Memory in Medieval England* (Oxford).

Schiller, Gertrud (1971–2). *Iconography of Christian Art*, trans. Janet Seligman, 2 vols. (London).

Scott, Kathleen (1996), *Later Gothic Manuscripts 1390–1490*, 2 vols. (London).

—— (2002), *Dated and Datable English Manuscript Borders c. 1395–1499* (London).

Scragg, D. G. (1974), *A History of English Spelling* (Manchester).

Shepherd, Geoffrey (1959) (ed.), *Ancrene Wisse* (London).

Short, Dorothy C. (1956), 'The Role of the Virgin in Giotto's Last Judgment', *Art Bulletin*, 38: 207–14.

Simmons, T. F. (1879) (ed.), *The Lay Folk's Mass Book*, EETS 71.

—— and H. E. Nolloth (1901) (ed.), *The Lay Folk's Catechism*, EETS 118.

[de Smedt, Charles] (C. D. S.) (1887) (ed.), 'Documenta de S. Wenefreda', *Analecta Bollandiana*, 6: 305–52.

Somerset, J. Alan B. (1994) (ed.), *Records of Early English Drama: Shropshire*, 2 vols. (Toronto, Buffalo, and London).

Somerset, Fiona (2004), 'Wycliffite Prose', in A. S. G. Edwards (ed.), *A Companion to Middle English Prose* (Woodbridge), 195–214.

Spalding, M. C. (1914) (ed.), *The Middle English Charters of Christ*, Bryn Mawr College Monographs, 15 (Bryn Mawr).

Sparks, H. F. D. (1984) (ed.), *The Apocryphal Old Testament* (Oxford).

Spencer, H. L. (1993), *English Preaching in the Late Middle Ages* (Oxford).

Staunton, Michael (2006), *Thomas Becket and his Biographers* (Woodbridge).

Steckman, Lillian L. (1934) (ed.), 'A Late Fifteenth-Century Festival-Book' (Ph.D. thesis, Yale University).

—— (1937), 'A Late Fifteenth-Century Revision of Mirk's Festial', *Studies in Philology*, 34: 36–48.

Steiner, Emily (2003), 'Lollardy and the Legal Document', in Fiona Somerset, Jill C. Havens, and Derrick G. Pitard (eds.), *Lollards and Their Influence in Late Medieval England* (Woodbridge), 155–74.

Stokes, G. T. (1891) (ed.), *Pococke's Tour in Ireland in 1752* (Dublin).

Stratmann, Francis Henry (1891) (ed.), rev. Henry Bradley, *A Middle-English Dictionary, containing Words used by English Writers between the Twelfth and the Fifteenth Century* (Oxford).

Sutton, Anne F. (2005), 'Caxton, the Cult of St. Winifred, and Shrewsbury', in Linda Clark (ed.), *Of Mice and Men: Image, Belief and Regulation in Late Medieval England*, The Fifteenth Century, 5 (Woodbridge), 109–26.

Swanson, R. N. (1993), *Catholic England: Faith, Religion and Observance before the Reformation* (Manchester).

Swanton, Michael (1970) (ed.), *The Dream of the Rood* (Manchester).

Thomas, E. C. (1960, 1880) (ed. and trans., re-ed. M. Maclagan), *The Philobiblon of Richard de Bury* (London).

Thomson, D. (1979) (ed.), *A Descriptive Catalogue of Middle English Grammatical Texts* (New York).

Thomson, R. M. (1989) (ed.), *Catalogue of the Manuscripts of Lincoln Cathedral Chapter Library* (Cambridge).

Thurston, Herbert, and Attwater, Donald (1956) (eds. and revs.), *Butler's Lives of the Saints*, 4 vols. (London).

Tite, C. G. C. (1984 ([1696, T. Smith]) (ed.), *Catalogue of the Manuscripts in the Cottonian Library (1696) (Catalogus librorum manuscriptorum bibliothecae Cottonianae). Reprinted from Sir Robert Harley's Copy, Annotated by Humfrey Wanley, together with Documents Relating to the Fire of 1731* (introductory essays trans. Godfrey E. Turton) (Cambridge).

Tite, C. G. C. (2003), *The Early Records of Sir Robert Cotton's Library: Formation, Cataloguing, Use* (London).

Trask, R. L. (1996), *Historical Linguistics* (London).

Tubach, Frederic C. (1969) (ed.), *Index Exemplorum: A Handbook of Medieval Religious Tales*, FF Communications, 204 (Helsinki).

Venn, John, and Venn, J. A. (1922–7) (ed.), *Alumni Cantabrigienses . . . from the Earliest Times to 1900: Part I, From the Earliest Times to 1751*, 4 vols. (Cambridge).

Vinaver, E. (1990, 1967, 1947) (ed.), *The Works of Sir Thomas Malory* (3rd edn. rev. P. J. C. Field,), 3 vols. (Oxford).

Wade-Evans, A. W. (1944) (trans.), *Vitae Sanctorum Britanniae et Genealogiae* (Cardiff).

Wakelin, M. F. (1960), 'An Edition of John Mirk's *Festial* as it is Contained in the Brotherton Collection MS.', 2 vols. (MA thesis, Leeds).

—— (1967), 'The Manuscripts of John Mirk's *Festial*', *LSE* NS 1: 93–118.

[Wanley, H., Casley, D., Hocker, W., et al.] (1808–12) (eds.), *Catalogue of the Harleian Manuscripts in the British Museum*, 4 vols. (London).

Ward, H. L. D., and Herbert, J. A. (1883–1910) (eds.), *A Catalogue of Romances in the Department of Manuscripts in the British Museum*, 3 vols. (London).

Warner, Marina (1976), *Alone of All her Sex: The Myth and the Cult of the Virgin Mary* (London).

Warren, F. E. (1911) (trans.), *The Sarum Missal*, Part 2 (London).

Warner, G. F. and Gilson, J. P. (1921) (eds.), *Catalogue of Western Manuscripts in the Old Royal and King's Collections*, 4 vols. (London).

Washburn, M. W. (1974) (ed.), 'The *Manuale Sacerdotis* of John Myrc: An Edition' (Ph.D. diss., University of Chicago).

Watson, Andrew G. (1969), *Manuscripts of Henry Savile of Banke* (London).

Weatherly, E. H. (1936 for 1935) (ed.), *Speculum Sacerdotale*, EETS 200.

Webber, Teresa (1997), 'Latin Devotional Texts and the Books of Augustinian Canons of Thurgarton Prior and Leicester Abbey in the Late Middle Ages', in James P. Carley and Colin G. C. Tite (eds.), *Books and Collectors 1200–1700: Essays Presented to Andrew Watson* (London), 27–41.

—— and Watson, A. G. (1998) (eds.), *The Libraries of the Augustinian Canons*, Corpus of British Medieval Library Catalogues, 6 (London).

Wenzel, Siegfried (1989) (ed. and trans.), *Fasciculus Morum: A Fourteenth-Century Preacher's Handbook* (University Park, Pa. and London).

—— (2005), *Latin Sermon Collections from Later Medieval England: Orthodox Preaching in the Age of Wyclif* (Cambridge).

Whiting, B. J., with Whiting, H. W. (1968), *Proverbs, Sentences, and Proverbial Phrases from English Writings Mainly before 1500* (Cambridge, Mass., and London).

Williamson, Keith (2000), 'Changing Spaces: Linguistic Relationships and the Dialect Continuum', in Irma Taavitsainen, Terttu Nevalainen, Päivi Pahta, and Matti Rissanen (eds.), *Placing Middle English in Context* (Berlin), 141–79.

Wilmart, A. (1932), *Auteurs spirituels et textes dévots du moyen âge latin* (Paris).

Wilson, Edward (1990), 'John Clerk, Author of *The Destruction of Troy*', *N&Q* NS 37: 391–6.

Wilson, E. F. (1946) (ed.), *The Stella Maris of John of Garland* (Cambridge, Mass.).

Woolf, Rosemary (1968), *The English Religious Lyric in the Middle Ages* (Oxford).

—— (1972), *The English Mystery Plays* (London).

Wormald, Francis (1936), 'The Revelation of the Hundred Paternosters: A Fifteenth-Century Meditation', *Laudate*, 14: 165–82.

Wright, Cyril Ernest (1972), *Fontes Harleiani: A Study of the Sources of the Harleian Collection of Manuscripts Preserved in the Department of Manuscripts in the British Museum* (London).

—— and Wright, Ruth C. (1966) (eds.), *The Diary of Humfrey Wanley 1715–1726*, 2 vols. (London).

Wordsworth, Christopher, and Littlehales, Henry (1904), *The Old Service-Books of the English Church* (London).

Wright, T. (1863) (ed.), *De Naturis Rerum Libri Duo (Alexander Neckam)*, Rolls Series 34, (London).

Young, Karl (1936), 'Instructions for Parish Priests', *Speculum*, 11: 224–31.

Zupitza, J. (1892), 'Die Gedichte des Franziskaners Jakob Ryman', *Archiv für das Studium der neueren Sprachen u. Litteraturen*, 89: 167–338.

Zutphen, J. P. W. M. van (1956) (ed.), *A Litil Tretys on the Seven Deadly Sins by Richard Lavynham, O. Carm.* (Rome).

THE *FESTIAL*

God, maker of alle thyng,
Be at oure begynnyng,
And ȝef vs alle hys blessyng,
And bryng vs alle to a good endyng.   5
Amen.

[Prologue]

By myne owne febul lettrure Y fele how yt faruth by othur that bene
in the same degre that hauen charge of soulus and bene holdyn to
teche hore pareschonus of alle the principale festus that cometh in the
ȝere, schewyng home what the seyntus soffreden and dedun for   5
Goddus loue, so that thay schuldon haue the more deuocion in
Goddus seyntys and wyth the better wylle com to the chyrche to
serue God and pray to holy seyntys of here help. But for mony
excuson ham by defaute of bokus and sympulnys of letture, ther`fore´
in helpe of suche mene clerkus as I am myselff I haue drawe this treti   10
sewyng owt of *Legenda Aurea* wyth more addyng to, so he that hathe
lust to study therein he schal fynde redy of alle the principale festis of
the ȝere a schort sermon nedful for hym to techy[n] and othur for to
lerne. And for this treti speketh alle of festis I wolle and pray that it be
called a *Festial*, the wyche begynnyth the forme Sonday of the Aduent   15
in worschup of God [and] of alle [the] seyntis that ben wryten therein.
Explicit prefacio.

Incipit liber qui vocatur Festial. In dei nomine. Amen.

[1 Advent]

Thys day ys kalled þe furst Sonday yn þe Aduent, þat ys, Sonday in   f. 4ʳ
Crystes comyng. Wherfore þ[ys] day Holy Chyrch makyth mencyon
of tw`o´ comynges of Crist. þe furst comyng of Crist, [God]es Sone of   5
heuen, was to bye monkynd out of þe deles bondage and to bryng alle

Prayer   2–6 God . . . Amen] *in red textura*   2 God] G- *in blue, dec., 3 ll. deep*
   Prologue   2–17 By . . . *prefacio*] *in red textura*   2 By] B- *in blue, dec.*   9 fore] *in*
red   13 techyn] techym   16 and] *om.*   the] *om.*
   [1]   assit principio sancta maria meo *in top margin with red paraph*   1 *Incipit* . . .
Amen] *in red textura*   3 Thys] T- *in red and blue, dec., 6 ll. deep*   4 þys] þe
5 two] -o *above* t-   5 Crist, Godes] cristes

gode doeres into þe blysse þat euer schal last. And `of` hys oþur comyng: þat schal ben at þe day of dome for to deme `alle` wykked doeres into þe put of helle for euermore.

10 But þe furst comyng of Crist into þys world brogh ioy and blysse wyth hym. þerfor Holy Chyrch vseth summe songes of melody as Alleluia and oþur. And for þe secunde comyng of Crist to þe dome schal be `so` cruel and so yrus þat no tonge may telle, þerfor Holy Chyrch layth doun somme songes of melody and of murth, as Te 15 Deum laudamus, Gloria in excelsis. And also weddyng[es], for aftur þat day schal neuer weddyng ben more. þus Holy Chyrch leyth doun songes of melody byfore, in tokenyng of vengians þat schal come aftur.

þen of þe furst comyng of Crist into þis world þus seth Seint 20 Austyn: 'þer ben', hee seth, 'þre þyngys þat ben ryvot in þis world—burth, trauel and deth.' þys is þe testament þat Adam oure fadur made to al hys ofspryng aftur hym, þat `ys` to be boren in seknes, for to lyuon in trauayl, and for to dyen in drede. But Crest, blessed be he, come to be excecutour of þys testament and was boren, trauayled and 25 dyed. He was bore for to bryng men out of seknes into erlastyng hele; he trauayled to bryng mon to erlastyng rest; he was ded to bryng mon into erlastyng lyf þat neuer schal haue ende. þis was þe cause of þe furst comyng of Crist.

þerfor he þat wol voyde þe perel and þe myschyf of þe secunde 30 comyng to þe dome he mot legge doun al maner of pride and hyghnes of hert and know hymself a wrech and slym of þe erþe, and so holde f. 4ᵛ mekenes | in hys herte. He mote trauayle hys body in gode werkes and geten hys lyflode wyth swynk of hys body and put away al ydulnes and slowth, for he þat wol not trauayl hire wyth men, as seyth Seynt 35 Bernard, he schal travayl euer `wyth` fendes of helle. And for drede of deth he mot maken hym redy to hys God when he wol sende aftur hym, þat ys to saye, scryve hym of alle `his` synnes þat ben in hys concyens, not for to abyde fro ȝer to ȝere, but also sone as he feleth hymself in synne to scryve hym and mekely take þe dom of hys scryf-40 fadur.

þen schal he haue at þe `day of` dom gret worschep. For ryght as a knyght schowuet þe wondes þat he hadde in batel in moch comendyng to hym, ryght so alle þe synnes þat a mon hath scryuen hym of and taken hys penans fore schul ben þer schewet to moch honour and 45 worschep to hym and moch confucyoun to þe fynd. And þyke þat he

15 weddynges] weddyng

hath not scryven hym of schul ben schewet to al þe worde in gret
confusyon and schame to hym. þys ys seyde for þe furst comyng of
Cryst into þe worde.

The secunde comyng of Crist to þe dom schal be ʻsoʼ cruel, fereful
and orribul þat þer schal come byfore fyftene tokenes of gret drede, so 50
þat, by þe euedens of þe tokenes komyng byfore, a mon may knowe in
party þe grede horribylyte and drede þat schal come at þe dom aftur.

þe furst day, as seth Seyn[t] Ierom, þe see schal ryson vp in h[u]re
stude, þat þe watur schal ben herre þen any hul by fowrty kubytes,
stondyng stylle in hure stude as hyt ʻwereʼ a wal. þe secunday þe see 55
[schal] falle adoun aȝeyn, so þat onneth heo schal ben seyn. þe þrydde
day alle þe see-swyn and gloppes of þis ʻseeʼ schul stondyn on þe see
and makyn a roryng and a noyse so hydewys þat no mon may telle hyt
but God. þe forth day þe see and alle wateres schal bren. þe fythe day
trees and herbes ʻschulʼ swete blod and alle foules schul come togedur 60
and neyþur ete ne drynk | for drede of þe dom comyng. þe sexte day f. 5ʳ
alle byldyngus and castellus schul fallen down to gronde and an
horrybyl fure schal ryson at þe sonne goyng doun and bren tylle þe
rysyng of þe sonne aȝeyn. þe seveʻneʼth day alle stones and roches
schal vchon breken oþer and bete togedur wyth an hydewys noyse, þe 65
whech noyse God hymself schal know and vndurstond. þe eghte day
þe erþe schal quake so orrybuly þat þer schal no mon stonde on hyt
but falle to gronde. þe ix day alle hullus and [mowntayns schal turne
into powdyr and] þe erþe schul be made playne and euen. þe x day
men schul gon owt of hure dennes and gon as þey were myndles, and 70
neuer on schal speke to oþur. þe xj day alle þe bones of dede men
schul ryse and stonde vpon hure graue, and þat day alle graues schul
opon. þe xij day sterres schul falle fro heuen and scheton out of ham
brenyng lemes, and also bestes schul come ʻinʼto þe feldes roryng and
cryng and schal neyþur ete ne drynke. þe xiij day alle men schal dye 75
for te ryse wyth ʻham þatʼ ben ded byfore. þe xiiij day heuen and erþe
schal bren so orribuly þat no mon may telle. þe xv day heuen and erþe
schul be made new, and alle men, wymmen ʻandʼ chyldre schul ʻryseʼ
vp in þe age of þrytte ȝere and come to þe dome.

þen schal Ihesu Crist, very God and mon, come to þe dome wyth 80
hys angeles and schewe hys wondes, fresch and new bledyng as þat
day þat he dyed on þe cros. And þer schal þe cros be al blody, þe
spere, þe scorges, þe nayles and alle þe instrumentes of hys passyon.

49 The] T- *in blue, dec.*, 2 *ll. deep*   53 Seynt] seyng   hure] harre   56 schal¹]
om.   59–61 þe¹ . . . comyng] *4th and 5th days trs.*   68–9 mowntayns . . . and¹] *om.*

þen sory may þey ben þat han be wond to swere by hys hert and oþur
85 lymes of God. þat schal ben a grete repryf and gret confusyon to ham
but `þey´ ben mended þerof in þis world. þen, lo, Crist schal heygly
þonken hame and prayson ham þat han don mercy to hure euen-
criston and wol saye to ham þus: 'My Fadyr blessed chylderen,
comeht to me. Reseyveth þe kyngdom of my Fadur þat ys ordeynot to
90 3ow fro þe bygynnyng. For `when Y was hongery ye fed me´, when Y
f. 5ᵛ was þursty 3e 3eue me drynke, and | so alle þe werkus of mercy. For
when 3e dude to any of myne, 3e dude to me, and þus for my loue 3e
dude `hit´ to me. For when 3e dude to þe lest of myne, 3e dude to me.'
þen schal he horybuly rebuke rych `men´ þat han don no mercy and
95 say to ham spytusly þus: 'Go, 3e cursed leftes, into þe peyne of helle.
For when Y was hungery 3e 3af me no mete', *et cetera, vt in euangelio.*
þen woo may þey ben þat Crist Ihesu þus schal rebuke. þer schal no
pledur helpe, ne no gold ne seluer ne non oþur 3yftes, but as a mon
hath don he schal haue. þer schal bee dyuers accusoures aboven hym,
100 wythinne hym, on eyþur sydes hym and vndur hym, þat he schal no
way schape. Aboven hym schal be Crist Ihesu, hys domus-man, so
wroght þat þer con no tonge telle, for `he´ dede no mercy. Wythinne
hym hys owne conscyens accusyng hym of þe leste þoght þat euer he
dede amys. Hys angel on þe ryght syde tellyng hym redyly where,
105 whenne and how ofte he hath don amys. On þe oþur syde fendus
chalangyng hym heres as by ryght for hys wyked dedes. Vndur hym
helle 3onyng and galpyng to swolewe ham þat ben evel and spyttyng
out fyre and stench. þoo þat ben `fond´ evel þat day þer schal ben in
payne and woo wythout ende.
110 þat day of dome pore men schul sytte in dom wyth Crist and deme
þe rich, for þe woo and þe dese[s]e þat pore mon han ys by rych men,
for, þagh þey han mych wrong, þay mowe geton non amendes tyl þay
come to þat dome þer þey schul haue alle hure owne wylle of ham.
For `whan´ þey han wronge, þey may gete non amendes but pray `to´
115 God ful hertefully to quyte ham at þe day of dome, and so wold he ful
well and trewly. For God seyth: 'Keputh 3owre vengeans to me and Y
wol quite.' þerfor whyl 3e ben here, makes amendus fore 3owre euel
dedus and makes ham 3owre frendes þat schal be 3owre domus-men at
þe day of dome and truste not to ham þat cometh aftur 3ow leste 3e
120 ben bygyled. Dredeth þe peyne þat schal last euer wythout ende.
Seyn[t] Bede telleth þat þer was an husbond-mon here in Englon
þat fel seke and lay as ded fro þe euentyde tyl þe morwoo. þen he

aroos and departed hys gode in þre partees. And hys parte he ȝaf to
pore men, and ȝede and was maked a monk in an abbey þat stod vpon
a wateres syde, into þe whech | watur vch nyght he ȝede, were hyt   f. 6ʳ
neuer so cold, and stod þerin long tyme of þe nyght. And whan he was   126
asked why he put hymself into so mich peyne, he sayde: to eschew þe
more peyne þat he hade seyn. And he ete barly bred and dronk watur
al hys lyf aftur and telles to relygyous men þe payne þat he segh, þat
was so gret þat he couthe not telly hyt opynly. He sayde þat a angel   130
ladde hym into `a´ place þer, on þe on syde, was such a colde þat no
tong myght telle þe peyne þerof. On þe oþur syde was so grete hete
þat no mon myght telle þe peyne þerof, and soules were kast out of þe
on into þe oþur. And so þe [angel] schowed hym þe fyre þat come out
of helle þat was so whot þat, al so fer as he myght see hyt, hym þoght   135
he brend for hete. And in þe lame þerof he segth soules bulmen vp
and doun, crying and waylyng for woo and sorwe, and horybul noyse
of fyndus crying: 'Sle, sle, sle. Sle, sle, sle! Put on `þe´ broch, rost
hote, kast into þe cawdren, seth fast in pych and kode and brenston
and hote led!'   140

þus þen þey þat ben dampned to helle
Ste[n]ton neuer to crye and ȝelle.
Woe ys hym þat þydur schal g[o—
God hymself scheld vs þerfro—
And bryng vs to þe blysse he boght vs to. Amen.]   145

[2] *De sancto Andrea apostolo*

Gode men, ȝe schul haue sech a day Seynt Andrewes Day and fast þe
evon, þe qwhech day ȝe schul come `to´ God and Holy Chyrch to see
þi God and do worschep to þis holy seynt, specyaly for þre virtues þat
he hadde. Won for he hadde gret holynes and was holy in lyuyng, þe   5
secunde for gret myracules doyng, þe þrydde for gret passyon
suffryng.
   He was a mon of holy lyuyng. For when he herde of Se[yn]t Ion
Ba[p]tyst preched in desert[e], he laft alle hys worly ocupacyoun and
ȝede to hym and was hys dyscypul. þen fel hyt hopon a day þat Crist   10
come walkyng. And when Seynt Ion seth hym walkyng, he sayde to

134 angel] *om.*   142 Stenton] steton   143 go] gg   144–5 God . . . Amen] *om.*
[2] 2 Gode] G- *in blue, dec., 2 ll. deep*   8 Seynt] senyt   9 Baptyst] bastyst
deserte] deserto

f. 6ᵛ hys dyscypeles: 'Lo, | ȝont ys Goddes lombe þat schal don away þe
sunne of þe world.' And [when] Seynt Andrew herde þat, anon he
lefte Seynt Ion and sewed Crist.

And when he herde Cryst prechen,
15 he lykud [hyt] so wel þat he fette Seynt Petre, hys brother, to Cryst to
here his prechyng. And `þen´ þey bothe kaston such a love to Crist
þat, on a day sone aftur, as þey weren in þe See of Galelye fyschyng,
Cryst com by ham and kalled ham. þan þey bothe anon laften hure
schyp and hure nettes and al þat þey hadden and sewed forth Cryst
20 euer tyl he stegh into heuen.

And when he was goo into heuen, Andrew preched þe worde of
God to þe pepul, amonk þe whech was on called Nycol þat hadde
lyvet syxty wyntur and more in lecchery. But by þe grace of God hee
þoght to mende hys lyf and lette wryte a gospel and hadde hyt `wyth´
25 hym, hopyng þat þe vertu of Goddes worde schulde put away
temptacyon. And so, by þe vertu of Goddus word, he abstened
hym of hys synne a whyle. But ȝete, by entysyng [of] þe fynde, on a
day he forȝet hymself and ȝede to þe bordel-hous, as he was woned.
And when he come þydur, þe wemen cryed on hym and sayde:
30 'Onsely olde mon, go ham, for Y se on þe mony merueles!'

þen þis Nycol byþoght hym þat he hadde þe gospel of God vpon
hym, and anon he ȝode to Seynt Andraw and tolde hym alle þe cas
and prayde hym to pray to God for hym þat hys sowle were not lore.
þan Seynt Andraw sayde þat he wolde neyþur ete ne drynk tyl he
35 wyst wheþur he schulde be savot or dampnet. þanne he faste fyve
dayes, prayng bysyle for hym. þenne at þe fyve dayes ende þer come a
voys to hym and sayde: 'Andraw, ryght as þou has fasted and prayed,
so make Nycol to don, and þen he schal be saff.' þen he called Nycol
to hym and bad hym faste fowrty dayes bred and watur and praye
40 bysyly to God, and so dede he. And whan þe fourty dayes were don,
sone aftur þis Nycol dyed. þan þer come a voys to Andraw and sayde:
'By þy prayere Y haue wonne Nycol, þat was ylost.'

Also a ȝong mon cam to Seynt Androw and priuyly sayde to hym:
'Syre, my modur hath soght me longe to lygge by hure. And for Y
45 wolde not do hure wylle, heo hath acused me to þe iustyse. Wherefore
wel Y wot Y schal be ded, and ȝet Y haue leuer take þe deth þan so
f. 7ʳ foule sclandere my modur. | Wherefore, syre, for þe loue of God,
praye for me þat Y may take my deth mekely.' þanne sayde Seynt
Andraw: 'Sone, go forth to þy dome and Y wol goe wyth þe.' þenne

13 when] *om.*   15 hyt] *om.*   27 of²] *om.*   43 Also] A- *in blue, dec., 2 ll. deep,*
narracio *in margin with red paraph*

anon come men and fatten hym to þe iustyse. And whan hys modur 50
accused hym stufly, he huld hys tong and sayde nothyng. þan
answered Seynt Andrew and sayde to þe modur: 'þou wyked
wommen, þat for lust of þy lechery art abowte to do þi sone to
deth. Vengyans wol falle vpon þe!' þen sayde heo to þe iustyse: 'Syre,
sethon my son myght not do þis horybul dede þat he wold haue don, 55
he hath drawe to þis mon for sokur.' þen þe iustyse commanded to
putte þe sone in a feet and kast hym into a watur to drowne, and
Androw into prison tyl he were avysot on what deth he schuld slee
hym. þen Seynt Androwe prayed to God bysyly to helpe hym. þan
anon com a hydeus þondur þat maked alle aferd þat were þer and 60
were fayn to fach Andraw out of prison. And þerwyth com a bolt of
leeyt and forbren þe modur in syght of alle men. And þus he saued þis
mon fro deth and turned þe iustyse and alle þe pepul to þe feyth of
Crist. Herby ȝe mon vndurstonde þat he was a mon of holy lyuyng.

He was also gret in myracules worchyng. For on a day, as he walked 65
vpon þe see-warth, he seygh a drownot mon cast out of þe watur. þan
he prayed to God for to reysen hym to lyve. þan anon þis body aros to
lyve. And when he was reysed to lyue, Seynt Androw asked hym how
he was drownot. þen he answered and sayd þus: 'We weren fourty
ȝong men yfere and herden of an holy mon þat was in þis contre and 70
woldon han gon to hym to ha herde of hys prechyng. But when we
weron in þe see, a tempas come on vs and dround ous alle togedre. But
wold God þat we hadden alle be cast vp yfere þat we myght ha ben alle
yreysed yfere.' þen, at þe prayere of Seynt Androw, alle þe bodyes
were cast to londe on dyuers partees. þen Seynt Androw maked for to 75
gedre hom togedre and knelud adoun, prayng longe for ham tyl heo
weron reysed alle. þanne Seynt Androw preched ham þe feyth of
Crist and followod ham alle. And whan þay were studfast in þe fayth,
he sende ham | hom to hure contre aȝeyn wyth much ioye and murth. f. 7ᵛ
Mony oþur miraculus he dede þat were to long to telle, but herby ȝe 80
may know þat he was myghti in worchyng of myraclus, þat þus reysed
fourty drounet bodyes yfere.

Also he suffred gret passyon for Crystes loue. For when he was in
'þe' cyty of Patras, he turned to þe feyth þe wyf of þe iustyse þat was
kalled Eggeas. He maked men to do mawmentry, þat ys, to offre to 85
fyndes. But for Seynt Andrew reprevet hym þerof, anon he maked to
taken hym and wold haue 'hadde' hym to haue do þe same. But he

58 into . . . avysot] *ink faded*   61 And] þan and *add.*   65 narracio *in margin with*
red paraph   71 ha] *foll. by eras.*

studfastly ȝeynstod hym and preved by mony resenes þat he and alle
men schulde worschep God almyghty and not þe fynd of helle. þan
90 Egeas wax wod for wrath and made men to take Androw and strype
hym naked and bete hym wyth scorges þat alle hys bode ran on blod.
And aftur he commandet to bynde hym fett and hond and don hym of
a cros, for he schulde payne long or he dyed. But whan Seynt Androw
com to þe place þer þe cros was, he kneled adow and sayde: 'Heyle be
95 þou cros, þat art mad holy by þe presyous body of Cryst! On þe
hanget my mayster Ihesu Cryst. Y worschep þe wyth al myn hert, Y
desyre to cluppe þe. Wherefore now take me to þe and ȝeld me to my
mayster þat dyed of þe.' `He´ stod vp and dede of hys cloþus and ȝaf
`ham´ to þe turmentures, and bad ham do as þey were charget of þe
100 iustyse. þanne þey bond hym to þe cros hond and foot, so harde and
strayt þat þe blod wrast out at vch a kutte. þus he hanget on þe cros
too dayes olyve prechyng þe pepul, so þat þer come to hys prechyng
mony þowsand of folk.

And for rewthe þat þey hadden of hym, þey bede Egeas do hym
105 doun of þe cros or ellys þey wold sle hym. þanne for fere of þe pepul
he com to haue take hym doun. þan Seynt Androw ȝaynstod and
seyde: 'Egeas, wyte þou wel þat þou schalt haue no myght to take me
downe, for here Y wol dyen on þis cros.' þen þer com a gret lyght, so
þat þer myght no mon see hym half an owre, and in þat lyght he ȝaf
f. 8ʳ vp | þe gost. þus when Egeas segh þat he was ded, he ȝode homward.
111 þan aftur þe way he wax wod, and sone aftur among alle men he starf
in þe way. And when Maximilla hys wyf herde þerof, anon heo made
for to take Seynt Androwes body and byryed hyt in a tombe, out of þe
whych tombe manna and oyle welleth out togedre, so þat men of þat
115 contre may know whenne þey schal haue derth and when gret cheppe.
For when hyt schal be dere, hyt welleth schaffly, and wen hyt schal be
gret chep, hyt welleth plente ynogh.

Aftur hyt fel þat þer was a byschop þat loued wel Seynt Androw so
þat alle þyng þat he dede he comendet hyt to God `and´ to Seynt
120 Androw. þen for þe deuel myght no way put hym out of þus purpos,
he come `to´ þys byschop in lykenes of a fayre womon, prayng hym
þat scho myght speke wyth hym in scryfte, [and h]e granted. þan heo
bygan þus: 'Syre,' heo sayde, 'Y am a kyngus doghtur and haue ben
chyr[s]lych noryschet. But for Y see þat þe wele of þus world ys but a
125 floure, Y vowet castyte. And when my fadur wolde haue maryed me to

118 narracio *in margin in the long hand*   121 lykenes] -ke- *over eras.*   122 and he]
be   124 chyrslych] chyrlych

a gret prince, for Y wold not brek my vowe, priuyly in a nyght Y stalle
away in pore wede. And when Y herde of ʒoure gret holynes, Y drogh
to ʒow to haue helpe of ʒow, consel and sokur. Werefor, syre, Y praye
ʒow þat ʒe ordeyne so for me þat Y may be holpon, þat þe fynde haue
no power to lette me of my purpus.' þen þe byschop confordet hure 130
and bad heo schulde haue trust in God, for hee þat hadde set so hegh a
purpos in hure hert wold ʒeu hure grace wyth. 'But þus day ʒe schul
ete wyth me, and aftur mete we schul by gode avyse ordeyne so for
ʒow þat `ʒe´ schul be wel holpon.' 'Nay, syre,' sayde scho, 'not so, lest
men wolde haue suspecyon of euel.' 'ʒe, þerof no charge,' sayde þe 135
byschop, 'for we schul be so fely in company þat þer schal no
suspecyoun be of mys.'

þan scho gentyly þonked hym, and was set in a chyere byfore þe
byschop at þe mete. But euer when þe byschop lokot vpon hure, hym
þoght hure so fayre þat he was so tempted vpon hure þat he hadde 140
nygh forʒeton hymself. þenne anon com þer a pylgrym to þe ʒate and
be[t] hopon þe ʒate so harde þat alle þat weren in þe halle weren
astoned. þen sayde þe byschop: 'Dame, schal þys mon comen yn or
no?' 'Syre,' sayde scho, 'furst let hym onswere to a questyon and
þanne let hym come in.' 'Dame,' sayde þe byschop, 'make ʒe þys 145
questyon, for we ben onavysed as now.' 'þan', say scho, 'let asken
hym what ys þe graste myracule þat euer God made in a fote of
erþe?' | þan when `þe´ pylgrym was asked þus, he answred and sayde: f. 8ᵛ
'A monnes faas, þat ys erþe, and but a monnes owne fote. For þagh
alle `þe´ men and wemmen þat euer were bore stode yfere, me schul 150
knowe on by anoþur by sum degre.' When he hadde made þys
onsw`e´re, he [was] gretly comendet for hys wyse onswere.

þanne sayde heo: 'For Y see he `ys´ wys, byd hym make anoþur
onswere. Aske hym where þe erþe ys herre þan heuene.' þan when
þys pylgrym was asked þys, he sayde: 'þeras Cryst ys bodyly. For 155
Crystes body ys of oure kynde, and oure kynde ys erþe. þerfor, þeras
Cristys body ys, þer þe erþe ys herre þan heuene, for Cryst ys herre
þen heuene.' When he hadde make þys onswere, he was wel alowet
and was bede comen in.

þen heo sayde: 'ʒet let hym as[o]yle þe þyrde questyon and þen let 160
hym come in. Aske hym how fer ys fro heuen to helle.' þen when he
was apposut of þys, he onswered and sayde to þe messanger: 'Go
aʒayn', he sayde, 'to hure þat syt byfore þe byschop in þe cheyre and
byd hure make þus onswere, for heo can bettur þen Y, for heo ys a

142 bet] bed   152 was] *om.*   159 bede] *partly er.*   160 asoyle] aseyle

165 fynde and hath met hyt, and so dude Y neuer—scho fell doun wyth
Lucyfer.' þen when þe messenger herde þys, he was al heuy, but ʒet
he made onswere þat alle mygtonn heron. þen anon þys fynd
vanysched away wyth a horybul stench.
þen þys byschop byþoght hym of hys temptacyon and was sory in
170 hys hert, and anon maked sende aftur þe pylgrym. But by þat þe
menssenger come to þe ʒate, þe pylgrym was gon. þen þe byschop
maked alle men to praye to God to sende wyttyng wahat þys pylgrym
was þat so godly hadde holpe hym in hys nede. þen þer com a voys to
hym and sayde hyt was Seynt Androw þen com forte sokur hym for
175 þe gode loue and seruyce þat he dude to hym, and bad hym bywar in
tyme comyng and preche þat to þe pepul in helpe of hure soules.

[3] De sancto Nicholao episcopo

Seche a day ʒe schal haue Seynt Nicholas day. He ys mych praysed in
Holy Chyrch for þre þynges specyaly: for hys mek lyuyng, for hys
heuenly chesyng, for hys gret compasyon hauyng.
5   He was of mek lyuyng. For we reden he hadde a fadur þat `was´
kalled Ephifanus and a modur þat was kalled Iohanna, þe qwech in
hure ʒowþe geton Seynt Nicholas. And when he was boren, þey
avoweden chastyte and deleden no more togedre, but hulde hem
payed vpon þys on chyld, þe whech þey maket for to crystene, and
f. 9ʳ wol[de] not kalle hym Nychol, þat ys | a mones name, but Nycholas,
11   þat ys a chyldes name, so þat al hys lyf-dayes he hadde þe name of a
chyld and þe vertues wyth, þat ys to say mekenes, sympulnes, and
wythout malys.
Also, whyl he was in hys kradul, he faste Whednesday and Fryday,
15   `þe´ whech dayes he wolde soke but ones in þe day and so halde hym
payed. And for he hulde forth þese vyrtues al hys lyf wyth his chyldes
name, ʒet chyldren doth hym worschyp specyaly byfore any oþur
seynt. þus al hys lyf-dayes he lyued so mekely and sympuly and so
wythout malys þat alle pepul hym loued and preysed hym for hys
20   meke lyuyng.
He was also by a voys þat come fro heuen choson to be byschop of
þe cyty of Myrre. For when þe byschop of þat cyte was ded, þe
byschopes of þe contre comen togedre to chese anoþur byschop. þen
com þer a voys to on of ham, þat was chyf of ham, and bede hym go

[3] 2 Seche] S- *in blue, dec., 2 ll. deep*   10 wolde] wol

erly on þe morwe to þe chyrch-dore and make hym byschop þat he 25
fond þere: 'and ys kalled Nycholas'. On þe morwe þys byschop was
erly vppe and ʒode to þe chyrch-dore, and fond þer Nycholas redy,
and sayde to hym: 'What ys þi nomen?' þen he, [as he] was ful meke,
mekely onswered and s[ay]de: 'Syre,' loutyng wyth hys hed, 'Nycholas, seruand to ʒoure holynes.' þen sayde þe byschop: 'Come, sone, 30
wyth me, for Y haue to speke wyth þe in priuyte', and ladde hym to þe
oþur byschoppes and sayde: 'Lo, syres, here he ys þat God hath
ordeyned to vs.' And so þey t[o]ken hym and sacred hym byschop.
þus was he mad byschop by heuenly chosyng.
He hadde alleso gret compacyon of alle þat weren in desese and 35
woo. For when hys fadur and hys modur were ded both, þey laften
hym worldes good ynoght, þe wheche he spende vpon hem þat were
nedy. þenne fel hyt so þat þer was a ryche mon þat hadde þre
doghteren, ʒonge fayre wymen, but by myschep he was fallen into
such pouerte þat for gret nede he ordeyned hys doghteren to be 40
comyn wymen and so to geton hure lyuyng and hys boþe. But qwen
Nycholas herde þerof, he hadde gret compassyon of hem. And on a
nyght priuyly at a wyndow he cast in `a´ bagge wyth a summe of gold
into þe monnes chambre. þenne in þe morw-tyde þys mon ros and
fond þys gold. He was so glad þat no mon cowde telle, and wyth þat 45
gold anon he maryed hys eldest doghtur. þen on anoþur nyght
Nycholas cast anoþur summe of gold into þe monnes chambur as
he dede byfore. | And so þe þrydde tyme tyl þey were alle maryed. f. 9ᵛ
But þe þrydde nyght, whan þys mon herde þys gold fallen, anon he
ʒede out and or-tok Nycholas and knewe þat hyt was he þat hadde so 50
holpe hym in hys myschef, and kneled adown and wolde ha cussed
hys feet. He wold not suffre [hym], but prayed hym to kepe consel
whyle he lyued.
Also anoþur tyme men weren in þe see in despeyre of hure lyf,
cryng to Seynt Nycholas for helpe. þen anon he com to ham, goyng 55
on þe watur, and sayde to ham: 'Loo, Y am redy at ʒoure kallyng', and
holp ham so þat þey com sonne to þe hauen.
Also þat tyme was þer such a derthe of corn and a hongur in al þat
contre þat al nygh spylled for defaut. þen hyt happed so þat þer
commyn schyppes of þe emperoures, fretted wyth whete, into þe 60
hauon. þan wente Seynt Nycholas to ham, praying ham to grante hym
of vch schyp a hundred buschel of whete for to releue þe pepul wyth,

28 as he] *om.*   29 sayde] syade   33 token] taken   41 comyn] *foll. by one-*
letter eras.   52 hym¹] *om.*

and he wolde vndurtake þat þey schulde wonte ryght noght of here
mete when þey comen hom. þan he `hadde´ hys askyng. And when
65 þese chypmen comen hom, þey hadden hure ful mete and wontud
noþyng. And þat corn þat Seynt Nycholas hadde þorgh hys holy
preyre was of so gret plente and vertu þat hyt fond alle þe pepul to
eton and to sowen ynoȝgh to ȝere aftur.

þre knygtes also weren empeched to þe emperour of traytury by
70 fals suggestyon and weron comandet to prison for to han ben slayn þat
nyght. But for þese knyghtus [were] wepyng and criyng to Seynt
Nycholas for helpe, he com þat nyght to þe emperour as he was in
bedde and sayde þys to hym: 'Why hast þou so wrongfully ydampned
þese knyghtes to deþe? Ryse vp anon and make for te delyuere hem,
75 or ellys Y wol praye to my God to reyse batel aȝeynus þe, in þe whech
þou schalt be ded and bestus schul ete þe.' þen sayde þe emperour:
'What art þou þat spekust so boldly to me?' 'I am', he sayde,
'Nicholas, þe byschop of Myrre.' þen was þys emperour afrayed, so
þat anon he sende aftur þe knyghtes to hym and sayde þus: 'What
80 wychecraft konne ȝe þat han trowbolud me so þus nyght? Knowe ȝe a
mon þat hette Nycholas, byschop of Myrre?' þen when þey herden
hys name, anon þey fellon to þe gronde on kneus and hulde vp `hure´
hondes, þonkyng God and Seynt Nycholas. And when þey hadde
tolde þe emperour of hys lyf, he bad hem go to hym and þonke hym
85 here lyf and praye hym heghly þat he schulde þrete hym no more so
f. 10ʳ but praye to God for hym `and´ for hys reme, and so duden. | þus ȝe
mon see þat he hadde gret compassyon vpon alle þat weren in dissese.

þen aftur when he wyste þat he schulde dye, he prayed God to
sende hym angelus and fache hys soule. And when he segh þe angelus
90 comen, he lowted to hem wyth hys hedde and sayde: *In manus tuas,
domine, commendo spiritum meum*, and so ȝold vp þe gost. And when he
was buryed, at þe hed of hys tombe sprong a wele of oyle þat dude
medicyne to alle seke. þen felle hyt so þat, mony ȝere aftur, Turkus
stryed þe cyte of Myrre þer Seynt Nycholas lay. And when men of þe
95 cyte of Barus herdon þat, seuen and fourty knyghtes wyth here helpes
ordeyned hom schyppus and ȝoden þydur. And `when´ þey comen
þydur, by tellyng of foure monkus þat weren laft þere þey knewen hys
tombe. And anon þey vnduden hyt and fonden hys bones swymyng in
oyle, and tokun ham vp and broghton ham into þe cyty of Bares wyth
100 mycul ioye and murthe.

þen aftur for gret myracles þat weren ywroght þere when Seynt

71 were] *om.*   80 trowbolud] -bo- *over eras.*   101 miraculum *in margin*

Nycholas was ded, anoþur good mon was chosun to be byschop in hys stede. þen aftur by envye of euel men he was put out of hys byschoprych. And þen `anon´ þe oyle cesed of rennyng out. þenne was he called aȝeyn to hys degre, and þen anon þe oyle sprang out as hyt dude byfore. 105
Also a crystene mon borewed a certeyn summe of gold at a Iewe. þe Iewe sayde [h]e wold lene non but he hadde a borgh. He sayde he hadde non but Seynt Nycholas. þan þe Iewe granted to take Seynt Nycholas to borgh. So þe cristene mon swere vpon þe `auter of´ Seynt 110 Nycholas þat `he´ wolde trewly paye hym aȝayn. þen þey wente forth and þe day of þe payment of þe money passed. þe Iew þanne asked þe cryston mon why he payed not hym hys money as he made connande. And he onswered and sayde he hadde payed hym vch peny, and he sayde nay. þe odur sayde he hadde payed, and þerto he wold don hys 115 lawe. þanne þys crysten mon made hym a holwe staf and put þe gold þerin and wente to do hys lawe. When he wold do hys lawe, he bytoke þe Iewe hys staf to holde whyle he swere. When he hadde don, he tok hys staf aȝeyn and wente homward. And as he wente by þe way, he was slepy and lay don and slept in þe way. þenne com a c[ar]t and 120 went ouer hym and slogh hym, and brak hys staf, and þe gold | fel f. 10ᵛ out. þoo men seen hyt was vangans for hys falshede and kalled þe Iew and bad hym take hys gold þer. He was sory and sayde he wold not but Seynt Nycholas wolde praye for to ryse hym to lyf. þan he wold be crystenet and leuen `on´ crysten feyth. And so by þe prayere of 125 Seynt Nycholas þe ded mon ros vp, and þen þe Iewe was crystenet by euedens of þys miracle.
Also a Iewe seygh þe grete myght of Seynt Nycholas by myracles worchyng and lette mak a ymage of Seynt Nycholas and sette in hys sch[o]ppe among hys good and bad hym kepe wel hys `good´ whyle he 130 wcre fro home or ellus he schulde ful dere abye. þen he wente out of þe towne. So when he was gon forth, comen þefus and stelon his good and beren hyt away. So when þys Iewe was comen hom and fond hys good ystolon, he was ful wrogh wyth Seynt Nycholas and toke a scorge and beet þys ymage of Seynt Nic`h´olas, as hyt hadde be Seynt 135 Nycholas hymself, and þus spak to hym: 'Y to[ke] þe my gode `to kepen, Nycholas, for gret trust þat Y hadde in þe, and þus´ þou hast þus foule seruet me. þou schalt abye hyt vche day tyl þou haue broght my good aȝeyn.' þenne as þe þefus weren yfere for te departe þus

140 stole good, com Seynt Nycholas to hem and sayde: 'See how ȝe han
maket me beton for þys good', and schewet ham hys sydus al blody.
'Go', seyde he, 'and bereth þys good aȝeyn, or ellus Goddus vengans
schal fallun vpon owe and 'ȝe' schul be honget vchon.' þenne sayden
þey to hym: 'Who art þou þat þretus vs þus?' þan sayde he: 'Y am
145 Nycho, Goddus seruant, þat þys Iewe bytok hys good to kepun.' þen
weren þey so afert þat anon þe same nyght þey beren aȝeyn alle þus
good. þenne on þe morwe when þys Iewe segh hys good broght hol
aȝeyn, anon he tok folþe and wes aftur a trewe cryston mon.

A mon for þe loue of a sone þat he hadde, clerke, he made euery
150 ȝere a fest of Seynt Nycholas. On a tyme þe fadur made a fest and
beed mony clerkus þerto. þen com þe deuel to þe ȝate in þe maner of
a pylgrym and askud sum good. þe fadur beed hys sone ȝeue þe
pylgrym almes. þe chylde wente to þe dore and þe pylgrym was gon.
þenne þe chyld folewed aftur. þen he caght þe chyld and strangulym.
155 When þe fadur herde, he was ful sory. He tok þe chyld and leyd hym
in hys chambre, crying for sorwe, and seyed: 'A, Seynt Nycholas, ys
f. 11ʳ þys þe hyre þat Y schal | haue for þe worschip þat Y do to þe?' Anon
wyth þat þe chylde ros vp, as hyt hadde be fro slep.

Also a mon prayed ' to' God and to Seynt Nycholas to ȝeue hym a
160 chyld and he wold lede þe chyld to hys chyrch and schuld offre þerre a
coppe of gold. þe chyld was boren, and he lette make þe coppe. When
hyt was mad, hyt was so fayre þat he lette make anoþur. þen he went
forth wyth þe chyld toward Seynt Nycholas chyrch ouer þe see. þen
in þe see þe fadur bed hys chylde: 'Take þe coppe and cleche watur.'
165 þe chyld went forth and stowpud doune rechelasly. þe coppe fel out
of hys hond, and he wold haue caght hyt aȝeyn and fel aftur and was
drownet. þe fadur mad much sorwe, but ȝet he went forth wyth þe
odur coppe to do hys pylgrimage. And when he wold 'han' offret vp
hys coppe, he set hyt on þe auter, and anon hyt was cast fro þe auter.
170 Efte he set hyt on þe auter and hyt was cast ferre fro. þe þryd tyme he
set hyt on þe auter and hyt was cast wel fyrre fro þe auter. Wyth þat
come þe chyld in wyth hys cuppe in hys hond. þen he tolde to alle folk
how Seynt Nycholas tok hym by þe hond when he fel into þe see and
ladde hym out saf. þan was þe fadur glad and offred vp bothe cuppes
175 ant 'wenten' hure way.

þer was also a ryche mon þe wheche, by þe prayere of Seynt
Nycholas, hadde a chyld. þen he byld a chapel in honore of Seynt
Nycholas, and euery ȝere he mad a fest in honore of Seynt Nycholas.
þen vpon a day þys chyld was taken of enmyes and lad into anoþur

lond and was in seruys of a kyng. On Seynt Nycholas [day], as he was 180
seruyng þe kyng, he þoght on þe murþe þat hys fadur mad on þat day,
and he sykud ful sore. þe kyng was war and sayde: 'Whatsoeuer þy
Nycholas may do, þou schalt dwelle here wyth vs.' þen sudenly a gret
wynt cam and smot þe hous, and þe chyld was caght vp wyth þe coppe
þat he bare in hys hond and was set byfore þe ʒates of þe chyrch þer 185
hys fadur mad þe fest. þan was þer gret ioy. þus he hadde gret
compassyon on hem þat were in desese. Summe bokus sayn þat þys
chyld was of Normandy and | was taken of a soudan byʒonde þe see f. 11ᵛ
and of[t] was beten. Onus he was beton on Seynt Nycholas day and
put into þe prison. þen he wept sore and wyth þat he fel on slepe. And 190
when he wok, he was in þe chapel of hys faderes yfound *et cetera.*

[4] *De concepcione beate Marie*

Suche a day ʒe schul haue þe concepcyon of oure Lady, þe whech day
Holy Chyrch makuth mensyon of þe concepcyon of hure for þre
specyal poyntes: for hure fadur holynes, for hure modur goodnes, and
for hure oune chesen mekenes.   5
Heo hadde a fadur þat was kallud Ioachym, þat was of such holynes
þat, when he was fyftene ʒere old, he departed hys good in þre
partyes: on to wydewes and faderles chyldren and oþur þat weren
pore and nedful, þat oþur part to ham `þat´ seruet God day and nyght
in þe temple, þe þryd part he kepte to hys houshold. And when he 10
was twenty ʒere old, for þe gret gudnes þat he herde and knewe by
Seynt Anne he weddet hure, and weron yfere twenty ʒere, þe whech
tyme Anne neuer dysplesyd hym by nyght ne by day for þe grete
gentelnes þat was wyth hure. But þagh þey were bothe good and holy,
God ʒaf ham no frut of hure body but were bareyn bothe. Wherfore 15
þey maden a vow to Godde: ʒef he wold ʒeu hem a chyld, þey wold
offren hyt in þe temple, þat schulden serue God day and nyght.
þen vpon a day, as Ioachym wyth hys neybores ʒod to þe temple to
don hys offryng, þe byschop, þat hette Ysacar, rebukud `hym´
opunlych and sayde: 'Ioachim,' quod he, 'hyt falluth not to þe, þat 20
art bareyn, for to offren in company wyth oþur þat God hath ʒeue frut
in Israel.' þen was Ioachym so asc`h´omot wyth þys rebuk þat he went
hom wepyng, and priuyly `tok´ hys schapardes wyth hys schep and

180 day] *om.*   189 oft] of
[4] 2 Suche] S- *in blue, dec., 2 ll. deep*   15 bareyn] -eyn *over eras.*
22 Ioachym] *over eras.*

зod forth in fer contre among hulles, and purposed hym to haue lyued
25 þere all hys lyf-dayes and neuer eft haue seyn Anne hys wyf.

þen was Anne sory and prayed to God and sayde þus: 'Lord, þat
me ys woo for y am bareyn and may haue no fryt, and now, more, myn
f. 12ʳ hosbond ys gon fro me, Y wot neuer wydur. Lord, haue mercy | of
me!' þen, as scho prayed þus, an angel com to hure and conford hure
30 and sayde: 'Anne, be of good conford—þou schal han a chyld such
wes neuer non lyk ne neuer schal bee.' þen was Anne aferd of þys
angel word and of þe sygh of hym and lay al daye in hure prayeres, as
heo hadde be ded.

þen went þys same angel to Ioachym and sayde þe same word, and
35 bad hym taken a lombe and offren hyt to God in sacryfyce, and so
dude. And when he hadde so ydon, fro mydday tyl euensong he lay
vpon þe erþe in hys preyeres, þonkyng God wyth al hys myght. þen
on þe morwen, as þe angel bad, he зode homward softe pas wyth hys
schep. And when he com nygh hom, þe angel com to Anne and bad
40 hure go to þe зate þat was kalled þe gyldon зate and abydon hure
husbond þere. þen was hoo glad, and toke hure maydenes wyth hire
and зode þydur, and mette þere wyth Ioachym hure husbond and
sayde: 'Lord, Y þonk þe heyly, for Y was a wydewe and now Y am a
wyf; Y was baren and now Y schal haue a chyld; Y was in woo and
45 wepyng and now Y schal ben in ioye and lykyng', and so conseyvet
oure Lady. And when heo was boren, heo was kalled Marya, as þe
angel bad byfore.

þen 'aftur' heo was wenet, þey broghton hure to þe templ[e] and
lafton hure among oþur maydenes to serue God day and nyght. þen
50 was heo so meke among 'alle' oþur vyrgines in al hure dowyng þat
oþur virgines kalled hure quene of maydenes, so þat зet heo ys þe
mekest seynt in heuen and most redy 'ys' to helpe alle þat kalle to hure
in nede.

Y rede þat þer was a lord þat hade a peny-reve þe 'whech' hadde
55 gedred hys lordes rent and зode to beren hyt to hym. þen were þefys
set for hym in a wode þat he most nedus goo þorgh. But when he
come into þe wode, he byþoght hym þat he hadde not sayde oure
Lady sauter þat he was woned to say vche day. þen anon he kneled
doun and bygan to say. þan anon com oure Lady lyke a fayre mayden
60 a set a garlon on hys hed, and at vch '*Aue*' heo sette a ros in þe
garlond, þat schon as bryght as a sterre. So by þat he hadde sayde, þe

---

48 temple] templo   54 narracio *in margin with blue paraph*   55 were] þere *add.*
and canc.   59 doun] a (*er.*) dount   61 So] *over eras.*

4. CONCEPTION OF THE VIRGIN 19

garlon was so | bryght þat alle þe wode schon þerof. þus, when he f. 12ᵛ
hadde don, he cussed þe erþe and ʒode hys way. þenne weren þe
þefus redy and broghton hym to here mayster, þat had seyen alle þys
doyng. þen sayde þe þeff to hym: 'Y wot þat þou art soch a lordus 65
seruant and hast hys money wyth þe, but telle me what woman þat
was þat set þys garlon on þy hed?' 'For soth,' he sayde, 'Y sagh no
woman ne haue no garlond þat Y know. But for Y hadde forʒeton to
say oure Lady sauter and was adred of ʒow, Y kneled adoun and sayde
hyt, prayng to hure to helpe me at my nede.' þen sayde þe þeff: 'For 70
hyre loue, `now´ go þy way and pray hure for vs', and so ʒede hys way
saf and sounde by sokur of oure Lady.

But now schul ʒe h[e]ren how þus fest was furst yfonden. þer was
in Englon a kyng was kalled Wylyam Conquerour. He sende þe abbat
of Ramesey to þe kyng of Denmark on message. But when he was in 75
þe see, þer come a darknes vpon hym and suche a tempest wyth, þat
he and alle þat weren wyth hym wende to haue be spyllyd anon. þan
vch mon prayed bysyly to dyuerse seyntes of heuen to helpe and sokur
ham in hure grete nede. þen as þe abbot prayed deuowtly to God, þer
come to hym a fayre mon and sayde to hym þus: 'ʒef þou wolt halwe 80
þe concepcyon of oure Lady, þat ys þe secunde day aftur Seynt
Nycholas day, heo wol sokur þe and alle þat ben wyth þe in þus nede.'
'Syre,' he sayde, 'wyth ful good wyll and þou woldest telle me what
`schal´ be þe seruyse of þys fest.' þen sayde he: 'þe same þat ys in
hure natiuite, saue turne þe natiuite into concepcyon.' 'Ful gladly', 85
sayde he, 'schal þus be don.' And þen anon þe tempest sesed and þe
wedur clered. He went forth and dude hys message, and cam aʒeyn to
spede wel in al hys doyng. And when he hadde told þe kyng of þus
vysyon, þe kyng mad to prechen hyt alle þe reme, and so was halwyt
in Holy Chyrch. 90

Also þer was a seculer chanon þat went ouer a watur to haue don
aduo|wtry. As he was in a bot, he bygan to saye matenes of oure Lady. f. 13ʳ
Whyl he sayed [þe] inuitat[o]rium, Aue Maria, þe deuel cast hym
doun and drouned hym and hadde hym to peyne. þen oure Lady cam
and sayde: 'Why haue ʒe tak þys mon?' þey sayde, he was in here 95
seruyse. Oure Lady sayde: 'Nay, he was in myn houres', and anon
restoret hym to lyve, and bed he schulde no more don auoutri, and
also halwe hure concepcyon, and so he dede and was a ful good mon
aftur.

100 Also Y rede þat þer was a clerk þat was wonot euery day to say matenes and seruyse of oure Lady. Hyt fel þat by consel of hys frendes he schulde han a wyf. And when he schulde be weddet he hadde a mynde þat he hadde not sayde þe seruyse of oure Lady þat day, and he made alle þat þer were to gon out of þe chyrch. And when
105 þey were gon, he kneled and sayde hys seruyse tyl he com to þe antyme: *Quam pulcra es et quam decora.* þen oure Lady appered to hym and sayde: 'Whyl þou sayst þat y am fayre and onest, why wyl þou leue me and takon anoþur?' þen anon he sayde: 'Lady, what wol þou þat Y do?' Heo sayde: 'And þou wolt leue þy flesly wyf and serue
110 my Sone and me, Y wyl be þy spose and þou schal haue wyth my Sone a crowne in kyngdam of heuen. And also þat þou wol worschep þe concepcyon of me.'

[5] *De sancto Thoma apostolo*

Suche a day ȝe schul haue Sent Thomas day, þat was Crystes holy apostel, and ȝe schul faste þe euen. And specyaly ȝe schal worschep hym for þre þyngus þat hys holy apostel hade, þat ys to say, for hys
5 heygh preuyng of oure fey, for grete wondres in hys way, and grete myraclus on hys day.

þys holy apostel preuet so oure fey þat he laft not scrupul in no part
f. 13ᵛ þerin. For when alle þe dyscypules | byleued and tolde hym þat Cryst was ryson fro deth to lyf and þey haddon seyen hym of lyue and
10 spoken wyth hym, Thomas onswered and sayde he wolde neuer l[e]ue tyl he hadde put hys hond in hys syde in þe wonde of þe spere. þenne eight dayes aftur, when alle þe dyscypules weren yfere and Thomas wyth ham, þenne come Ihesus bodyly to ham and sayde to hem: 'Pees be wyth owe.' And `þen´ he sayde to Thomas: 'Come and put þi
15 fyngur in` to´ þe holus of þe nayles þat persed my hondus and put þy hondes into my syde, and be no lengur out of þe byleve, but be hereaftur studefast in þe leue.' þen when Thomas hadde so don, anon he cryed for wondur and for fere and sayde: 'My Lord and my God', þat ys forte to saye: now Y beleue þat Ihesu art very God and mon.
20 þenne sayde Ihesu to Thomas: 'þou hast yseye me, þerfore þou leuest, but blesset be þey þat seye me not and byleven in me.' þus þe tarying of Thomas leue broght vs in ful byleue and to þe beneson of Ihesu Cryst. Of þys seyth Seynt Gregory þus: 'Meche more Thomas

100 narracio *in margin in the long hand*
[5] 2 Suche] S- *in blue, dec., 2 ll. deep* 10 leue] lyue

of Ynde help me to þe feyth, þat wold not byleue tyl he hadde
hondeled and groput þe wondes of Cryst, þen Mary Madeleyn þat 25
byleued anon at forme syght.' þus Thomas preued oure fey.
He made also wondrus in hys waye. For when þe kyng of Ynde
hadde sende hys messenger, þat hette Abbanes, into þe contre of
Cesarce to seche[n] hym a carpunter þat couþe makun hym a palys,
þen Cryst spak wyth þys Abbanes and sende Thomas to Ynde wyth 30
hym. And when þey weren passed ouer þe see, þey comen into a cyty,
of þe whech þe kynges doghtur was wedded þat day. Wherfore vch
mon was comandet for to come into þe mete. þen among oþur
Thomas and Abbanes comen into þe fest. But for Thomas hadde all
hys þoght on God and hadde no lust to ete, þe bo | teler smot hym on f. 14ʳ
þe cheke and bad hym eton. þen Thomas sayde to hym: 'Y wol not 36
ryson of þys place tyl þat hond be gnawen of wyth dogges and be
broght hydur before me.' þen anon aftur þys boteler ȝede aftur watur,
and a lyon slogh hym anon and dronk hys blod and doggus eton hys
body, among þe whech was on black dogge þat tok þys honde in hys 40
mogh and broȝt hym into þe halle in sygh of alle men and leyde hyt
doun byfore Thomas. þen was þer a womon, a mynstrel, þat
vndurstod Thomas wordes, þe `whech´ anon fel doun to Thomas
fet and cryed þat alle men herdon: 'Ouþer þ[ou] art God or ellus
Goddes dyscypul. For ryght as þou saydest, hyt [ys] befallen.' þen 45
was þe kyng and alle men abasched and prayed Thomas to blessen hys
doghtur and hure husbond. þen Thomas preched hem bothe so þat he
maket þe husbonde byschop of [þe] cyte and þe wyf a nunne, þat were
bothe aftur martyres for Goddus sake.

þenne went Thomas forth to Ynde to þe kyng and byhette þe kyng 50
to mak hym a palys, a bolde for a kyng. Wherfore þe kyng was glad
and made to delyueren hym a grete somme of gold forto mak þe palys
wyth, and so wente fer into anoþur contre whyle Thomas schuld haue
made þat palys. But for Thomas þoght hit was bettur to mak hym a
palys in heuen þen in erþe, þerfore he tok þys money and dalte hyt 55
among pore men and wemen and oþur þat were nedy, and so aftur
went about and preched Goddus word to þe pepul and turned mony
of hem to þe feyth of Cryst. þen aftur, when þe kyng com hom and
hadde grete hope to haue fond hys palys mad redy, and herde how
Thomas hadde don, he was wod wrogh and wold haue don Thomas 60
and Abbanes to deþe. But for hys broþur was ded þat same tyme,

29 sechen] sechem   42 womon] -on *over eras.*   44 þou] þat   45 ys] *om.*
48 þe²] *om.*

þerfore he made to do ham boþe in preson tyl þe tyme `þat´ he hadde
buryed hys broþur.

þen, as God wolde, when hys broþur hadde long be ded, he ros fro
65 deth to lyf and tolde þe kyng þat he hadde sayen þe palys þat Thomas
f. 14ᵛ hadde maket for hym: 'Wherfore Y | praye þe, let me bugge hyt and
Y schal ȝeu þe as mych as hyt coste þe.' þe kyng þen byþoght hym,
and by good conseyl he sayde: 'Nay, þat schal be myn; let hym mak þe
anoþur.' For hys broþur sayde he hadde seyen hyt in paradyse yrayed
70 wyth gold, seluer and presyous stones. þen he toke fo[l]þe and mony
þowsand pepul wyth. þenne seyen þe byschoppes of mawmetry þat
alle þe [pepul] laft here lawe and ȝedon to cryston fey. Wherfore þey
were so wrogh wyth Thomas þat on of ham sayde he wolde wreken
hys god, and wyth a spere rouet Thomas þo`r´ghtout þe body and
75 slogh hym. þen crystemen buryed hym in a tombe of crystal þer God
wroght mony wondur myraclus for hym, for þe honde þat was in
Crystes cyde hyt wol neuer into þe tombe but lay euer wythout.

Also in hys prechyng he taghte *xij gradus virtutum assignare. Primus
est vt in Deum crederent, qui est vnus in essencia et trinus in personis. Dedit*
80 *eis triplex exemplum sensibile quomodo sint in vna essencia tres persone.*
Primum est quod vna est in omni sapiencia et de illa vna procedit
intellectus, memoria et ingenium. Memoria est vt non obliuiscaris que
disceris; intellectus vt intelligas que ostendi possunt vel doceri; ingenium
est, inquit, vt quod didiceris inuenias. Secundum est quod in vna vinea tria
85 *sunt, scilicet, lignum, folium et fructus, et hec omnia tria sunt vna vinea.*
Tercia est quod caput vnum ex quatuor sensibus constat. In vno enim capite
sunt visus, auditus, odoratus et gustus, et hec plura sunt et vnum caput.
Secundus gradus est vt baptismum susciperent. Tercius vt se a fornicacione
abstinerent. Quartus vt se ab auaricia temptarent. Quintus vt gulam
90 *destringerent. Sextus vt penitenciam tenerent. Septimus vt in hijs*
perseuerarent. Octauus vt hospitalitatem amarent. Nonus vt voluntatem
Dei quererent et ea opere complerent. xus est vt non facienda quererent et
ea vitarent. xius vt caritatem amicis et inimicis impenderent. xijus vt in
custodiendis hijs vigilem curam exhiberent. Item apostolus omnes qui
95 *adorant Deum de tribus breuiter instruxit, scilicet, vt ecclesiam diligerent,*
f. 15ʳ *sacerdotes honorarent, et assidue vt au|diendum verbum Dei conuenirent.*

He doth also mony wondrus on hys day. For alle þe contre cometh
þedur on hys day and takun hosul of þat hond in þys wyse: þe
byschop of þat cyte synguth þe masse þat day, and, when he

---

70 folþe] forþe   72 pepul] *om.*   78 nota cc *in margin with blue paraph*
97 nota bene *in margin in the long hand*

bygynneth þe masse, er he seye hys *Confiteor*, he takuth a branch of a 100
vyne and puteth in Thomas hond and so goth forth to masse. þen þys
branch burgeneth out grapus, and so, by þat þe gospel be seyd, þe
byschop takuþ þys grapus and wrengeth into hys chalis and synguth
wyth þat wyn and hoseleth alle þe pepul þerwyth, and puteth þe ost in
Thomas honde and so hoseleth alle þe pepul. But when any comuth 105
þat ys vnworþy, anon þe hond closeth togedur and wol not opun tyl
he be scryven klene, and þen hyt wol opun and hoselen hym. Also
when men ben in debate, þey ben brogh byfore þe tombe of Thomas
and set on twyn. And when þe cause of debate ys rehersed, þen wol þe
hond turne to hym þat ys in þe ryght, and so ben þey mad at on *et* 110
cetera. þus he prevet oure fey and dede wondrus in hys way and grete
myraclus on hys day.

Ion Crysostom sayth þat Thomas com into þat contre where þe þre
kyngus of Coleyn weron and folewet am and mad ham crystene men.
For þath þey hadden worscheppe Cryst in hys borth, þey herdon no 115
more of hym, and þerfore Thomas come to hom and taght hem þe
feyth.

[6] *De natiuitate Christi*

Gode crysten men, as 3e sen and heren, þys day al Holy Church
maketh melody and myrth in mynde of þe blessed burth of oure Lord
Ihesu, veri God and mon, þat was þys day boren of hys modur Seynt
Mary in grete help and sokur to al monkynde, but specyalych for þre 5
causes: for to 3eue pees to men of good wylle, for te lyghton ham þat
lokon | ylle, and for te draw vs wyth loue hym tylle.   f. 15ᵛ

þen, as to þe forme cause, þat he was boren to 3eue pees to men of
good wylle, Y may preue þus. For when he was boren, angeles songon
þus: '*Gloria in excelsis Deo*', þat ys to sayn: ioye be to God þat ys hyegh 10
in heuen and pees be in erþe to men of gode wylle. At mydnyght
Cryst was yboren, for þen al thyng by kynde takuth rest in schowyng
þat he ys prince of pees and was comyn to make pees bytwynne God
and mon, bytwynne angel and mon, and bytwynne mon and mon.

He made pees bytwynne 'God' and mon. Wherfore for te bee a true 15
m[e]dyatour bytwynne ham too, he tok kynde of boþe and was very
God and mon, and by hys medyacyon he knytte þe loue of God to

114 am] a- *over eras.*
[6]   1 *De natiuitate Christi*] *red paraph with red pointing hands*   2 Gode] *G- in blue,*
dec., 2 ll. deep   16 medyatour] madyatour

mon so sadly þat þe fadur of heuen sparet not hym þat was hys owne
Sone, but sende hym to ȝeynbye mon wyth hys holy blod and bryng
20 hym by way of mekenes aȝeyn to þe ioye of paradyse þat mon lost by
couetyse and pride. þus he makuth pees bytwyxe God and mon.
He makuth pees bytwynne angyl and mon. For when angelus syen
þat here Lord was wroth wyth mon for hys vnbuxomnesse, þey weren
also wroth wyth hym, for vnbuxomnes ys a synne þat angelus haton
25 heyghly. Wherfore þey kepton þe ȝates of paradyse and letten no
soule in tyl þey seyen here Lord boren in monkynde. þen anon for
loue of hure Lord þey dedon mon wyrschep and speken louyngly to
þe pore schepardus þat kepton here schep in contre by, and bad ham
gon in to þe cyte of Bedlem, for þer þey schuldon fyndon a chylde
30 yboren and layde in a crache and don hym worschep, and so þey
dudon, þat euer sethon angelus han ben fryndes and seruandes to alle
gode men and wemen, and alle in reuerens of þe incarnacyon of oure
Lord Ihesu Crist. þus he made pees bytwynne angel and mon.
f. 16ʳ   He made also pees bytwyxe mon and mon. | For aȝeyn þe tyme þat
35 he wolde be bore, he made so [grete] pees al þe world þat, þereas
kyngdames and contrees were at þe bate and werre vchon wyth odur,
in hys tyme of burth wes so grete pees þat on mon, þat was kalled
Octouyan, was imperour of Rome and hadde þe gouernans of al þe
world—for alle þe world was suget to þe emperour of Rome—and
40 dured so þrytty wyntur, insomuch þat þenne was sende out a
mandement al ȝent þe world, comandyng þat vche mon schuld gon
to þe cyte þat he drow lynage of a legge a peny vpon hys hed and so
offren hyt vp, knawlachyng þat he was suget to þe emperour of Rome.
þenne most I[o]seph, oure Lady husbonde, nedus go to þe cyte of
45 Bedleem for to offren wyth oþur men. But for he hadde no monay, he
tok a nox wyth hym for te selle þer and for te make hym money of.
But for he durst not leue oure Lady byhynde hym, for ho was so nygh
tyme of burthe, he sette hure vpon a nasse and tok hure wyth hym.
But when þey comon into þe cyte, hyt was so ful of pepul þat þey
50 myght[e] geton no herbor but turnet into a cave þat was bytwisse too
houses, þeras men setten hore kapulus when þey comen to þe market,
and þey fondun þer a crach wyth hey and setton þe oxe and þe asse
þerto.
þenne a lytyl byfore mydnyght owre Lady bad Ioseph geton hure
55 mydwyves for heo schuˋlˊde be delyuer. But whyl he was in þe toune

---

34 mon²] ffor aȝeyn *catchwords f. 15ᵛ with red pointing hand*   35 grete] *om.*
44 Ioseph] ieseph   50 myghte] myghto

aftur mydwyves, oure Lady was delyuered and lappud hure Sone in cloþus and layd hym in þe crach byfore þe oxe and þe asse. And þey anon knewen here Lord and fellon downe on knoes and worschepput hym and eton no more of þe hey. þat same tyme, as men in þe contre ȝedon 'at' þe plogh, oxen speken to þe ploghmen and seydon þus: 60 'Sedus schul encrese and men schul waxen fewe.'

þen sone aftur come I[o]seph wyth too [m]ydwyves, ȝebel and Salome. But when ȝebel fond wel þat oure Lady was klene maydon, heo cryed anon and sayde: 'A maydon hath boren a chyld.' þen þe oþur, Salome, wol not leue þat but boysturly hondeled oure Lady, 65 and þerwyth anon hure hondes dryed vp. þen co[m] þer an | angel f. 16ᵛ and bad hure towch þe chyld and heo schul be hol, and so dude and was hol. þen went Ioseph and dude hys offryng wyth oþur men and kepte oure Lady in þat same caba[n] whyl heo was in chyldebed. þus ȝe mowen vndurston how God ȝeveth pees to hem þat ben men and 70 wymen of good wylle and kalleth hem hys chyldren.

In veryfying of þys þyng, þe forme masse þat ys songon þys day ys sayde sone aftur mydnyght and bygynneth þus: *Dominus dixit ad me, filius meus es tu*—God seyde to me: þou art my sone. God kalleth hym hys sone þat lyveth here in pees and rest, and when 'he' parteth fro 75 þys world, he wol bryng hym to þe pees þat euer schal laste, and þoo þat wol haue no pees here þey schul gon heþen to erlestyng woo. þus Cryst ȝeveth pees.

He lyghteth also þoo þat loketh ille. Herby, gode men, ȝe schul vndurstonde þat Cryst heluth not onlych hem þat weren blynde in 80 body but mony moe þat weren blynd in soule and combret wyth darkenes of synful lyuyng. For as Seynt Austyn sayeth, when Cryst schuld be boren, þe world was so ful of darkenes of synne, and namely of synne of lecchery and of synne aȝeyn kynde, þat he hadde nygh laft of to haue be bore of monkynde. Wherfore þat nyght þat Cryst was 85 boren, alle þat duden synne aȝeyn kynde dyodyn sodenly al þe world, in schewyng how horrybul [þat] synne ys byfore Goddus enon. þen lokut þey ful ylle and hadde gret nede to be lyghtnet þat hadden euer hure herte to synne. Wherfore Cryst was boren at mydnyght and turned þe darkenes of nyght in to daylyght, schewyng þat þenne was 90 [boren] þe sonne of ryghtwysnes and comen for to lyghten alle þat weren combret wythinforth wyth darkenes of synne.

Also | þat same tyme þat he was boren, as mony doctorus seyn, f. 17ʳ

62 Ioseph] ieseph   mydwyves] wyd/wyves   66 com] con   69 caban] caba
87 þat] *om.*   91 boren] *om.*

Cryst appered in a brygt sterre to þre kynges in est and bad hem gon
95 to Bedlem and worschep þer a chylde þat schulde be kyng of Iuwes
þat was þoo boren, and so dudun, sewyng þe sterre tyl þey comen
þydur. þus he lyghtud hom þat byfore lokut ful ylle, for byfore þey
weren paynymes and leued on mawmentrye and false goddes, but
aftur þey leued on Cryst and weren holy lyueres and now lyth at
100 Coleyne.

þus þe burth of Cryst makuth to se ful wel þat byfore lokut ful ille.
For he lokut ful ille þat hath algate hys þoght on hys good and on
worldus worschep, for þese makuth `a´ mon blynde, so þat he
forȝetuth hys God and hath no lust to desyron þe rychese of heuen
105 ne for te se þe lyght þat ys þer, but such machuth `hys good´ hys God
and hys mawment. þen, for Cryst was boren to destrue such
mawmentrie, when þat Herod pursued hym and wolde han slayn
hym, hys modur bar hym into þe lond of Egypt. And when he come
þydur, anon alle þe mawmentus þat weren in þat lond þey fellon doun
110 to gronde, doyng to vndurstonde þat he was come into þys world þat
schuld caston doun `in´ mennes hertes þe mawmentry of couetyse of
good and of worldus worschep and pompe and pride þat men vson
þerin. Herfore, þahht he hymself were Lord of alle lordus, he wes
boren ful porelych, and of a pore maydon, and in a pore place, and in a
115 ful `pore´ aray, ȝeuyng ensample to alle men to sette noght by worldy
rychese ny by `þe´ pride of þys world. For haue a mon neuer so mych
good ne neuer so mych worschep, here he fy[n]deth hyt `and´ here he
leuyth hyt. þus Cryst, by myraclus þat he schewet in hys burth, he
lyghteth mony wythinneforth þat weren byfore ful blynde.

f. 17ᵛ In tokenyng [of] þys, þe secunde | masse of þys day ys sayde in þe
121 dayng when nyght and day parteth, þe whech masse bygynneth þus:
Lux fulgebit hodie super nos—lyght schal schyne þys day vpon vs. For
þe Fadur of heuen sendeth grace of gostly lyght vpon alle men þat
leueth þat Cryst was þys day boren, very God and mon, of hys modur
125 Marye, very modur and mayden, and setteht noght by þe vanyte of
þys world, but setteht al hys hope in Cryst and in hys modur Marie.
þus Crystes burth lyghteth mony ful wel þat byfore lokut ful ille.

Also wyth loue he drogh vs hym tylle. Chyldren drawen loue of
þylk þat sen hem, and þey make hem to haue lykyng to speke and to
130 playe wyth hem. þus Cryst was boren a chyld, þe ferest þat euer was
boren of womon, for te drawe mannes loue to hym. For whyle a chyld
ys ȝong and wythoute synne, hyt ys more amyabul þen hyt ys aftur

117 fyndeth] fydeth   120 of¹] om.

when hyt comyth to monnes state. þus not only for hys bevte, but also for hys bounte, vche mon hath mater for te drawe to hym and don hym worschep, as dude Octouian þe emperour, þe whech emperour 135 plesud so mych þe pepul of hys empyre of Rome þat þey wolde haue worscheped hym as for God. But þenne þys emperour was wyse and knew wel þat he was but a mon as oþur weren and durst not take vpon hym þat nome, but sende aftur Sybyl þe sage and askud hure wheþur þer schuld be aftur hym any yboren þat schuld be grattur þen he. þen 140 Sybul lokud in þe sonne and segh at mydday a cerkul of gold abowte þe sonne and in þe myddul of þe cerkul a wondur fayre mayden wyth a chyld in hure barm. And when Sybul hadde schewot þys to þe emperour, heo sayde to hym: 'þys chyld schal be grettur þen þou [art] or euer were or euer schalt be—þerfore do hym worschip and 145 reuerence!' þenne þe emperatour tok cense and dude sa|crifyce to f. 18ʳ hym, and charget alle men þat þey schuld don þe same and callen þat chyld God and not hym. By þys e[n]sampul vch crystene mon and womon schuld lerne to do seruyse and honour þys day to þys chyld.

Wherfore þe þrydde masse of þys day ys sayde at mydday, in 150 schewyng þat vche mon and womon ys holde for to come and offreon in þe worschep of þys chyld and of hys modur, and schowe hym seruand and suget to hym, and knowlach þys chyld for hys God and hys Lord. And for vch mon schulde do þus for loue and not for eye, þe masse bygynneth þus: *Puer natus est nobis*—a chylde ys boren to vs. 155 A chyld, he seth, and not a mon, so þat alle men and wemen for loue schulden haue boldnes to come to hym to sech grace. And for he ys ful of grace and redy to ӡeue mercy to hem þat askuth hyt mekely wyth du reuerence, he ys aye ʻredyʼ to ӡeue grace and mercy. In tokenyng of þys þyng, þat same day þat Crist was boren in Bedlem, a welle of 160 watur in Rome turned to oyle and renned so alle þat day, schowyng þat þe welle of grace and of mercy was boren þat day þat schulde ӡeu grace and mercy to alle þat woldon come to hym.

þerfore y rede of a womon þat was defouled wyth þe synne of lecchery and almost fel in despeyre. For when heo þoght vpon 165 Crystus dome, scho knewe hure gult and þat scho schulde come to ʻþeʼ dome þerfore; when heo þoght vpon þe peynus of helle, heo knewe wel þat þylk peynus weron ordeyned for such as heo was; [when] heo þoght on þe ioye of paradyse, heo wyst heo myght not come þer, for heo was vnworþy; when heo þoght on þe passyon of 170

Crist, heo wyst wel þat heo was vnkynde to hym þat suffred so much for hure. At þe last, heo byþoght hyre how þat chyldren don no vangians but lyghtly beth saght, þagh þei ben worth. Wherfore heo cryed to Crist, prayng hym for hys chyldhod þat he wolde haue mercy

f. 18ᵛ on hyre and | forȝeuen hyre hure trespas. þen anon heo herde a voys
176 on hegh and seyde: 'þi trespas ys forȝeue.'

[7] *De sancto Stephano*

Blessed pepul of Goddes moght, þat ben comen þys day to Holy Chyrch in worschip of God and of þys holy martyr Seynt Steuen, þat ys kalled Goddus form[e] martyre for encheson þat he was þe furst
5 martir þat suffred deth for þe loue of Crist aftur þe ascencyon of God—þen forte steren ȝoure deuocyon þe more to þys holy martir, ȝe schul now heren what he suffred for Goddus loue, as þe bok of þe dedus of þe posteles telleth.

When Crist was ascended into heuen, þe appostelus tendeet al to
10 prechyng of Goddes worde and to holy praire. And [for] þey myth not seruon al þat turned to þe fey, þey cheson sixe holy men and gode out of syxty and ten þat weren Crystus dyscypules for te helpen hem in Goddes seruyse, of þe whech Seynt Steuen was þe forme and þe wysest, and was so ful of grace and myght of þe Holy Gost þat he
15 dude mony wondrus and myraclus in þe pepul. But þagh a mon be neuer so holy a lyuer, ȝet he schal haue enemys. Werfore mony Iewes of dyuerse contreys þat hadden envie to Seynt Steven ryson aȝeynes hym and 'spysed and spyted aȝeynes hym and' aȝeynes Cristes fey, hauyng ful purpose, ȝef þei myght not ouercome hym by dysputyson
20 ny by fals wytnes, for te do hym to deþe. But wen Seynt Steven know hore malys, he þoght for te seson hem by on of þese þre ways: by schamyng in disputyson, or by drede of reuelacyon, or by loue and holy oryson.

But furst he seyde by schamyng in disputyson. For [when] þei
25 bygan to spyte wyth hym, he was so ful of þe Holi Gost þat þei hadden no wyt ne pousti for te ȝenstonde hym, but opunly or-kom hem in al here materes and preued here wytnes fals and sayde he was

f. 19ʳ redy to | take deth in veryfying of al þat he sayde, and preued wel þat hyt was a gret schame to al hem, þat weren gret clerkus and knewen þe

[7] 2 Blessed] B- *in blue, dec., 2 ll. deep*   moght] -g-?   4 forme] formo
10 for] *om.*   18 spysed . . . and³] *marked by red-dotted caret,* spysed *prec. by red dot*
24 when] *om.*

lawe and þe prophecyus þat schuldon comen—and weren fulfulled in 30
Ihesu Crist þat he preched, and ȝet þey wold not leue in hym but
algate ȝeynstonden þe Holy Gost þat spak in hertus and schewuet
hem in consciens þat þey duden amys. And þeras þey seyen þat þe
comyn pepul turned to þe feyth for wordus and myraclus þat 'God'
schewed in hure sygh, þei algate ȝeynstoden stufly and setton Goddus 35
werkus at noght only by malys of envies hertes and by no maner reson
of scripture. þenne were þey more angrud aȝeyn hym, and freton here
hertus wyth envie wythin, and grysbat wyth hure teth aȝeyn hym.
And for þei myght not ouercome hym wyth disputyng, þey soghton
ȝef þei myghton taken hym wyth som worde of sclandur in God 40
wherby þei myghton laufully haue mater and cause to do hym 'to'
deth.

þenne knew Seynt Steven hure malys and lufte vp hys eyen to
heuen and seygh Ihesus, Goddes Sone, stonden of hys fadur ryght
honde. And þen sayde Seynt Steven: 'Lo, Y se Ihesus stondyng at hys 45
fadur ryght hond redy to help me', and þerwyth annon hys face schon
bryght as he had ben an angel of heuen. But when þei herdon hym
speke so, þei were fayn and stopput here heres, as þey hadden herde
hym spek fals and sclandur of God, and hadden ben horribul for any
mon to haue herde 'hym' lye so. þenne anon þei drowyn hym out of 50
þe cyte for te stonen hym to deþe as for a dyssclaunderer of [God],
and cheson two men þat cowþen best hurle stones at hym, and
despoyled hym of hys cloþes and leyden ham at þe feet of a ȝong mon
þat was kalled Saule, þat was aftur Seynt Paule, for he was on of þe
chyf of hem þat deden Seynt Steven to deth. 55

But when Seynt Steuen seygh þat he myght not seson hem by fere
of | reuelacyon, þenne he turned to dewovte oresenes. And when þey f. 19ᵛ
horlet at hym stones and smot oute hys brayn, he cryed to God and
sayde: 'Lorde Ihesu, tak my soule!' And for he wolde praye more
devowtly for hys enmyes þen for hymself, he kneled adown to þe erþe 60
and seyde: 'Lord Ihesu, let þe synne of hem be forȝefne and þys gult,
for þei wyt not wat þey don.' And when he hadde sayde soo, anon he
slepte in God.

Nowe takuth hede whech a brennyng loue þys mon hadde in hys
herte, þat prayed more devowtly for hys dedly enemys þen he dede 65
for hymself. In þys he ȝaf an hegh ensampul to al crystene pepul to
haue charite vchon to oþur and to prayen hertyly for here enemys and
for þylk þat pursuen hem or don hem dysese. For he [þat] prayeth

51 God] *om.*   68 þat²] *om.*

deuowtly for hys enemy in þat he ys a martir, for martyrdom falleth
70 by þre wayes: þat ys, by passyon and wylle þerto, by wylle wythouten
passyon, by passyon wythouten wylle.

In schewyng of þese þre martirdomus, þe þre festus þat sewyth þe
burthe of Cryst ben set togedur in tokenyng þat who so suffreth any of
þese he schal be set euen to Ihesu in heuen. Seynt Steuen he ys set
75 nest for he hadde passyon and wylle þerto; Seynt Ion hadde wylle but
no passyon; þe Innocentes he'o' suffred deth but þey hadde no wylle
þerto—but not aʒeynus wylle. þus may a mon be a martir, þagh he
schede [not] hys blud, þat ys, when he suffreth wronge and pursewt of
euel men and þonketh God þerof, and takuth hyt wyth gode wyl, and
80 preyeth for hys enymys to God in ful charite. For martyrdom
wythouten charite, as Seynt Paule seyth, profeteth noght. Wherfore
takuth gode hede, and ʒe schul fynde þat þese þre weren ful of charite:
Seynt Steven [when] he schulde dyon, he kneled doun for te preye for
hys enemys; Seynt Ion when he wente to hys deth, he sayde to hem
85 þat ladden hym: 'Chyldren, loueth to[g]e[d]re and þat ys ynoght'; þe
Innocentes, for þey weren so ʒong þat þey cowþe not speke, þey
schewet hare loue by opun syne, for þey dede lagh vpon hem þat slogh
ham and pleyed wyth here hondes for ioye when þey seyen here
brygte swyddes schyne.

90   þen for encheson þat Seynt Steuen was so glorius a martyr, God
f. 20ʳ schewed mony myraclus for hym, of þe whech þys ys on. Ther | was an
honest womon and hadde seuen sones and þre doghtrus. But in a
myshap on a day alle þey wrathed hure modur þat heo in a gret malys
cursed hem alle, and anon þerwyth fel vangya[n]s vpon hem so þat þe
95 membres of hem quokon þat al þat syen hem hadden gret compassyon
of hem and reuwet hem gretly. And for þey myght not do no werk, þey
ʒedon as mased bestes al ʒent þe contre. þenne happed hyt so þat a
broþur of hem þat hette Paule and a cystur þat hette Pallida comen into
a chyrch of Seynt Steven. And when þys mon herde how deuowtly [he]
100 prayed for ham þat slowen hym, he hadde ful trust þat 'he' wold praye
for hym, and he wolde be hys seruand euer aftur. And so in þys ful
hope he ʒode into þe chansel, and wyth al hys herte he prayed Seynt
Steven of help. And anon in syght of alle men he was hol. þen when þe
systur sygh hure broþur hol, heo prayed þe same wyse to Seynt Steuen.
105 And þenne as heo prayed, heo fel on slepe, and when heo wok, hoe was
hol, and wyth alle hure herte þonked God and Seynt Steven.

Anoþur myracle Seynt Austyn telleth þus: A senatour of Rome
wyth hys wyf 3ede to Ierusalem and þer bulde a fayre chapell in
worschip of Seynt Steuen. And when `he´ was ded, he ordeynet
hymself to be byryed þerin by Seynt Steuen. But long aftur hys deth   110
hys wyf wolde gon a3eyn to hure contre, and heo wold haue þe bonus
of hure mayster wyth hure. And so wyth preyre and wyth 3eftes þe
byschop broghte to hure þe bonus of Seynt Stephon and of hure
husbond, and sayde to hure: 'Y knowe not wheþer ben þe bonus of þy
mayster.' þen seyde heo: 'Syre, Y knwe ful wel þese ben my maystres   115
bones', and tok Seynt Stephenes bones in stude of hure maystres
bones, vnwytyng to hure. þen when heo com to þe see, angelus
songen in `þe´ eyre and a swete sauur com oute of þe bones þat passed
any spycery, and þerwyth fendes cryed: 'Woo ys ows for Steuen goth
and bitturly brenneth ous and betuth ous', and þerwyth rered a   120
tempest þat þe schipmen wenden to haue be drowned and cryed to
Seynt Steven. And he [anon appered to hem and seyde: 'Be not
adrad', and] | anon þe tempest sesed. þen herdon heo þese fyndus   f. 20ᵛ
cryen: 'þou wykked prynste, owre mayster, brenneth þe schyppe, for
Steuen, þat ys owre aduersari[e], ys þerinne.' þen þe prince of fyndus   125
sende fyue fyndes for to haue brend þe schip. But þenne was þe angel
of God redy and drowned hem into þe grownd of þe see. And when
þey comen wyth þe schip to londe, fendus cryed: 'Goddes seruand
comeþ þat was stened to deþe wyth Iewes wy[k]kut.' þenne in
worschep of Seynt Steuen men makut a chyrch and put hys bones   130
þerin, where God wyrched mony myraclus aftur for hym.

[8] *De sancto Iohanne euangelista*

Goddes blessed pepul, 3e ben ycomen þys day to Holy Chyrch to
worschep God, oure Lady, and Seynt Ion þe euangelyst þat ys
Goddus owne derlyng. Wherfore al Holy Chirch þys day maketh
mensyon of þe specyal grace þat Cryst 3af hym byfore alle oþur   5
dyscypules: he 3af hym grace of virginite, and grace of kepyng hys
modur fre, and grace of schewyng hys priuyte.

He 3af hym grace of virginite, þat ys, of mayden-hod, for, as storyes
telleth and somme han in opyneon, when he schulde haue wedded
Mary Magdaleyn, Cryst kalled hym and bad he schulde sue hym. And   10

107 narracio *in margin with red paraph*   122–3 anon . . . and] *om.*
125 aduersarie] aduersario   129 wykkut] wylkut
[8]   2 Goddes] G- *in blue, dec., 2 ll. deep*

he anon laft alle þe worldes vanite and sewed Cryst forth and kepte
hym clene mayden tyl hys endyng day. In preuyng of þis, as we
redeth, when Domycyan þe emperour of Rome herde þat Ion preched
in a contre þat ys kalled Asya and bulde mony chyrches, he was wrogh
15 þerwyth and sende aftur Ion, and made to putte hym in a brason
tonne ful of oyle and soe seþen hym þerin. But when he hadde longe
ysodon þerin, and alle men wenden he hadde ben al forsodon to pesus,
þenne þe emperour bad opon þe tonne. And when þe tonne was
'opon', Ion come oute of þe oyle and of þe brennyng of þe fyre as hol
20 and sound in vche part of hys body as he was clene of part of womones
body, of þoght, and of dede.

Anoþur assaye he hadde ful harde. When he sagh a temple of Iewes
ful of mawmentry, he prayed 'to' God for te destryen hyt. And
þerwyth anon hyt felle doun into powder. Wherfore Arostodinus, a
25 byschop of þe temple, pursewed Ion to þe deth. þenne sayde Ion to
hym: 'What wolt þou þat Y do for te make þe to byleue on Ihesu Cryst
my Lord?' þen sayde he: 'Y wol mak venym and do men for te drynk
f. 21ʳ hyt by | fore þe, and when þou seest hem ded, drynk þou þat wythout
harm, and þenne schal Y leuen on þy God.' þen sayde Ion: 'Goo and
30 do as þou sayst.' þenne ordened þys byschop þe poyson and geet too
men þat weren dampned to þe dcth and mak ham drynke of þys
poyson byfore Ion, and when þey hadden dronken, þey were ded anon
ryght. þenne Ion tok þat poyson and blessed hyt and so dronke hyt of,
and wes ner þe worse, but semed þe lylokur aftur þen he wes byfore.
35 [For as clene as he was wythout venym of lechery], so clene he was of
þat poyson aftur he hadde dronk hyt. But ȝet þys byschop seyde he
myght not leuen tyl he segh þe men reysed aȝeyn to lyve þat weren
slayn by drynkyng of þat poyson. þen Ion caste of hys kote and sayde:
'Haue þys, and lay hyt vpon þe ded bodyes and say þys: "Ion, Crystes
40 apostel, sende me to ȝow þat ȝe ryson vp in Crystes nome."' And
when he hadde do so, þey ryson aȝeyn to lyve. þen þys byschop wyth
mony oþur leueden in Cryst and weren folwed of Ion and was aftur a
ful holy mon. þus he þat hath grace to kepen hym clene in body and
soule, þagh þe fynd helde into hym venym of lecchery or of oþur
45 synne, hyt schal not don hym no harm, but in þe ȝeynstondyng of hys
lust he ys a martyr byfore God and schal be taken as for worþy to be
keper of Crystes modur.

þus for þe grete clannes þat Cryst seygh in Ion byfore alle oþur,
when he schulde dye, he charget Ion wyth þe kepyng of hys modur.

33 hyt²] *over eras.*   35 For . . . lechery] *om.*   43 mon] mony

And he, as a good sone schulde do, tok hyr into hys kepyng, so þat 50
when Cryst was ded and layde in hys tombe, Ion, wyth oþur, help to
bere hure into hys hous and kept hure þere tyl Cryst was ryson aȝeyn
to lyf. And also when Cryst was styed into heuen, he kepte hure in þe
same chambur also longe as heo lyvede after here in erþe. þus hadde
he grace of kepyng of Crystes modur free. 55
    He hadde also grace of knowyng of Goddes priuete. þys was fyrst
when Cryst sat at hys soper on Schere þursday. For gret loue þat he
hadde to Cryst, he lened hys hed to Crystes breste, and þenne, ryght
as a mon leneth to a w[e]ll and drynketh hys body | ful of watur, rygh f. 21ᵛ
[so] Ion dronk of þe welle of wysdam þat ys Crystes brest and fulled 60
hys soule ful of gostly wysdam, so þat after he passed alle oþur in
wysdam. þus Cryst schewed hym of hys priuyte byforen oþur.
    Also, for he wold not stynton to prechen Goddes worde, þe
emperour exyled hym alone into þe yle of Pa[t]hmos. But wyl he
was þer hys one, God schewed hym hys apocalips of þe world þat wes 65
to come, and most of Antecryst, and of þe worldes endeng, and of þe
day of dome. And as he seygh hyt, he wrote hyt in a gret confirmacyon
of Holy Chyrche. But aftur when þe emperour was ded, Ion was
kalled aȝeyn to þe cyte of Ephesim, þer he was byschop. And when he
come þydur, a wydewe þat hette Drusyana lay ded on bere. þenne for 70
Ion segh mony wepon for hure, Ion sayde to hure: 'Drusyan, ryse vp
and goo mak me som mete.' And heo anon ros vp and ȝede forth, as
þagh heo hadde ryson from slepe.
    Anoþur day too ȝong men and rych by prechyng of Ion þey soldon
alle hure good and sewedon Ion. þenne on a day, as þey comyn into þe 75
cyte of Pargame, when þey seyon þyke þat weren hure seruandes byfore
gon in rych aray and heo hemself in pore wede, by temptacyon of þe
fynd þey forþoghton here purpos and weren sory þat þey hadden lafte
soo hure good. þenne anon by reuelacyon of þe priuete of `God´ Ion
kn[e]w here þoght and sayde to ham: 'Y see how þe deuyl tempteth ȝow 80
and maketh ȝow to forþynk ȝoure purpos þat ȝe were in. Wherfore goth
to þe wode and bryngeth eyþur of ȝow hys burþon of ȝerdes, and aftur
goth to þe see and bryngeth eyþur of ȝow hys burþon of smale stones',
and þey dudon soo. þen at þe preyre of Ion þe ȝerdus turned into gold
and þe stones into precyous ieweles, and þen Ion seyde to hem: 'Now 85
taketh þys gold and þese precyous stones and beth also rych as ȝe were
byfore, and knoweth wel þat ȝe han l[os]t þe kyndam of heuen.'

f. 22ʳ þen happed hyt þat men broghton a ded body to byryon. | But
when þe modur of þe cors seygh Ion, heo fel doun on hure knees to
90 hym, prayng hym þat he wolde hure sone reyse to lyue, as he reysed
Drusyan þe wedewe to lyue. þenne Ion prayed to God and anon he
þat was ded ros vp. þenne Ion sayde to hym: 'Y bydde þe telle þese
men what þou hast yse þen and what ioye þese men han ylost.' þen
he, in heryng of alle men, tolde of þe ioye of paradyse and of þe
95 peynes of helle, how strong and `how´ horribul þey weren, and how
hegh gloryse place were ordeyned for þylke men, and now how sore
hure angeles dude wepe for lure of hem, and how mych ioye þat
fendes made for heo weren so turned from hure perfet lyuyng. þenne
anon þese men weren sory in here hertus and repented hure doyng
100 and, wepyng, cryeden to Ion þat he schulde praye to God for hem.
þenne when Ion segh ham wepen for sorw, he prayed to God for ham
and ȝaf ham penans. And when þey hadden don hure penance, anon
þe golde turned aȝeyn into ȝerdes and þe ieweles into stones, and þey
weren holy men aftur.
105 Anoþur reuelacyon Ion hadde by schewyng of Goddes priuyte. For
on a day he segh a chylde þat was like to ben a good mon. Whefore Ion
broght hym to a byschop and bad hym kepen wel and techen hym.
þenne þys chyld woxe a mon and ȝaf hym al to foly, and so fel to a
company of þefus and was sone aftur a mayster of hem. þenne by
110 reuelacyon of God Ion kn[e]w þat, and anon he ȝede to þe byschop
and blamed hym swyþe for myskepyng of hys chyld, and bad hym
tellen where he was. þen þe byschop wyth much fere sayde he was a
leder of þeves in such a place. þen Ion, for he was old and myght not
wel gon, tok an hors and rod þydur. And when þys þef sagh Ion, he
115 was so aschamed þat he flogh. þen Ion rod aftur crying, and sayde:
f. 22ᵛ 'My swete sone, my | dere sone, abyde and speke wyth þin old fadur.'
So at þe laste þys mon abod. þen Ion preched hym so þat he lafte al
hys foly and was aftur so holy a mon þat he was a byschop aftur. þys
Ion hadde reuelacyon of Goddes priuyte.
120 In þe lyf of Seynt Edward þe Confessour þat lygh at Westmonester
ys wryton þat Seynt Ion appered to Seynt Edward on a day as he ȝode
in processyon, and prayed hym to ȝeve hym som good for Seynt
Ionnes sake euangeliste, for he loued hym much. But for þe kyng had
nothyng ellys redy to ȝeven hym, he tok þe ryng of hys fyngur and ȝaf
125 hym. And so Seynt Ion had þe ryng seven ȝere, and at þe seuen ȝeres

105 narracio *in margin with blue paraph*   110 knew] know   120 narracio *in
margin*   124 he] *to add.*

ende Seynt Ion appered to a knyght of þe kynges byȝonde þe see and
bad hym bere þat ryng to þe kyng, and bed he schuld beþenk hym wel
for whos loue he ȝaf hyt away, and sayde þat he grete hym wel and bad
hym make hym redy, for he schuld dye sone aftur, and so dude.

Anoþur reuelacyon he had when he was syxty ȝere old and seuen.   130
þen com Ihesu Crist to hym wyth hys dyscypules and seyde þys to
hym: 'My derlyng, com now to me, for now hyt ys tyme for þe to ete
wyth me and þi bredren in my fest.' þen he ros vp anon and wold
haue gon. þen sayde Cryst to hym: 'Vpon Sonday þou schalt come to
me.' þen by Sonday he was so febul þat he made to lede hym to   135
chyrch, and, euer as he myght speken, he sayde to hem þat ladden
hym: 'Chyldren, loueth vchon oþur.' þen sayde on to hym: 'Fadur,
why saye ȝe so þus ofte?' þen sayde he: 'For, ȝef ȝe louen togedre, hyt
ys ynogh to saluacyon.' Also he bed ham þat þey schulde be stabul in
þe feyth and feruent in þe commandementes. þen he commandet to   140
make hym a graue byfore þe auter, and, when hyt was mad, h[e] lay
doun in hyt, and þen þer come such a lyght vpon hym a gret whyle
þat | no mon myght sen hym. And when þys lyght was gon, þe put   f. 23ʳ
was ful of manna and welleth vp as doth sond in a welle wyth watur.

[9] De festo innocencium et martirum

Gode crysten chyldren, þys day ys kalled in Holy Chyrch Innocentes
Day, þat ys [in] Englysse Chyldremas Day, for chyldren þat were
slayn for Crystes loue þey ben kalled Innocentes, þat ys, wythout nye.
For þey weren not nyvs to God by pride, for God ys euer nyed wyth   5
pride and aȝeynstondeth prowde men; [þey were not nyvs, ny] to hure
neghbores by no wronge doyng ny to hamself by no consent of synne.
Wherfore Y may wel seyn þey lyueden here clanly wythout schame,
þey dyeden wythout blame, and were yfollewed in hure blod at hame.

þese Innocentes þat Holy Chyrch redeth and syngeht of lyueden   10
here wythout schame, for þey weren alle wythinne too ȝere of age,
wherfore þey were not aschamed of hure owne schap. For whyl a
chyld ys wythinne þe state of innocentry, he ys not aschamed of hys
schap, for he ys not defouled wyth fulþe of synne but wyth þe synne
þat he hath by þe draght of kynde of Adam and of Eve. For so ferdon   15
heo þe same wyse, for þey weren in paradyse in þe stat of innocens:

141 he] ho
[9] 2 Gode] G- in blue, dec., 2 ll. deep   3 in] om.   6 þey . . . ny] me
10 syngeht] over eras.

þey weren naked but þey were not schamed of here schap, for þey
weren wythout synne. But as sone as þey hadden synned, þey seyen
hure schap and weren aschamed þerof and hudden hyt wyth leues of a
20 fygge tre. þus, when synne bygynneth for te take rote in a chyld,
þenne innocens goth away. For þen he bygynneth to knowen þe gode
by þe evel, and when he leueth þe gode and taketh þe evyl, þen he
sungeth, and in þat he ys ˋnoˊ innocent, but in þat he greveth hys
f. 23ᵛ God. But þese chyldren | leuet not so longe for to knowe good by þe
25 euyl but weren yslayn wythinne þe degre of innocens. Wherfore þey
lyueden here wythout schame.

þey dyed also wythout blame. For Herod, kyng of Iewes, made to
slen hem wythout gylte. For when þe kynges comen to Herode and
asked where þe kyng [of] Iewes was ybore and bad tellen hem, for þey
30 were come to wyrschepen hym fer out of þe est, þen was Herode al
astoned of hure wordus and asked hys clerkes where he schulde be
boren. þen sayden þey: 'In þe cyte of Bethleem.' þenne tolde Herod
þe kyngus soo, and bad ham goo þydur and don hym worschyp and
comen aȝayn by hym and telle hym alle hure doyng, þat he myght gon
35 and wyrschepon hym also. But when þus kynges hadde[n do]n hure
offryng to Crist, þey ȝedon hom anoþur way, for an angel in hure slep
bed hem go anoþur way hom, and so deden. þenne was Herod
wondur wrogh and schapped anon to haue slayn Cryst.

But when he hadde maket hym redy þerfore, þat same tyme þe
40 emperour of Rome sende to hym by letter for te come to hym in al þe
hast þat he myght, for two hys owne sones hadden appeched hym to
þe emperour of traytury. So ˋatˊ þat tyme he lafte þe sleyng of Crist
and ȝede [to] Rome and had þe [b]ettur of hys sonus, and so cam hom
wyth more worschep þen he had byfore. Wherfore he þoghte to slen
45 Cryst, lest when he hadde come to monnes state, he wolde haue put
hym out of hys kyngdam. þen sende he men anon and bad hem slen al
þe chyldren þat weren in Bedleem and in al þe contre aboute þat
weren too ȝere old and wythin too, and a chyld þat was bore þat same
day, and so deden. For he wes aferd lest Cryst, þat made a sterre
50 bryngyng þe kynges so fer, cowþe haue turned hymself into diuers
ages and made hym hymself aldur or ȝongur at hys owne wylle, and
for he wes a ȝer in goyng and comyng to Rome, þerfore he made to
slen al þe chyldren þat weren too ȝer old and wythinne. And for
f. 24ʳ wrache schulde fallen vpon hysself in partee | þerfore, a chyld of hys
55 owne was slayn among oþur. But þen com þer an angel to Ioseph and

29 of] *om.*   35 hadden don] haddeyn   43 to] *om.*   bettur] lettur

bad hym taken þe chyld and hys modur and flen to þe lond of Egypt
and be þer tyl he warnd hym, and so dude. þus þys Innocens were
slayn wythout blame.

þey weren also folwed in hure same, þat ys, in hure owne blod, in
no font but in schedyng of hure blod. Wherfore ȝe schul vndurstond 60
þat folth cometh þre wayes: in watur, as we crysten men ben folwed in
þe font ston at þe chyrch; in schedyng of blod, as þese chyldren and
mony þowsand of oþur martyres þat sch[e]dden hure blod for Crystes
loue; [þe] þrydde folþe ys in feyth, in þe whech feyth al patriarchus
and prophetus and al oþur holy fadres þat weren byfore Crystes 65
incarnacyon, þat leueden in Cristes comyng, þey weren folwed in þe
folþe of feyth. þus ȝe m[o]n se how mych cruelte þys mon had in
herte þat slogh so mony þowsand of gultles chyldren for `envye´ þat
`he´ hadde to Criste, þat noght gult hym ne non oþur. þen for he
made mony a modur chyldlas and sore wepe for here deth, God 70
wroght so for hym þat he made slen hys owne chyldren. And aftur, as
he pared a nappul, wyth þat same knyf he styked hymself. þus he þat
was lusty for te schedon gultles blod, at þe laste he sched hys owne
herte-blod. For he þat ys wythout mercy, vengyans falleth on
hymself. And he þat loueth to do mercy, God wol ȝeue hym mercy. 75

And þat Y may afferme by ensampul þat Y fynde in þe lyf of Seynt
Syluester. þer Y fynde þat Constantyn þe emperour was mesel, and
by consel of hys leches he made to gedre þre þowsand of chyldren
yfere for te haue ben slayn, and alle hure blod schulde haue be don in a
vessel and þe emperour haue ben bathet þerin whyl hyt hade ben hot. 80
And þenne when þese chyldren were gedred in a place, þys emperour
com rydyng þydur in a chare. But when he com nygh, þe modres of
þese chyldren wepton aȝeyn hym, crying and wepyng and on-fax,
makyng a dulful noyse. þen asked | þe emperour what wemen þat f. 24ᵛ
were. þen sayde oþur þat þey were þe modres of þe chyldren þat 85
schuld be dede, and þey made þat noyse for sorwe of hure chyldre.
þen sayde þe emperour: 'Hyt were a cruel dede of vs to make so mony
bodyes be slayn for to hele my body þat am but on mon. And mony of
ham may be eraftur `ful´ worþy men and stonden oure empyre in ful
gret stude. Nay,' quod he, 'Y wol not so. Let hem gon hom hol and 90
sound. And `Y´ wol take þe penance þat ys ordeynet for me,' and
made to ȝeue þe modres gret ȝyftes, and so bad ham gon hom wyth

---

57 warnd] *over eras.*   61 we] ben *add.*   63 schedden] schodden   64 þe¹] in
67 mon] men   68 envye] *marked by red dots*   69 he¹] *marked by red dots*
76 narracio *in margin with red paraph*   89 ful] *marked by red-dotted caret*

myrthe and gladnes þat comyn þydur wyth sorwe and wepyng. þenne
þe nyght aftur, as þe emperour lay in hys bed sclepyng, Petur and
95 Paule comen to hym and sayden: for þat gret compassyon þat he
hadde on þe chyldren and hure modres, God sende hym worde þat he
wolde haue compassyon on hym, and bad hym senden aftur Seynt
Siluester and folwy[n] hym, and þen he schulde ben hol, and so he
dude. þen when he was folwot þer, anon in þe watur þe lepur fel away
100 fro hym, and he `was´ as clene of hude and skyn as any chyld þat he
delyuered byfore.

þus ȝe may sen how þat he þat wol ay do mercy schal haue mercy.
And he þat loueth to do vengyans, vengyans schal fallen on hymself.
Soo dude Herod: he dude ve[n]gians [and vengians] fel on hym. And
105 for þus oþur mon dude mercy, he hadde mercy and grace bothe here
and henne.

[10] *De sancto Thoma Cantuariensi episcopo*

Thys day ys Sent Thomas Day, a marter þat was slayn for þe law of
Holy Chyrch and for þe ryght of þys reeme. þys holy Seynt Thomas
was boren in þe cyte of London and hadde a fadur was kalled Gylbard
5 þat was schyref of London. þen fel hyt as þys Gylbert ȝede into þe
Holy Lond, he was taken and put in dystresse. þen come þer a
wyrschepful womon of þe contre to hym and sayde: ȝef he wolde
f. 25ʳ plyghte hure trowþe for te wedde hure, | heo wolde helpon hym out
of dystresse, and so deden. þen went Gylbard hom to Engelon, and
10 heo, when heo segh hure tyme, com aftur and mette wyth hym in þe
chyrch of Sent Poule at London. þen made Gylbard þe byschop of þe
cyte to folwe hure and aftur for te wedde hem togedur. And so
Gylbard gat Thomas on þus womon.

And when heo was wyth chyld, heo mette in a nyght þat heo cam to
15 Sent Poule chyrch, but, when heo wolde han gon in, here wombe was
[so] gret þat heo myght by no way in. þen on þe morwe scho ȝede to
hure scryf-fadur and tolde hym hure sweuen. þen sayde he: 'Dame,
be glad and þonke God ȝurne, for þou hast a chyld in þy baly þat schal
ben so holy þat al Holy Chyrch schal be to lytyl to reseyve hym.' þen
20 was heo glad and þonk God ȝurne, and sone aftur, whyn þys chyld
was boren, he was folwed and called Thomas, þat ys vndurstonden al

---

98 folwyn] folwym   100 as¹] *over eras.*   104 vengians] vegians and vengians]
om.

[10] 2 Thys] T- *in blue, dec., 2 ll. deep*   16 so] *om.*

mon, for he was aftur a mon at al. For he serued þe kyng monly, he
serued God devowtly, and dyed for þe lawes ful mekely.
He serued þe kyng monfully. For what tyme þat he was mad
chanseler, þys 'lond' was ful of Flemmynges and so ouerset wyth ham   25
þat no mon myght gon bytwynne townes for ham onrobbed. But in a
schert tyme aftur, Thomas, what wyth wysdam, what wyth monhode,
he drof hem out of þys lond and mad such reste and pees al þe lond
þat a mon myght gon where he wold, vnrobbod wyth hys gold in hys
hond. He was also monful in raparayleyng of þe kynges maneres þat   30
weren destryed, and nomely of þe kynges palys in London þat was al
forlet. But bytwysse Astur and Wytnestyde Thomas made reparen hyt
aӡeyn, for he hadde 'þer' so mony werkmen of diuers craftes þat a
mon schulde | vnneþe here hys felow speken for dun of strokes. He   f. 25ᵛ
was also monful in dedus 'of' armys. For þeras þe kyng hadde   35
beӡonde see mony castellus and townes out of hys hond and had
spende much gold and sched much blod for te geton ham and myght
not gaynon, þeras Thomas wyth hys wyt and monhed geet ham aӡeyn.
And also in þe werres of þe kynges of Fraunce he bar hym so þat
þeraftur þe kyng louede hym cherely and was aftur hys best frend in   40
hys exulyng and hys chyf help and sokur.
He was also monful in hys araye. For he was cloþed in þe rychest
cloþ and furreur þat myght ben yfond. He hadde also þe best hors þat
myght ben yfond in þe reme, and al hys sadules and brydeles schon al
of seluer. He was also monful in houshold. Hys halle was vche day of   45
þe ӡere new stryed in somur wyth grene rusches and in wyntur wyth
clene hey forto save knyghtus cloþus þat seton on þe flore for defaute
of place on þe bench, so fele comen vch day to hys mete. For of alle
deynteyþus þat weron wythinne þe reme, in hys hows weren
pleynteþ, so þat þe kyng hymself wolde ofton tyme vnwarnd come   50
to þe mete and syt doun, bothe for love þat he hadde to Thomas and
also for þe raye of Thomas howshold þat al men speken so mych of.
For trewer loue ne bettur was þer neuer bytwyxen too men þen was
bytwynne þe kyng and Thomas, whyl hyt laste.
Wherefore Y putte hyre þus ensampul. In a colde wyntures day, as   55
þe kyng and Thomas rydon yfere in Chepe at London, þen was þe
kyng war of a pore mon sore acolde wyth toren cloþus, and seyde to
Thomas: 'Hyt were almes to ӡeu þe ӡonder pore mon warmur cloþus
þen he hath—he semeth ful sore acolde.' 'Syre,' quod Thomas, 'so
hyt were, and to such ӡe schulden taken hede.' þen seyde þe kyng: 60

37 blod] *over eras.*

'He schal haue þus.' þen hadde Thomas a cloþ vpon hym of fyn scarlet wel yfurred wyth grys. þys cloþ þe kyng pulled atte faste for

f. 26ʳ to | haue drawen hyt of hym, but he loggud aȝeyn faste. And þus þey wrastelen longe, so þat sum tyme þey weren nygh to han fallen boo to

65 gronde. But for fauur Thomas suffred þe kyng to pullen hyt of. And when he had hyt of hym, þe kyng caste hyt to þe pore mon and bad hym rennen away faste and sayde: 'Haue þys and sel hyt and bye þe oþur, for, and þou besette hyt wel, þou myght fare þe bettur al þo dayes of þy lyf.' þen Thomas feyned hym wrogh, but he [was] wel

70 apayed þerof, þat hys cloþ was so wel bysette. þen hadde men furst gret maruayl what come bytwysse þe kyng and Thomas, but, when þey wyston and kn[e]wen how hyt was, alle men lowen and maden gret borde þerof. þys Y say for te schewen by ensampul how þey louet togedre, for bettur love ne trewer myght non haue ben bytwynne too

75 breþren þen was bytwyn þe kyng and Thomas, whyl hyt laste. þus Thomas serued þe kyng monfully.

He serued also God devowtly. For also sone `as´ he was arche-byschop of Canturbury, anon he wox anoþur mon and turned al hys lyf into bettur, and þoght to serue þe kyng of heuen aftur þat as wel as

80 he hadde don þe kyng in erþe byfore. þen anon he layde away scarlet and ryche furres and wered blake cloþes of myddel prys, and cast away selke and sandel and wered nexte hys flessche an hard here and a broch syde to hys hommes of þe same, þat bredden so mych vermyn on hym þat hyt was an horrybul þyng for te sen, but þys penance no

85 mon kn[e]w but he þat hadde seyn hyt. But he euer hudde hyt so þat þer were but fewe þat kn[e]wen hyt. Also vche Wednesday and vch Fryde he made hys confessour to beton hym wyth a ȝard on þe bare bak, as a chyld ys beton in a scole. Also vch day he vsed for te wasche þe feet of þrytty pore men knelyng and ȝeue vchon of ham foure

f. 26ᵛ penees. | Muche oþur penans he vsed in hys leuyng of preyng [and] of

91 wakyng þat were to longe to telle.

But for to scwen þat God loued hym specyaly, þys ensampul Y telle. When Thomas wes exiled and dwelled in þe abbey of Pountney, on a day when he hadde sey[de] hys masse, he knelled adoun byfore

95 þe auter in hys preyeres. And as he knelled þer, þe abbot of þe place hadde to speke wyth hym and abood hym wythouton priuyly vndur a pyler. And as he stod þer, he herde oure Lord Ihesu Cryst speke wyth Thomas and tolde hym how he schulde be slayn in hys owne chyrch

69 was] *om.*   70 hys] *dot under* h-   72 knewen] knowen   85 knew] know
86 knewen] knowen   90 and] *om.*   94 seyde] seyn

for hys loue. Wherfore he bad hym be studfast and holde forth as he
hadde bygonnon. þen when Thomas com out of hys chapel, þe abbot 100
fel doun to grond and sayde: 'Syre, ȝe mon blesse þe tyme þat ȝe
weron yboren for to haue such a visytacyon as Y now haue yherde.'
þen sayde Thomas: 'Ȝef þou haue oght herd, we chargeth þe þat þou
neuer telle hyt mon whyl we ben on lyue.' So whyl he lyued he huld
hyt clos, but, when Thomas was ded, he told hyt opunly to al men. 105
þus Y seye Thomas serued God devowtly.

He dyud also ful mekely. For when he soght how þe kyng ouer-
sette Holy Chyrch and made lawes in suche þat schuld haue destryed
þe lond, þen Thomas put hym forth and repreued þe kyng of hys
mysdoyng. þenne wes þe kyng wroth and made a parlemend at 110
Northamton al in misanse of Thomas. And for Thomas wolde not
setton hys seeal to cursed lawes þat þe kyng and hys sory counsayle
hadde imaked, he was demot as traytur to þe kyng and | exuled howt f. 27ʳ
of þe lond. þen wente Thomas to þe kyng of Fraunce for sokure, and
he louyngly reseyved hym and alle hys clerkus and fond hem almast 115
seuen ȝere al þat ham byhoued. þenne aftur mony deseses and greues
and wronges þat he hadde mekely suffred of þe kyng of Engelond and
of hys offyceres, boþe in Englon and beȝond see, by trete of þe pope
and of þe kyng of Fraunce þer was mad a feynod loue-day bytwysson
þe kyng of Engelon and Thomas. But when þe 'kyng' schuld haue 120
cussed Thomas, he wold not, for he sayde he hadde mad a vow þat he
wolde neuer cusse Thomas, but bad hym boldly gon hom to hys
chyrche. þen, wat by consayl of þe kyng of Fraunce and princepaly
for þe byddyng of þe pope, he ȝede hom to Canturbyry.

þen were þer foure knyghtes of cursed lyuyng þat, for gret hope þat 125
þey hadden to haue a gret þongk of þe kyng, þey madden a vowe yfere
to slen Thomas. And so in Chyldermas Day, almost at nyght, þey
comen to Canturbury into Thomas halle: Syre Reynald Beresone,
Syre Wyllyam Tracy, Syr Richard Bryton, and Syre Hugo Moruyle.
þen Reynald Beresone, for he was boystrus of kynde, wythouten any 130
gretyng he sayde þus to Thomas: 'þe kyng þat ys byȝonde see sende
vs to þe and bed þat þou assoyle þe byschoppes þat þou hast cursed.'
þen sayde Thomas: 'Syres, þey ben acursed by þe pope and not by
me, and Y may not asoyle þat þe pope acurseth.' 'Wel,' quod Reynald,
'þen we seen þou wolt not doun þe kynges byddyng—by þe enon of 135
God, þou schalt be ded þerfore!' þen cryed þat oþur knyghtes: 'Sle,
sle,' and ȝedon doun into þe court and armed ham.

104 huld] schuld

þen clerkus and monkus drowen Thomas into þe chyrch and
sparreden þe dores to hym. But when Thomas herd þe k[n]yghtes |
f. 27ᵛ armed in þe cloystre and wolde haue comen in and moght not,
141 Thomas ʒod to þe dore and vnbarred þe dore, and tok a knyght by þe
hond and sayde: 'Hyt bysemeth not to maken Holy Chyrche a
castel—cometh in, my chyldren.' þen, for hyt was dark þat þey
myght not wel knowen Thomas by anoþur, he sayde: 'Where ys þys
145 traytur?' 'Nay,' quod Thomas, 'no traytur but þe erchebyschop.' þen
sayde he aʒeyn: 'Fle, for þou ard but ded.' 'Nay,' quod Thomas, 'Y
cam not for te flen but forte abyden and taken my deth for Goddes
loue and for þe ryght of Holy Chyrch.'
þen Reynald wyth hys swerdes poynt put of Thomas cappe þat he
150 hadde on hys hed, and smot at hym, and kutte half hys crowne. þen
anoþur smot aftur, and hutte in þe same stroke, and smot hys croune
`al´ of, þat hyt honget by as hyt hadde ben a dysch. þen Thomas fel
doun on hys knees and elboes and sayde: 'God, into þy hondes Y
betake my cause and þe ryght of þys chyrch', and so dyud. þen þe
155 þrydde knyght smot and hut half hys stroke vpon a clerkus arm þat
held Thomas [crosse] byforen hym, and þat oþur del fel doun to
Thomas hed. And he þat hadde þat half strok anon wythdrowe hys
arm and flogh away. þen smot þe fyrþe knyght hys swerd to þe
pamand and brast þe poynt of hys swerd. And when þey hadde so
160 don, þey sayden: 'He ys ded—go we hennes.' But when þey weren at
þe chyrch dore outward, won Robert Brok ʒede aʒeyn, and set hys fot
in Thomas necke, and scrypput out þe brayn of þe skolle abouton on
þe pament. þus for ryght of Holy Chyrch and þe lawes of þus lond
Thomas tok hys deth ful mekely.
f. 28ʳ   þen how þus martyrdom was knowen in Ierusalem hyt fel | þus: in
166 Ierusalem was an abbey of monkus, in þe wheche, þat same tyme þat
Thomas dyed and þat same day, a monk lay [at] þe poynt of deth. þen
for he was a gode mon of lyuynng, hys abbot [b]ad hym, ʒef God were
payed, þat he schulde comen to hym aftur hys deth and tellen hym of
170 hys fare. And so aftur he was ded, he com aʒeyn and told hys abbot
þat, when he dyud, angelus broghton hym byfore God, and anon, þer
he stod, he seght a byschop com wyth a gret company of angelus and
oþur seyntus, and, as he stod byfore God, hys hed droppud doun of
blod of hys wondes þat he hadde. þen sayde God to hym: 'Thomas,
175 þus hyt bysemyth þe for to comyn into þy Lordes cowrt', and sette a

139 knyghtes] kyghtes   141 ʒod] -o- *over eras.*   156 crosse] *om.*   165 fel]
þus in ierusalem *catchwords f.* 27ᵛ   167 at] *om.*   168 bad] had

gret crowne of brende gold vpon hys hed þat was wounded, and
sayde: 'Also much ioye as Y haue ʒeuen to Seynt Petur, so much Y
ʒeue þe.' And þen he sayde: 'Herby Y knowe wel þat þyke gret
byschop of Canturbyry ys þys day yslayn for þe loue of God, and so
kn[o]we wel þat Y go to þe blysse.' þys told þe patriark of Ierusalem   180
sone aftur hys deth, þat come into Engelond aftur men for to fygthon
aʒeynes þe Sarysenes.

And a bryd þat cowþe speken, as he herde þe pepul þat come on
pylgrimage to seynt Thomas, as he was out of hys cage, a sparhauke
wolde haue slayn hym. þen þys bryd cryed: 'Seynt Thomas, helpe,   185
Seynt Thomas, help!' And anon þe sparhauke fel doun ded. þe[n],
insomuch þat Thomas herde so sone a bryd þat wyst not wat he
mante, much sanner he hereth ham þat calleth to hym in hure herte.

Anoþur mon þat Seynt Thomas loued in hys lyue was sek and come
to Seynt Thomas prayng hym of help, and anon he was helud. But,   190
aftur, he þoghte þat God sende hym þat sykenes for myche more
encreces of sowle mede, and ʒode to Seynt Thomas, preyng hym, ʒef
hyt were more help to hys soule for to be sek þen hol, þat he moste be
seke aʒeyn. þen anon þe sekenes toke hym aʒeyn and he þo|ngket   f. 28ᵛ
God and Seynt Thomas.   195

And when þe kyng herde how God wroghte so mony myracles for
Seynt Thomas, he come to Canterbyry wolward, and barefot, and al
naked but a febul cote to hyde hys body, goyng in þe fen and þe lake as
he hadde ben þe porest mon of þe rem, cryng and [sykyng] ful sore
and prayng to Seynt Thomas of help and forʒefne[s]. So w'h'en he   200
com to Seynt Thomas toumbe, he made al þe couent of þe place by
and by to ʒeu hym dyscypline on hys bare bak wyth a ʒerde. And þer
al þe sory costend and þe lawes þat maden þe debate bytwyxen
Thomas and hym byfore hys tombe he dampned hem and granted þe
chyrche hure fredames aʒayn, and so ʒede hys way.   205

þese foure knyghtes, when þey herdon how God wroghte for Seynt
Thomas, þey weren ful sore of here cursed dede and cursed þe tyme
þat hyt byfel ham so, and lafton alle hure lorschep, þes londes and
rentes þat þey hadden, and wenton to Ierusalem, and þere werredon
on Goddes enemys. But Wyllyam Tracy, by lettyng þat he hadde, he   210
taryed byhynde and fel sek by þe way and roted al hys body, so þat
hymself lompemal wyth hys hondes kaste away hys flesche into þe
flore and dyed an horrybul deth. þe oþur þre also dyed on pytewys

deth, so þat, wythin þre ȝere aftur Thomas deth, heo weren ded alle.
215 But also longe as þey lyued, þey cryed euer of mersy to God and to
Seynt Thomas.

[11] *De festo circumcisionis domini*

Gode crysten men, þys day [ys] kalled Newe ȝerus Day as endyng of
þe ȝere þat hys gon and þe bygynyng of þe ȝere þat ys comyng.
Wherfore, has Y hope, ȝe ben comen as þys day to Holy Chy[r]ch for
5 to contynue ȝoure seruyse forth þys ȝer þat ys to come as wel or
betture as [ȝ]e haue don þe ȝer þat ys gon, wythout any newe
couenand makyng. For a gode seruand þat hath a gode mayster he
maketh but ones couenand wyth hym [but so holdeth forth fro ȝer to
ȝer, hauyng full trayst in hys mayster þat he wol for hys gode seruyce
10 ȝeu hym a gode reward at hys ende and at hys nede. Now ryght so
Goddys seruand maketh couenand wyth hym] ones at þe font when he
hys crystened and so halt forth hys couenand, hauyng ful trayst in hys
God þat he wol at hys nede ben hys sykur frynde and ȝeu hym
f. 29ʳ auansement in hys court of heuen. þen schal | ȝe þat ben Goddes
15 seruandes knowe wel þat þys day ys kalled Newe ȝeres Day, and also
þe cyrcumcysyon of oure Lord, and also þe vtas of þe natyuyte.
Hyt ys kalled Newe ȝeres Day for hyt ys furst day of þe kalender.
þen for þe [ȝ]er ys rewled and gouerned by þe kalender and þys day
ston in þe bygynnyng þerof, þerfore hyt ys kalled ȝeres Day. þenne
20 setht Seynt Austyn þat þus nyght paynemus vson mony false
opiniyones of whychcraft and of fals feyth, þe whyche byn not for
to tellen among crystene men, lest þey weren drawen into vse.
Wherfore, ȝe þat ben Goddes seruandes, be ȝe wel war, lest ȝe ben
deseyuot by any sorsory or by mys[by]l[e]ue, as by takyng honsel of
25 on mon raþur þen of anoþur, oþur for to bygge or sulle and asken or
borwe, in þe wheche somme han mony dyuerse opynyonus, þat, ȝef
þey were c[l]ene scryuen, þey weron worþy gret penans for mysby-
leue, for þat comyth of þe fynde and not of God.
þys day also ys kalled þe cyrcumcysyon of howre Lord. For, as al
30 Holy Chyrch techet þys, he was cyrcumsysed and sched hys blod þys
day for oure sake, for when hys flessche was kut fro hym he bledde

---

[11] 2 Gode] G- *in blue, dec., 2 ll. deep*   ys] *om.*   4 Chyrch] chych   6 ȝe] he
8–11 but² . . . hym] *om.*   18 ȝer] her   21 þe] *rep.*   24 mysbyleue] mysloue
27 clene] chene

ȝurne and was ful sor to hym, for he was but ȝong and tendur, not but
eghte dayes old, and þerfore he bledde þe more.
þen ȝe schul knowe þat he bled for vs fyue tymes. þe forme was as
þys day when he was cyrcumsysed. þe odur tyme was when he for 35
fere of hys passyon, as he prayed to hys Fadur, þen he swat blod for
drede. For ryght as a chyld weputh for fere when he sygh þe ȝe[r]de
and ȝet hath he no strok, ryght so þe flesse of Cryst was aferd of þe
stronge passyon þat was comy[n]g and swat blod for drede. þe þrydde
tyme was in hys flagellacyon, when he was wyth feres kynghtus bete 40
wyth scorges vpon hys bare body, þat he was ronnyng blod al about.
þe forþe tyme was when he was nayld hond and fot to þe cros and
heuen vp þat þe body pesed doun and þe blod of hys hondus stremed
down by hys harmes doun by hys body. þe fyfþe tyme was when þe
spere oponed hys syde and blod and watur ran out. þe fyue tymes he 45
sched hys blod for vs.
þen | soþen Cr[y]st was wythout synne cyrcumsod, and syr- f. 29ᵛ
cumcyson was ordeyned in reme[d]y of synne, why wold he ben
cyrcumsysud? Seynt Austyn seth: for foure causes. On was for to
maken a syth wyth þe Iewes, ellus þey myghton skylfully han seyd to 50
hym: 'þou art not of oure lawe, whe[r]fore we reseyue þe not ne
consenton to þy techyng.' þe secunde wa`s´ for te deseyue þe fynde.
For ryght as he deseyuot Ewe, owre allur mod[ur], and so dampned al
monkynde, ryght so hyt lee to Cr[y]st to de[se]yue hym, wherþoȝgh al
monkynde schulde be broght aȝeyn to blysse. þen when þe fynd sygh 55
Cr[y]st cyrcumcysyd as oþur weren, he wende he hadde taken þat
penance in remedy of orygynal synne and so knew hym noght by
anoþur synful mon. For ȝef he hadde knowen hym redyly þat he
hadde comon for to buggen monkynde out of hys þraldam, he wolde
neuer ha tysud mon to haue don hym to þe deth. þys was also þe 60
cause why oure Lady was wedded to Iosep[h]: for to deseyve þe fynde,
þat he schuld wenon þat Ioseph hadde ben hys fadur and not
conseyuot of þe Holy Gost. [þe] þrydde cause why he was cyrcum-
sysod was to confermon þe Olde Lawe in gret comford of fadrus of þe
old testament. For ȝef he hade be folwod and not cyrcumcysed, hyt 65
hadde ben a gret dysconford to alle þat weren byfore þe `in´carnacyon
of Cr[y]st. þe fourþe cause of hys cyrcumcysyon was for he weste wel

---

37 ȝerde] ȝede   39 comyng] comyg   47 Cryst] crst   48 remedy] remekyon
51 wherfore]whefore   52 was] -s *over eras.*   53 modur] mod   54 Cryst] crst
deseye] deyue   56 Cryst] crst   57 in] þe *add. and canc.*   61 Ioseph] iosepl
63 þe] *om.*   67 Cryst] crst

þat þe herytekus schuldo[n] comme þat wolden sayn þat Cr[y]st
hadde a body of þe eyre by fantesy and not very flesse and blud as we
70 hauen. þen for a body of þe eyre may not bledon ny hath no blod in
hym, þerfore, to putten away þat error, Cryst was cyrcumcysod and
bl[e]dde in þe cuttyng of hys flesse, þe wheche flesse þat was cut f[ro]
hus membre an angel aftur broght to Kyng Charles for þe moste
vertues rele[k] of þe world, and he, for þe grast worschep þat he couþe
75 do þerto, broght hyt into Rome to þe chyrch þat ys challed *Sancta
Sanctorum.* For þese foure causes Ihesu Cryst was cyrcumcysed.

þys day also ys kalled þe vtas of þe natyuyte, þat ys, þe [e]ghte day
of oure Lordes burth, in techynng to vs þat ben Crystus seruandes to
þenken on þe eghte dayes þat sewon hys burth-day. þe furste day ys
f. 30ʳ to þenke inwardly on þe sed þat he ys conseyvot of, þat ys | so foule in
81 hymself and so wlateful þat mon or wommon, be þey neuer so fayre,
and þey seen þat mater, hure hert wol wlaten and ben schamot of
hymself to þenkon þat he were conseyuot of so foule þyng. þe
secunde day ys for to þenken how greuesly he payned hys modur
85 in hys burth-tyme, insomuche þat hyt was an hegh myracul of God
þat heo skapud to lyue. þe þrydde day ys to þenken how febul and
how wrechet he ys borun, for alle bestus of kynde somwhat con help
hamself, saue mon: he neyþur may ne con not help hymself in a degre,
but schulde dyon anon ȝef he where not holpun of oþur. þe ferþe day
90 ys for to þenken in how myche drede and perel he lyueht euer, for
euermore in vche place deth scheweth hym, redy for to falle on hym,
what tyme ne where he not neuer. þe fyfþe day ys for to þenken how
ho`r´rybul deth ys when he cometh, for in schert tyme he makuth hym
so to stynke þat alle hys best frendes ben bysy for to putton hym into
95 þe herþe and hydon hym þere. þe sexte day ys for to þenken how
rowþeful ys þe partyng of þe soule fro þe body, þat m[o]w not be
departed tyl þe hert in þe body breke for drede of syghþes þat þe
sowle syth. þe seuenthtes day ys to þenken how dredeful schal be þe
day of dome þat he goht to anon. þen he [þat] þenketh bysylyche on
100 þese seuen dayes he schal [ben cyrcumsysed þe eghte day, þat ys to
saye, he schal] [k]utte away from hym þe luste of ys flessch and
worldes lykyng, and so schal he comen to þe vtas of Cr[y]st, þat ys, to
þe ioye þat ys in heuen blysse. To þat b[ly]sse God bryng vs et cetera.

---

68 schuldon] schuldom   Cryst] crst   69 not] no(t? *er.*)   72 bledde] blodde
fro] for   74 relek] relef   77 eghte] (S?)ghte   96 mow] mew   99 þat²] *om.*
100–1 ben . . . schal] *om.*   101 kutte] putte   102 Cryst] crst   103 blysse²]
bylsse

[12] *De ep[ip]hania domini*

þys day ys kalled Tolþe Day, but al amys, for hyt ys þe þretteneth day
of Crystemas, þe wheche day Holy Chyrche challeth þe Epiphany, þat
ys, in englys, þe schewyng of oure Lord Ihesu very God and mon þat
he was. þys day, as Holy Chyrch maketh mynde, Ihesu Cryst was 5
schewed verey God and mon þre vayes: by þre kynges offryng, in hys
owne folwyng, and by watur turnyng into wyn. þe þrotteneth day
aftur hys burth he wes schewod by þe offryng of þre kynges; and þat
same day, nyne and twenty 3er and þryttene dayes aftur, he was
folwod in þe watur of flom Iordan; and þat same day twelmoneth aftur 10
he turned watur | into wyn at a weddyng in þe Cane of Galylee.   f. 30ᵛ

But þys fest makuth most mynde of þese kyngus offeryng. þerfore
pursewe we þe forme of Holy Chyrche and telle we howe by hore
offryng Ihesu Cryst was schowot very God and mon. þese þre kyngus
weron of þe lynage of Balaham, þat profesyed how þat a [s]te[r]re 15
schulde spryngen of Iacob. And þagh þey were no Iewes of kynde,
[n]erþeles þey hodden yhorde by aunsetrye of þe sterre. Wherfore þey
wylled muche for to seyn hoe, and often tymus nyghtus comen
togedur vpon serteyn hullus for to dysspyte by astromony of þys
sterre. þen vpon Crystenmas nyght, þe same tyme þat Cryst was 20
boren, as þey weren yfere spytyng of þe steˋrˊre, a sterre come to ham
bryghtur þen any sonne, and in þe sterre a fayre chyld and vndur hys
hed a bryght cros of gold, and sayde þus to ham: 'Goght anon wyth
alle hast into þe lond of Ievrye and takuth wyth how gold and ensense
and myrre, and offreth þese þre to hym þat ys þer now yboren kyng of 25
Iewes, verey God and mon, and Y wol ben 3oure gyde and ledon 3ow
þe nexte way þydur.'

þen þey wyth gret hast token dromedaryuus, þat ben of kynde so
swyfte þat þey wol rennen in on day forre þen any hors in þre dayes,
and so rydon to Ierusalem, þat ys þe hedd cyte of þewry, hopyng for 30
to wyte þer sone were þys chyld was boren. But anon as þey turned
into þys cyte, þe leston þe syght [of þe sterre, þat glode euer byfore
ham tyl þey comon þydur, bryghtur] þen þe sonne. þenne for Kyng
Herod was þere, þey 3odon to hym and asked where þe kyng of Iewes
was yboren, and sayde: 'We seyen hys sterre in þe est and ben comon 35
wyth offryng to worschep hym.' þen was Herod al trowblod, and al þe

[12] 1 *epiphania*] ephania   2 þys] þ- *in red, dec., 4 ll. deep*   3 day Holy
Chyrche] *rep.*   5 as] ades?   15 a sterre] aftere   17 nerþeles] þˋaˊerþeles
32–3 of . . . bryghtur] *om.*

cyte wyth hym, mor for te glauereng of ham þen for any loue þat þey
hadden to hym. þen asked Herod hys clerkus: 'Wherre ys þe chyld
schulde be boren?' And þey sayde: 'In Bedlem.' þen Herod priuyly
40 asked þese kynges of þe sterre and bad ham gon to Bedlem and
wyrscheppon þys chyld, and comen aӡayn by hym and tellen hym
where he myght fynde þys chyld, þat he myght goo and wyrschep
hym as þey dude.
   þen when þese kyngus were passed þe town toward Bedlem, anon
f. 31ʳ þe sterre apered aӡeyn to ham. And when þey seyen þe | sterre comen
46 aӡeyn, þey were wondur gretly ioyed in hure hert. þen as hyt ys mony
plases peynted and koruen, þat þe kyng þat ys in þe myddel, for gret
ioye þat he hadde, wryed on bakward to hys felow byhynde and put
hys honde vp, schewyng þe sterre to hym. Lewot men han opynyon
50 and sayn þat he hadde slayn a mon, wherfore he myght not se God in
þe face. But God forbede þat þys opynyon where trewe, for now ys
mony hundred of gret seyntes in heuen þat where byfore monsleeres
and duden mony an holy martyr to deþe, but aftur þey weren turned
and holy marteres hamself and sen God in þe face euermore.
55   þen þese kyngus sewen þys sterre forth tyl þey comen into Bedlem,
and when hyt come ouer þe hows þer Cryst was, hyt stod stylle. þen
þese lyghton down and ӡodon into þe hous and fondon þe chyld wyth
hys modur. And þen, wyth all þe reuerens þat þey couþon, þey kneled
doun and offred vche of hem þese þre þyngus: gold, ensence, and
60 myrre, knowlachyng by þe gold þat he was kyng of alle kynges, and by
þe encence þat he was verey God, and by þe myrre þat he was very
mon, þat schulde be ded and layd in graue wythouten rotyng. For
gold ys kyng of metel; ensence ys brend in holy chyrche in worschep
of God; myrre ys an vnement þat keputh ded bodyes from rotyng.
65 þus when þese kynges haddon don hure offryng, by thechyng of [an]
angel þey lafton Hero[d] and ӡedon hom by anoþur way, and [þe]
sterre vaneschod away into hure forme kynde. þenne Ioseph, as Seynt
Bernard sayth, kepte of þe gold as meche `as´ hym nede[t] for hys
trybut þat he schulde to þe emperour, and more þat hym nedet for
70 oure Lady whyle heo lay in chyldbed, and þe remenand he dalde to
such þat hadden nede. þe s[e]n[c]e he brend to put away þe stenche of
þe stabul þer scho lay. And wyth þe myrre oure Lady wasche þe chyld
to kepon hyt fro wormes and oþur fulþes.

41 aӡayn] aӡanyn   50 he¹] ha *add.*   65 an] *om.*   66 Herod] heron   þe] *om.*
68 as] *marked by cross* nedet] neden   71 sence] sone   72 Lady] laydy (-y- *marked*
by dot)

But what fel aftur [of] þese kynges Y fynde noþyng put in serteyn
but by opynyonus, þat sayen | how Thomas of Ynde, whan he come   f. 31ᵛ
into [þe] contre, he folwot ham, and þen, ryght as þe sterre lyghte   76
ham to Cristus burth, ryght so þe [H]oly Gost lyght ham wythin and
schewot ham what was þe perfet way to heuen, so þat þey lafton al
hure remes and hure lordschoppes and 30den forth as pylgrymes to
Ierusalem and to oþur plases þer Cryst suffred deth, and so forth þey   80
comen to Melayn and þer dyedon. But aftur þey weren translated to
Colayn and so beth kalled kynges of Colayn.

Now 3e haue herde how oure Lord Ihesu Cryst was þys day
schewed by þese kynges offryng. Wherfore, as þey offred þen [to hym,
so schulde 3e do 30ure offryng to hym þus. When 3e com] to Holy   85
Chyrche, wyth al þe reuerens and mekenes þat 3e con, kneluth doun,
not on 30wre on kne, as to a lord temporal, but on boo 30wre knees,
and doth hym worschep. And 3e so don, þen 3e offren to [hym]
þrecyous gold, for þer nys no gold in þys world so precyous in þe
syght of God as ys þe preyere of a meke mon and logh hert of a mon or   90
woman. þen herewyth holdeth vp 30wre hondes to hym [wyth a]
deuowt hert and seyth þus: 'Lord God, haue mercy of me synful.'
And þen 3e offren to hym sence, for þer ys no s[enc]e brennyng þat
sauereth so sote in monnes nese as doth a deuowt preyere in Goddes
nese [and] in al þe angelus of heuen. And sethen mekely maket a cros   95
on þe erþe and cusse hyt and seyth: 'Lord, when [Y] þat am erþe schal
dyen and turne into erþe, þen, Lord God, haue my soule.' And þen 3e
offreth to hym myrre, for ryght as myrre keputh a body fro stench and
rotyng, so mynde of deth keputh þe soule fro stench and rotyng in
dedly synne. þese wyse do 3e 30wre offryng and getheth 30u also   100
meche mede as þese kyngus hadden.

He was also schewed [at] hys folwyng. For when he com to fl[o]m
Iorda[n], he 3ede into þe watur and halwed hyt. For ryght as he was
cyrcumsysed to fulfullen and conferme þe Holde Law, [ryght so he
was folwed to halowe and to begynne þe Newe Law,] for no nede þat   105
he hadde þerto, for he was clene wythout synne, but | for te [make]   f. 32ʳ
þat sacrament þat schuld waschen and clansen ham þat token
crystondam in hys name of al synne. þen was Ihon Baptyst redy
þer, and mech pepul wyth hym þat come þydur to benne folwed, and

74 of] om.   76 þe¹] om.   77 Holy] loly   83 Lord] lorld   84-5 to . . .
com] om.   87 lord] lorld   88 hym²] om.   91 wyth a] and   93 sence²] soule
95 and] om.   96 cusse] cussed   Y] om.   102 at] om.   flom] fflem   103 Iordan]
Iordam   104-5 ryght . . . Law] om.   106 make] om.

110 sayde to Crist, quakyng and tremelyng for [fe]re of hym, and sayde:
'Lord, þou art Goddus lombe wythowt synne: þou ast no nede to ben
folwed of me. But Y þat ham a mon geton and bore in synnes most
come to þe to ben folwed in remyssyon of my synnes.' þan sayde Crist
to Iohn: 'Suffur at þys tyme, for þus we moten fulfulle al ryght
115 wylfulleche.' þan Iohn folwed Ihesus Cryst, and, as hys credybul,
oure Lady wes folwed wyth, and oþur þat weren Crystes dyscypules
aftur, and al pepul þat weren comen þydur. þen when al weron
f[ol]we[d], oure Lord Ihesu went out of þe watur, and, as he preyut on
þe wateres brynke and al þe pepul wyth, a gret lyght vmbecluppud
120 hym, and so, in syght of Seynt Iohn and al þe pepul, þe Holy Gost in
lykenes of a whyt coluer lyght on Crystus hed, and þe Fadur of heuen
spak þus in heryng of al: 'þys ys my Sone wel byloued þat wel pleseth
me.'
   Al þys was donne for to techen vche cristene mon hys byleve, for
125 vche criston mon ys holdon for to leuen in þe Fadur and in þe Sone
and in þe Holy Gost, þat ben þre persones in on Godhed. And þagh
þe Fadur spak abouen, and þe Sone Ihesus Cryst were þer bodyly,
and þe Holy Gost in lykenes of a koluer, ȝe schul byleue þat þer ben
þre persones and on God in trynite. þys byleue ȝe knowlache on þe
130 watur brynke, þat ys, vpon þe brynke of þe font wen ȝe ben folwed.
Wherfore he þat byleueth þys and doth þe werkes of þe byleue,
wythout drede he schal be saued, and he þat byleueth not schal be
dampned. þe werkes of þe byleue ben mekenes and charyte. For
wythout þese too schal neuer non be saued, and he þat hath þese too
135 be wryton in þe genelogye of Ihesu Cryst. Wherfore in þe wytenes of
[þis, þe] genelogye þat ys red in Crystenemas nyght bygynneth aboue
f. 32ᵛ at A|braham and so cometh donward tyl Ioseph and so to oure Lady
Marye, in sch[ow]yng þat he þat ys most mekust of hert he ys nexte to
oure Lord and scuche he avanseth. And þerfore þe genelagye þat ys
140 red þys nyght bygynneth at Ihesu Cryst and goth vpward into
Habraham and so into God, in schewyng þat he þat hath perfet
loue to God and hys euen crystun þys ys wryton in þe genelogye of
God in heuen and schal ben as cosyn and nygh derlyng to God
wythout en. þus Cryst was schewed in hys holy folwyng.
145   He was also schewed by watur into wyn t[u]r[n]yng at þe weddyng
of Iohn euangeliste and Marye Magdaleny. þen, for Iohn was Cristus

110 fere] sorre   115 Iohn] -n *over eras.*   118 folwed] flowen   120 so, in]
written as som   136 þis, þe] *om.*   138 schowyng] sc(-hw- *partly oblit.*)oyng
141 so into] *written as* som to   145 wyn turnyng] wyntryng

aunte sone, he and hys modur and mo of hys dyscypules weron callud
þydur. þen hyt happud so þat he wonted wyn at þe m[e]te. þen bad
Ihesus þe seruandes fulle syxe stenes þat stoden wyth watur, and,
w[hen] þey hadden do so, Ihesu blessed ham and bad held and bere to 150
hym þat byganne þe [b]ord. þen sayde he: 'þat was passyng wyn
bettur þen any oþur.' þus Ihesu schewed hym þer werey God and
mon: very God in þat he turned watur into wyn, and very mon in þat
he ete and dronk wyth ham. þys meracule he dede at þys weddyng in
schewyng þat he blessed þe weddyng þat ys doun as þe lawe of Holy 155
Chyrch ordeyneth. þerfore kepe ȝe ȝow in worschepyng of God
mekely, kepyth ȝowre feth strongly, and ȝoure weddyng trewly, and
þen schal ȝe come to þe ioye þat hath no ende veryly.

[13] *De conuersione sancti Pauli apostoli*

Suche a day ȝe schal haue þe fest of Sent Poule, þat ys kalled þ[e]
co[n]uersyon, þat [ys] to say, þe conuertyng of Seynt Poule, for þat
day he was conuerted and yturned fro a cursed tyrand into Goddes
seruand, fro an hegh mon and a proud into a meke mon and a 5
deuo|wt, and fro þe dys`c´ypul of þe deuel into Goddes holy apostel. f. 33ʳ
So for þys mon was þus turned from alle wyckedenes [into godenes]
in gret strenth and help to Holy Chyrch, þerfore Holy Chyrch
halweth hys conuersyon, and so heo doth of non oþur seynt, but
onlych of hym, and þat ys for þre s[k]eles: furst, for gret myracul in 10
hys turnyng, and for gret ioye of hys de[f]endyng, and for hegh
ensampul of amendyng.

Furst þys mon, er he was turned, he was kalled Saule. For, ryght as
Saul, þe kyng of Ierusalem, pursewed þe holy Dauid for to haue slayn
hym, ryght so þys Saul pursewed Cryst and hys dyscypulus and hy[s] 15
seruandes to bryng hem to þe deth. Wherfore, whyl Cryst ȝode on
erþe, he wold nere comen to hym to heren hys thechyng. But al son as
he was styed into heuen, þen anon, for he was lered and cowþe þe
Iewes law, he bygan to ȝeynstonde Crystus dyscypulus, spytyng
aȝeynes ham and pursewyng ham in al þat [he] myght, in ful entent 20
for te haue destryed Crystus lawe. þen on a day he spytud wyth Seynt

148 mete] mote   150 when] wyne   151 bord] lord
[13] 1 *apostoli*] -p- *add. in red*   2 Suche] S- *in red, dec.,* 2 *ll. deep*   þe²] þo
3 conuersyon] couersyon   ys] om.   4–6 was . . . deuo] *written in small bottom f. 32ᵛ*
7 into godenes] *om.*   10 skeles] sveles   11 defendyng] desendyng   15 hys²] hy
17 nere . . . heren] *over eras.*   18 heuen] he huen   20 he] om.

Steuene, and, for he myght not ouercome hym, he schapud how he
myght bryng hym to þe deth, so þat he lafte hym neuer tyl he was
stenud to deth. þen, as yt [ys] þe maner of þe [deuel]es chyldren,
25 when þey han don a foule dede, þen þey ben fayn þerof and prowde in
here herte and encresud in here malys, so was þys Saule glad of þe
deth of Seynt Steuen.

And for he wold geton hym a name of wykednes passynt al hys
felowes, he ȝode to hym þat hadde þe lawe of Iewes to kepon and gat
30 hym a lettur of warand for to takyn and byndon al þat caldon on
Crystes name, where þat þey myghton ben [f]o[n]don, and bryngon
ham bowndon to Ierusalem for to takon hure deth þere. And when he
hadde þese letteres, he tok such a pride þerwyth and such envye in
hys herte aȝeyn criston men þat, when he herde spekon of hem, anon
f. 33ᵛ he wold freþon at þ[e] nese and at þe mowþe for | angur, þretyng and
36 manaschyng so heghly toward ham þat vch cryston mon was wondur
sore aferd of hym.

þen for he herd þat [in] þe syte of Damasce weron mony cryston
men hud for drede, anon he tok hys hors and hys men by hym and rod
40 þydurward in al hast. But þen oure Lord Ihesu Cryst—blessed mot he
be—schewod þe swetnesse of hys grace þus: when þys Saule was in
hys heghest pride and malis and in þe purpos for to haue don most
harm, þen abowton mydday, when þe sonne schon allor clerest, þen
Cryst cast a lyght of grace abowt Saule þat was myche lyghtur þen þe
45 sonne, and in þat lyght spak þus to hym: 'Saul, why pursuest þou
me?' þen he anon was so aferd þat he [f]el doun of hys hors and for
gret fere sayde: 'Lord, what art þou?' þen sayde oure Lord: 'Y am
Ihesus of Nasareht þat þou pursuest.' He sayde not: Y am God of
heuen [ne Goddes Sone of heuen. But for] þey leueden þat he was
50 ryson fro deth to lyue, þerfore Saul pursued hem most and sayde þat
þey leuedon on a ded mon, herfore oure Lord Ihesu sayde: Y am
Ihesu of Nasareth, þat ys þe name of hys monhed. þen leuede Saul on
hym anon and sayde: 'Lord, what wolt þou make me to don?' þen
sayde Ihesu oure Lord: 'Ryse and go into þe cyte, and þer schal ben
55 ysayde to þe wat þou schalt don.'

þen see hys men þys lyght and herdon þe voys but þey seon no
mon, but ȝedon to Saul and tokyn hym by þe honde, for he was blynd,
and ladden hym into þe cyte to a goode monnes hous. And þer he was

24 ys] om.   deueles] iewes   31 fondon] stodon   34 herte] hertet   35 þe¹]
þis   38 he] *rep.*   in] *om.*   44 cast . . . Saule] *over eras.*   46 fel] sel   49 ne . . .
for] *om.*   52 leuede] *over eras.*

þre dayes and þre nyght[es] fastyng and myght not seen, but euer he
prayed to God for þe drede þat [h]e hadde of þat vysyon, þe wheche 60
tyme þe Holy Gost taght [hym] Crystes lawe. þe þrydde day come to
[hym] on of Crystus dyscyplus þat hette Ananias, as God bad hym,
and sayde, ful sore aferd: 'Saul, broþur, oure Lord Ihesu hath sende
me to þe þat þou schalt soen and ben fo[l]wed.' And, when he layde
hys hond on hys hed, anon he seght, and þen þer fel from hys enon 65
lyke skales of a fysche. And when he hadde folwod hym, he kalled |
hym Poule. And when he hadde eton, he was comforded and had hys f. 34ʳ
strenth aȝeyn and was wyth þe dyscyplus þat weren þer a [f]ewe
dayes. And þen he wente into þe temple and opunly preched of Ihesu
Cryst, preuyng clerkly þat he was Crist and non oþur, so þat vche 70
mon wondred of hys sodeyn conuercyon and sayde to hymself þat hyt
was an heght myracul of God þat he [þat] was so cursed of lyuyng was
so sone turned into so blessed a mon. þus, gode men, ȝe moue heren
how gret a myracul God schewed in hys conuertyng.

Holy Chyrche also makuth gret ioye for hys de[f]endyng. Hyt was 75
gret gladnesse to al crysten men for to syn hym þat was a lytyl byforen
bysy for to [destrye hem þen so sodenly bysy for to encrese hem, and
he þat was glad for to] schedden hure blod þen was redy for to schede
hys blod for hem, and he þat ȝode to put ham to deth þen wente
bodyly to take þe deth for ham. And þeras non durst preche Goddes 80
lawe ne Goddus word for hym, aftur, by conford of [hym], þey spared
neyþur for kyng ne for oþur lord, but oponly preched þe feyth of
Ihesu Cryst in vche place. And he þat was so prod byfore, aftur he fel
to vche cristen monnes fot þat he hadde gylt to, askyng mercy wyth
ful meke herte. Wherfore Seynt Austyn lyconeth hym to a vnicorn 85
and s[e]th how þe vnicorn of kynde bereth an horn in hys nase, and
wyth þat horn he sleth al þe bestus þat he fyghteh`t´ wyth and ys so
ferus þat þer may no hunter takyn hym by no crafte. But þus he wol
aspyen wher and when hys walke ys, and þer he setteth a womon þat
ys clene mayden. And when þys vnicorn syth hure, anon of kynde he 90
falleth doun and leth hys hed on hure barm mygh[t]las wythout
strenth and so ys takon. þus, he seyth, Seynt Poule was furst so ferus
and prowd þat þer durst no precher dele wyth hym. But when God
schewed hym þys maydon, þat ys, þe [f]eyth of Holy Chyrche, anon

59 nyghtes] nyght   60 he] ȝe   61 hym] om.   þe] þen   name of hym/
cristyned paul/nanias *cropped in margin in later hand*   62 hym¹] om.   64 folwed]
fowed   layde] *over eras.*   68 fewe] sewe   72 þat²] om.   75 defendyng]
desendyng   77–8 destrye . . . to¹] om.   81 hym²] om.   86 seth] soth
91 myghtlas] mygh las   94 feyth] seyth

95　he fel doun of hys pride and was sympul and meke and suget to al
　　cryston seruans. Herfore Holy Chyrche was glad of hys defendyng.
　　He was also set for ensampul of heth amendyng. God ys so
　　gracyous in hymself þat he wol þat no mon be loren, but he wol
　　þat alle men and women ben saued. Werfore, in heght ensampul and
100　comforde to al synful, he seyt seynt Poule to lokon on. For þagh a

f. 34ᵛ　mon or a womon haue | don neuer so hegh a synne or lyuot so cursed
　　lyf, ȝef he wol taken ensampul of Seynt Poul, þat ys, to leue pride and
　　be meke, lef synne [and] be bysy to amende, and þen schal he make
　　God and al þe court of heuen to make more murþe in heuen of hys
105　conuersyon þen doth Holy Chyrche in erþe of Seynt Poule con-
　　uersyon. But, more harm ys, þer ben mony men and wemen þat louen
　　more hure synne þen God, þat nol nowþur for loue of God ne for
　　drede of p[e]ynes of helle leuen hure synne, but seyun þat God wol
　　not leson þat he dere boght wyth hys blod. But þou þat sayst so, be þe
110　war þat þou lese not þiself, for, whyl þou louest þi synne more þen
　　þou louest þi God and hast leuerer ben þe delus seruand þen Goddes,
　　þou dampnest þiself and art cause of þi owne damp[na]cyon.
　　Wherfore [for] s[uc]h God hath ordeyned [f]endes for to turmenten
　　hem and bry[n]gon hem into þe peyne þat hath non ende. For as
115　Seynt Gregory seyth, heo þat schal be dampned þey begynneth hur
　　penance in party here and so aftur hur deth contynueth forth.
　　　Wherfore Y t[e]lle þys ensampul: þer was a mon, a cursed lyuer,
　　þat was an offycer to a lord, and, as he r[o]d to a maner of þe lordus,
　　he fel wod and, so on-brydul, hys hors bar hym into a maner of hys
120　lordus. But when he come in, anon þe baylyf sagh what þe mon eyled
　　and made anon hys hynon to bynde hym to a post in þe berne. þen,
　　when þe bayly hadde soupud, he bad on of hys hynes gon and lokon
　　how þys mon f[a]rede. And wen he come to þe berne, he segh þre gret
　　doggus blak as cole on uch syde pluked away hys flesse. þen was þys
125　hyne sore afred þat vnneþe he hulde hys whyt, but ȝode to hys bed
　　and lay þer longe syk aftur. On þe morwen when men comen to þe
　　berne, þey fundon no more of þe mon but hys bare bones and al þe
　　flesch away.
　　　þus woso lyueth a fowle lyf he may ben sykur of a foule ende, and
130　þagh hys ende be fayre to monnes eye, hyt ys ryght foule in Goddus
　　syght and al hys angelus. Wherfore vch mon take ensampul by Seynt

---

103 and¹] *om.*　108 peynes] poynes　112 dampnacyon] dampcyon　113 for]
om.　such] seth　fendes] sendes　114 bryngon] brygon　117 telle] tolle
118 rod] red　123 farede] frede

Poule and amende | hym whyl he ys here and hath space and tyme of f. 35ʳ
amendyng. For aftur þat a mon ys ded, þer ys no tyme of amendyng,
and he þat doth schal come to Seynt Poule and dwelle wyth hym for
euer. Amen.   135

[14] De purificacione beate Marie

Suche a day 3e schul haue Candelmasse Day. Wherfore doth in þat
euen as 3oure deuocion techuth 3ou, for þat day Holy Chyrche
maketh myche melody in worschep of oure Lady and of hure swete
Sone, oure Lord Ihesu Cryst, specyalyche in þre þynges: in oure Lady 5
p[uryf]lying, in Sym[e]ones metyng and in candeles offryng.

þys day, gode men, ys kalled þe puryfycacyon of oure Lady, þat ys
in Englys, þe clansyng of oure Lady—for no nede þat heo hadde
þerto, for heo was clansed so wyth þe wyrchyng of þe Holy Gost in þe
conseyuyng of hure Sone þat þer was laft in hure no mater of synne ne 10
of non oþur fulþe, but for þat day was þe fortyþe day f[ro] þe burth of
hure Sone and [was] kalled in þe Iewes lawe þe day of purgacyon, not
onlyche for oure Lady but for alle oþur wymen of þat lawe. Wherfore
3et we callen hyt þe puryficacyon of oure Lady.

þe law of þe Iewes was þen such þat a womon þat was delyuered of 15
a knaue-chyld schulde be holden v[n]clene seuen dayes aftur hure
burth, and þen þe lawe 3af hure leue to go to hure husbondus bed. But
3et heo was unclene by þe law by þre and þrytty dayes aftur, so þat, tyl
fourty dayes weron fullud, heo schuld not come wythin þe temple.
[þen þat day heo schuld come to þe temple] wyth hure offryng and 20
wyth hure sone, and offren for a rych a lombe and for a pore a payre of
turtures or too bryddes. And so offrot oure Lady for [hure S]one. And
3ef a womon were delyuered of a mayde-chyld, heo schuld dowbul þe
dayes of comyng to hure husbond bed and of comyng into þe temple.
For as clerkus techun, hyt ys seuen dayes aftur a womon conceiueth of 25
þe mon er þe sed turne to blod, and þre and þrytty dayes aftur er hyt
haue schap of mon, and þen God sende lyue into hyt. And 3ef hyt be a
maydon-chyld, hyt dowbeleth al þe dayes, bothe into turnyng into
blod and into schap of body. And þys ys þe chause: for by encheson

[14] 1 De ... Marie] in red; de p/ficac/arie cropped in margin   2 Suche] S- in red,
dec., 2 ll. deep   6 puryfying] praysyng   Symeones] symones   11 fro] for
12 was] om.   15 such] schuch   16 vnclene] vp clene   20 þen ... temple] om.
21 for¹] rep.   22 offrot] offront   hure Sone] fone   24 nota bene in margin in the
long hand

30 þat þe forme womon Eue vexud God more þen dude þe mon, þerfore
heo ys lengur in formyng þen þe mon.

f. 35ᵛ   þus for fleschly | cowpul of mon and womon ys vnclene in hymself,
þerfore leue wel þat oure Lady hadde no nede to þys clansyng, for heo
conseyved not of coupul of mon, but only of þe Holy Gost, so þat heo
35 [was] clene of al maner fulþe touchyng conseyt of mon. Nerþeles heo
ȝode to þe temple as oþur wemen duden for foure skyles. þe furst was
to fulfulen þe scripture þat byddeth þus: þe grettur þou be, þe meker
mak þe in alle þyng. þus dude oure Lady: þagh heo wyst þat heo was
modur to Goddus Sone of heuen and was so of worschep passyng alle
40 oþur wymmen, ȝet heo mekud hure as lowe as þe porest wommon þat
was in hure company. þe secunde skyle was to fulfulle þe lawe. For
ryght as he[o] fulfulled þe law in þe cyrcumcysyon of hure Sone,
ryght so heo fulfulled hyt in hure puryfycacyon and in offryng of hure
Sone into þe temple, doyng for hym as oþur por wymmen duden for
45 hure chyldres. þe þredde skyle was for to stoppon Iewes mowþes, lest
þey haddon sayde þat heo dude not þe lawe and so caht a gret
sklandur aȝeynes hom tym aftur commyng. þe ferþe skyle was for
ensampul to alle crysten wymmen þat þey schulden come to chyrche
aftur here burth and þonke God þat hadde saued ham f[ro] perel of
50 deth in hure trauay[ly]ng of hure chyld. For þer nys non euel þat goth
so nygh þe deth wyth skapyng as doth hyt. For þese skeles Holy
Chyrche maket mynde of oure Lady puryfyng.

Heo also makuth mynde of þe comyng of Symeon and Anne. þys
Symeon was a passyng old mon, but for he prayed bysyly day and
55 nyght to God þat he most sen Crist bodyly er he dyed and God
grantud hym hys bone, and þys Anne also—but not Anne, oure Lady
modur, but anoþur þat was wedded seuen ȝere, and þen, when hure
husbond was ded, heo lyued tyl heo were foure skore ȝer old and
serued God in þe temple day and nyght. Heo hadde also grant of God
60 to sen hym or heo dyed. þen wen oure Lady com toward þe tempul
wyth hure Sone, þe Holy Gost warned Symeon and þys Anne. And
heo þen wyth mychul ioye ȝode aȝeynes ham and br[o]ght hym into
þe tempul. þen Symeon to[k] hym in hys armes wyth al þe reuerence
þat he cowþe and kussed hym and þonked hym heghly þat let hym
65 lyuen tyl þat tyme for to sen hym bodyly wyth hys eynon. Wherefore
ȝet in mynde of þys processyon, when a womon cometh to chyrch of

      34 conseyved] *over eras.*   35 was] *om.*   41 þe] þen   42 heo] he   49 fro]
for   50 trauaylyng] trauayng   62 broght] breght   63 tok] tol   66 of¹] þe
add.

chyld, heo bydyth at þe chyrche-dore tyl þe prist com and cast holy |
watur on hure and clanseth hure, and so takut[h] hure by þe honde f. 36ʳ
and bryngeth hure into þe chyrche, ȝeuyng hure leue to comen into þe
chyrche and to gon to hure husbonddus bed. For and heo haue [ben] 70
at hys bed byfore, heo mot taken hure penance þerfore, and he both.
Holy Chyrche also maketh mynde þys day of candelys offryng. Ȝe
sene þat hyt ys a comyn vse of al Holy Chyrche to come to chyrche
þys day and beren a candel in processyon, as þagh þey wente bodyly
to chyrch wyth oure Lady and aftur offrede wyth hure in worschep 75
and hegh reuerence of hure.

þen now hereth how þys worschep was furst yfonde. Ȝe schul here:
when þe Romanus by gret chyualry conquered al þe world, for þey
hadden euore in here doyng, þey rotton not þat God of heuen ȝaf ham
þat euer but madon hem dyuers goddes aftur hure owne lust. And so 80
amonge oþur þey hadden a god þat þey kallud Mars, þat was byfore
tyme a chyualous knyt and an euorus in batel. Wherefore þey kallud
hym god of batel, prayng ȝerne to hym for to help. And for þey wold
sped þe bettur, [þey dyd gret worschep to his modyr, þat was called
Februa, aftur] þe wheche womon, as mony han opunyon, þys mone 85
þat now ys was called February. Wherfore þe forme day of þe mone,
þat ys now Candelmas Day, þys Romans woldon gon al nyght abowte
þe cyte of Rome wyth torches and blases and candeles brenny[n]g in
worschep of þys womon Februa, hopyng for þys worchep to haue þe
sandur help of hure sone Mars in here doyng. 90

þen was þer a pope þat was called Sergius. For he segh cristen men
drawen to þys mawmentry, he þoght for to turne þat [f]oule coston
into Goddus worchep and oure Lady Seynt Mar[y]e, and commendut
þat alle cristen men and wymmen to come þys day to chyrche and
vchon offren a candel brenny[n]g in worschep of oure Lady and hure 95
swete Sone. So vche mon aftur by pros[e]se of tyme lafton þe
worschep þat þey dude to þat wommon Februa and dudon worschep
to oure Lady and to hure Sone, so þat now þys s[o]lempnyte ys
halwod al cristendam, and vche mon and womon and chyld of age
cometh þys day to chyrche and off[r]yn candeles, as þaght [þ]e wente 100
bodyly wyth oure Lady to chyrch on chyld, hopyng for þe reuerans
þat þey don to hure in erþe to haue a gret rew[ar]d þerfore in heuen.

---

68 takuth] takutk   70 ben] *om.*   80 madon] ma(-y- *er.*)don   84–5 þey . . .
aftur] *om.*   88 brennyng] brennyg   92 foule] soule   93 Marye] marre
95 brennyng] brennyg   96 prosese] prosse   98 hure] de *add. at end of line*
solempnyte] selempnyte   100 offryn] offyng   þe] ȝe   102 reward] rewerend

f. 36ᵛ   And so þey mon be sekur þerof, for a | candel brenyng bytokeneth
oure Lady and hure Sone [and] a monvs self. For a candel ys mad of
105 weke and of wax brenny[n]g wyth fere. þus Crystes swete soule was
hude wyth hys monhed and [brende] wyth þe fyre of hys Godhed.
Hyt bytokeneth also oure Ladyes modurhed and maydonhed lyghtod
wyth þe fyre of loue. Hyt bytokeneth also vch god mon and womon
þat doth dedus wyth good entent and in ful loue and charyte to God
110 and to hys euen-crysten. Wherfore ȝef any of ȝow haue so trespassud
to hys heuen-cryston wherby þat hys candul of charyte be queynt,
furst go he and be at one wyth hys neghbur and so tend hys candul
aȝeyn, and þen offere hys candel to þe prest. þys ys Goddes
commandemente, and elles he lesud hys meret of ys offryng.
115   Y rede in þe lyue of Seynt Dunstane how þat hys modur, when heo
was gret wyth chyld wyth hym, heo com on a Candelemas Day to
chyrch. And whon alle þe pepul hadde gon on precessyon wyth
candeles brenny[n]g and stodon al in þe chyrche, yche wyth hys lyght
in hys honde, sodenly al þe candeles in þe chyrche veren que[yn]t and
120 gret darkenes come wythal, so þat vnneþe on myght sen anoþur. And
when þey hadden stonde so longe sore agast, þen com a fayre lyght
from heuen and lyght þe candul þat Donustannes modur bare in here
hond, and so of hure al oþur tokon lyght. So in a whyle al þe chyrche
was lyght aȝeyn in tokenny[n]g þat he þat was in here wombe schuld
125 aftur tende mony monnes charyte þat was byfore quent by enuye.
    I rede of anoþur womon þat was so dewowt in oure Lady seruyse
þat heo [ȝaf] for hure loue al þe cloþs þat heo hadde saue þe febullest
þat heo ȝode in hureself. Hyt fel so þat on a Candelmas Day heo wold
haue gon to chyrche, but, for heo was an honest womon, heo durst
130 no[t for] schame, for heo hadde non honest cloþs as heo was wonud
for to haue. þen when oþur men ȝode to chyrche, heo was wondur
sory þat heo schulde ben bout masse þat holy fest. Wherfore heo went
into a chapel þat was nyght hure place, and þer was in hure prayeres.
f. 37ʳ   And so as heo prayed, | heo fel on slepe. And þan hure þoght þat scho
135 was in a feyre [chyrche] and seygh a gret company of maydenes
comyng into þe chyrch, and on was passyng fayrere þen any of ham al
and went byforen wyth a fayre corone on hure hed of schynyng gold.
þan heo sat doun, and al þe oþur wyth. And when þey weren set, þer

104 and²] *om.*   a monvs] Amoncvs   105 brennyng] brennyg   106 brende] *om.*
116 was] narracio *add.*   118 brennyng] brennyg   119 veren queynt] verenquenyt
124 tokennyng] tokennyg   126 dewowt] narracio *add.*   127 ȝaf] *om.*
129–30 durst not for] durstnon   135 chyrche] *om.*

com in on wyth a gret burþon of condeles and furst 3of þe chyf
maydon þat hadde [þe] corone a candel, and so afture al þe odur   140
maydenes and al þat weren in chyrche. And þen he come to þys
womon and 3af hure a candel. þan heo was fayn. þen segh heo a prest
and too dekenes, honestly reuescht, [and ij] wyth too serges brennyng
goyng to þe auter, and, as hure þoght, Cryst was þe prest, too angelus
þe too dekenes, and La[uren]s and Vyncent þat beren þe serges. And   145
so too fayre 3ong men begonnon þe masse wyth a myry note. So when
þe gospel was red, þe quene of maydenes furst offred hure candel to
þe prest, and so aftur vchon in rew. But when al hadden offred, þe
prest abod aftur þys womon. þe quene sende to hure and bad hure
com offren. And when þe messanger hadde sayde hys ernde, þys   150
womon sayde: nay, heo wold not leuen hure syrge, but heo wold
kepon hyt for gret deuocyon. þen s[en]de þe quene anoþur messanger
and bad say`e´ to hure þat heo was vnkurteyse for te tarye þe prest so,
and, but heo [wold] offren wyth good wylle, he[o] bad hym take hyt of
h[ure]. 3et heo sayde nay and wold not offreren vp þe syrge. þen þys   155
messanger wold haue taken hyt of hure wyth strenþe, but, for heo
huld fast, by[t]wysse ham too þe serge brake in myddus, and half þe
messanger b[ar] forth, and þe oþur half þe womon huld wyth hure.
And so in þat wraste[l]yng þys womon awoke of hure slep and fond
half þe serge in hure honde. And þen heo þonkod oure Lady he[rty]ly   160
þat heo was not wythout masse þat day and for heo 3af hure such a
relyk to kepon whyl heo lyuod.
   Item. Y rede þat þer was a womon of so eul lyuyng þat heo dud
neuer no gode dede in hur lyf, but only fonde a serge brennyng byfore
an ymage of hure Lady in þe chyrche. þen fel hyt, whe[n] heo was   165
dede, fendus comon and fatton hure sowle t[o]ward helle. But | when   f. 37ᵛ
þey were goyng, þer comen too angelus and rebuked þe fendes þat heo
weren so bold to fache any soule forth wythout dom. þen sayden þey
þat þer nedeht no dom, for [heo] hadde neuer don gode dede in al
hure lyue. þen sayden þe angelus: 'Bryngh`u´t þe soul byfore oure   170
Lady', and so þey dedon. But when hyt was fonde þat heo dede neuer
gode, heo most nedus go to helle. þen sayde oure Lady: 'Heo fond a
serge brennyng byfore me, and wold euer whyl heo hadde lyued—
þerfore Y wol ben as kynde to hure as heo was to me', wher heo bad an

---

140 þe¹] *om.*   143 and ij] *om.*   145 and¹] *rep.* Laurens] lampus   152 sende]
sayde   154 wold] *om.*   heo²] he   155 hure] hym   157 bytwysse] bywysse
158 bar forth] braforth   159 wrastelyng] wrastebyng   160 hertyly] heytly
165 when] whem   166 toward] tward   169 heo] þay   171 dede] deden

175 angel take a gret serge and lyghton hyt, and bad hym setten hyt so
brennyng byforen hure in helle, and commandet þat no fynd schuld
be so hardy for to come nygh hyt but lette [hyt] brenne þer for
euermore. þen sayde[n þe fendus] þat hyt schuld ben an hoget confor
to al þat ben in helle, wherfore þey haddon leuer leue þe soule þen
180 don such an ese to alle þe soules þat wher in helle in payne. þen bad
houre Lady an angel bere þe soule aʒayn to þe body, and so dude. And
when heo was comen aʒeyn to lyue, þen heo byþoght hure on þat hard
dom þat heo was ate, and ʒede and scrof hure, and was aftur a gode
womon and serued oure Lady deuowtly alle hure lyue aftur.

[15] *Dominica in Septuagesima*

Gode men, ʒe schul knowen al þat þys day ys kalled in Holy Chyrch
Sonday in Septuagesun. þen for encheson þat Holy Chyrch ys modur
to al criston pepul, heo takuth hede to hure chyldren as [a gode modur
5 owuth for to do, and syth hem alle sore syke yn þe syknes] of synne,
and fele of hem wondet to deth wyth þe swyrde of synne, þe wheche
syknes þey han c[a]ght al þe ʒere byforon, but namely þe Crystonmas
dayes, þat weren ordeynot in Holy Chyrche to gret solempnyte to
vche. For vche mon schuld þat tyme more solemply, more bysyly,
10 more mekely, more deuowtly serue God þen anoþur tyme of þe ʒere,
for cause þat God schewed al monkynde þylke dayes hegh swetnnes of
hys loue, þat he wolde loghe hymself so for ben boren in þe same
flesse and blod as [on] of ous was, and leyd in a crache more porely
þen any of ous, and aftur was folwod in watur as on of ous, and came
f. 38ʳ to a weddyng hym|self [and] ys modur wyth ys dyscyples, for to hal
16 weddyng and for to clanse hyt of synne, al to maken vs holy and
breþeron to hym and eyres of þe kyndam of heuen.

For þese causus men and wymen in old tyme were ful glad in sowle
þys tyme and madon gret solempnite, makyng ham clene in body and
20 soule of al maner of fulþe and onclannes of synne and grondud hem in
sad loue to God and to hure euon-cryston, doyng gret almes, vche
aftur hys hauyng, to hem þat hadde nede. But now, more ys þe harm
þat solempnite and holynesse ys turned into fulþe of synne and syknes

---

177 hyt²] *om.*   178 sayden þe fendus] sayde   180 wher] wher(-en *canc. by red dots*)

[15] 2 Gode] G- *in blue, dec.*, 2 *ll. deep*   4 pepul] p(-h- *canc. by dots*)epul
4–5 a . . . syknes] *om.*   7 caght] chght   11 swetnnes] swetn/nes   13 on] *om.*
15 and] *om.*

of soule: into pr[y]de by dyuers gyse of cloþyng; into couetyse,
wylnyng wyrschep on byfore anoþur onskylfully; into enuye, for 25
[on] ys bettur rayed þen anoþur; into gloteny by surfet of diuers
metus and drynkus; into lechery þat scheweth alway gloteny; into
slowþe of Goddus seruyse, ly`g´ing in mor-tyd long in bedde, for
outrage wakyng ouer nyght in roytyng, in reuel, in pleying of
vanyteus, in iapis makyng of ryba[u]dy and harlotry, so þat he ys 30
haldon most worþy þat rybaudy con makon and speken. þus þese holy
dayes of þat fest, þat weron ordeynot in hegh worschep to God and to
hys seyntus, now ben turned into gret offens of God and into gret
hyndryng of monnes soule.

Wherfore Holy Chyrch, seyn[g] here chyldes fare þys, as a modur 35
ful of compassyon, for þe grete myslykyng þat heo hath in hert for
hem, þys day heo legh don *Alleluya* and oþur songes of melody and
takuth forth tractus, þat ben songes of mornyng and sykyng and
longyng. And also, for þat holy sacrament of weddyng ys myche
de[f]ouled by suche vanyte, heo legh hem don þys dayes þat ben 40
com`me´yng and in þe Aduente also, for new-weddud ȝeyu ham al to
lykyng and lust of hure body and þenken al on þys lyf and noght on
deth. But as an holy clerk seyth, hyt ys myche more spedful to monnes
soule to gon to þe hous þer ys a c[or]s and weputh þen to þe hous þer
alle reuoleth and loghuth, for suche worldes murþe maketh a mon 45
forȝeten hys God and hymself also. But þer ys þe syght of a c[or]s and
wepyng, þat makuth a mon to þenke on hys deth, þat ys þe chyf help
to put auay synne and worldus vanite. For so toght Salomon hys sone,
and bad hym haue hys last ende in hy[s] mynde and þen he | schuld f. 38ᵛ
neuer synne dedly. 50

þen Holy Chyrch, hauyng gret compassyon of hure chyldren,
ordeyneth þre maner salu[es] to hele hure chyldre wyth, þ[at] ben to
þenk on deth inwardly, to laber bysyly, and for to chasteyse þe body
resenabyly.

To þe forme, þat ys, þenk on deth inwardly, Holy Chyrche ȝef 55
hensampul þys day in þe offys of þe masse þer he[o] seth þys:
Circumde[de]runt me gemitus mortis, þat ys [yn] Englys: þe sykynges of
deth han vmbecluppud me. þus sayth heo, techyng vche Goddes
chyld to haue in mynde how hard he ys bystad wyth deth on vche a

24 pryde] prode   26 on] *om.*   30 rybaudy] rybandy   35 seyng] seynt
40 defouled] desouled   44 cors] cros   46 cors] cros   51 thynges/ þat
trewly(?)/ þou schall/ syn dedly/ on thynk/ deth/ wardly/ laubour/ syly and/ to chasty/
body/ sonable *cropped in margin in later hand*   52 salues] saluo   þat] þre   56 heo]
he   57 Circumdederunt] circumderunt   yn] *om.*

60 syde, in so harde þat he may no way schape but euer deth sewyth hym
wyth hys bowe drawen and an arwe þ[er]in redy to scheten hem, he
not ner where ne what tyme. þys ys a princypal salue to vch mon þat
takuth þys to hert for te putton away al maner worldly vanyte and
vayn murþe and reuel.

65   But for te vndurstonde þys þe bettur, Y schewe by ensampul. I
rede of [a] kyng þat was a mon euer of heuy chyre and wolde neuer
laght ny makon glad chere, but euer was in mornyng and in hevynes.
þen for hys mayne and alle oþur men weron greuot þerwyth, þey
ȝodon to þe kynges broþur, prayng hym to speke wyth þe kyng þat he
70 were of gladdur chyre in comford of al hys meyne and of al oþur. þen
went þe broþur to þe kyng and sayde þat he greuot al þat weron
aboute hym wyth hys chere, and consayled hym to leue þat heuy
contenans and takon lygtur chere to hym in tyme comyng. þen was þe
kyng wyse and þoght to chastyse hys broþur by a w[y]le, and wroghly
75 bad hym to gon hom radly and medelen hym in þat he hadde to don of
and noght of hym.

þen was hyt þe maner of þe contre þat, when a mon schuld be don
to deth, þer schuld com trumperes to trompe byfore hys ȝate. þen
sende þe kyng tromperes, byddyng hem trumpe byfore hys broþur
80 ȝate, and men wyth for te areste hym and bryngc hym to þe kyng. But
þe mene-whyl þe kyng kalled to hym seuen men þat he trust and bad
ham, when hys broþur com, for te drawen here swerdus and [stonde
aboute hym] wyth þe poyntes set anont [hys] hert. So when þus
broþur was com, anon þe seuen men dudon as þe kyng bad ham. þen
85 þe kyng commandet al men to danson and maken al þe reuel þat þey
cowþe on vch a syde, and so dudon. þen sayde þe kyng to hys broþur:
'Why art þou of so heuy chere? Hef vp þy hert and make mery. Lo, al
þys murþe ys mad in comford of þe.' þen onswered he and sayde:
'How schuld Y ben of any chere and see her seuon swyrdus set to myn
90 herte, and wot newer wheche of hem schal furst ben my deth?' þen
sayde þe kyng: 'Put vp ȝowre swerdus', and þen spak to hys broþur:
'þys hyt faruth wyth [me]—where þat euer Y be, þe seuen dedly
f. 39ʳ synnes ben euer redy to roue my soule to | þe hert, and þys makuth
me þat Y may neuer be glad ne of glad chere, but euer am aferd of
95 deth of my soule, þat ys þe lyf of my body.' þen sayde he: 'Y crye ȝow
mercy, for Y knewe neuer þys er now. Y schal be þe wyser euer aftur.'
þys Y say boldly: he þat wol tak þys to herte he schal haue bettur lust

61 þerin] þus in   66 a] *om.*   74 a wyle] awle   81 þe] *written in small*
82–3 stonde aboute hym] *om.*   83 poyntes] and *add.*   hys] om.   92 me] *om.*

to louren þen to laghon, to sykon þen to be glad, to wepe þen to synge,
so þat he schal fynde þe mynde of þe deth þe pryncypal salue to alle
maner synne.   100
þat oþur salue ys for te labren bysyly. To þys labor Seynt Poule in
þe pystul of þys day [t]echet and sayth: *Sic currite vt compre[hen]datis.*
'Renneth so', he seyth, 'þat ȝe mowen haue þe gamen.' By þys
rennyng ȝe schul vndurstonde bysy labur, for he þat renneth for þe
gamen he enforseth hym in al hys myght to renen swy[ft]ly. So mot   105
vch seruand of God enforson hym to laberon in þys gre þat God hath
set hym in: men of Holy Chyrche schuld laberen bysyly in prayng and
studying for to techen Goddes pepul; lordus schuld laberen, and oþur
rentud men schul bysy ham to kepe Holy Chy[r]che in pesse and in
reste, and al oþur comyn pepul; þe comyn pepul schuld labore bysyly 110
to geton lyflode to hemself and for al oþur.
   For no mon ne wommon schuld excusen ham of oþur labor, God in
þe gospel of þys day ȝeueth ensampul, seyng þys: An husbondman
ȝede in þe mor-tyd at prime, eftsonus at vndur, eft at mydday,
ȝeftsonus at none of þys day, and euesong-tyme, and hered mon into 115
hys vyne-ȝord for to laberon. So by al þese tydus of þe day, al þat 'a'ges
and al þe degrees of men ben vndurstonde and ben hyred by God for to
laberon whyl þey ben in þys world. For as Iob seyth: 'A mon ys boren
to labur.' [And Seynt Bernard seyth: 'He þat wyl not labur here] wyth
[men] he schal laberen henes wyth fendus.' For þat ys þe testament of 120
Adam þat he laft to alle hys osspryng: labor and sorewe.
   To þys labor [Holy] Chyrche ȝeueth ensampul þeras heo þys day
rehersoth how God mad Adam and Eue for to laberon and to kepon
paradyse, and bad hem eton of alle þe tren in paradys excepte on tre
þat he kapte as for hyms[el]f for chef, so þat, as ofton as þey seynne 125
þat tre, þey schuldon þenkon on hym and k[n]owen hym as for God.
And for þey sculdon not ben forȝetful in hor wele, [þer]for he bad
hem not eton þerof in peyne of deth. þen for þe fynd sagh hom in so
myche vele and hemself in so mych peyne, þat hadde enuye to ham,
and ȝode to Eue and askud here why þey ete not þe tre. þen sayde 130
heo: 'For God hath forbodon vs þat tre in peyne of deth.' þen sayde
þe fynd: 'He wot wel, þat tyme ȝe 'e'ton þerof ȝe schud ben seke as
goddus both, knowyng gode and euel. And ȝef ȝe wol preue þat Y saye

102 techet] ce/chet   comprehendatis] compredatis   105 swyftly] swysly
109 Chyrche] chyche   113 ensampul] enspampul   116 ages] a- *in darker ink*
119 And ... here] *om.*   120 men] *om.*   122 Holy] *om.*   125 hymself] hymslef
126 knowen] kowen   127 þer] *om.*

sogh, ete of þe tre and saye.' þen Eue eete of þe tre and ȝaf Adam and
f. 39ᵛ byd eton. And for | Adam louode here and wold not wrath here, he
136 toke a nappul and ete. And anon þerwyth eyþur sagh oþur schap and
weren aschamet of hyt, and tok leues of fygge-tre and huled hyt. þen
com God anon, and, for þey mygh not dyen in paradyse ne suffre
penans þer, he drof ham naked out of paradyse into þys wrechet
140 world, whepyng and sore sykeyng, þer þey schuld drye woo and sorwe
and geton hure mete wyth labor and swot, and dyed at þe last.

þen prayed Adam God, sore whepyng, þat he schul not setton to
hard vangyans on hym but ha mercy on hym, and haue reward how he
syngut by innocens and not by malys and was deseyuot by enuye of þe
145 fend. þen hadde God rewthe of hym, and, for þey weron nakud, he
cloþod ham in pylchys, and bad Adam laboron and `g´eton hys bred
wyth swot and Eue boren hure burþenes in woo and peyne, and ȝaf
Adam diuers instrumentes for to labere wyth and laft hym þere. By
þys ensampul ȝe schul takon ensampul for to laberon bysyly. For ȝef
150 Adam and Eue hadden bysyed hem in labor, þe feynd schuld not han
ouerkomen hem so sone. For þe fynd keput no more when he wol
tempton hym but fyndon a mon ydul. Wherfore ȝe schul kon wel þat
hyt [ys] a ryche salue to hele synne to laboren bysyly.

þe þredde salue ys for to ch[a]steyse þe body dyscre[t]ly. Hereto
155 seyth Poule in þe pystul of þys day: *Castigo corpus meum et in seruitute
redigo*, þat ys in Englis: Y chasteyse my body and dresse hyt into
seruage of þe soul. For monnes flesse ys so wylde and so lusty to synne
þat hyt wol no way leuen hys lyst and serue þe soule tyl hyt be
f. 40ʳ chasteysed wyt penance, so þat by sc[h]appnes of penans þe | [lyking
160 of syn]ne schal ben slayne in þe flesse þat doth þe synne.

þus dude Adam and Eve in ensampul of alle þat comen of þem, for,
fele ȝerus before deth, oyþur of hem stode in a uattur nythes, fer fro
oþur, vp to þe chyn for penaunce. þan whan here flesse was grene as
gresse for colde, þe fende com to Heue, bryght as an angel, and sayde
165 to Eue þat God hadde sende hym fro heuen, and badde hur gone to
Adam and seyn hym how þat God badde hym seson of hys penaunce:
'For he hath don inogh for hys gylte, and þou also for þine.' þan ȝode
Eue to Adam and sayde hym soo. Bot for Adam wyst wel þat þis cam
of þe fende and not of Goddys sonde, he seyde to hure: 'Whan God
170 drof vs oute of paradyse for oure synne and hadde compassioun of vs
for we wepton on hym and mekely prayde hym of mercy, he sette vs

153 ys] *om.*   154 chasteyse] chsteyse   dyscretly] dyscrely   159 schappnes]
sclappnes   159–60 lyking of syn] *om.*   162 a uattur] auentur? *alt. to* auattur?

here to do penaunce into oure lyues ende. þan for suche a grete synne
may not ben quyte bot wyth grete penaunce, þerfore þe more
penaunce we don, þe more is oure mede before God.' Wherefore
he sayde to Eve: 'Go aȝeyne and do þi penance in Goddys name.'   175
Efte þe fende com aȝeyn to Eve and sayde: 'God hath take rewarde
to ȝoure grete penance þat ȝe suffren for ȝoure grete synne. Wherefore
byd Adam be gladde and leuen of hys penance, lest God be wroth
wyth hym þat he takyth no rewarde to hys sond.' þan whan Eve hadde
sayde þus to Adam, he answered and sayde: 'I wotte he is oure enmy   180
þat sayth so, for oure penance greuyth hym more þan vs, and he is
aboute in alle þat he may for to make vs to leven of and so leson oure
mede. Bot do we forth oure penance to oure lyues ende, for God
rewardeth þe gode ende and not þe gode begynnyng wythoute gode
ende.'   185
Ȝytte þe þrydde tyme he com aȝeyne to hure and sayde: 'Go to
Adam and say þat þe begynnyng was foule and wel fouler ȝe wil ende.
For ȝe gylton furste be innocentri and be seyte of þe fende, and now
ȝe gylton by godde wylle and knowon wel ȝe done mysse. Wherefore
ȝoure gylte is worthy þe doubul dampnacion oure þat it was before.'   190
þan was Eue aferde and ȝode to Adam and sayde hym so. þan sykud
Adam sore and sayde hyre: 'Vnsely womman, God of hys godenesse
made þe of one of my rybbes for to helpe me, and now þou arte bysy
be tysing of þe fende to cumbur me efsonus. But þenkon on, þat oure
forme synne stank so in Goddys sythe þat alle oure osspring schal be   195
enfected and repreuid þerof into þe worldes ende. Wherefore, þagh
we mythe do also myche penance as alle oure ospring mythe do, it
were to lytyl to quyton vs to oure Lorde God. Bot, for God of hys
grace aloweth a gode wylle [þeras myght fayleth. þerfore do we oure
penance wyth a gode wylle, þagh hit be lytyll whyll we ben here. And   200
þen I hope] þat God wyl ȝevon vs þe oyle of mercy whan þe tyme of
mercy comyth.' þanne ȝode Eue aȝayne and dude hyr penance mekely
to þe lyues ende. And whan þei hadde lyued nyne hundred ȝere and
thrytte and haddon þrytty sones and þrytty doghteres, þan þei dyed
and weron beryed infere. þus ȝe schul know wel þat Adam and Eve   205
were ful holy er þei dyed, and thouthon on deth inwardely, and
labordon bothe besely, and schastysid here body re[so]nabully, and so
moton | alle þat comon of hem þat wil com to þe ioy of paradice and   f. 40ᵛ
to þe lyue þat eure schal laste.

210   In tokenyng of þis, Sonday ys callyd Sonday in Septuagesun, þat is
a nombur of syxti dayes and ten, þe whyche noumbur begynnyth þis
day and endeth þe Saturday in Astur weke, so þat Holy Chyrch is in
murnyng for here schylderon fro þis day tyl Saturday in Astron Even.
þan scheo takuth comforde to hyr in parte and synguth on *Alleluya*
215   wyth a tracte, for encheson þat scheo is not 3itte in ful murthe tyl
[Sa]turday afftur, þat is callud Saturday *in albys.* þan scheo leythe
away tractus and grayeles and synguth dobul *Alleluya*, techyng vche
schylde of God to do penance and laburon til he com to Astur
Saturday, þat is, tyl hys soule passe to reste. But 3ytte þe soule is not
220   in ful ioy tyl Saturday *in albys*, þat is, til þe day of dome, whan þe
body and þe soule schul come togydyr and ben iclothed *in albys*, þat
is, in whyte, seven sythes brytar þan þe sonne. And þan schul þei syng
in fere dobul *Alleluya* in þe ioy of heuen þat eure schal laste, *et cetera.*

[16] *Dominica in Sexagesima sermo*

þis day is called in Holy Chyrch Sunday in Sexagesime. 3e schul
knowe wel þat Sexagesime is sette for a nombur of þre score, [by] þe
wyche nombur 3e schul vndurstonde þat Holy Chyrch techeth boþe
5   man and wommam to þenkon how schorte is mannus lyf now in oure
dayes or it was in holde tyme before. For sum tyme men lyuod nyne
hundred 3ere and more, bot now he þat lyueth iij schore 3ere or
sumwhatte more it is takon for a long lyfe. But 3ytte þe goddenesse of
God [is suche þat, yf we wyl be besy in oure schorte lyf to plese God]
10   and sauyng of oure soules, he wyl 3eue vs as myche mede in heuen os
he 3af hem þat lyuyd so many 3eres. þan he þat wyl haue þat mede of
God he mote haue þre thyngys: þat one is, he motte soffur tribulacion
mekely; he mote done almus-dede descretely; and hate synne namely.
þan for mannus dayes ben schorte, he motte suffron þe mo
15   tribulaciones wyth godde wylle and not wyth grutchyng, for God
louith a man of gode wille and is wroth wyth a man þat is grutchyng
a3eynus hym. For it comyth of a special grace of God wen he sent to a
man any tribulacion or any desese, for ouþur it is in remedy of synne
to haue hys penance here, or ellys in eghe encresse of ioy before God.
20   þan for Seynt Poule, Goddys holy apostel, wil þat vche man take
ensampul by hym for to suffur tribulacion wyth gode wille, he
reherseth in þe pystyll of þis day myche of tribulacion þat he suffred,

215 for encheson] *rep.*   216 Saturday[1]] asturday
[16]   2 þis] þ- *in blue, dec., 2 ll. deep*   3 by] *om.*   9 is . . . God] *om.*

and seyth þus: 'I haue ben putte in prison ofte tymes, and suffred in
bondys of kene schaynus and oþur dyuerse ernes, and fyue sythes
beton wyth scowreges [of þe Iewes and hadde vche tyme nyne and 25
thrytty strokes] on my bare body, and þryes beton wyth ȝardus of
paynemus, and onus beton wyth stonus, and þryes ben in schyppe-
wrake in þe see and was in þe grounde of þe see on nyght and on day,
and ofte tymes in perel of flodys, in perel of þeues, and in perel of
falce breþeren þat schewyth hem to me louyng and trewe, and weron | 30
false and entysed oþur to do me wrong and desese. He rehersed also f. 41ʳ
þe woo þat he sufred in diuerse desese, travayles, in myscheues, in
colde, in nakydschep, in þruste, in hongur, in longe wakyngus, in
fastyng, and in many oþur myscheues þat he suffred þat were to longe
to telle. And alle he suffred wyth gode wylle and eure þankud God of 35
hys swete sonde, for wel he wyste þat alle þe desese þat God sende to
hym it was for synne þat he dydde before and for encres of mede
aftur. Wherefore yche man þat wole plese God, whatte maner desese
þat cometh to hym, be it sekenesse, be it long of worledes gode, oþer
deth of any frende, take it as esely as he may for þe tyme, and aftur, 40
whan he is maystur of hymselfe, þan þank he God and pray hym
mekely of mercy for hys paciens. God knoweth oure frayelte, and
þerfore he forȝeueth sone alle þat askyth hym mercy wyth a meke
herte. þus motte a man suffur tribulacion mekely.

He mote also do almus-dede discretely, þe wyche ben fygured be 45
þis Sexagesym, þat ben syxti dayes. For sixti ben syx sythe ten, so þat
be þe syxe ȝe schul hundurstande þe syx werkys of charite þat cometh
oute of þe x commandementes of God, þe wheche werkes ben: for to
ȝeu mete to hongry; to ȝeue drynk to hem þat ben thrusty; to cloþe
hem þat ben akolde for defaute of cloþus; for to ȝeue hem herbar þat 50
han none; for to helpon hem þat ben seke of þat hem nedeth; [for to
vysyt presoners and socoure hem wyth mete and drynke and oþer þat
hem nedeth]. Anoþur werke Holy Chyrche lythe to: þat is to byrion
þe pore þat hath none helpe as to byry hymself. þese ben þe werkus of
charite and of mercy, þe wyche vche man and womman mote nedely 55
done þat wyl haue mercy of God at þe dredeful day of dome.

Wherefore þis Sexagesine bygynneth þis day and endeth þe
Wednesday in þe Astur weke, þe wyche day Holy Chyrche syngeth
and sayth: *Uenite, benedicti patris mei, et cetera*, þat is in Ynglys to
seyne: come, ȝe my Fader blessyd chylderen, and takuth þe kyngdam 60
of heuen þat is ordenyd to ȝow. þese same wordys God schal sayne in

29 þeues] þeuoges   47 ȝe] ȝere   51–3 for² . . . nedeth] *om.*

þe day of dome to alle þat haue [don þe werkes of mercy discretely. Wherefore all þat han] whereof, þei moton donn hem in dede, and þei þat haue not whereof þei mote haue gode wille for to donn, ȝyf þei 65 haddon whereof, so þat here gode wylle schal fulfulle here nownepower.

þan for þeise werkus moton ben done dyscretely lest a man lese alle yfere, God techeth be ensampul be þe gospel of þis day [h]ow þa[y] sul be done and sayth þus: A man ȝede owte to sow hys sede, and, os 70 he sew, [som sede fel by þe way and fowles of þe ayre etyn hit; and som fel on a stone and hit dryet vp for defaute of humore; and] som fel among thornys and in þe growing it turnyd to kokul; and sum fel in gode erþe and hyt browthe forthe froyte an hundred folde—þis was Cryste, þat seyth þis: 'I am the way to heuen.'

75   Wherefore hys sede falleth besyde þe way þat ȝeuyth not hys almys only for Cristes loue bot for pompe of þe worlde and veyne glory and for to ben holdon an holy man, and so leseth alle in fere. I rede þat þere was a wondur ryche man sum tyme in Yrelonde, and dede so many almys-dedus in hys lyue þat alle men wendon he hadde ben a 80 grete seynte before God. But whan he was dedde, he aperyd to on þat f. 41ᵛ louid hym well | in hys lyue, alle blake as pyche wyth an horrybul stynche, and sayde to hym: 'Ȝe weneth þat I be a seynte, but now I am seche os þou seste.' þan seyde þat oþur: 'Where ben all þine almusdedys bycomyn?' þan seyde he: 'þe w[ynde] of veyne glory hath 85 blowen hem all away.' þus he þat doth almus-dede for vayne glorye he lesuth alle hys mede and fendys of þe ayre stroyeth hytte.

Hys sedde falleth on a stone þat ȝeuyth hys almys-dede to suche þat he knoweth wel ben grounded in dedly synne [and woll not leue it, and so he mantayneth hem yn here synne] and leseth hys mede. Hys 90 sede also falluth among þornys þat ȝeffeth hys almys to ryche men þat haue none nede þerto, and so leseth hys mede. And also ȝeuith it to hys seruandus in rewarde of here hyre, and so leseth hys mede. But hys sedde falleth in gode erþe þat geffyth hys almys to gode trewe men and pore, þat ben Goddys erþe, and oþur, were he wotte h[it] ys 95 almys to ȝeue. And þis sede sal ȝeldon an hundred folde froyte and ben eure lastyng fode to hym in heuen. þus he þat doth almys-dede discretely schal haue hys fode in heuen perpetualy.

He mot[e] also hattyn synne namely and flen it in alle he may. For

---

62–3 don . . . han] *om.*   68 how] now   þay] þan   70–1 som . . . and²] *om.*
84 þe wynde] þei weron   88–9 and . . . synne] *om.*   94 hit ys] hys   98 mote]
moton

he þat [ha]tteth synne he louyth Gode, and [God] louyth hym, and so
he is made one spyrite of hys Gode. God hatuth synne so mech þat he 100
toke vengeauns on alle þe worlde, as Holy Chyrch now makuth
mynde, and namely for þe synne of lechery and of avowterye and for
synne aȝeyne kynde. þerefore God sayth þe wykkydnesse namely of
þis synne reynyng in þe worlde. He sayde þis: 'Me forthynkyth þat I
made man.' Wherefore he sayde to Noye: 'Alle þe worlde is 105
envenummed wyth synne so greuysly þat I wil stroy it wyth a
flode. Wherefore make þe a scheppe, as I wil teche þe, of planed
burdes, and make schaumburres þerine. And take of alle clene bestes
þre coupull and one be hymselfe, and of vnclene bestys take in on
coupul, and mete wyth hem.' þan makud Noe þis schypp os God 110
badde hym, square in þe bothum, and þre hundur cubytes in lenthe,
and [in] brede fyfty cubytes, and in þe heygth þrytty cubytes, so þat
þis schyppe was in makyng an hundred wyntur to schewon [h]ow
merciabul God is and how loth to do vengeans, and how longe he
abydeth for to take vengeans. And alle he doth for to lokyn if men 115
wolde amende and askon mercy. But for þe pepul wyl not amendon
bot was euere þe lengar þe worse, alle maner bestes, as God badde
before, were brogth to Noe be help of angellys and were done into þe
schyppe. And whan alle were browthe in, as God bad Noe, and hys
þre sonnus gon into þe schyppe be hemselfe, and Noes wyf and hys 120
sones wyues be hemselfe, for encheson þat in tyme of aflyxion men
schuldon abstyne hem fro cowpul of wommen—so, whan þei were
alle in, God closyd þe dore aftur hem wythouteforth.

And þan reynyd so grettely fowrety dayes and fourety nythes þat þe
watur bare þe schyppe heyer þan any hull be fyftene cubytes and 125
stode so stylle an hundred dayes and fyfty. And so was alle þe worlde
drowned, boþe man and beste, owtetakyn hem þat weron in þe
schyppe. Nereþeles Iosaphus saythe þat in Armeny is an hull þat is
callud Barys, þat was herre þan þe watur, where many men and
wommen were sauid, as me[n] haue opynion þere. þus was Noe in þe 130
schyppe | twelue moneth. And þan Noe put oute a rawne for to bring f. 42ʳ
worde if þe watur were sesud or nay. þan fond þis raven a drowned
careyn and fyllyd hym þerof, and com not aȝeyne. Aftur þat Noe sent
oute a coluer, þe wyche come aȝeyn wyth a braunch of olyue in hyre
bylle, whereby Noe knewe þat þe watur was sesed and thankud God 135
heghly. þan whan God badde hym, he ȝode owte and toke þe odde

beste of þe clene bestes and brende hym in offryng to God. Wherefore God was so wel payed þat he ȝaf hym and alle men aftur hym leue for to eton flesse of `clene´ bestes and for to drynke wynne, þeras before
140 þe flode men eton no flesse no dronkon not ellys bot watur. For þe erþe was batefull before, þat men nedud none oþur fode but seche os com of þe erþe.

þus, gode men, ȝe mon vndurstande how grete vengeans God toke on alle þe worlde for wykkydnesse of synne. And now, more harme is,
145 þe pepul is as ful of synne as it was þat tyme, and God wolde takon vengeans nere þer prayere of Holy Chyrche and of holy seyntus, and specialy of oure Lady. For þus I rede in þe lyue of Seynt Dominek: whan he was in a nythe in hys deuocion, he seth oure Lorde Ihesu holdyng þre speres in hys hande redy for to schote to þe worlde for
150 vengeans. þan com our Lady anone and knelud before hym and sayde: 'My dere swete Sone, whatte wo[l]te þou done?' þan sayde he: 'My dere modur, þe worlde is so ful of pride and couetyse and leccherye. Wherefore wyth þeyse þre speres I wol schoton hem.' þan sayde oure Lady: 'My swete Sone, haue mercy on hem and ȝitte abyde a whyle. I
155 haue one trewe servaunte, þe whyche schal gone and prechen Goddus worde and turne þe pepul and alle þe worlde to þe.' And so he abode. And þanne sche sente forthe Seynte Dominek and badde hym gone and prechon Goddys worde and turne þe pepul. And so he dede.

þus, gode men, ȝe haue herde how, be þe preyer of oure Lady and
160 be þe prechyng of þis holy man, God sparod to do vengeans þat tyme. But now, more is þe harme, þe pepul is combred wyth þe same synne and is ful lyk to ben smytton wyth þe same vengeans oþur wyth worse, for now þe pepul sette lytul be Goddys worde. For þogh þei heren it, þei sette bot lytyl þerby, for þei wil not do þeraftur and
165 amenden hem and levyn þer synne. Wherefore God smyteth a lytil now and w[o]l here aftur wel harder, bot amendes be made þe sonner, *et cetera*.

[17] *Dominica in Quinquagesima sermo*

Gode men, þis [day] is called in Holy Chyrch Sonday in Quinqua-gesin[e]. þan schal ȝe know þat þis worde Quinquagesime is a nombur

---

139 clene] *replaces* chef (*canc.*)   147 of Seynt] osseynt *add.*   151 wolte] woste
166 wol] wel
[17] 2 Gode] G- *in blue, dec., 2 ll. deep*   day] *om.*   2–3 Quinquagesine]
Quinquagesino

of fyfty, þe whiche nombur betokeneth remission and ioy. For in þe
Olde Lawe vche fyfty ȝere alle men and wommen þat weren ouresette 5
wyth seruice of bondage þey [we]ren makyd fre in grete ioy and
mirthe to hem. Wherfore þis nombur begynnyth þis day and endith
on Astur Day, schewing þat vche Goddus seruande þat is here
oppressud be trybulacion and takuth it mekly in hys lyue he schal
ben makyd free in hys resurrexion, þat is þe day of dome, and ben 10
made eyre of þe kyndam of heuene.

And ȝitte, in more comforde of alle | Goddus pepul, vche fyfty ȝere f. 42ᵛ
þe pope of Rome graunteth a ful remission of alle synnus to vche man
and womman þat cometh to Rome þat ȝere. Bot for alle mow not com
þidur and haue þis pardon, þe pope of heuen, Ihesu Criste, of hys 15
special grace graunteth alle men and wommen ful pardon of hure
synnus in here deth-day, so þat þei wol kepon be here lyve þre
thyngus þat ben nedeful to hem, þe wheche ben þese: ful contricion
wyth schryuing, hol charite wythoute feynyng, and stabul fayth
wythowtyn flo[t]tering. Sothly, wythowtyn þese þre þer may no 20
man haue pardon at Rome ne ellys where.

Wherefore he þat wyl ben asoyled of þe pope of heven and haue
playne remission of hys synnes he mote ben ful contrite, þat is, he
mote be inwardely sori for hys gyltus, schryuen hym clene, and ben in
ful purpos nere to syngen more. Whoso doth þus, leue he wel þat God 25
forȝefveth hym hys trespas and ful pardon of hys synnus. For a man
may haue suche contricion þat it schal quenche alle þe peynus þat
weron ordeyned to hym. Ensaumpul we haue of Petur þat forsoke
Criste wyth hegh oþus, bot, for he was contrite and wepe bytturly,
God, þat is ful of mercy, forȝaf hym hys trespase and makyd more 30
che[re] aftur to hym þan he was before.

Anoþer ensampul: [I fynde] þat þer was a grete man and was so
wykkyd of lyuing þat alle men demot hym to helle. þan happond hym
so þat he fel sek in hys deth-bed, and whan he felde þat he schulde be
dede, he þoght how wykkyd he hadde ben in lyuinge before, and caute 35
suche a contricion in hys herte þat he wepte day and nythe and neurer
sesed of seven dayes þat he leuet, and made prestus to be wyth hym
day and nyght. And eure os hys synne [come] to mynde, wyth hegh
repentans he schrof hym and euere cryed to God of mercy so dolfully
þat vche man hadde rewth of hym, and so dyed forth. 40

þan was þer besyde in an abbey a monk þat dyed þat same tyme þat

6 þey weren] þey/ren   20 flottering] floctering   31 chere] chef   32 I fynde]
om.   38 come] *om.*

þus mon dude and was bedu[n] be hys abbotte to comyn aȝeyne and
tellyn of hys state, and so dude. þan he sayde to hys abbote: 'Sir, I am
comyn as ȝe badde me. ȝef me leue to gone my way, for I go to ioy.'
45 þan sayde þe abbotte: 'Was þer any sowle þat ȝode wyth þe to þe ioy
wythoute any peyne þat day þat þou dedust dye?' þan sayde þe monk:
'For soth, one and no moo, þat [was] þe soule of suche a man', and
tolde hys name. þan sayde þe abbotte: 'Now I se wel þat þou arte a
fende and note my monk, þat arte icomen for to temp me. For wel I
50 wotte, ȝef any soule be in peyne, þan ys hys soule.' þan sayde þe
monke: 'Ful vnworthy is a man to know þe priuete of Goddus dome.
þat man hadde such contricion and wepte so bytturly or he dyed þat
þe watur of hys eynon persud alle hys cloþus and þe bed-stre and so
doun into þe erthe. Wherefore goo þidur tomorwe, and, when þou
55 fyndust soth þat I say, lefe þat I am trewe and go to þe ioye.' þan ȝode
þe abbotte þidur, and whan he fonde alle soth as þe monk tolde, þan
he knelud doun and heryed God and bad all men ben gladde, for he
was þus certyfyed þat þis soule was in þe blysse. þus þe grete
contricion þat þis man hadde here he dyed quyte fro þe grete
60 peyne þat was ordeyned to hym.

Hereby ȝe mow knowon oponly how spedeful it is to a man to be
contryte for hys synnes. Wherefore, for to make men to [com to]
f. 43ʳ contricioun, | namely þese fyfty dayes, þe fefte[þ]e salme of þe sauter,
þat is, *Miserere mei, Deus*, y[s] more rehersed þese dayis þan any other
65 tyme of þe ȝere, þe whyche is þus myche to sayne in Englys: God,
aftur þine grete mercy, haue [mercy] of me, and aftur þi multitud[e]
of þine mercies do away [m]ine wykkydnesse, and so forth. þus whan
a man is sory for hys synnes and seythe þese wordys wyth ful herte,
God hereth hys prayere and forȝefeth hym hys synnes, so þat he be in
70 ful wylle to mende hym in tyme comyng.

An also ful of scharite wythoute feyning. For whatte kyn uertu þat a
man hath, bot he be in charite, it stondeth in none avayle to hym. For
þagh he [wepe and crye to God, whyl he ys wythoute charite to] any of
hys euen-cristyn God hereth hym noghte. Hereto acordeth Seyn
75 Poule in þe pestel of þis day and sayth þus: 'þogh I wore so eloquent
in speche as any man or any angel, or þow I hadde profesye and knew
þe priuete of God, or þogh I hadde so ful fayth þat I myghte remeve

42 bedun] bedum   47 was] *om.*   52 þat] he dyed *add. and canc.*   62 com to]
om.   63 fefteþe] feftene   64 ys] y   66 aftur] *over eras.*   mercy] *om.*
multitude] multitudo   67 mine] þine   69 synnes] and sayth þese wordys wyth ful
herte god hereth hys prayere and forȝefuet hym hys trespace *rep.*   73 wepe . . . to] haue

hylles, or þat I dalte alle my godys to pore men for Goddys sake, or
þagh I putte my body to brennyng fyre for Goddus loue, ȝef I haue no
charite, alle profyteth me rythe noghte.' Wherefore þogh a man 80
weneth þat he louith hys God, and louith notte hys evenn-criston
and alle Goddus pepul, he is disseyuid, for he þat louith God he louid
alle þat God louid. For þus mote a man haue ful scharite þat wyl ben
sauid before God, for he þat dyeth in charite schal ben sauid and he
þat dyeth in dedly hatte schal be dampned. þerfore of alle vertues 85
charite is moste necessarye.

ȝi[t] he mot haue stabul fayth wyth oute flotering, so þat he leue
saddely as Holy Chyrche techet and leueth, þat is, in þe Fadur and in
þe Sone and in þe Holy Goste, þe Fadur ful God, þe Sone ful God,
and þe Holy Gost ful God, and ȝe[t] þese þree ben bot one God, þat 90
alle þing made of noghte. þis fayth was furste schewod in þe holy
patriarch, Abraham, as Holy Chyrch þis day makyth mynde and sayth
þat Habraham was in þe vale of Mambre and segh þre fayre men
comyng towarde hym. And þanne he ȝode aȝeynus hem and, þagh he
segh þre, he worcheppud bot on, ȝeuing ensampul to alle men to sene 95
[in] hure spyryte þe Fadur and þe Sone and þe Holy Goste, þre
persones in one God.

And also ȝe schal levin one þe incarnacion of oure Lorde Ihesu
Criste, þat oure Lady conseyuid of þe Holy Gost wythowtyn wem of
hur body, and was borne of hur in fless[he] and blode as one of vs, and 100
he very God and man, þat aftur was dede vpon þe crosse and beried
and rosse fro deth to lyue þe þridday and step into heuen on Holy
þrusday and schal com aȝeynne to deme þe quyke and þe ded. þis
[was] fygured be Ysaac, þat was sone to Habraham, þe whyche
Abraham gatte of hys wyf Sare þoroght þe behest of God whanne 105
þei weren boþe paste age to bryng forth schyldron, of þe whyche sone
God behette Abraham þat he schulde haue frutte as fele as werren
sterres in þe firmament.

þan, whan þis schylde was borne, he was called Ysaac. [But whan
he was xxv ȝere olde, God asayde Abraham in þys wyse: he bad hym 110
take hys sone Ysaac] þat he louid and gone to suche an hul þat he
wolde schewen hym and þere | offren hym in sacrifice, þat was, to f. 43ᵛ
slene hym and to brenne hym, os þe maner was þat tyme. þan
Abraham, þogh he louid hys sone myche and hadde beh[e]st of God

87 ȝit] ȝif   90 ȝet] ȝef   96 in] *om.*   98 þe incarnacion] in þe carnacion
100 flesshe] flesseh   104 was¹] *om.*   107 God] badde *add.*   109 he was] *rep.*
109–11 But . . . Ysaac] *om.*   114 behest] behost

115 for to haue grete vssu of hym, nerþeles he toke hym anone wythowtyn
groschyng and ʒode to þat hull and made Ysaac bere wode to brenne
hymselfe wyth. And whan þei comyn to þe hulles toppe, Habraham
makyd an auter of þe brondys and sette hem on fyre, and þan toke hys
sone Ysaac and wolde han slayne hym and offred hym so to God. þan
120 anone spake an angel to hym and bad hym leven of and tak þe wether
þat was behynd hym teyed be þe hornys in þe breres and offren hym
in stede of hys sone, and so dude.

þan [by] Habraham ʒe schul vndurstande þe Fadur of heuen, and
be Ysaac, hys Sone Ihesu Criste, þe wheche he spared notte for no
125 loue þat he hadde to hym bot suffred þe Iewes to leggen [wode] vpon
hym, þat was þe cros vpon hys schuldur, and ledon hym to þe hulle of
Caluarye, and þer duden hym on þe auter of wode þat was þe crosse,
þat was made of foure tren, cedur, cypur, olyfe, and palme, and þere
dyed for alle mankynde. þus may Cryste wel be called Ysaac, þat is to
130 vndurstande, laghtur, for many a soule he browght owte of helle
lawhyng þat ʒode þidur ful sore wepyng.

þan os þis was a fygure of Cristes passion long or he were borne,
ryght so Criste hymselfe þis day in þe gospel tolde hys dysciplus how
he schulde ben scornyd and beton wyth scowreges and done to dethe
135 on þe crosse and ryson þe þrid day aʒeyne to lyue. And for þei
schuldon haue ful leue hereto, anone before hem he makyd a blynde
man to sene, þat cryed to hym and sayde: 'Ihesu, Dauid sone, haue
mercy on me.' þan sayde Cryste: 'Whate wylte þat I do to þe?' And
[he] sayde: 'Lorde, þat I mow sene.' þan sayde Ihesu: 'þi fayth hath
140 helyd þe—beholde forthe!' And anone he segh greythely and þankud
God hertyly. þis mote vche man þat wyl haue pardon of God: he mote
haue ful contricion wyth schryfte, and hol scharite wythough feynyng,
and studefaste beleue wythoute fl[o]tering.

I rede þat þer was a byschoppe of Lyncolne þat hytte Roberde
145 Grosthed, þat was holdon þe grattest clerke in þe worlde in hys tyme.
And ʒette whan he lay in hys deth-bedde, þer come to hym a grete
multitude of fyndes and spytyd wyth hym so of þe feyth þat þei
haddyn nygh turnyd hym and putte hym into dyspeyre. But þan was
oure Lady redy, þat is euer redy in nede, and sayde to hym: 'My
150 seruande, say þat þou beleuyst as Holy Chyrche doth.' And þan he
cryed and sayde: 'I beleue as Holy Chyrch doth.' And þerwyth anone
þe fendys vanysched away and he ʒaf vp þe spyryte, *et cetera.*

120 hym[1]] hymd   123 by] *om.*   125 wode] hondus   139 he] *om.*
140 And anone] *trs.*   143 flotering] flatering

[18] *De festo sancti Math[ie]*

Gode men and wommen, such a day ȝe schul haue Seynt Matheyus day, þat is Goddys holy apostyl, þe wheche hath none evyn isette in certyne for to faston bot at a mannus deuocion, as Iohn Belet seyth, þat is a doctur of Holy Chyrch, for cause þat he was notte choson of 5 Cryste hymself.

Whyl he was here in erþe, he chese hym twelue apostelles | to f. 44ʳ sewon hym, to sen and to heron alle þat he dude and preched, for þei schuldon beron wyttenesse to þe pepul aftur hys ascencion of alle þing þat he dude. For þe Iewes weron so harde aȝeynus hym in alle þing 10 þat he dude, þat þei wolde not leue nothyng þat he dude bot þat mythe be preued be wyttenesse. þan was Iudas Schariote one of þe twelue þat Cryste hadde schoson to hym, þe whyche Iudas hadde beforon slayne hys owne fadur and byleyne hys owne modur, and so cam to Cryste to ben on of hys dyscyplus. But for he was wonte before 15 to s[t]el[e] and cowde not levyn hys olde wone, he wex wery of Cristes holy lyuing, and for grete couetyse of money he solde hys Lorde Ihesu Criste to þe Iewes for þritti penyes.

And whan he segh þat Cryst was takon and demod to þe deth be hys sale, anone he fel in dyspeyre, and ȝode anone and hengyd 20 hymselfe wyth þe grenne of a roppe. So be ryght dome þat þrote þat spake þe wordys of trayturye aȝeynus hys Lorde, þat same þ[ro]t[e] was strangullyd wyth a roppe. For he wold a sayde mony ele wordus be hys Lorde aftur hys deth þat dude so foule be hym in hys lyue. And for þe fende mythe notte drowen hys sowle owte be hys mowthe, þat 25 hadde cussid þe mowthe of God so late beforne, he braste hys wombe and schedde oute hys guttys, and þat way drewe oute hys sowle and bare hit into helle.

But ȝitte, for encheson þat God is so gode in hymself and wol þat iche gode dede be rewardyd and þat vche synne be ponyschode, we 30 rede þat Seynt Brendan, as he scheppud in þe see, he sagh þis Iudas sytton vpon a stone, and a cloth hangud before hym þat hette in þe watur and bete hym in þe face ȝarne and þike. þan Brendan wende he hadde ben som holy man þat hadde sufred þat for penaunce, and askyd hym in þe name of God whatte þat he was. þan answered he 35 and sayde: 'I am Iudas, Goddys traytur, þat haue þis place of Goddys curtesye for þe refressing of þe grete hete þat I suffur wythin me, an

[18] 1 *Mathie*] mathei   2 Gode] G- *in blue, dec., 2 ll. deep*   16 stele] sellyng
22 þrote] þat   24 hym] hymself

note for no merete þat euer I deserued. Me þinketh þat I am in
paradyce whyl I am here.' þan sayde Brandan: 'Why hast þou þat
40 stone vndur þe? and why þis clothe þat beteth þe þus?' þan sayde he:
'I layde þat stone in a heygh-way þeras þe comyn pepul schulde
tredon þeronne and bene esed þerby, and þe clothe I ȝaf to a pore
man, a mesel. Bot for þe cloþe was anoþur mannus and not myne,
þerfore it doth not me bot half þe refressing os it schulde, hadde it ben
45 myn owne.' þan sayde Brendan: 'How long haste þou þis ese?' þan
sayde he: 'Vche Sonday fro[m] euensong to euenson, and from
Cristonmes Day tyl Twelue Day, and fro[m] Astur Day tyl Wytson-
tyde, and in þe Assumpcion of oure Lady, and in Candulmas Day.'
þan Brendan þankud God þat he is so merciabul in alle þing, and
50 badde hys felowes rowe forth fast þat [þei] weron gone, for þei
schulde here tythyngus sone. And þerwyth comyn oute of an hull þat
was besyde many fendys and caston blomys of brennyng yren into þe
see aftur [hem], þat þe see brande on vche a syde of hem. Bot God
kepte hem soo þat þei haddon no harme.

f. 44ᵛ   þan for | encheson þat þis Iudas was of þe twelue aposteles and þe
56 nombur of hem most nedys ben fulfillyd, aftur þat Cryste was steyed
into heuen þe ellevne apostollys wyth mony othyr dyscipulus of
Cryste weron togydur in a place. þan sayde Petur to [hem] alle: 'Gode
men and breþeren, hyt is knowen to ȝow how þat Iudas was on of
60 apostolys. And for encheson þat þe nombur may not be vnperfette, it
is nedeful [to chese] one of þese men þat haue ben wyth oure Lorde
Ihesu f[ro] þe tyme þat he was fulwode into þe tyme þat he stey into
heuen, for to be wyttenes of hys vprysing wyth vs.' þan þei setton
oute too men, Ioseph Barsabas and Mathy, and leydon lotte vpon
65 hem, preing God for to cheson wheþer he wolde haue of hem too.
And so lotte fel vpon Mathey and was nombered wyth þe oþur
ellevne apostolys.

þan went Mathey anone into Iuri and preched Goddus worde. And
for he hadde grete grace to do myracles, he turnid myche pepul to þe
70 feythe. þan was þe fend sory, and aperud to þe byschoppe of þe Iues
laue in þe lyknes of a ȝung chylde wyth long herus and hore an
vnschewly, and bad hym takon Mathey and done hym to þe deth: 'Or
ellys he wyl turne alle þe pepul to Cristes feyth and þanne schuldon ȝe
ben sette at noght and ben wretches and beggares euremore aftur.'
75 þan þeis byschopus wheron wode wrothe and sendon men to takon

---

46 from] fron   47 Day²] dayes   from] fron   50 þei¹] *om.*   53 hem¹] *om.*
58 hem] *om.*   61 to chese] *om.*   62 fro] for   66 Mathey] *over eras.*

Seynt Mathey, and so dydun, and boundon hys handus behyndon hym and caston a roppe abowton hys nek, and laddon hym to preson and boundon hym faste wyth scheynus. But þat nythe aftur, oure Lorde Ihesu Cryste come to hym wyth myche lyghte and loused hys bandys. And whan he hadde wel comfordeth hym, he oponyd þe 80 preson dore and badde hym gone preche þe fayth and spare for no man, and so dude.

þan os he preched, þere weron summe þat aȝeynestode hym and lettud oþur þat wolde haue turnyd to þe fayth. þan seyde Mathey to h[e]m: 'I telle ȝow beforon þat ȝe schullen fallyn doun into helle.' And 85 þerwyth anone, in sythe of alle þe pepul, þe erþe oponyd and swollowod hem body and soule, and nere was more seyne of hem. þan was þe pepul sore aferde of þat syght and turned to þe fayth a grete nombur of hem. þan, whan þe byschoppus herdon hereof, þ[ei] madon men to takon Mathey eftesonus and setton men for to þrowon 90 stonus at hym, and so dudon. And whan þat [he] was nyghe þe deth, he badde crysten men bery þe stonus þat [he] was slayne [wyth] wyth hym in hys graue, in wyttenes of hys martirdam. And þan he knelud doun and hof vp hys handys to God and ȝaf vp hys gost.

Reynalde of Chestur in hys croniclus telluth anoþur myracul lek 95 þis, and sayth þat whan Seyn Wlstane vysyted hys byschopryche, men broghtyn a man beforon hym þat dyde hys neygthburres myche desese and wolde neure ben in pes, preyng þat holy byschoppe þat he wolde schastyse hym. But whan þis byschoppe had preched hym alle þat he cowþe and fonde hym ere lengar þe warse, þan he prayed to 100 God and Seynt Mathey to sende and schewe hys my[r]acul | by hym a f. 45ʳ ȝeue hym þat he was worthy. þan anone in syghte of alle men þer comen outhe of þe erthe too fendys wyth too brennyng hokys and pullud þis man all quyk doun into helle, wherby þe pepul was wel comforted and aftur lyuid in pes and reste þe bettur. 105

[19] De dominica in Quadragesim[a] sermo

þis day is callyd in Holy Chyrch Sonday in Quadragesine. þan is Quadragesine a nombur of fourety, for fro þis day to Astur ben fourty dayes, þe teþþes dayes of þe ȝere. And for vche man doth surfete vche day more or lesse, þerfore to makon satysfaccion for þat gylte vche 5

85 hem] hym   89 þei] þat   91 he] it   92 he²] om.   wyth¹] om.
101 myracul] mycacul   102 ȝeue] ȝene   102–3 alle . . . of] rep.
[19] 1 Quadragesima] Quadragesime   2 þis] þ- in blue, dec., 2 ll. deep

man is holdon be þe law of God and Holy Chyrch to faston þese
fourety dayes, [ow]takon hem þat þe lawe dispenseth wyth for nede,
þat ben schyldron wythinne age, wymmen wyth schylde, olde men
passed age and myght not faston, pylgrymes and seke, pore men and
10 þilk þat laboreth sore for here lyflode. þeise þe law dispensith wyth
vpon here consciens.

þan for encheson þat Sonday is no day of fastyng, þerfore ȝe schul
begynne ȝou[r]e faste on Aske Wednesday, and þat day comyth to þe
Chyrch holly and take askus of þe prestes hande, and bere forth in
15 ȝoure herte þat he sayth to ȝow whan he layth askys on ȝoure hedde.
þan he sayth þus: 'Man, þenk þou arte bot askus, and [to] askus þou
schalte aȝeyne turne.'

þen ben þ[er] dyuerse skyllys why ȝe schul faste þeyse fourety
dayes. On hys for encheson, os þe gospell of þis day telleth, how þat
20 þe Holy Gost ladde oure Lorde Ihesu into a deserte þat was betwyson
Ierusalem and Ierico to be temptud of þe fende, and was þere fourety
dayes and so many nythes fastyng for oure loue, schewing to vs and
alle criston pepul þe vertu and þe mede þat comyth be fastyng, þe
wyche uertu and mede bene expressed in þe preface of þe messe þat is
25 sayde in Holy Chyrche þeis fourety dayes, þere is sayde þus: þat
bodely faste þrusteth doune vices and lyfteth vp þoght of man to God
and ȝeth hym uertu and mede. It ȝeth hym mede in heuen þat schal
laston eurer and grete [uertu] in erþe. For os clerkus techon, þe
sp[yt]ell of a fasting mon schal slene a neddur [bodyly. þan moche
30 more it schall sle þe myght of þe olde neddur], þat is þe fend of helle,
þat come to Eue in paradyse in lyknesse of a neddur to tempton hur of
glotonye, of veyne glory, and of couetyse. Rythe so he com to Cryste
in lykenesse of a man, leste he hadde ben knowon, and temptud hym
of þe same synnus.

35 þis, as þe gospell tellyth, whan Criste [hadde] fast so longe and was be
kynde of manhed onhungred, þe fend come to hym and schewod hym
stonus and sayde: 'If þou be Goddys Sone, make þesse stones bredde',
þat ryght os Eue, whan scheo see þe appul, scheo was raput to eten þerof,
ryght so he hadde hope to haue made Cryste, and so be gloteny to haue
40 eton of þe bredde. For glotery is notte in a mannus mete but in hys foule
apetyte. þan sayde Cryste to hym: 'A mon schal not lyuen only in bredde
bot in vche worde þat goth outhe of Goddys mowth.'

---

7 owtakon] and takon   13 ȝoure] ȝoue   16 to] *om.*   18 þer] þre
23 fastyng] in *add.*   28 uertu] *om.*   29 spytell] gospeil   29–30 bodyly . . .
neddur] *om.*   35 hadde] whan

þan þe fende toke Criste and sette hym vpon a pynnakul of þe tempul, and sayde: 'If þou be Goddys Sone, bring þiself doun wythoute mannus helpe, þat I may knowen þe for Goddus | Sone.' f. 45ᵛ þan sayde Cryste: 'þou scalte notte temp þi God, þi Lorde.' ȝette þe 46 þrid tyme he toke hym and sette hym on an hye hull and schewed hym all þe kyngdam of þe worlde be [c]alkyng, and all þe ioy of hem. And whan he hadde tolde hym, he sayde þus to hym: 'Alle þis I schal ȝefe þe, so þat þou falle doune to þe erþe and worchep me.' þan 50 answered God and sayde: 'Go forth, þou blak Sathanas. It is wrytton: þou schalt worchep þi Lorde God and only serue hym.' þan þe fende laf hym, and angelus comyn and browton hym mete fro heuen.

þan þe fende is moste bysy to makon eury man to gylton in þeyse þre þinggus moste þese fourety dayes. þerefore ȝow nedeth þre 55 helpys aȝeyne hem, þat ben: aȝeyne gloteny, abstynens, for in eting he tempteth a man moste and raþethurrest; mekenesse aȝeyne pride; largenes aȝeyne couetyse.

þan aȝeyne glotenye, ȝe moton faston, þat is, note to eton before tyme bot abyde tyl none of þe day. And whanne ȝe ben at ȝoure mete, 60 ete ȝe note to freschelych, no more þan anoþer tyme, ne s[ytte] for luste ne lengar þan anoþer day. And beth wel ware þat ȝe faston boþe day and nyghte as Cryste dude, for þer ben many þat faston þe day at on mel, and þei wyl sytton myche of þe nyght and drynkon, and so fyllon here wombe wyth drynkyng as ful os of mete, and þere þei done 65 for volupte as myche [a]s glotonrye. Also ȝe muste faste fro alle maner flesse-mete [and] w[hyt]-mete, as [I]erom sayth: 'Egges and chese ben molton flessch and mylke ys blode.' Also for to schewon ensampul of Holy Chyrch, take hede on þe preste þat goth to masse, þat is, to Goddys borde, how he at hys begynnyng boweth hys kneus downe to 70 God and byd alle oþur for to done so. And also þe mydul and þe ende of hys masse he bytte alle men bowen here hedys to God. So do ȝe whan ȝe gon to ȝoure borde: furste worchep ȝe God wyth a Paternoster and an Aue Maria, [or] mo as ȝoure deuocion is, and makuth a cros vpon ȝoure mete, and aftur mete [þanke God wyth 75 anoþur Paternoster and an Aue, þat eure sendyth ȝou mete] at ȝoure nede. þus schul ȝe faste aȝeyne glotonry.

Aȝeynus veyne glorye þat is [in] a mannus herte, ȝe motyn faston wythineforth gostly. ȝe schul putton away alle euel þoghtes of heygnesse and haue þoghtes of lownes, þenkyng how a man is 80

48 calkyng] talkyng   61 sytte] schurter   66 as] þat is   67 and¹] *om.*   whyt] wyth   Ierom] rerom   74 or] *om.*   75–6 þanke . . . mete] *om.*   78 in] *om.*

borne febul and seke, nakud and pore, and how he goth yche day a
iorney towarde hys deth. And thenk how at þe laste deth comyth and
takyth hym, and casteth hym doun seke in hys bedde [gronyng and
sykyng, and sone castyth vp] hys drynk and hys mete [and] turneth
85 hyde and hewe. And þan hys breth stynkyth, hys lyppus waxon bloo,
hys face pale, hys eyen holowe, hys mowth frotheth, and so at þe laste
wyth depe syyngus and sore ȝoldeth vp þe goste. þan lyght þere bot a
stynkyng stok of erþe and is hydde and putte in þe erþe and lafte þere
and ful sone forȝeton. Holduth þis in ȝoure mynde and I hope it schal
90 put away pride.

Aȝeyne couetyse, ȝe schal faston wythine and wythoute: wythine
from horribul thoutys of wordly occupacion and of hardenes to
holdyn gode aȝeynus [Goddys] byddyng. Also wythoute: ȝoure
f. 46ʳ handys, þat haue ben eurer redy to takon, now | ȝe schul makyn
95 hem as redy to rechyn to hem þat ȝe oweth anyþing and to hem þat ȝe
haue done wrong to, and to rechyn to þe pore pepul mete and drink
and þat þei han nede to. For þeke handys ben vnworthy [to] heven vp
to God þat be not wonte to reche pore [men] mete and drink. And
þeke fete þat haue bene bysy erly and late to wa[l]ke aboute wordely
100 gode now schul ben as bysy to visyte pore and seke, and gone on
pylgrymage, and gone to chyrch to here Goddys seruyse. And he þat
hath faste before to spare [hys gode for] chynchese now schulde spare
owte of hys owne mo[uþe to ȝefe hem] þe whyche þat haue nede. þis
faste pleseth God and helputh þe sowle hegly. For rythe os watur
105 quenchith fyre, ryght so almusdede quencheth synne. Herefore sayth
þe profytte þus: 'Ȝeueth almus, and alle þing schal be clene to ȝow, so
þat it be ȝeven wyth gode wille.' Bot more harme is, þer ben mony þat
haue more lust to fedun ere owne body in lusti metys and drynkys þan
for to ȝeuon a pore man an hyse of hys bredde.

110 I rede þat þer was an nobul knythe of hys owne handde and a grete
lorde, bot he scherysched hys body to myche wyth deynteth metys
and drinkys. So it fel þat he was dede and byried in a tombe of stone,
as lordys ben. þan hadde he a sone þat was a gode man and hadde
vche day in custom to segge before mete *De profundis* for hys fadur
115 soule beforne hys tombe. þan it felon a day þat he made a grete feste
of lordys and grete men of hys cuntre. And whan þei were redy to
waschon, hys sone þowthe þat he hadde not seyde hys deuocion, and

---

83–4 gronyng . . . vp] *om.*   84 and³] *om.*   93 Goddys] *om.*   97 to²] *om.*
98 men] *om.*   99 walke] wake   102 hys gode for] *om.*   103 mouþe . . . hem]
moke

prayde hem to abydon a whyle whylle he ʒode and sayde *De profundis*. þan saydon þai þat þei woldon gon wyth hym. þan whyl þei saydon *De profundis*, þer fel such a lust at þis sones herte to sene hys fadur, þat 120 hym þoght he schulde be dede bot he segh hym. þan made he men to vndo þe tombe. þan see he a passing grete tode as blak as pyche, wyth eynon brennyng as fyre, þat hadde beclyppod wyth hure foule fette hys fadures þrote and gnew faste þeron. þan whan þe sone segh þat, he sayde: 'Oo fadur, myche swete mete and drynk hath gone doune þat 125 þrotte, and now arte strangelode wyth þat foule helle-beste.' þan badde he hulle þe body aʒeyne, and ʒodon to mete. And whan he hadde seruid alle men ryalich, priuely he ʒode forth and lafte wyfe [and schylde] and all hys lordeschep, and ʒode to Ierusalem and þer lyued among beggarus alle hys lyfe aftur in grete penaunce, *et cetera*. 130

[20] *Dominica secunda Quadragesime*

Gode men and wommen, þis day is þe secunde Sonday in clene Lenton. Wherefore, os ʒe haue ben bysy alle þis ʒere before for to make ʒow clene and honest wythouteforth in body, now ʒe schul ben as bysy for to clense ʒow wythineforth in ʒoure soule, for þat is 5 Goddys wille þat ʒe so done. Wherefore þis tyme of Lenton is ordeynod only for to schow[r]on and to clenson ʒoure conscience of alle maner ruste and fylthe of synne þat he is defouled inne, so þat ʒe mowen wyth a clene consciens reseyuen on Astur Day þe clene body of oure Lorde Ihesu Criste. 10

Wherefore Seynt Poule techuth ʒowe in þe pystell of þis day and sayth þis: *Hec est uoluntas Dei*, þis is Goddus wylle þat [ʒ]e ben holy and þat ʒe cone holde ʒowre vessel aʒeyne in holynesse and worchep. þan it preueth wel þat [h]e doth God | worchep þat bysyeth hym for f. 46ᵛ to clenson his vessel aʒeyne þe comyng of hys [l]orde. þan schul ʒe 15 know wel þat þis vesell is noght ellys, as Seynt Bernarde [sayth], bot a mannus consciens. Hit is a trew vessell and a hol, and keputh trewly alle þat is put þerine to þat day of dome. For þat day vche mannus vesell, þat is to say, vche mannus consciens, schal ben oponed, so þat þe worlde schal sene what a man hath kepte þerine, be it bettur, be it 20 worse. þan wel schal hym bene þat bryngeth þat day a clene vessel before þe iustice.

---

122 passing grete] *trs.*   128 and schylde] *om.*
[20]   2 Gode] G- *in blue, dec.*, 2 *ll. deep*   7 schowron] schowon   12 ʒe] he
14 he] ʒe   15 lorde] horde   16 sayth] *om.*

þan how a man schal kepe hymself clene Holy Chyrch techeth be
ensaumpul of an holy man þat is a patriarch, Iacob, þat is red and
25 songon of alle þis whyle, and sayth þus: þis Iacob hadde a fadur þat
[was] callud Ysaac, and a modur þat was kallud Rebecca. þan h[adde]
þis Rebecca be hur husband too chyldron att onus, and þat on þat
[was] furst borne hette Esaw, and þe oþur hatte Iacob. þan God
ordeynyd so þat þe fadur louid Esau, and þe modur louid Iacob. But
30 for þis story is long, we schul at þis tyme takon þat is spedeful and
leue þat oþur.

þan God ȝaf þe patriarches suche a grace þat, whate maner blessing
þei ȝefuen here chyldron, þei schuldon haue it. þan for þis Ysaac was
olde and blynde and nygh hys deth, he badde hys sone Esau gone and
35 hunton and geton hym som mete þat he mythe eton of, and þan he
wolde ȝeven hym hys blessing. But whan þis Esaw was gone, be tysing
and sleyte of hys modur, Iacob, þat was þe ȝongar, gate ys fadur
blessyng and was made eyre and lorde of alle hys breþeron, and [hys
fadur] cursyd alle þat cursyd hym and blessed alle þat blessed hym.
40 þan Esau com hom and knew þis, he hatyd hys broþer Iacob and
þoghte to haue slayne hym. Wherefore be counsel of hys modur he
ȝode oute of cuntre to an vnkul þat he hadde þat hatte Laban.

And as he went be þe way, he com into a cuntre of euel-lyfuing men
and durste not herbar wyth hym, but lay alle nythe be þe way, and
45 layde a stone vndur hys heued and so sleppe. And os he sclepe, hym
þoght he saw a laddur [þat raghte from þe erthe to heuen, and God
ioynyd to þe laddur], and angellus going vp and dounn þe laddur. þan
spake God to hym and sayde: 'I am God of Habraham and of Ysaac
and wol ȝeue þe þis londe and ben þi keper in þis way.' þan woke
50 Iacob and sayde: 'For soþe God is in þis place, and I wyste notte.' And
so ȝode forth to hys vnkul, and was wyth hym xx ȝere hys servaunte,
and weddud hys too doghteron. þe on hette Rachel, and þat oþur Lya.

And whan he hadde ben þer so long, he hadde longyng to gone
home into hys owne cuntre, and toke wyth hym hys wyfes and hys
55 schylder and alle þe catell and gode þat he hadde, and ȝode forth. But
ȝit for he dredde hys broþer, þer com to hym þan a grete multitude of
angellus to helpe hym, in lyknesse of men. þan whan he com to a
forth, þis Iacob made hys mene and alle hys catell go before oure þe
f. 47ʳ forþe, and he is one abode be|hynde in hys preyeres. And os he was in
60 hys preyeres, an angele cam to hym in lyknes of a man and wrasteled

26 was¹] *om.*   hadde] hys   28 was] *om.*   38–9 hys fadur] *om.*   40 þis] þat
add.   46–7 þat . . . laddur] *om.*   47 going] g- *alt. from* d-

wyth hym alle þe nyght tyl on þe morow, and towched þe grete synow
of hys þegh and made hym to halton euremore aftur. þan seyde þe
angel to Iacob: 'What is þine name?' He seyde: 'Iacob.' 'Nay,' quoth
he, 'þou schalt hette no lengar Iacob, but Israel schal be þine name',
and so blessyd hym and lafte hym þer halte, and so 3ode home into 65
hys cuntre in myche prosperite.

þis story is redde in Holy Chyrch in heygh ensaumpul to vche
Goddys servaunte þat desyreth for to gete blesyng of þe fadur of
heuen and haue þe eritage þat is þere. He mote furste ben Iacob and
aftur Israel, for Iacob is vndurstondon a wrasteler and Israel a [m]on 70
þat seth God. For he þat wol see God in heuen he mote wrastelen in
erþe wyth þe euel angel, þat is þe fende, and wyth hys owne flesch.
þus whan he goth to schryuing hym and hath done an horrybul synne,
þe fende putteth suche a schame in hys herte so, þogh it be in hys
mouth, he may not for schame telle it owte. þan motte he wrastel 75
wyth þe fende and ourecomyn hym, and so tellon oponly alle þe
circumstaunce of hys synne. þan wyl hys flesse ben aferde of þe
penaunce and doth it noght aftur, as he is bydon, for drede þerof. But
þan he motte also wrastelyn wyth hys flesse and, magreyth it, done
hys penaunce fully os he is bedon, takyng also ensampul of þe 80
womman [þat come] of fer to Cryste, os þe gospel telleth of þis
day, for to geton hele to hur doghtyr þat was trauaylde wyth a fende.

þan among oþur wordus, whan scheo cryed to [Cryste for helpe, he
answerde and sayde: 'It is not gode to] take brede of schyldren and
3euen houndes for to eton.' But þus rebuk[e] þis womman tok mekly 85
and sayde: '3is, Lorde, forwhy whelppys eton of crommys þat fallon
fro here lordys borde.' þan sayde Cryste: 'Womman, þou hast a grete
feyth. Wherefore os þou wylte, be þi doghtur hole.'

þis womman and hur doghtyr betokeneth a man þat hath hys
conciens trauaylyd wyth þe fende of dedly synne, þat may no way ben 90
holpon bot he go to God and to Holy Chyrch and þer oponly schryue
hym to þe prest, sparing for no rebuke ne for no schame no drede, but
mekly suffyr þat þe preste sayth to hym and take hys penaunce
devoutely. And so schal he be delyuered of þe fende þat traueyleth
hys consciens. For þat man þat doth a dedly synne, 3ef he schal be 95
sauid, he schal neure haue reste in hys consciens tyl he be schryuen.
þerfore, ryght as a hound gnaweth a bone, ryght so þat synne schal
gnawe hys consciens, schewing hym be experiens how howndes of

70 a mon] anone   81 þat come] *om.*   fer] frer   83–4 Cryste . . . to] *om.*
85 rebuke] rebukyd

helle schal gnawe hys soule euremore wythoute reste þat dyeth
100 wytinly in dedly synne þat he moste haue ben schryuen of and
wolde notte.

I rede of a womman þat hadde don an horybul synne, and ofte sche
wolde a schryuen hur þerof but scheo mythe neure for schame tellyn
hytte to þe preste. þan in a nyght scheo lay and thoght eure myche
105 how scho mythe done for schame. þan cam Criste to hure bodyly and
sayde to hure: 'My doghtyr, why schryuest þe notte of þat synne?'
f. 47ᵛ þan sayde scheo: 'Lorde, I | may not for schame.' þan sayde Criste to
hyr: 'Schew me þine hande', and tok hyr hand and put it in h[y]s syde
vp to þe elbowe, and sayde: 'Whatte felys þou?' And scheo quakyd for
110 fere and sayde: 'Lorde, I fele þine herte.' þan sayde Cryste: 'Be þou
no more aschamyd to schew me þine herte þan I am to suffyr þe to
felon myn herte.' þan þe womman rose and wyth a candul se hure
hand alle blody. And þan sche wolde haue wasson hur hande bot it
wolde not ben, tyl scheo ȝode on þe morowe to þe chyrch and schrof
115 hure. And whan scheo was schryuon, þan anone was hur hande as
whyte os þe oþur, *et cetera.*

[21] *Dominica tercia Quadragesime*

Gode men, þis day is þe þrydde Sonnynday of Lenton. Wherefore we
rede in þe gospel of þis day how oure Lorde Ihesu Criste caste oute a
dome fende of a man. And whan þe fende was oute of hym, þan þe
5 man spake. þan schul ȝe vndurstande be þis dome man alle þike þat
haue no pouste in þer tonge to schryuyn þem of ydul othys, of ydul
wordus, and of ydul thowtus þa[t] a man wyth delyte ocupieth hys
herte ine. And whan he cometh to [s]c[h]ri[f]te, þan he is dome and
spekyth note of hem, wenyng þat it be no synne to þenkon on ydul
10 þoghte, ne for to spekon an ydul worde þat makon men to laghon, ne
for to sweron a nothe doth men no harme. ȝus, for soth, it is suche a
synne to sweren an oth, as Criste sayth hymselfe, þat a man schal ȝeue
acownte of in þe day of dome, of vche ydul worde þat a man spekuth.

Wherefore to wythstrayne alle men from suche othus, Seynt Poule
15 in þe pystyl of þus day forbeduth vche criston man to spekon alle
maner foly speche and rybaudy and harlotry and alle oþer speche þat
turnyth to foly and to noght, and byd hym speke such wordus þat ben

---

102 Narracio bona *in margin in the long hand*   108 hys] hus *alt. from* hur
[21] 2 Gode] G- *in blue, dec., 2 ll. deep*   7 þat] þan   8 schrifte] criste
10 an] and

worchep to God and profytte to hem þat heruth hem, and byddyth
þat suche foly wordus and harlotry schulde not ben nemod among
Goddus pepul. For þereos þei ben oftyn nemod, þei ben þoght on, 20
and so falleth into þe ded of synne, and þogh þe dede of synne sueth
not, nerþeles þe luste þat a man hath in spekyng is a grete synne.
I rede of an abbas þat was a clene womman of hur body os for dede
of lechery, but scheo hadde grete lust and gamon to talk þerof. So
whan scheo was dede, scheo was byried in þe schyrch. On þe nyghte 25
aftur, fendus commyn and tokon vp þe body and beton it wyth
brennyng schoureges fro þe navel vpwarde, þat it was also blake as
pyche; bot from þe nauel dounwarde þei myght do noght þerto, for
þat parte schone os þe sonne. But eure os þe fendes beton hur, scheo
cryed so pytuesly[c]h þat too of hur susteres, þat weron sextenus, 30
weron sore agrysyd þerof. But ȝit eyther comforded oþur, þat þei
comyn where þe body lay and seyn how þe fendys ferdon wyth hur.
þan sayde scheo to hur systeren: 'ȝe knoweth wel inogh þat I was
clene maydon as for any dede of flesche, wherefore þat party of my
body þat was clene þat schynyth nogh os ȝe sene. But for I hadde grete 35
luste to spekon of fylthe of þe flesshe and oþur rybaudy, þerfore þat
parte of my body þat is gylty it hath þe penaunce as ȝe sene.
Wherefore I prey ȝow þat ȝe preyen for me, for þorgh ȝoure preyeres
I may ben holpyn. And beth ware | be me in tyme comyng.'   f. 48ʳ
Be þis ensaumpul ȝe mown knowon how grete synne it is to spekon 40
of rybaudy. Wherefore þe same postyl byddyth ȝow abstene ȝow from
such doing and swe Cryste, and walkon in loue as Criste dude and
suffred for ȝow many skornes and rebucus and despytys and many
deseses. And alle he toke softely and mekly and in charite, ȝeuyng
ensampul to alle hys pepul to do ryghte so, for þat is nedeful to vche 45
Goddys seruaunde. For he þat schaputh hym for to lyuon in reste and
pes he schal haue grete persecucion of vle men, but, ȝef he take it
mekely and in charyte, he is a martir before God.
Wherefore in comfordyng of alle suche Goddus seruandus, Holy
Chyrch makyth mynde þis [day and alle þe weke aftur] of an holy man 50
þat was callud Ioseph, þat sufred grete persecucion, but for he toke it
mekely, God aftur browth hym into grete worchep, and how ȝe schul
here. But for þe story is oure-long, we schul take þereof þat neduth
and leue þat oþur.
þis Ioseph hadde a fadur þat hatte Iacob and hadde ellewne 55

23 nota *in margin with red paraph*   30 pytueslych] spytueslyth   49 seruandus] of
add.   50 day . . . aftur] *om.*

breþeren to Ioseph. And [for] hys fadur louid hym specialy before alle
þe oþur, þei hatud hym, and muche more for a sweven þat he mette,
þe wheche he tolde to hys breþeren, whereby þei haddon oure-
trowing þat he schulde ben a lorde to ham and alle schulde do hym
60 worchep. þerfore þei schapud to han slayne hym. But for þei durste
notte, for þe eye of God, schedon hys blode, þei soldon hym into þe
londe of Egypte to a man for þrytty penyes. þan for God was wyth
hym, þe maystur of þe kyngus knytus þat hatte Putyfer bogth Ioseph
and made hym schef of hys howsolde. But ȝette þe deuel hadde envye
65 to hym and makyd þe lady of þe houce to coueton hym to haue lyne by
hur. And so on a day whanne scheo segh tyme, scheo toke hym be þe
mantyl and spak to hym of þat mater. But whan he herde þat, anone
he flogh away and lafte hys mantyl þere. þan þis womman rerud a cry
and tolde hur lorde how þat Ioseph wolde a lyne by hur, and for he
70 schulde notte seyn nay, scheo hulde hys mantyl in wyttenesse aȝeynus
hym. Wherefore þe lorde anone made caston Ioseph in preson, þeras
Kyng Pharao hadde done hys butler and hys baxstere byfore.

þanne mette þei too swevenus, þe whyche Ioseph dudde rec[c]hon
and sayde þat wythinne þre dayes aftur þe kyng wolde restore hys
75 botteler aȝeyne into hys offyce, and þe bakster schulde ben hongod
wythinne þre dayes. And so it was os he sayde. þan felle it so þat þe
kyng mette a sweven hymself. But for þer cowþe no man telle whatte
schulde falle þerof, be stering of þe butteler þe kyng send aftur
Ioseph. And whan þe kyng hadde tolde hym hys s[wev]en, þan sayde
80 Ioseph þat God hadde sent warning to þe kyng to be ware and puruey
hym before, for he schulde haue sewuen ȝere plentevous of corne and
alle oþur vytayles, and aftur hem schul come odur seven ȝere of
hungur þat schuldon eton vp and destroyen alle þat mythe ben geton
in þe seven gode ȝerus before. þan sayde þe kyng: 'I know no man þat
85 coude do þis bettur þan þou. Wherefore I make þe grattest vndur me
in my reme, and alle schal bowe to þe as to me and don þi
commaundement in alle þing.'

þan Ioseph lete makon þe gretest barnus þat eure weren seyne and
gadered corne alle þik seven ȝere. So atte þe seven ȝerus ende, as he
90 sayde, dere ȝere and hungur com, and [whan] alle men hadden
f. 48ᵛ spended | þat þei hadden, [þan þei come to Ioseph þat hadde inogh
and solde hem corne and oþur vytayles]. þan þat Iacob, Ioseph fadur,
harde þat þere was corn to sellen in Egypte, he send þidur hys ten

sonus for to byge corne. And whan þei sen Ioseph, os his swevon
wolde, too and twenti ȝere beforon, alle þei fellon on kneus and ₉₅
honured hym, for þei knew not Ioseph, bot he knew hem wel. He
spake harde wordys to hem be a latimer, lest he hadde ben knowen,
and sayde þei weron spyeres and were comyn to spye þe londe. And
þei saydon: nay, þei weron alle on mannus sones, and one broþer þei
haddon lefte at home wyth here fadur, and anoþer broþer þei haddon, ₁₀₀
bot þei wyste hym not on lyue—þan þei speke be Ioseph. þan he
wolde preue hem if þei weron trewe, and made byndon on of hem þat
hythe Symeon, and sayde he wolde holde hym faste tyl þei hadde
broght to hym þat broþer þat was at home, and made fyllon here
sakkes wyth corne and put þe money in þe mowthes of vche sake, ₁₀₅
vnwyttyng hem, an so made hem to go hom to hur fadur.

So whanne þe comyn hom and poured oute þe corne, þei fondon þe
money in here sakkys, and þei tolde hure fadur alle þing. þan was þe
fadur wondur sory for hys sone þat was lafte behynde in bondus, ande
moste nede sende hym forth þat he louid moste, for he was Ioseps ₁₁₀
owne broþur—þe other weron hys half-breþeren. But þohg hym were
loth to levyn hym, whan hys corne faylyd he moste nedus haue more,
and sende forth Beniamyn to Ioseph. And whan Ioseph segh hym, he
mythe not forberon to wepon, and ȝode into hys schaumbur, and
badde delyueron here oþur broþur Symeon to hem and setton hem to ₁₁₅
mete, and bad fullon hure sakkus wyth corne and putton priuelych
hys coupe þat he drank of hymself in Beniamynnus fettus, and so
made hem gon here way.

But whan þei weron gone in gode spede, as þei wendon han done,
þan sende Ioseph aftur hem men, þat saydon þat þei were wykkyd ₁₂₀
men þat, aftur þat here lorde hadde made hem wel at ese, haddon
stolne hys coupe þat he louid moste. þan were þei sory and sayden it
was not soth, and badde he[m] ransake hem vchone by and by. And so
þei gonnon at þe eldest tyl þei come to þe ȝongest, and tokon hym, for
þei foundon hyt wyth hym. þei laddon hym aȝeyne to here lorde, for ₁₂₅
þei þoght þe were sykur þat it hadde not ben so. þan whanne þei
comyn to Beniamyn, þat was Ioseph broþer, þei foundon þe coupe in
þe boþom of þe sak. þanne þe weron alle sory and turnyd aȝayne and
comyn alle wepyng before Ioseph. But whan he sawe hem alle wepon
and [hys] owne broþer makyng moste sorow, for it was fondon wyth ₁₃₀
hym, þan Ioseph spak to hem and badde hem ben of gode comforde
and sayde: 'I am Ioseph, ȝoure broþur: be ȝe not aferde. Gode hath

123 hem] hen   130 hys] *om.*

sente me before 30w hydur for 30ure gode.' And sente aftur hys fadur and dwellud þere eure aftur in þat lond in grete wele and prosperite.

135 þis story is redde þis weke in Holy Chyrch for Goddys schyldron schuldon takon ensaumpul to holde holy faderes to suffron desese and persecucion wyth meke herte and in ful charite for Goddys loue, as he suffred for vs. And he þat takuth persecucon a3eyne herte, and grucheth a3eyne God, and sayth: 'Why doth God þus wyth me?

140 Whatte haue I trespased þat he fareth þus wyth me?', þeise moste schryue hem þerof and askon God mercy of hys inpaciens and of alle oþur synnus, be þei neure so smale in hys eye, for þe trespace of synne may letton myche grace.

I rede in þe myracles of Seynte Wynefrede þat a man com to hur on

f. 49ʳ a nyght vpon too crotches full of alle maner | whoo. þan by help of þis

146 holy virgine he was helud, and so went alle þe day aftur holle in vche houce of alle þe abbey, heygly þankyng God and þe holy maydon of his hele. But at nyght he 3ode to hys bedde þer he lay before, hopyng to han gone on þe morowgh al hol. As sone as he cam to hys bedde,

150 anoone þe seknes toke hym wors þan it dude before, and so lay alle þe nyght crying, þat it was rewthe to here hym. þan on þe morogh monkus comon and askud hym what he hadde gylte þat hys sekenesse was comyn a3eyne, and he sayde: 'Noþing.' þan sayde one of þe monkus: 'Hast þou ben schriuen seth þou come?' And he sayde: 'Nay,

155 for sothe, for he hadde no nede, and sayde he stal neyþer ox no cowe ne hors ne mare, ne neure dude no grete greves synne, wherefore he hadde no nede to schryuyn hym.' þan sayde þe monke a3eyne þus: '3is,' quoth he, '3ow a man do notte no grete dedly synnus, he may do so many venial þat þei schul turne into a dedly synne. For ryghte as a

160 man may wyth many smale cornus oure-schargen a strong horse, so wyth oure-many venial synnus vnschryuen he may schargeon hys soule þat it schal fallon into þe lake of helle.' þan þis man toke a preste and schrof hym, and whan he was schryuen, anone he hadde hys hele and was hol eure aftur, and þankud God heygly þat he was helud body

165 and soule, in soule be confession, in body be helpe of preyer of þat holy mayden, *et cetera.*

[22] *Dominica iiijᵃ Quadragesime sermo*

As 3e knowen wel, þis is þe furþe Sunday of Lenton, in þe whyche alle Holy Chyrch makuth mynde of han holy profytte þat was callud

[22] 2 As] A- *in blue, dec., 2 ll. deep*

Moyses, þe wych was a fugure of oure Lorde Ihesu Cryste many ȝerus
or God was borne of oure Lady. þan as we reduth þis weke in Holy 5
Chyrche, as þis Moyses was in deserte of Synay, God spake to þis
Moyses and sayde to hym þus: 'Pharao þe kyng of Egypt oppressuth
þe pepul of Israel wyth bondage [and] vnresonabul warkus, and þei
for whoo and oppressyng kryedon to me for sokur and helpe.
Wherefore goo þou þidur and fache hom oute of here bondage, and 10
bryng hem hydur, and offreth to me in þis stede. And I wil bryng hem
into a londe pleyntevous of alle godenesse.' So whan he hadde taghte
Moyses alle how he schulde done, þan he ȝode ȝydur and gedered alle
þe holde men of hem þat knewon be profecy how þei schuldon ben
ladde oute of þat londe, and sayde to ham as God badde hym. þan 15
were þei wondur gladde and fayne, and sewed hym forth, more an
lasse, tyl þei comyn to þe Redde See. And God was beforne hem in þe
day in a pyler of a clowde to refresson hem for þe hete of þe sonne and
in þe nyght in a pyler of fyre to lyghten hem from harme of nedderes
and of othur venummus bestus. 20

But whan Pharao herde þat Moyses hadde ledde forth þis pepul, he
toke þree hundred of chariotus of hys owne and oþur þree hundred of
þe londe and fyfty thowsand of horse-men and too hundred thowsand
of fotte-men, and ȝode aftur hem. But whan Moyses seygh þis pepul
commyn, he prayed to God for help. And God badde hym smyte þe 25
see wyth hys ȝerde and it schulde opyn and ȝeu way to hys pepul. And
whanne he hadde smyton þe see, it cleue on [ij] partyes so þat þe
watur stode on eyþur syde os a wall and þe grounde was drye sonde.
þan ȝode Moyses ine and alle þe pepul aftur hym, tyl þei woron
passyd alle oure. þan | w[e]n[de] Pharao to haue [d]one soo and ȝode f. 49ᵛ
ine aftur. Bot whan he and alle hys oste weren in þe see, þe watur 31
went aȝeyne togydur and drownyd hym and all hys oste, so þat þere
lefte of hem not one man. þan whan Moyses and hys pepul seygh þat,
þei thankyd God wyth hegh stewen and dwellyd þer seuen dayes
aftur, and vche day ȝedon to þe see wyth melodye, thankyng God of 35
hure wondurful schapyng. And ȝit in mynde hereof alle þe Astur
weke procession is made to þe fonte.

þan went Moyses forth wyth hys pepyl into deserte tyl þei comyn
to þe hul of Synay, and þer lafte þe pepul beneþen. And he hymselfe
ȝode vppe into þe hulle þer God was, and was þer fourety dayes and 40
fourety nygthes wythoute mete and drink. þan God ȝaf hym too
tabullus of stone, in þe wyche God wrotte wyth hys fyngurres þe ten

8 and¹] om.   27 ij] om.   30 wende] whan   done] gone

commaundementus and badde Moyses techen hem hys pepul. And
whan he com doun to þe pepul, hys faas was so bryght as þe sonne and
45 too spyres sto[don] oute of hys heued lek too hornys, so þat þe pepul
myghte not spekon wyth hym for clerenesse tyl he toke a kerchef and
heled hys face. þan were þere wrytton in þe one lef þree commandementis þat longuth to God, and seven in þe tother lef þat longuth to
þe neygbur.

50 þe þree commandementis þat longuth to God ben þese: þou schalte
luf þi God and worcheppon hym beforon alle þing, so þat þou salte in
alle thyng putton Goddus wylle before þi wylle, and so sewe hys wylle
and not þine. þe oþur is: þou schalt not takon þi Goddys name in
vayne, þat is, þou schalt not be callud a criston man but þou lyf a
55 criston lyve. For þagh þou be called a criston man and seruyst moste
þe fende, þat name standeth þe in veyne. And also þou schalt not
sweron be God, ne by no parte of hys body, ne by noþing þat he made,
bot in affermyng of trewth and ȝitte whan þou arte constreynod
þertoo. þe þrydde is: þou schalte holde þine haly-day, þat is, þou
60 schalte bene as erly vppe and as late doune and ben also [besy] on þe
haly-day to serue God as þou arte on þe werke-day to serue þe worlde.
þe ferthe is: þou schalte honouren þi fadur and þi modur þat haue
broght þe into þis worlde, and þi god-fadur and þi god-modur þat
holpon to make þe a cristen man, and þi fadur vndur God þat hathe
65 charge of þine soule and schal answere þerfore before God. þe fyfte is:
þou sc[h]alte no[t] slene no man neþur wyth þine hande, ne wyth þine
tonge, ne wyth euel ensampul, ne wythdrawe lore and techyng fro
þem þat þou arte holde to teche. þe syxte is: þou schalt do no lechery
in no degre wythoute weddelok. þe seuent is: þou schalte stele no
70 þing grete ne smalle. þe eyghte is: þou schalte bere no falce
wyttenesse aȝeynus no man be no way. þe nynthe is: þou schalte
couette neyþur seruaunte ne horce no noo thyng þat is þine
neytheburres aȝeynus hys wylle. þe tenþe is: þou schalte not desyre
þi neyhburres wyf ne consayle hur be no way to done euel ne þat is
75 harme and vyleny to hur husbonde. þeis ben þe ten commendementes
þe wyche iche criston man is boundon to kepon.

þus was Moyses a fugur and a tokyn of Criste. For Moyses com
before and ȝaf þe lawe, and Criste com aftur and ȝaf grace and mercy
and trewthe. For ryght as Moyses fatte þe pepul oute of Egypte |
f. 50ʳ þorogh þe see to þe hul of Synay, rygh so Cryste, whan he com, be hys
81 preching and miracles doing, fatte þe pepul oute of darkenesse of

45 stodon] stonus   60 besy] *om.*   66 schalte] sclalte   not] none

synne and of ele lyving þorogh þe watur of folowyng to þe hul of
uertues. For he þat wyl schryuen hym klene and leuen hys foule
lyving and [holde] þe cownandes þat he made wyth God in hys
folwyng he schal gedure togydur [uertues] so þat he schal encreson 85
hem herer þan any hul in erþe.

But he þat wol do þus, he mote ben fedde of God wyth fyve loves
and too fysches. We reduth þis day in þe gospell how he fedde fyve
þousande of pepul wyth fyve loues and too fysches. þe forme lof of þe
fyve is contricion of herte. þe secunde is trew schryfte of mowþe. þe 90
þridde is satisfaccion of hys trespace. þe ferþe is drogh of resydyva-
cion, þat is, ofte turnyng aȝeyne to hys synne, for he þat is algate
aferde he schal do wel. þe fyfte is perseuerans in gode. þe too fysches
ben orysonus and almus dedus, for þeis ben noressyd in teres of
deuocion. þeis too susteres geton of God whatte þei askyn of hym. 95

I rede þer was sum tyme a man þat was callud Pers and was ful
rych, bot he was so herde þat no beggar myth geton no gode of hym be
no maner wyse. þan felle it so þat a company of beggarres comon an
seton togydur, and spekon of þis Pers and how þei mythe gette no
gode of hym. þan spake on þat was a maystur of hem and sayde: 100
'Whatte wyl ȝe leyne wyth me þat I schal gete no gode of hym?' So þei
madon a waiore. þan wente þis man forth and sette hym in þis Pers
halle-porche to habydon hym tyl he com. þanne anone as he seygh
hym comyn, þis beggar began to halson hym so hyghly and so
horrybully þat þis Pers for grete angur þat he hadde of hys grete 105
halsyng, os hys seruante com by hym wyth a basketful of bredde, he
kaghte a lof and wyth alle hys myghte he cast at hym wyth þe lof and
smotte þis beggar on þe breste, and sayde: 'Stoppe þi mouthe
þerwyth! þe deuel of helle choke þe! How beg[g]yst þou on me!'
þan þof þis beggar hadde ane euel strok, ȝette he was fayn þat he 110
hadde sumwhatte to wynne wyth hys waior, and toke þe lof and ȝode
to hys felows, and sayde: 'þis I haue geton', and hadde hys waior.

þan in þe nyghte aftur hyt happud so þat þis Pers steruyd in hys
bedde. And anone fendes comyn and tokon hys soule to helle. But þan
was oure Lady redy and badde bryng þe sowle furste to þe dome, and 115
so dudon. þan was þer no thyng to helpe þe soule but only þat lof þat
he caste atte þe pore man. þan sayde þe fendys þat he ȝaf it aȝeynus
hys wylle, wherefore be ryght it schulde notte helpon hym. þan went
oure Lady to hur Sone, preying hym to graunte þe soule to gone

84 holde] leue   85 uertues] *om.*   96 tyme] was *add.*   109 beggyst]
begynnyst

120 aʒeyne to þe body to loke ʒif he wolde amende hym. þan badde he
    bryng þe soule aʒeyne to þe body. And whanne þe soule was putte
    into þe body to lokon if he wolde amende hym, þe body anone satte vp
    and ʒaf a grete syk, and kallyd to hym alle hys manye and tolde hem
    how harde a dome he was atte, and how he hadde ben dampned ne
125 hadde þat lof ben þat he caste at þe beggar. Wherefore anone he made
    sellon alle hys gode and delon it to pore men for Goddus luf. And
f. 50ᵛ whan he | hadde [so don], he was made a man of religion and was
    aftur ane holy man.
        Hereby ʒe may knowon how grete vertu is wyth almys dede. And
130 prayer, þat makuth a man priuey wyth God for ofte spekyng wyth
    hym. For as ofte os a man preyeth devoutely, so ofte he spekuth wyth
    God. And almus dede makuth hym sykur aʒeynus þe day of dome.
    For alle þat haue done almus dede for Goddys loue schullyn ben sauid
    þat day ʒif þei ben oute of dedly synne.
135   Also for we spekon of þe synne of avoutry above, þat is, a man to
    lyggen be hys neyghburres wyf, or þe wyf to takon anoþer man þan
    hur husbande, þerfore I telle ʒow þis ensaumpul. þere was a man þat
    makud charkolus in a grete lordys parke. And whan he hadde made a
    grete fyre, he lay by it alle a nyght. þan a lytul before mydnythe þer
140 com a womman half-nakud also faste os scheo myghte renne, and
    scheo ferde os scheo were oute of hur wytte, and aftur hur a knythe
    rydyng on a blak horce also faste os he myght prekon, and hunted
    hure wyth a drawen swerde alle abowte þe col[e] fyre. And so at þe
    laste þis knythe slew þis womman and hew hyre alle to smale peces,
145 and caste hem into þe fyre, and rode aʒeyne wyth alle hys mythe. So
    whan þis man saw þis done fele nygthes, at þe laste he ʒode to hys
    lorde and tolde hym alle togydur.
        þan was þis lorde a bowlde knyte and sayde he wolde wytton
    whatte þat mythe ben, and com þidur þe nyghte nex aftur and see alle
150 os þe man hadde tolde before. þan whanne þe knyth hadde slayne þe
    womman and caste hur into þe fyre, þat oþur knythe spake and halsed
    þe knythe þat dude so, and badde hym tellyn hym whatte he was and
    why he dude so. þan he answered and sayde þat he was swoche a man
    þat was hys servaunte a lytul before, and þat womman was suche
155 anoþur knytus wyfe. And for he hadde ley by hyr vndur hur
    husbande, þerfore þe weron boþe putte to suche a penaunce, and
    sayde þat vche nyghte he al to-hew hur and brende hur þere, and þe

horce þat he rode onne was a fende þat brennyd hym an hundred
foulde hatter þan any erthely fyre. And so þat penaunce þei moste
suffron tyl þei weron holpon by certeyn masses and almes-dedes, and 160
tolde hym whatte. þan þat oþur knythe byhatte hym þat alle schulde
be done for hem, and dude it alle togydur, and so halpe hem of hure
peyne be þe grace of God.

[23] *De annunciacione beate Marie uirginis*

Suche a day ȝe schul haue an hygh feste in Holy Chirche þat is callud
þe Annunciacion of oure Lady, þe evon of þe whyche whosoeure hath
avowed or is ioynyd he mote faste. ȝe schul know þat þis [feste] is
kalled þe Annunciacion, for þe fadur of heuen send hys holy angel 5
Gabriel doun oute of heuen into þe cyte of Nazareth to oure Lady, þat
was new weddud be þe byddyng of God and reuelacion of þe Holy
Gost to ane olde man þat was callyd Ioseph.

And os scheo was in hur chambur in hure preyeres, þe angel
Gabriel com to hure and grette hur wyth mylde chere, and sayde: 10
'Hayle be þou ful of grace! God is wyth þe! Blessyd be þou of alle
wommen!' þan was scheo gretly abassched of þis greting, for þer was
þat tyme in þat cuntre a man þat cowth myche of wychecrafte. And so
be help of þe fende he made hym lyk an angel and com to diuerse
may|denes, and sayde he was sent fro God to hem on þis message, f. 51ʳ
and so lay by ham and dude hem grete vylany. þan for oure Lady 16
hadde herde telle of þat monnus doing, scheo was sore adredde lest it
hadde ben he, for ofte before scheo hadde spokun wyth angellus but
suche wordus ne suche gretyng þei made neure to hure.

þan þis angel comfordeth hure and sayde: 'Mary, be not adrede. 20
þou haste fondon grace wyth God. For among all maydenes þat ben
and schullyn bene God hath choson þe for þe mekest to hys owne
Sone to be modur. And hym þou schalte conseyven be fayth and be
loue of þe Holy Goste, wythowtyn any werke of mon, þat schal
schadowe þe and quenchyn alle maner flescly luste and tendon þe fyre 25
of gostly loue in þine herte. And so þou by fayth and loue schal
conseyue þe Sone of þe hegh God of heven, and þus schalt þou be
modur and maydon infere, and so was neure none before þe ne aftur
schal ben.' þan whan oure Lady herde þis worde, anone þer com
suche a spirutual swetnesse and a ioy in hure herte þat none er[th]ly 30

160 by] a *add.*
[23] 2 Suche] S- *in blue, dec., 2 ll. deep*   4 feste] *om.*   9 preyeres] preyeyeres
30 erthly] erly

man cowde telle. And so, wyth alle þe reuerens and mekenes þat scheo cowþe, scheo answered þus: 'Loo here, Goddes owne meke mayden redy to done Goddys owne wylle, preyng þat it mot ben don to me ryght os þou sayste.'

35 Þus scheo conseyuid oure Lorde Ihesus Criste in ere-lasting ioye to alle þe worlde, and þus may I lykon oure Lady resonnabully to a precious ston þat is callyd onix, and is as clere as crystall, and schal of kynde, whan þe soune schyneth hote on hym, opon and so reyseyvon on drope of þe dewe of heuon into hym, and closon hym aȝeyne tyl

40 nyne mones ende aftur. And þan it oponeth, an falleth oute a stone of þe same kynde, and so closyth aȝeyne, as clene os eure it was wythoute any wem, and neure opon aftur. Þus oure Lady, þat was clene as any cristall, at þe hotte love of þe Holy Goste oponeth hure herte and reseyvoth þe vertu of þe Holy Goste, and at þe nyne moneth ende was

45 delyuered of hyre Sone Ihesu Cryste, and scheo aftur as clos a maydon as scheo was before.

Þan whan þe angel hadde done hys message and was went aȝeyne to heuen, oure Lady anone ȝode to hyre cosyn Elysabeth, þat was grette wyth Seynt Ionh Baptiste. And so whan scheo com to Elysabeth,

50 scheo gret[te] hur mekely, and so anone os oure Lady spak to Elysabeth, þe chylde in Elysabeth wombe pleyed and makud grete ioye, for he sagh þat oure Lorde hadde takon mankynde and was comyn to savon hem þat weron forlorne. Þan oure Lady dwellyd þer wyth hur cosyn tyl Seynt Iohn was borne, and was mydwyfe to

55 Elysabeth, and toke Iohn from þe erth, and so lernd alle þat hur neduth for to knowen aȝeyn þe tyme þat hur Sone schuldyn ben borne of hur. Sethon, whan scheo was perfette þerof, mekly scheo toke here leue and ȝode hom aȝeyne into Nazareth.

Þan þogth Ioseph þat he wolde gone and lokon how hys wyf ferde.

60 And whan oure Lady herde of hys comyng, scheo ȝode aȝeyne hym and gret[te] hym ful mekly, as scheo cowthe ful wel. But whan Ioseph saw hyr grete wyth schylde, he merveylyd gretly how þat myght ben, for wel he wyst it was not hys, for he hadde neuer parte of hur body, and also he knew þat scheo hadde made a vowe beforne þat scheo

f. 51ᵛ wolde neurer | haue parte of mannus body. Þan he þoghte how he was

66 madde to wedde hyr be þe byddyng of God and grette schewing of miraclus, and þoght in hys herte þat he was not worthy to duelle in hur company, and schappud hym priuely to gon hom aȝeyne and leven hur þere. Þan com an angel to hym and sayde: 'Ioseph, be not

32 owne meke] *trs.*   50 grette] gretly   61 grette] gretly

aferde to takyn Mary to þi wyfe into þi kepyng. Hyt is of þe Holy 70
Goste þat is quik to hyr wombe. For þou schalte ben hur keper and
noryth to hur chylde. And whan it is borne, calle þou it Ihesus, for he
schal be sauer to mankynde.'

þus schal ʒe knowe þat for foure skyllys, os Seynt Ambros seyth,
our Lady was weddud to þis holy holde man Ioseph. þe forme was: ʒif 75
scheo hadde conseyvode oute of weddelok, þe Iewes wolde han sayde
þat scheo hadde ben a lecchur and so a stonod hur to deth. þe secund
cause was for scheo was to schamefaste, for and scheo hadde herde any
man putte any mysse-fame on hur, scheo wolde a ben dedde for ferde.
þe þridde cause was for Ioseph schulde bere wyttenesse to hyr of hure 80
maydonhedde, for whan þe wyf trespaseth in þat wyse, þe husbande
bysyeth hym moste to know þe sothe. þe ferþe caus was moste þat
Ioseph schulde ben helper to hur in hur burthe, and brynggon hur to
Beddelem and aftur into Egypte and so aʒeyne into hure owne cuntre.
For þese causes scheo was weddud to þis holy man, and so to begyle 85
þe fende þat he schulde notte knowon hym be anoþur chylde. þus,
gode men, ʒe haue now herde of þis Annunciacion.

þan ben þer somme þat askon why þere stonte a wyne-potte and a
lyly þerine betwyn oure Lady and Gabryel at hure salutacion. þis is
þe skylle: for oure Lady at hure salutacion conseyuveth by fayth, and 90
þat was þe forme miracul þat was wroghte in prevyng of criston fayth.
And fel þus þat a criston man and a Iewe setton togydur talkyng of þe
concepcion of oure Lady, and þereas þei weron, a wyne-potte stode by
ham. þan sayde þe criston man to þe Iewe: 'We belevyn þat rythe as
þe stalk of a lyly growing conseyveth þe coloure of grene and aftur 95
bryngyth forth a whyte floure wythoute crafte of man or any payring
of þe stalke, rythe so oure Lady conseyvod of þe Holy Goste and aftur
broghte forth hure Sone wythoute wem of hur body, þat is floure and
chef froyte of alle wommen.' þan sayde þe Iewe: 'Whan I see a lyly
spryng oute of þis potte, I wil leue þat, and ere notte.' þan anone 100
þerwyth a lyly sprong oute of þe potte, þe fayrest þat euere was sayne.
And whan þe Iewe seygh þat, anone he fel downe on knees and sayde:
'Lady, now I leve þat þou conseyued of þe Holy Goste Ihesus Criste,
Goddys Sone of heven, and þou klene maydon beforon and afture',
and þanne ʒode and was cristened, and he was an holy man aftur. For 105
þis skylle þe potte and þe lylye ben sette betwene hour Lady and
Gabryel, for, ryghte os þe Iew sputed wyth þe cristyn man of þe
maner of þe conseyte of oure Lady, ryghte so oure Lady sputed wyth

86 he] scheo

þe angel of þe maner and how scheo schulde conseyu[e] and be
110 maydon, er scheo assentud þerto.

þan ȝe þat fasten þe fyve evenes of oure Lady in worchep of þe fyve
ioyes of oure Lady, ȝe schul leue wel þat þis day was þe forme ioy þat
scheo hadde of hur Sone: whan scheo conseyved of þe Holy Goste and
so was may [and] modur to Goddus Sone of heven. þe secunde ioy
115 was on Cristenmes Day, whan sche was delyuered of hure Sone
f. 52ʳ wythoute any peyne of hure body. Ryght os scheo | conseyued hym
wythowten luste of flesse, rythe so scheo was delyuered of hur Sonn
wythowten payne of flesse. þe þrydde ioy was on Estur Day, whan
hur Sonne rose frome deth to lyue, and com to hur and cussud hur,
120 and makud hur more ioyful of hys vpryste þan scheo was sory before
of his deth. þe furþe ioy was whanne scheo seghe hym steyon vp into
heven on Holy þursday in þe same flesse and blode þat he toke of hur
body. þe fyfte ioy was in hur assumpcione, whan scheo sey hur Sonne
comen wyth grete multitude of aungellus and seyntes and fett hur into
125 heven, and krowned hur quene of heven and emperryse of helle and
lady of alle þe worlde. Syþen, alle þat ben in heven schul euer do hur
reuerens and worchep, and þilke þat ben in helle schul be buxum to
hur byddyng, and þylke þat bene in erþe schul done hur seruyce and
gretyng. þese ben þe fyue ioyes þat scheo hadde of hur swette Sonne
130 Ihesu. þan schul ȝe know wel þat he schal neuer fele þe sorowes of
helle þat wil devowtely vche day gretyn hur wyth þese v. ioyes in
erþe.

I rede of an holy maydon þat was devowte in oure Lady seruice and
vche a day grette hur wyth hur v ioyes. þan hit felle þat sche was seke,
135 and whan sche felde wel þat scheo schulde be dedde, scheo syed
wondur sore and makyd grete mone for encheson þat scheo wyst notte
wydur scheo schulde gone aftur hur dethe. þen com oure Lady to hur
and sayde: 'Why arte þou so sory þat hast makyd me so ofte ioy,
greting me wyth þe v ioyes þat I hadde of my Sonne? Wherefore know
140 wel þat þou schalte go wyth me to þe ioy þat eure schal laste.'

Narracio. I redde also of Seynte Fylberde, þat was neghe dede on
þe quynasy. And whan hys throte was so grete iswollon þat he mythe
vnnethe drawen brethe, oure Lady come to hym and sayde: 'Fylberte,
my servawnte, hit were euel idone þat þin throtte schulde lengar

---

109 angel] and *add.*   conseyue] conseyuyd   114 and] *om.*   116 scheo]
conseyved *catchword bottom f. 51ᵛ/* þe secunde ioy was on cristenmesse day whan scheo was
delyuered of hur sone wythowten any payne of hur body. ffor rythe os scheo (was *canc.*) *rep.*
f. 52ʳ   123 sey] schey (-c- *canc.*)   133 narracio *in margin*   143 Fylberte]
ffylberte

suffur þis penaunce þat hath so ofte gladud me wyth my v ioyes', and 145
þarwyth toke oute hur swete pappe and mylkyd on hys throte, and so
ʒode hur way. And anone þerwyth he was hole asse ffysche, and
þankud oure Lady heghly and taute alle other to do so þe same. And
at hys ende he hadde blysse of heven, to wyche blysse God bryng vs
alle to. Amen. 150

[24] *Dominica in passione domini: sermo ad parochianos: hoc modo*

Gode men and wymmen, þis day is callyd in Holy Chirche Sonday in
þe Passioun, for encheson þat oure Lorde Ihesu Criste began his
passion þis day. þe Iewes and þe Sarsynnes hadde swyche envye to
hym for encheson þat he tolde hem her vysus and repreuid here 5
wykkyd lyfving, þat þis day [þei] weron fully asentud for to done hym
to dethe. Offt beforone þei weron abowton for to haue slayne hym bot
ay | þai weron lettyd be drede of þe pepul, for þe pepul heldon him a f. 52ᵛ
prophette. Botte þis day þai knytten hem so togydur þat þei nolde
spare no lengar bot allewayes he schulde be dede. Wherefore os þe 10
gospel tellys of þis day, as Criste preched in þe tempul, þe Iues
spytwsly rebukyd hym so fowle þat þei sayde to hym þat he hadde a
deuel wythinne hym, and alle for to tempytun hym for to haue made
[hym] to a spokun summe worde be þe whyche þei mythe haue putte
hym to repreue. And for he tolde hem þat he was Goddys Sonne of 15
heven, þei weren redy for to a stoned hym to þe deth. Bot for he knew
wel here malys, he hydde hym and ʒode from hem oute of þe tempul.

þus, gode men, Cryste began þis day his passion. Wherfore Holy
Chirche reduth þis weke þe boke of þe prophette Ieromy, þat furste
propheted of Cristes passion, and tolde how and whatte maner Iues 20
schuldon done hym to þe deth. þan schul ʒe know wel þat, rythe os þe
Iewes pursueden Criste to þe deth whyl he was in erthe, rythe so be
þere now many false men cristened þat pursuen hym reynyng in
heven. And Seynt Austyn sayth þat he syngeth more greuowsly þat
pursueth hym reynyng in heven þan þe Iewes þat dyden hym to deth 25
in erthe. þan ʒif ʒe wil know wy[c]he þeise bene, takyth hede how
Cryste wyth his owne mowthe markys hem, þareos he saythe þus in
þe gospell of þis day, where he saythe þus: 'Who þat is of God he
heres Goddes worde. Wherefore ʒe here notte, for ʒe be notte of
Godde.' þus Criste hymself scheweth whyche þay bene þat pursueth 30

---

[24] 2 Gode] G- *in blue, dec., 3 ll. deep* Holy] -o- *over* -a-? 6 þei] *om.*
12 hym²] hymself 14 hym] *om.* 24 nota *cropped in margin* 26 wyche] wythe

hym now in heven. þais bene gladde whan þai haue done a foule dede,
and bene grownded in foule leuing and wil notte amende hem for no
preching ne for no teching, but euer defendeth here gulte be
ensaumpul of suche other os þei bene, and ben wrothe and redy for
35 to fyten with hym þat telleth hem bot sothe. For, more harme is, þe
worlde is suche now þat he schal haue many enmyes þat sayth þe
sothe now allegate.

Herby I may schewen ȝow an ensaumpul, as I rede how þere was
sum tyme a mawment in a cyte þat wolde telle of alle stolne þing and
40 who hit hadde. So was þare a ȝung man þat hadde stollon a thyng and
was adrede of þat mawment leste he hadde dyscured hym, and anone
ȝode to hym and sayde: 'Wel I wotte þou mythe do me schame and
vylany ȝif þou wilte, bot, be þat God I leue on, and þou discure me, I
wil breke þine heuede', and so ȝode forth his way. þan sone afftur
45 comon þai þat miston here þing, preying þe mawment for to tellen
hem who hit hadde. And whan þei hadde preyed longe, at þe last þis
mawment spake and sayde þus: 'Tyme is chaunged, men bene
f. 53ʳ worsed, and now þer may no man say þe sothe bot ȝif | his heued
be brokon'.

50 þus, wo is þe trew man þat schal lyuen in þis worlde. For he schal
bene so plu[ck]ud at on vche a syde þat he schal not wytton to whom
he schal discuron his counsayle. For þilk þat wil furst disc[eyu]en a
man, þai willon speke fayrest on hym. For os we redon in þe Boke of
Kyngus, how þere weron too knytus þat envyed other, Ioab and
55 Amasa. þan on a day os þei metton, Ioab l[o]gh on Amasa and sayde:
'Hayle, broþur Amasa!' and toke hym be þe chyn and kyste hym, bot
wyth þat oþur hand he smotte hym in þe bak and sclowe hym. þus
fareth myche pepul now-on-dayus: þay wil speke fayre before a man,
bot behynden hym þei wil sclene hym with here tonge. þeyse bene
60 þoo þat here notte Goddys worde ne settyth nowte þereby, for þof þei
heron hitte wyth her heres, i[t] synkus notte in her hertus.

Wherefore God compleyneth greuosly be þis holy prophete
Ieremye and sayth þus: 'Whatte gylte foundon ȝoure fadurres why
þat þei ȝodon fro me? Ȝif I haue trespassed to ȝow in any þinge,
65 telluþe!' Allas for schame to owre pride, God his in þe rythe, and ȝitte
he tretuth wyth vs þat bene in þe vronge. He profurreth mercy or we
hit askon, he mekuth hym to vs þat displesuth hym, and scheweth luf

---

35 bot] b- *over* n-?   38 nota *cropped in margin*   43 leue on] *trs.*   50 wo] who
51 pluckud] plukcud   52 disceyuen] discuren   53 redon] rededon   55 logh]
legh   61 it] in   62 þis] þis / þe

þere none is worthe. þus bene oure hertes harder þan stonus! þus
bene we werse þan Iewes! þus bene we vnkynde to hym þat scheweth
vs alle maner of kyndenesse and euer cryes to vs and saythe þus: 'I am 70
lyfte on hygh for alle schal heron me spekon. Turne aȝeyne to me and
I wol reseyven ȝow! Lo, myne armus bene spredde of brode redy for
to clyppon ȝow. My heued is bowed redy for to kysse ȝow. My syde is
opon to schewon my herte to ȝow, my [handes and] my fette blody for
to schewne ȝow whatte I suffred for ȝow. And ȝet ȝe wry away and 75
gruche for to cum to me. And ȝif ȝe wil not come for lof to me, come
to me for ȝeftus. Cometh to me and I wil ȝef ȝow tresoure witowten
nowmbur! I schal avawnse ȝow wythowton comparrison! I wil ȝeue
ȝow lyfe in reste and pes witowten ende, so þat alle þe defawte schal
be in [me] and notte in [ȝow].' þus God precheþ and techeth. And ȝet 80
beth þere bot fewe þat wil heron hym, luyte þat haue þeis wordys
sadde in here herte, butte alle ben besy for to be ryche and weltheful
in þis lyue þat is here and recchyþ lytul of þe lyue þat is comyng, and
takuþ bot lytul hede how sore Cryste sufred for to bringon vs to blysse
þat euer schal lasten. 85

Wherefore Seynt Bernarde in Cristes persoun maketh grete
waymentacion for vnkyndenesse þat he sethe in men and sayþe þus:
'þow, man, for vanite syngust and ioyust, and I for þe crye and wepe.
þou hast on þi heued a garlande of flowres, and I for þe suffur a wreþe
of strong þornes. þou hast on þi | handes whyte glouys, and I for þi f. 53ᵛ
loue haue blody handes. þou haste þi harmes spradde on brode ledyng 91
karolus, and I for þi luf haue myne harmes spradde on þe tre and
tackyd wyth grete nayles. þou hast þi cloþes pynched smalle, and I
haue my body for þi luf ful of grete walus. And ouer þis, þat greues
me moste: þou settyst notte be my passione þat I sufferud for þe, bot 95
be [m]e orybull swerus[t], [and] alle day vmbreydust me, sweryng be
my face, be my ȝene, be my nayles, be myne armes, be myne herte, be
myne blode, and so forthe be alle myne body. And so þou de-marrust
me be foule vse and custome of sweringe, þat schuldust done reuerens
and worschep to my woundes and to my passioun þat I suffered so 100
sore for þi sake.'

Narracio. I rede in þe *Gestus of þe Romaynus* þat þe emperoure
sende a grete man to a londe for to a bene a iustice oure hem. Botte
before hys comynge þere was no man þat kowthe swere none oþus but

---

74 handes and] heued   80 me] ȝow   ȝow] me   83 recchyþ] -þ *over* -d?
91 þi] -i *oblit. by blue ink of* G *initial (f. 54ᵛ)*   96 me] þe   swerust] swerus   and] *om.*
97 ȝene] be my face *rep.*   102 nota *cropped in margin*

105 '3e' and 'nay'. þan aftur þat þis iustice come, he made alle men to
sweron on bokus in schyrus [and] in hundrus. And he and alle his men
weron so wonte for to sweron be Goddys passyon, and armes, and
sydes, and blody woundys, þat alle þe pepul toke at hem so in vse þat
alle sworon orybullyche os þei dyddyn. þan on a day os þis iustyce
110 satte in his iusterye in sythe of alle men, þere come inne þe fayrest
womman þat euer þay seyne, alle cladde in grene, and browte a fayre
childe in hir lappe, bledyng and alle to-marryd, and sayde to þe
iustice: 'Sur, whatte bene þai worthi þat haue þus ferde with my
chylde?' þan sayde þe iustyce: 'þai ben worthi to haue deth.' þan
115 answerud þe womman and sayde þus: 'þou and þi men wyth 3oure
oribul othus haue þus demembrud my Sonne Ihesu Cryste þat I am
modur to. And so 3e haue tawte now alle þis lande. Wherefore þou
schalte haue now þine awne dome.' þanne anone in syte of alle þe
pepul þe erþe oponed and þe iustice fel downe into helle. And so aftur
120 þe pepul weron sorily agast and amendud hem of þare othus and
sweryng.

Wharefore, syrres and dames, do 3e as criston men schul done:
leuyth 3owre othus and 3oure swering, and doþe reuerence to Cristes
passion and to his woundus, and techeth other for to do þe same. And
125 kneluth now adowne, preing to God þat he for3ef 3ow þat 3e haue
trespased a3eynus hym be recheles swering, besecheing hym for his
grete mercy for to so kepon 3ow in tyme comyng þat 3e may amende
þat 3e haue done mysse a3aynus hym and his swete modur and haue
þe blisse þat he bowte 3ow to. Amen.

[25] *De dominica in ramis palmarum sermo breuis ad*
perochianos vestros |

f. 54ʳ Gode cryston men and wommen, as 3e know welle alle, þis day is
calde Palme Sonnenday. Botte for encheson þat þe seruice of þis day
5 is lengar, I wil schortely telle 3ow why þis day is callyd so.

þis day, os Seynt Ione telluth, oure Lorde Ihesus Criste was in
Betanye, where he reysed a man from deth to lyue þat hadde layne
stynkyng in his tombe fowre dayes, þat was callud Lazarus and was
broþur to Mari Mawdeleyne and Martha hur systur. þan wyst Ihesus
10 þat his passioun was neght and toke Lazar wyth hym, and so, ryding
on [an] asse, he 3ode towerde Ierusalem. And whanne þe pepul

108 nota *cropped in margin*
[25] 2 Gode] G- *in blue, dec., 3 ll. deep*   11 an] *om.*

herdun þat, alle ȝode aȝenus him, boþe for wondur of þe man þat was
reysyd from deth to lyue, and also for to done Cryste w[o]rchep.
Wherefore many [straw]don flowres in his way, and many brokon
brawnches of olyfe and of palme and keston in þe way, and spreddon 15
cloþus in þe way, makyng melody and singynge þus: 'Blessed be þou
þat comyst in þe name of oure Lorde, Kyngge [of] Israel!'
Wherefore Holy Chirche þis day [makuth] a sollempe procession in
mynde of þat processione þat Criste makyd þis day, and also for þere
bene many of ȝow raysyd frome dethe to lyue þat hath lyne dede 20
fowre dayes, þat bene synful thoutus, synful speches, synful werkys,
[a]n[d] sinful customes. But now I hope þat ȝe bene reysud from deth
of evel leuyng to þe lyue of grace ande þat angelys in heuen makon a[s]
myche melody in heuen for ȝoure rysinge os þe pepul dede for
wondur of þe reysing of þe Lazar. But for encheson we haue none olyf 25
þat beruth grene leues, we takon in stede of hit hew and palmes wyth,
and beruth abowte on procession, and so þis day we callyn Palme
Sonnenday.
And os þei songon and dyden worchep to Cryste in here
processioun, rythe so we worchep þis day þe crosse in oure 30
processioun, þries knelyng to þe crosse in worchep and in þe
mynde of hym þat was for vs done on þe crosse, and welcomyng
hym with songe into þe chirche, os þei welcommod hym syngyng into
þe cyte of Ierusalem. þan askuth Ion Belette a question: 'Syþen þat
Criste hadde þe grattest worchep rydyng on an asse þat eure he hade 35
in þis worlde, and aftur of þe same pepull was done on þe crosse in þe
grattest vylany þat euer he hade in þis worlde, why worchep we þe
crosse and noute þe asse?' To þis question he answeruth hymself, and
saythe þat alle þe worchep of þis worlde turneth alle to vanite and to
no nother, and makyth a man forȝeton hys God and hymself, þare þoȝ 40
mischef and woo makuth a man to thenkon on hys God and to know
hymself. Herfore cryston men puttuth away vanite a[s] a thyng of
noȝte þat brynguth a man to euerlasting peyne and worchepus þe
crosse þat was cause of oure saluacion and of þe ioy þat we alle hopon
for to cum to. 45
þen | whan Criste was comen into þe cyte, anone he ȝode into f. 54ᵛ
þe tempul and droff oute alle þe byers and þe sellerres þat he
fonde þereinne, and sayde to hem: 'My Fadur houce is a howce of
preyer and of orisoun, and ȝe haue makyd hit a den of þeffus',

13 worchep] wrchep   14 strawdon] haddon   17 of²] *om.*   18 makuth] *om.*
22 and] in   23 as] and   37 nota *in margin with red paraph*   42 as] *om.*

50 ȝeueing iche a criston man heghe ensaumpul for to leuyng schafferyng
on Sonnondayes, and namely in chirche.

Another skylle is why þis day is callyd Palme Sonnenday: for
encheson þat palme betokonyth victori. Wherefore iche criston man
and womman schal þis day beron palmus in processioun, schewing
55 þat he hath fowton wyth þe fende and hath þe victorye of hym bi
clene schryuing of mowþe, repentaunce of herte, and mekely done his
penaunce, and in þis wyse ouercommyn is oure enmye.

Hytte was þe maner som tyme, os we redyn in *Gestus of þe*
*Romaynus—narracio—*þat whan any londe of þe worlde rose aȝeyne
60 þe emperoure of Rome, anone þe emperoure wolde sende a worthi
knyte wyth pepul inowh to þat londe for to sette hit doune and make
hit sogette to þe emperoure. Ande whan þis knyte hade so done, þan
schulde he ben sette in a char as ryche as he mythe, wyth clathus of
golde drawen oure hym and a palme in his hande, schewing þat he
65 hade þe victory, and so with grete worchep schulde be lade aȝeyne to
Rome. But whan he come thorowg any cite, þere schulde a man
s[ta]nden by hym in þe chare and beton hym in þe mowthe with a
braunch of olyf, sayng þus: '*Anothe delytes*', þat is to sayne: know
þiself! know þiself! As þoȝ he sayde to hym þus: 'þoȝ þou haue þe
70 victori now, hit may happon þat þou schalte anoþur tyme haue þe
werre, and so turne þe into also mykul vilanye os now is done þe
worchep. Wherefore be nowte proude of þineself!'

þus, gode men and wommen, þus ȝe schal beton ȝoure seluen in
[þe] mowþe of ȝoure sowle wythinneforþe wyth þe braunche of olyf,
75 þat is, wyth þe vertu of mekenes, and so holde ȝow meke in herte,
being algate adrede leste ȝe falle aȝeyne to ȝoure synne, and so leson
þe worchep þat ȝe haue now wonnonn, wyttyng wel þat mekenesse is
þe vertu þat moste ourecometh ȝoure enmy and most growndeth a
man in doing of gode werkys in vertues. Wherefore ȝe schul alle now
80 prey to God þat he wil of his hye grace ȝyf ȝow myȝte and strenghe in
tyme comyng so to ouercom ȝoure enmy þat ȝe may haue þe victori of
hym and haue þe blysse þat euer schal laste. Amen.

---

50 nota *in margin with red paraph*   67 standen] satnden   71 þe into] to þe in
74 þe¹] *om.*

[26] *Sermo iste debet dici ad Tenebras post matutinas dictas priusquam detur disciplina. Perachianis suis hoc modo incipietur.* |

Gode men and wymmen, os ӡe leue, [Holy Chirche vsyth] þeise þre f. 55r
dayes for to sayne seruice in þe evontyde in derknesse. Wherfore hit is
callyd wyth ӡow Tenabulles, but Holy Chirche callyth hit Tenebras, 5
þat is to say, derkenesse.

þan why þis seruice is done in derkenesse holy faderes wrytuth to
vs þre skylles. One skylle is for encheson þat Criste þis nythe, before
þat he was takon, he ӡode þre tymes into þe hulle of Olyuete and
prayed hys Fadur to putton away þe harde payne þat hym was 10
towarde, ӡiff hit were his wille, and ellys noӡte. And so for drede of þe
passioun þat he felte in his spiryte commyng, he swatte blode and
watur.

Anothur skyll is for anone aftur mydnyӡte Iudas gedurred ffyffty
knytus strongge and bolde wyth oþur grete cumpany of misse-doerres 15
and come for to takon Cryste. But for hit was dark nyӡte and þei
kowde not wel know hym be Seynt Iames, þat was so leke Criste þat
he was callud Crystus broþur, leste þei haddon takon Iames in stede of
Cryste, þan Iudas badde hem takon hym þat he custe, and so with a
cusse betrayed hys maystur, and so token Criste alle in darkenesse and 20
deden hym alle þe despyte and vylany, bobeting hym and spytting in
hys lufly face.

þe þrydde skylle is for whan Cryste was naylud fote and hande,
hanggyng on þe crosse þre owrus on þe day from vndren to none, þe
sonne withdrew hur lyӡte and was also derke os nyӡte oure alle þe 25
worlde, schewyng þat þe maker of lyӡte peynyd þat tyme to þe deþe.

For þeis þre skylles þe seruyce of þeyse þre nyӡtes is done in
darkenesse, þe whyche seruyce makuth mynde how Iudas betrayed
Cryste and how þeis Iewes comen wyth force and armes as pryuely os
þei cowden for drede of þe pepull. Wherefore to þis seruice is no belle 30
irongon bot a sownde makuth of treo, whereby vche criston man and
womman is enformode for to comon to þis seruise wythowtyn noyse
makyng, and alle þat þei spekon going and comynge schal sowne of þe
tree þat Cryste was done onne and of þe wordys þe whyche þat Cryste
spake hongyng on þe treo, þat ben: how he commendud his modur to 35
Seynt Ion his discipul, and how he grauntud þe þeff paradyse þat
askud mercy, and how he betoke his sowle into hys Fadur hande, and
so ӡolde vp þe goste. þus comynge and goynge to þis seruise, vche

[26] 3 Gode] G- *in blue, dec., 3 ll. deep*   Holy Chirche vsyth] *om.*

criston man and womman schal leuon talkynge of alle vanite and only
40 tal[k]ynge [of þe tree], þat is þe crosse.

Anoþur skyl is: whan þat Iudas had trayed Cryste and seghe þat be
his traytury he schulde be dede, anone he felle into dispayre and 30de
and hangud hymselfe on a treo, so þat he wraþthud Criste more for
hongyng hymselfe so in dyspayre þan dud þe traytury þat he dud
45 before. For Cryst is so merciabull in hymselue þat he wolde haue
3euen hym mercy and he wolde haue askud hit wyth contrite herte.

f. 55ᵛ   Allso at þis seruice is sette an herce | wyth candulles brennyng,
aftur os þe vce is, in some place mo, in some place lesse, þe whyche
bene quenchyd vchone aftur othur, in schewing how Cristes dis-
50 cipulus stolne from hym whan he was takon, vchon aftur oþer. But
whan alle bene quenchyd, 3it one leuyth ly3te, þe wyche is borne away
a wyle, wyl þat þe clerkus syngone *Kyrius* and þe versus wyth, þe
wyche betokeneth þe wymmen þat madon waymentac[i]on at Crystus
sepulcur. þan aftur þis, þe candul is browte a3eyne, and alle oþur at
55 hit bene ly3te, þe whyche betokenyth Crist, þat was for a qwyle dede
and hyd in hys sepulcur, but sone aftur he ros frome deth to lyue and
3aff ly3te of lyue to alle hem þat weron quenchud be dispayre. þe
strokys þat þe prestes 3eueth on þe boke betokynneth þe clappus of
thundur þat Crist brake helle-3atys wyth whan he com þidur and
60 spylud helle.

Now, gode men, 3e haue herde what þis seruise betokeneþ.
Wherefore holduth hit in 3oure herte, and be 3e nowte vnkynde to
3owre Godde þat þus suffrud for 30w, for vnkyndenesse is a synne þat
he hathuth hegly. Wherefore Seynt Ambros sayth þat þer may no man
65 fynde a payne for to ponychon dewlich þe vyce of vnkyndenesse.

Narracio. Ensawmpul to þis I fynde, os Allessaunder Nekkam
telluth, and is þis: þere was sum tyme a knyte þat went owte of his
cuntrey into fer cuntrey for to sekon auentures. And so hit felle þat he
come into a grete forest and harde a grete noyse of a beste þat was, os
70 hym thouthe, in grete dystresse. þan for he wolde sene whatte hit was,
he 3ode neght and saw how an orybul eddur of grettenesse and of
lenthe hade v[m]clyppud a lyon and so bownden hym to a treo as he
lenyd hym to sclepe. And whan þis lyon awoke and fonde hymself
faste and my3te not help hymselfe, he made a hoged noyse. And whan
75 he saw þis knythe, þan made he grette noyse, willyng helpe of hym.
þan hade þis knythe compassion of þis lyon, but 3itte he dredde

---

40 talkynge] talbynge   of þe tree] *om.*   46 contrite] of *add.*   53 waymentacion]
waymentacon   66 nota *in margin with blue paraph*   72 vmclyppud] vnclyppud

leste, whan he were lose, he wolde a fallon to hym and fowtyn wyth hym. But ʒet for encheson þat he was a knyʒte and seghe þis lyon, þat is kyng of alle bestes, in dystresse, he drow owte hys swerde and smotte þe eddur asondur. þan anone þe lyon, felyng hym losse, he 80 felle downe to þe knytes fete as meke as a spaynell, and so algate aftur, nyʒte and day, in vche place, he sued þis knyʒte, and lay at hys beddys fette vche nyʒte, and in vche turnement and batayle he helpud hys maystur, so þat alle men spokyn of þis knyʒte and of þis lyon.

ʒit be cownsel of som men, he hadde þis lyon in suspexcion. 85 Wherfore whan he ʒode aʒayne home to his owne cuntrey, pryueliche, whil þe lyon sclepud, he | ʒode into a chyppe and so saylyd forthe. f. 56ʳ But whan þe lyon awoke and myste hys maystur, anone he ʒaff a grete rerde and ʒode aftur hym to þe see. And whan he seghe no noþer bote, he wode into þe see and so swamme aftur also ferre os he mythe. And 90 whan hys myʒte faylud hym, þan was he drownyd.

Be þis knythe we may vndurstande Criste, Goddys Sone of heuen, þat come of a ferre cuntre, þat is, owte of heuen into þis worlde, and fonde mankynde bow[n]den wyth þe olde eddur, þat is, wyth þe bondus of þe fende, to þe treo of inobediens. Wherefore wyth þe 95 swerde of [hys] holy worde and wyth hys harde passyon he bowte mankynde of hys bandus and makyth hym free. Wherefore vche man þat is kynde to hys God, he wil þank hym for þat losyng, and louen hym, and be buxum to hym alle þe tyme þat he is lyuyng here, schewing þe lore and þe teching of hys Godde. And so whan he 100 passuth thorogh þe salte watur of peyne of deth, he schal come to þe ioy þat euer schal laste. To wyche ioy God brynge ʒow and me. Amen.

[27] *Sermo dicend[u]s ad parachianos in Parasceue domini: hoc modo.*

Gode men and wymmen, [ʒe schal vndurstonde] þat Cryste þis day schede hys blode for [vs]. As ʒe alle know welle, þis day is callyd Gode Fryday for alle þ[y]nge turned þe pepul to godd þat Cryste þis day suffrud for hem vndur Pownce Pylate. þan for hit is ofton sayne þat a 5 fowle begynnyng hath a fowle endyng, wherefore see we nowh how þis Pylate began and how he endud, and for he began cursudly, he endud cursedly. For os Seynt Austyn sayth, a cursyd lyuyng before

---

94 bownden] bowden   96 hysꜟ] *om.*   98 losyng] losesyng
[27] 1 *dicendus*] dicendis   2 Gode] G- *in blue, dec., 3 ll. deep*   ʒe schal
vndurstonde] *om.*   3 vs] *om.*   4 þynge] þnge   5 a] alle

askuth a cursyd ende aftur, and he þat forȝetuth God in hys lyuyng he
10 sal forȝete hy[m]selue in hys endynge.

Thys Pylate was a kyngus son, þat was callyd Tyrus, þat gate hym
on a woman þat hette Pylle and hadde a fadur þat hette Ato. So þat
whan þis childe was borne, þan setton þay þe modur name beforne
and þe graunsyre name aftur, and so of boþe here names kalde hym
15 Pilate. þan aftur þat he was thre ȝere olde, þe modur browte hym to
þe kyngus cowrte to hys fadur. þan hadde þe kyng be his wyf anoþur
sone ney ewen-olde to Pylate. But for þis sone in alle his doing was
more gentul and more manful, Pylate hadde envy to hym and oftyn
tyme fawte wyth hym, so at þe laste he slowghe hym.
20 So whan þis chylde was dede, þe kyng was wondur sory for hym.
But for he wolde note slene hym þo anone aftur þat othur and so make
too harmes of one, he sente Pylate to Rome for to bene þare in ostage
for a trybute þat þe kynge schulde ȝeff to þe emperoure. þan felle hit
soo þat þe kyng of Fraunce hade sent hys sone þidur also for þe same
25 cause. þan for Pylate seghe þat he hade more loue, and for men dydon
f. 56ᵛ þe kynggus | sone more reuerens þen hym, he hade envy þerto and on
a day wayted hys tyme and sloghe hym.

þan for he was so ferus and kursud, þe emperoure be cownsayle of
þe Romayns senden hym into a cuntray þat was called Pownce,
30 whereinne were men so cursyd þat þei slew alle þat were sent for to be
maystur oure hem. So whan Pylate come þidur, he confermed hym to
here maneres, þat wyth wylus and sleytus he hadde þe maystry oure
hem and so gederud hys name, as was Pilate of Pownce. þan whan
Herode, kynge off Ierusalem, knew þe fersed of Pylate, he sende aftur
35 hym and maked hym leuetenawnte vndur hym of alle hys londe off
Iury. þan for Pilate lekyd wel þat offyce, priuely he sende to þe
emperoure and hadde hys offyce confermed of hym, vnwyttyng
H[e]r[o]d[e] þe kyng. Wherefore Herowde and he weron enmyes til
þe tyme þat Cryste was takon, and so in þe assent of Cry[s]te[s] deth
40 þai becomyn frendys.

Then felle hit so þat þe emperoure was seke and sende aftur Cryste
for to helyn hym, for hit was tolde hym þat Criste hellyd alle men þat
comen to hym [of all maner of evel. But for þat Pylate had don hym to
deth, þe emperoure made Pylate to come to hym.] þan was Pilate
45 adrede and toke on hym Cry[s]tes cote, so þat euer wille þat cote was
on hym, þe emperoure and alle oþur makud hym grete chere. þan

10 hymselue] hyn(c?)selue   11 nota *in margin with red paraph*   38 Herode]
hyred   39 Crystes] cryteth   43–4 of . . . hym] *om.*   45 Crystes] crytes

haddon many othur grete wondur why þe emperoure made hym so
grete disporte, þat beforon hade sworne his deth, and cownsaylyd þe
emperoure for to dispoyle hym. And anone as Pylate was dyspoylud of
Crystes cote, anone þe emperoure was grettely agreuid aȝanys hym, 50
þat he makud to caston hym in preson tyl he hade takon consayle on
whatte fowle deth he schulde dyen. þan whan Pylate knew þat, anone
wyth his owne knyfe he sclow hymselfe. þan whan þe emperoure
herde, he made to bynde a grete stone to hys nekke and caston hym
into þe watur of Tybur. But for fendus madon swyche a noyce 55
aboutyn hym þere, þat alle þe cyte was affrayed þeroff, he was caste
into a watur betwyx too hilles, þere were longe tyme orybul sythes
iseyne.

Vndur þis cursyd m[a]n, oure Lorde þis day, Ihesus Cryste, suffred
deth for alle criston pepull. For whan he was takon, þei buffettud hym 60
and hubud hym and bobud hym, and aftur strypud hym nakud and
bete hym so dispytowslyche wyth scowreges alle hys body, so þat
from hys toppe to his to was noþing lafte holle on hym, bot alle ranne
on blode. And aftur þai wry[þ]en a crowne of thornes and setton on
hys heued, and so beten hit downe wyth staffes of redys þat þe þornus 65
persud his brayne. And when þay haddon peynud hym soo, þai
laddon hym alle blody towarde þe hul of Caluery for to bene done to
þe deth.

þan wymmen, þat sene hym so ferde wyth, haddon compassion of
hym and waylid and wepud | ffor hym. þan spake Cryste to hem and f. 57ʳ
sayde: 'Doȝteres of Ierusalem, wepe ȝe not [on] me, but weputh vpon 71
ȝoureselfe and vpon ȝoure schilderon, for þere sal dayes come in þe
wyche ȝe sal bleson þe wombus þat weron b[a]r[en] and þe pappes þat
neuer ȝyffon soke.' þus he þan profecied before of wrache þat afftur
felle on þat cite of Ierusalem for vengeaunce of hys deþe. þe whyche 75
veniaunce Ieromy þe profytte spekys of *in Trenis*, þat is redde þoses
þre dayes at Tenebras, þe wyche was so oribul of diuerse mischeuus
and specialiche of hongur, of þe wyche Iosaphus telluth þat þere was
þan in þe cyte of Ierusalem, whan hit was beseged, so grete hongur þat
schildur lay þe stretus fulle and dyed for defaute of mete, crying to 80
her modures aftur mete.

Narracio. Than was þere a wymman of grete kynne, þat for hongur
toke hur owne chylde, þat scheo fedde wyth hur owne pappus, and
sclew hit and partyd hit on too. So þe half scheo rosted at þe fyre and

---

59 man] men   64 wryþen] wryen   71 on] *om.*   73 baren] beried
76 spekys] þat *add.*   77 wyche] þat *add.*   82 nota *in margin with red paraph*

85 half kepud til on þe mo[r]oȝhe. þan as men comyn be þe strete, þei
haddon savowre of þe roste and comen in for to haue parte. But whan
þei sene how þe modur rostyd hir owne chylde, þei weron grettely
astonyed and hugged sore þerewyth and myȝte not eton. þan toke þe
modur and ete þeroff boldely, and sayde: 'þis is myne owne childe þat
90 I bare of my awne body and fede of my brestys. Bot ȝit wil I rather
eton hit þan dyen for hungur.' þis I telle for to schew þe vengaunce in
þat cite aftur for Cristus dethe.

So aftur þat þei haddyn browte hym to Caluarye, þei streyned hym
so wyth cordes on þe crosse þat vche a bone of his body myȝte haue
95 bene tolde, and so nayled his handes and his fette to þe crosse and
heven hym vppe þat þe body peysid so doune þat þe blode ranne
downe be his harmes and be his sydes downe to þe grownde. And so
whan he schulde dyen, he began, as Ion Bellette telleth, and saythe:
'*Deus meus, Deus meus, respice*', and so forth alle þe ix psalmus sewing
100 forþe til he come to: *In te, domine, speraui*, and so at þe vers: *In manus
tuas, domine*, wyth [þat] he ȝaf vp þe goste, ȝefvyng a hegh ensampull
to vche criston man and womman for to haue þat verse in mynde
whan he scal ȝoldon vp þe goste. Wherefore vche man þat can rede
schulde say þaise psalmus þis day, and he þat sayse hem vche Fryday
105 he sal newre dyon none evel deþe.

þan aftur þe passion þere sew[en] orisones wyth knelyng at vche
orison, saf at þe orisone þat is sayde for þe Iewes: at hit Holy Chirch
kneluth notte, for þe Iewes os þis day þries scorned oure Lorde
knelynge. þan in þeis orison[es] Holy Chirche prayes for alle maner
110 folke: for Iewes and Sarsynes, for heretykkes, for sismatus, but for
f. 57ᵛ cursyd men Holy Chirche | preyeth noȝte, for wil a man or womman
standuth acursud he is dampnud before God and schal be dampned
for euer, bot he repent and aske mercy. Wherefore Seynt Austyn
saythe þus: 'ȝof I wyste for certeyne þat my fadur were dampned, I
115 wolde prey no more for hym þan for a hounde of helle. For þere is no
suffrage of Holy Chirche þat may helpon a dampned man.' þan aftur
þe orisones þe crosse is browte forth, þe wyche yche criston man and
womman schal worchep þis day in worchep of hym þat as þis day
dyed on þe crosse. And pray to God to forȝeuen alle þat has trespased
120 aȝeynus ȝow, as Cryste prayed hys Fadur to forȝeuen þilke þat dedon
hym to þe deth, þis day hongynge on þe crosse.

   85 moroȝhe] moȝoȝhe   98 nota *in margin with red paraph*   101 þat] *om.*   he]
sayde and so *add.*   þe] spryte *add. and canc.*   106 þere] are *add.*   sewen] sewne
109 orisones] orison

Narracio. Thus dud a knyte þat was a grete lorde and hade a ȝung man to sone þat schulde haue bene hys eyre, þe wyche sone anoþur knythe þat woned besyde hem, as þei fellon at debate, he slow þis ȝong man. Wherefore þe fadur of þis man þat was dede gedurred 125 grete cumpanye and pursued þe knythe þat so hade slayne hys sone nyȝte and day, þat he myȝte noȝwhere abyde nor reste, bot ay flowe for fere of deþ. þan felle hit on Gode Fryday whan he sawe alle criston men and wommen drawe to þe chyrche for to worchep here God, he thowte þat [Cryste] dyed þat day on þe crosse for alle 130 mankynde, and put hym holy in Godys mercy, and yode to þe chirch wyth oþur men to heron and sene Goddus seruice.

But whan he was in þe chyrche, anone þat oþur knythe hade warnynge and come wyth grete cumpanye of men wyth hym into þe chirche wyth his swerde drawen in his hande. And whan þat oþur 135 knythe seghe þat and knew wel þat he hade trespased to heygly aȝeynus hym, he ȝode aȝeynus þat othur knythe and felle downe flatte to þe grounde wyth his armes spradde abrode, as Cryste sprade his armes on þe crosse, and sayde to hym: 'For hys lofe þat þis day sprade his armes on þe crosse and dyed for þe and me and alle mankynde, 140 and forȝaue alle þat dydu[n] hym to þe deth, haue mercy on me and forȝef me þat I haue trespased aȝeynus þe.' þan þis oþur knythe þoȝte welle hit hade bene a to horybul synne for to haue done oȝte amysse to hym þare in þe chirche whille þat he mekud hym so and so lowly prayde hym of mercy for Cristes sake. And whan he hade welle 145 beþoȝte hym, he answerud and sayde: 'Now for his loue þat þis day dyed on þe crosse for mankynde, I forȝeue þe', and toke hym vp and kyste hym, and soo wenton togedur to worcheppe þe crosse. þen whan þis knythe come crepyng to þe crosse and kyste þe fette, þe ymage [losud] his armys and klyppud þe knythe abowte þe nekke and 150 kyste hym, and sayde þus, þat alle þe chyrche herde: 'I forȝeff þe, os þow | hast forȝeuen for me.' þus schulde ȝe vchone forȝeue oþur for f. 58ʳ Cristus luff, and klyppon and kysson and ben frendus, and þan wil Cryste klyppon and kysson ȝow and ȝeffon ȝow þe ioy þat eure sal laston, to þe wyche ioy God bryng vs alle. Amen. 155

122 nota *in margin with red paraph* 130 Cryste] *om.* 135 hande] and whan he was in þe chirche with his swerde idrawen in hys hande *rep.* 136 seghe] *alt. from* segere?* 139 þat] dyed *add.* 141 dydun] dydum 149 nota *in margin with blue paraph* 150 losud] kauthe

[28] *Sermo iste sequens non dicendus est ad Parasceues sed quedam [in]formacio neccessaria capellanis: hoc modo.*

For hit is ofton seyne þat lewed men, þe wyche beth of many wordus and prowde in here wytte, wollon askon prestus diuerse questions of
5 þinggus þat towchon þe seruice of Holy Chirche, and namely of þis tyme, and gladly suche prestys þat cun not makon a grayth answere, so for to putt[e] hem to aschame, wherefore I haue here tytulled diuerse poyntus, wyche þat bene nedefull for vche preste to knowen, so he þat wol lokon [oure þis redyly] and holde hit in his herte he may
10 makon in his answere so þat hit schal done hymself worchep and oþur profythe.

Furste, ȝef men aske why Schere þursday is calde so, say þat in Holy Chyrche hit is calde oure Lordys soper-day. For þat day he soupud with his dissipulles oponly, and aftur soper ȝaff hem hys flesse
15 and his blode for to eton and for to drynkon, and sone aftur wasse hor ale fette, schewing þe heghe mekenesse þat was in hym and þe grete loue þat he hade to hem.

Hit is also in englis tong Schere þursday, for in owre elde fadur dayes men woldon þat day makon scheron hem honest, and dode here
20 hedes and clyppon here berdes, and so makon hem honest aȝayne Astur Day. For on þe moroȝe þei woldon done here body non ese, but suffur penaunce in mynde of hym þat suffrud so harde for hem. On Saturday þai myȝte noȝte [haue] whyle, whate for longe seruice, whate for oþur occupacion þat þei haddon for þe weke comynge, and afftur
25 m[e]te was no tyme for haly-day.

Narracio. For I rede in þe lyue of Seynt Rycharde, þat was bysy on a S[atur]day before none, þat he makud to schauon his berde one a Saturday aftur none. And þan was þe fende redy and gedured vp þe heres. Bot whan þis holy man seghe þat, he coniured þe fende and
30 bade hym tellon why he dud so. þan sayde þe fende: 'For þou doste no reuerens to þe Sonday, þat is Goddys owne day, to þe wyche day vche man þat is crystened is holdon for to do reuerens in worchep of Crystes resurreccion. Wherefore þeis herus I wil kepe to þe day of dome in hyȝe repreue to þe.' þan anone þis man made to leuon of hys
35 schavynge, and toke þe herus of þe fende and made for to brenne hem

[28]   2 *informacio*] formacio   3 For] F- *in blue, dec., 2 ll. deep*   7 putte] putto
9 oure þis redyly] *om.*   12 Furst] F- *in blue, dec., 2 ll. deep*   23 haue] *om.*
25 mete] mote   26 Narracio *cropped in margin in the long hand*   27 Saturday]
sonnonday   berde] and *add.*   30 nota *in margin with blue paraph*

in hys owne h[an]d for penawnce, and so abode half-schauon and half-vnschauon tylle þe Monday aftur. þis [I] sette here in a repreue of hem þat sparuth notte for to worschon on | Saturdayes aftur mete.   f. 58ᵛ
þan as Ion Belette telluth and techuth, on Schere þursday a man 40
schal dodun his heued and clypponde his berde, and a prest schal 40
schaue his crowne, so þat þere schal no þinge bene betwene Gode
almython and hym. He schal also schauen þe herus of his berde, þat
cometh of superfluite of humeres of þe stomak, and pare þe nayles of
his handes, þat cometh of superfluite of humerus of þe herte. So þat
ryʒte os we schauyn and scheron away þe superfluite of filthe 45
withowtyn, so we schalle schauon and scheron away þe superfluite
of synne and off vices withineforthe.
   þe vayle, þat alle þe Lenton haue bene drawen betwix þe auter and
þe quere, þat betokeneth þe professye of Cri[s]tes passion þat was
hullud and vnknowen tille þeise dayes comyn, þe wyche þeis dayes 50
bene done away and þe awter oponly schewed to alle men. For þeis
dayes Cryste suffrud oponly his passyon, þat he sayde hangyng on þe
crosse: *Consumatum est*, þat is, alle þe profesye of my passyon now
hath an ende. Wherefore þe cloþes of þe auter ben takon away. For
Cristus cloþus were drawen of hym and done alle nakyd, saue oure 55
Lady, his modur, wonde hur kercheff abowtyn hym to hulle his
memburres. þe auter stone betokeneth Crystus body, þat was drawon
on þe crosse os is a skyn of parchemyne on a harow, so þat alle hys
bonus myten be tolde. þe besommes þat hit is wassen wyth
betokeneth þe scowreges þat beton his body and þe thornes þat he 60
was crownyd wythalle. þe watur and þe wyne þat hit is wasson wyth
betokeneth þe blode and þe watur þat rane downe aftur þe spere fro
Crystes herte, þat wasched hys body. þe wyne þat is pouryd o[n þe] v
crosses, þat betokeneþ þe blode þat ranne oute of þe v woundes
pryncepaly owte of hys body. 65
   þis day is no pax ʒeven at masse. For Iudas trayed Cryste þis nyʒte
wyth a cusse. þis was þe prophesye of his passion þis day endud.
Wherefore þis nyʒte whan he hade sowpode, he made þe sakurmente
of his owne body, and ʒaf hit to his dyssypullys for to eton and for to
drynkon, and so began þe sakurmente of þe masse and of þe Newe 70
Lawe. And aftur þis soper he wassed hys discipulles fette, þat was a
maner of [þe] new [lawe of] folowhe. For os he sayde þan to Petur:

36 hand] heued   37 I] was   38 on] Sonnondayes aftur / ne *add.*
41 no] iewes *add. and canc.*   49 Cristes] crites   63 on þe] of   72 þe] *om.*
lawe of] *om.*

'He þat is waschen wit watur of folghe of alle dedly [synne], he hath no nede bot for to wasse his fete.' For þat betokeneth þe affection of
75 venial synne.

þan ʒif a man askuth why prestus done [not] hore masse aftur soper os Cryste dude, say þou: for þat was turnyd into more honeste and more saluacion of mannus sowle. For as Haymo tellyth vpon þe pystull of Seynte Poule, mony in þe begynnynge of þe faythe comyn
80 to chyrche vpon þis Schere þurresday, and þilk þat wheron ryche
f. 59ʳ browton mete and drynke | wyth hem and þere eton and dronkon til þei were dronkon and to ffulle of mete, and so at nyʒte tokun here hosul, sayng þat Cryste ʒaf hem þat ensaumpul. But whil þe ryche eton and dronkon to myche, þe pore þat nowte haddon, þei bydon til
85 þe ryche haddon done, sore in hungur, and þan eton of here relef and so aftur tokun here howsel. Wherefore os þe pystul of þe day telleth, Seynte Pole rebukeþ hem þeroff and turneth þat fowle vse into more honeste and holynese, þat is for to seyne þe masse fastynge and alle men for to takon here howsel fastynge.

90 On Astur Evon þe paschal is makud, þat betokenyth Cryste. For as þe paschal is c[h]e[f]e ta[pur] þat is in þe chirche, so is Criste þe chef seynte þat is in Haly Chirche. Also þis paschal betokyneth þe pyler of fure þat ʒode before þe schildron of Israel whan þei wenton owte of Egyppe into þe londe of byheste þat is now Ierusalem. Ande os þei
95 ʒedon þoroʒ þe Rede See holle and sownde, sevon dayes aftur þei commyn alle vche day to þe see and þankud God for here passage. Herefore Holy Chirche alle þe Astur weke goth in procession to þe fonte, þat is now Red[e] See to alle criston pepul þat bene fowloed in fonte. For þe watur in þe fonte betokeneth þe rede blode and watur
100 þat ranne downe of þe wounde of Cri[s]tes syde, in þe whyche þe power of Pharao, þat is þe verrey fende, is drowned, and alle his myʒte lorne, and alle cristen pepul sauyd.

þe fonte is on Astur Evon halowode, and on Wysson Evon. For at þe begynnynge of Haly Chirche alle men, wommen and chyldren were
105 keppet to bene ifolowode in þis dayes at þe fonte-halowinge. But now, for encheson þat many in so longe abydynge dyede bowte fologhe, þerefore Holy Chirche ordeyneth to folown alle þe tyme of þe ʒere, saue viij dayes before þese evonus a childe schal bene kepud to þe fonte-halowinge, ʒiff þat he may sauely for perel of deth, and ellus notte.

73 synne] *om.*   76 not] *om.*   83 hosul] þat cryste *add. and canc.*   85 done] (c?)eton *add.*   91 chefe tapur] clene takyn   98 Rede] redy   100 Cristes] crites 104 wommen and] *trs.*

þus is þe paskal holowd and lyȝte with ne[w]e fure, and of hit alle 110
oþur tapurers bene lyȝte. For alle holynesse and lyȝte of godde
worchinge cometh of Crystes lore, and Holy Chirche is lyȝte wyth
brennynge charite of his behestus. Fyue pepynce of encense bene
stekyd in þe paschall lyke to þe crosse, þat betokenes þe v wondes, as
Bede saythe, þat Cryste suffred in his body and schul be keppt fresse 115
and sote as ensence tylle þe day of dome, in rebuke of hem þat schul
be dampned, þat hadden none beleue in Crystes passyon ne woldon
askun hym no mercy for here synnes.

In þe fonte-halowing þe preste cast[us] watur oute in fowre partyes
of þe fonte. For Cryste badde his disciplus gone in fowre partyes of þe 120
worlde and prechon and techon þe foure gospelles and folowinge in þe
name | of þe Fadur and þe Sone and of þe Holy Gost, Amen. Aftur, f. 59ᵛ
þe preste breþus in þe watur, ffor þe Holy Gost in þe makynge of þe
worlde was borne on þe waturres. Wherefore when Gode for Adamus
synne cursed þe erþe, he spared þe watur. [Wherefore it is lawefull for 125
a man to ete in Lente þat comuþ of þe watur.] Afftur, he droppuþ in
þe watur wax of a tapur brennynge, þe wyche betokeneþ þe manhede
of Cryste þat was folowode in watur and in hys fologhe halowode alle
þe watur of fologhe. Aftur, oyle and creme bene put in þat watur, ffor
in þat sacurmente þilke þat bene in heven and þilke þat bene in erþe 130
ben ioyned togydur. þat was preuode in Cristes baptem, ffor þere þe
Fadur of heuen spake þat alle þe pepul herde, þe Holy Goste was
seyne leke a culuor. þus was þe fonte halowode twyes in þe ȝere at þe
begynnynge off Holy Chyrche, a[nd] none [o]ftur be þe ȝere. þat was
on Astur Even, ffor þan alle þe pepul was broȝte oute of þraldam of þe 135
fende be Crystus passyon, and on Wysson Evon, for þan is þe Holy
Goste ȝeue, þat is remissyon of alle synnes. þan frome þe fonte men
gone to þe quere syngynge þe letanye, preynge alle þe seyntus of
heuen for to pray to God ȝeuen hem þat bene folowode grace for
kepon þat heghe couenande þat þei haue made in her folowynge. 140

þan me goþþe to masse þat is begynnynge wythowtyn offyce, þat is
called þe heued of þe masse. For Cryste þat is heued of alle Holy
Chirche is note ȝete ryson frome dethe to lyue. *Kyrieleyson* is sayde,
for in vche office of Holy Chirche, and namely in þe masse, hit is grete
nede to ascon helpe and sokour of God for to defende vs of diuerse 145
temptacions þat assayluth ouse namely in Goddys seruyce. *Gloria in*

110 newe] nede   112 Chirche] and of holy chirche *add.*   113 Fyue] ffyue
119 preste castus] prestes caste   125–6 Wherefore . . . watur] *om.*   134 and none
oftur] anone aftur   144 office] is sayde *add.*

excelsis is sayde, for þe Fadur of hevon is gretly ioyued for to beholde
þe pepul þat his Sone hath bowthe wyth his passyone, þat lyuon in
charite and in pes vchone wyth oþur. Grayel nis none sayde, for þilk
150 þat bene folowode be note anone perfyte to walkon in þe gre[c]e of
vertues. *Alleluya* is songon, for hit [is] grete ioy to angelys to sene þe
ruyne of angelus bene restored be þilke þat bene folowode. Aftur þe
Allely, þe tracte is songon. For þoȝf þei bene in þer fologhe wassyn of
alle synnus, ȝit þei muston trauayle besyly for to kepe hem owte of
155 cumburraunce of þe fende, þat he falle not into dedly sinne aȝayne.
Offratory is none sayde, for þe wommen þat comyn for to offron to
Crystus body oynementys, þei fonde hym not in his tombe. *Agnus dei*
is sayde, botte no pese is borne, ffor Cryste, þat is hede of pese, was
not ȝitte aryson. Postcomyne nis none sayde, ffor heo þat bene
160 folowod schal not ben howselled not þis day bot on morowne. For
in begynny[n]g of Holy Chirche þere commen ʼmoʼ to fologhe of grete
f. 60ʳ ache þan of childruns. A sorte evensonge | is done, laste þei þat bene
folowde, for colde [o]þur sekenes, weron [anuy]de of longe seruyce.
þan is alle þis seruyce endud vndur one colette, ffor alle þe
165 s[akurment]e of Holy Chirche and of fologhe is endud in þe passyon
of Cryste.

[29] *De festo Pasche sermo breuis ad parochianos post resurreccionem*

Gode men and wommen, os ȝe alle know welle, þis day is called in
some place Astur Day, and in some place Pasch Day, and in some
place Goddus Sonunday.
5   Hit is callde Astur Day as Kandulmasse Day of kandulles and
Palme Sonunday of palmus. For w[e]l n[e]ȝ in vche place hit is þe
maner þis day for to done fyre oute of þe houce, a[nd] þe astur, þat
hath bene alle þe wyntur brente wyt fuyre and blakud wyth smoke, hit
schal þis day bene arayed wyth grene rusches and swete floures
10 strawde alle aboute, schewyng a heyghe ensaumpul to alle men and
wommen þat, ryȝte os þei machen clene þe houce alle wythine, bering
owte þe fyre and strawing þare flowres, ryȝte so ȝe schulde clanson þe
houce of ȝoure sowle, doing away þe fyre of lecherye and of dedly
wrathe and of envye, and straw þare swete erbys and floures—and þat

150 grece] grene   151 is] *om.*   161 begynnyng] begynnyg   163 oþur] eþur
anuyde] of mynde   165 sakurmente] seruyce
    [29] 2 Gode] G- *in blue, dec., 3 ll. deep*   alle know] *trs.*   6 wel] wol   neȝ] noȝ
7 and] at

bene vertues of godenesse and of mekenesse, of k[yn]denesse, of loue 15
and charite, of pese and of reson—and so make þe houce of ʒowre
sowle abulle to reseyuen ʒoure Godde. For ryʒte os ʒe wil note suffur
no þinge in ʒoure howce þat stynkuth or sauereth ille, whereby þat ʒe
may be desesud, rytʒ so Criste, whan he cometh into þe howce of
ʒoure sowle and fynde þere heny stynkyng thynge of wrathe and of 20
envy or any othur dedly synne, he wil not abydun thare, bot anone he
gothe owte, and þe fende cometh in and abyduth þare.

þan may þat sowle be ful sory þat so his forsakyn of God and
betakon to þe fende. þus done þay þat holdyn dedly wrath wythin
hym and dedely envye in here hertus and wil note forʒeuon hem þat 25
hauon trespased to hem for no prayoure. Wherefore take hit in
certeyne: þof ʒe mowne wyth glosyng wordus dyssayue me and
sayne þat ʒe bene [in] fulle scharite os ʒe awne for to bene, þoʒ ʒe
bene noʒte so, ʒe gaynot for to begyle Gode þat sethe vche cornel of
ʒoure hertus. Wherefore for Goddys loue dysseyue ʒe note ʒoure 30
sowle and ʒoureselfe, bot bene as besy for to make ʒoureselue and
ʒoure sowle klene wythinne to Goddes syʒte os ʒe bene to makon
ʒoure howces clene to manus syʒte. And ryʒte os ʒe klens ʒoure houses
with fayre fresse floures and sote, [ryʒ]te so cloþe [þ]e a[s]tur of ʒoure
sowle, þat is ʒoure herte, in fayre cloþe of charite and of loue and of 35
pese and of reste wyth alle Goddys pepul, þat ʒe mowne be abul for to
reseyuen þe best frende þat ʒe haue, þat is Cryste, Goddys Sone of
heuen, þat þis tyme suffrid deth for to bryng ʒow into þe lyue þat eure
schal laste.

þis day is also | called Pashe Day, þat is in englys tonge a passyng f. 60ᵛ
day, and so hit is for too skyllus. One: for þis day vche criston man in 41
reuerens of Godde schulde forʒeuen hym þat hath gylte hym, and
bene in fule luf and charite to alle Goddys pepul passyng alle oþur
dayes of þe ʒere, for alle þat is mysdone alle þe ʒere beforon schal be
helud þis day wyth þe salue of scharite. Hit is also a passinge day, for 45
vche criston man schulde passon owte of euel lyuing into gode
lyuynge, owte of vices into vertues, owte of pryde into meknesse,
owte of couetyse into largenesse, owte of sclowthe into holynesse or
bysines, owte of envye into loue and charite, owte of wrathe into
mercy, owte of glotonrye into abstinens, owte of lecherye into 50
chastite, owte of þe fendus clokus into Goddus barme, and so of
Goddus enmy make hym hys dere frende and derlynge. Whoso passus

15 kyndenesse] knydenesse   28 in] *om.*   32 makon] goddys ho *add. and canc.*
34 ryʒte] and ʒitte   þe astur] ʒe aftur   40 þis] Tþis

þus he is worthy for to cum to þat grete feste þat God makyth þis day
to alle þat þis passage makyth.

55 þis day is callyd Goddys Sonnonday, for Criste, Goddys Sone of
heuen, þis day ros fro deth to lyue and so gladud alle his servauntes
and frendus wyth his vpriste. Wherefore alle Holy Chirche makyth
myrthe þis day and synguþ þus: 'þis is þe day þat oure lorde makud:
be we gladde and ioyful in hur.' þe Fadur of heuen wit alle his
60 angellus makuth so grete melody for þe vpriste of his Sone þat he
makyth þis day a grete passinge feste, and bydduth alle his pepul
þereto, also welle hem þat bene in heue[n] os þilke þat bene in erþe.
þan also welle os hym schalle bene þat comyth to þis feste welle
arayed in Goddus lyuerey, kloþed in loue and charite, alse evel sal
65 hym be þat comyth in þe fendus lyueray, cloþud in enuye and dedly
wrathe. For þese, as þe gospel telluth, schal be takon and kaste into
preson of helle. So w[ille] þat oþur laȝe and make mery, þe oþur wepe
and be sory, and wille þat oþur eton and drynkkon at Goddus borde,
þei schul grenne wyth here tethe for peyne of helle-wormes þat
70 gnawon hem. For as þay eton oþur with bakbyting here in erþe, þei
schul ete hym bak and body wythowten ende in þe peynes of helle.

Wherefore, gode men and wommen, I scharge ȝow heȝly in Goddus
behalue þat none of ȝow today come to Goddus borde but he be in ful
charite to alle Goddus pepul, and also þat ȝe be clene chryuen and in
75 ful wylle for to leuon ȝoure synne. For ȝif I woste whyche weron owte
of scharite and vnschryuon, I moste be teching of holy wrytte wit a
fulle mowthe say þus to hym in audiens of alle men: 'I ȝeue þe here
not þi howsell bot þi dampnacion into euerlasting peyne til þou come
to amendement.' Wherefore for Cristes loue vche man seche wele hys
f. 61ʳ conciens and clense hit, þat ȝe may abully ressey|von hys sauyoure.
81 And ȝitte, for to ster ȝow more in conciens, I schal telle ȝow þis
ensampul.

Narracio. I rede of a holy byschope þat prayed God bysyly to ȝeuon
hym grace for to sene whyche weren worthy to reseyvon þat
85 sacurment and wyche vnworthi. þan whan þe pepul come to
Goddus borde, he saw some comyn wit here faces redde os blode
and blode droppynge oute of her mowthes, some here faces weron
blace as any pyche, some as whyte as snowe, and some fayre and rody
and lysty for to beholdon. Than among oþur he saw tweyon comyn
90 wommen, and here faces schone as bryte as þe sonne. þan hadde he

62 heuen] heue   63 schalle . . . comyth] þat comyth schalle ben   67 wille]
wollon   83 nota *cropped in margin with red paraph*

myche wondur of this sythe and prayde God to ȝef hym reuelacion
and knowinge whate alle þis betokened.

þan come þere an angel to hym and sayde: 'þese þat haue blody
faces, and blode dropput owte of here mowthes, þo ben envyous men
and wommen and ful of dedly wrathe, and wyl not amende hem, and 95
gnawen hem behende, and bene vsed for to swere orybul oþus be
Goddys blode and hys sydus and v[m]breydon God of hys passioun
and done hym no reuerens. Wherefore here mowthes schul droppon
of blode tul þei comyn to amendement. Heo þat hath blake fasus bene
lecherus men and wommen þat wil not leue here synne no here lust, 100
ne wil not schriue hem of hit. They þat haue whyte faces as snowe
bene þay þat haue done grete synnus and bene schryuen þereof, and
wit weping of here eyen hathe wasschon here sowlys so whyte and
clene. þilke þat bene fayre and rody of face bene gode comyn lyueres
þat leuen trewly be here mayn swynke and so keputh hem owte of 105
dedely synne. And þese tway women þat schyned passynge alle oþur
where too comyn wommen and off ful euel leuynge, bot whan þei
comyn into þe chyrche, þe tokon suche repentawnce in her hertus þat
þei madon a vow to God þat þei woldon do neure more of mysse wit
helpe of his grace. Wherefore God of hys heȝe mercy hath forȝeuen 110
hem here synne and so clene wasschon here sowlus þat þei schyne þus
passing alle oþur.' þan þis angel wente his way, and þis byschoppe
thankud God of his heȝe grace þat he schewed hym þat reuelacione,
and serue[d] hym eure aftur wit alle his myȝte, and hadde þe blysse of
heuen, þe wyche blysse God grawnte ȝow and me. Amen. 115

[30] *De festo sancti Georgij sermo dicendus ad parochianos vbi sanctus
Georgius est patronus ecclesie, quia alibi festum istud celebratur*

Gode men and wommen, suche a day ȝe schal haue þe fest of Seynt
George, þe whiche day ȝe schal comyn to Holy Chirche in worschep
of God and of þe holy martyr Seynte George þat bowthe hys day ful 5
dere.

For os I rede in his lyfe, I fynde þat þere was a oribul dragon þat
men | of þe cite weron so aferde þat, be consayle of þe kynge, vche a f. 61ᵛ
day þai ȝef hym a schepe and a childe for to eton for he sculde not
come into þe cite and eton hem. þan whan alle þe schildur of þe cite 10
weron eton, for encheson þat þe kynge ȝaf hem þat consayle, þay

constreynud hym þat hade but one doȝtur for to ȝevon hur to þe
dragon, os þai haddon done here chylderon before. þan þe kynge for
fer of þe pepul wit wepynge and grete sorow makynge delyuerod hem
15 his doȝtur in hur best aray. þan þei setton hur in þe place þareas þai
were wonte to setton oþur chylderon and a schepe wyth hur, for to
abydon tyme tul þe dragon wolde comen.

But þan be ordenaunce of Godde Seynte George come rydynge þat
way. And whan he saw þe aray of þat damessel, hym þoȝte wel þat hit
20 schulde be a womman of grete renowne and askud hur why scheo
stode þere wit so mornynge a chere. þan answerud scheo and sayde:
'Gentul knyte, wel may I be of heuy chere þat am a kyngus doȝtur of
þis cite and now am sette here for to be deuowred anone of an orribul
dragowne þat hath eton alle þe childur of þis cite. And for alle ben
25 eton, now mote I be eton, for my fadur ȝaf þe cite þis cownsayle.
Wherefore, gentul knyȝte, go hene faste and saue þiselue, leste he lese
þe as he wil me.' 'Damysel,' quoth George, 'þat were a grete vylany to
me þat am a knyte wel i-armode, þat I schulde flene, and þou þat arte
a womman schulde abyde.'

30 þan wit þis worde þe orribul worme put vp his heued and
spyttynge owte fyre proforod batayle to George. þan makud
George a crosse before hym and sette his spere in þe grate, and wit
suche myȝte bare downe þe dragone into þe erþe þat he bade þis
damyssayle bynde hym [wyth hur] gyrdul aboute hys neke and ledon
35 hym aftur hur into þe cite. þan þis dragone sued hur forth os hit hade
bene a gentul hownde, mekely witowtyn any mysdoing.

But whan þe pepul of þe cite seghe þe dragone come, þei flowne
vche man into hys hyron for ferde of hym. þan called George þe
pepul aȝayne and bade þay schulde note bene aferde. For ȝyf þai
40 woldon levon in Cryste and take folowgh, he wolde befor hem alle
slene hym and so delyuer hem of here enmye. þan weron þai alle so
glade þat x[x] thowsand of men withowtyn wommen and childron
weron folowde, and þe kyng was furste folowde and alle hys howsalde.
þan George slewe þis dragoun and badde teyon oxon to hym and
45 drawe hym ferre owte of þe cite, þat þe sauor of hym schulde hem
note greue, and bade þe kyng belde faste in euery hyron of hys londe
chirches, and be lusty for to here Goddys seruice, and done honoure
to alle men of Holy Chirche, and euer haue mynde and compassion of
49 alle þat weron nedy and pore.

f. 62ʳ   þan whan | þat George hade þus turnyd þis londe to Goddys

34 wyth hur] *om.*   39 þai] sch *add. and canc.*   42 xx] x

faythe, he harde how þe emperoure Dyoclisiane dude many criston
men to þe dethe. He wente to hym boldely and repreuid hym of þat
cursyd dede. þan þis emperoure anone commawndud for to done
hym into preson and ley hym þare vpry3te and a mylne-stone on hys
breste for to haue so crusched hym to deþe. But whan he was seruid 55
so, he prayed to God of helpe, and God kep hym so þat he felte no
harme, nor no party of hys body. But whan þe emperoure harde
þereof, he bade makon a qwelle, sette ful of hokus in þe one syde, and
swerde-poyntus in þat othur syde of þe whele a3ayne hit, and sette
George in þe myddus, and so for to turne þe whelus abowte and alle 60
to-rase hys body on eyþur syde. But whan he was in þis turment, he
prayde to Criste of sokoure and was holpen anone. Afftur he was put
in [a] hotte brennynge lyme-[kyl]ne and closyd þerine for to haue
bene brente, but [God] of hys my3te he turned þe hete into colde
d[e]we. 3ete þe þridday aftur, whan alle men wende he hade bene 65
brente to dethe and to colus, þan was he [f]ounde ly3te and mery and
þankyng Godde.

Afftur, whan he was fette and sette before þe emperoure, he
repreuid hym of hys falce goddys and sayde þe weron but fendus
and wito3ten my3te and falce at nede. þan made þe emperoure for to 70
beton his mowþe wit stonus til hit was alle to-poned, and made to
beton his body wit drye bulle-synowes tylle þe flesse felle fro þe bone
and hys guttys myten ben seyne. Yitte aftur þei makud hym to drynk
venym, þat was makud stronge for þe nonus, for to a poysnd hym
anone to þe dethe. But whan George hade made þe syne of þe crosse 75
on hit, he drank hit witowtyn any greffe, so þat for wondur þerof þe
man þat makud þe poyson anone turnyd to cryston faythe and anone
was done to deþe for Crystes sake.

þan þe ny3the aftur, as George was in preson praynge to Gode,
God come to hym wit grete ly3te and bade hym bene of gode 80
comforde, for in þe morowen he schulde makon hys ende of his
passyoune and so come to hym into þe ioy þat euer schulde laston.
And whan he hade sette a crowne of golde vpon hys heuede, he 3af
hym hys blessinge and stey into heuen. þan on þe morowne, for he
wolde note done sacrifice to þe emperoures falce goddus, he makud to 85
smyton off his heued, and so passyd to God. And whan þe emperoure
wolde haue gone to hys palice, þe ley3te brente hym and alle hys
seruandus.

63 a] *om.*   kylne] and talne   64 God] *om.*   65 dewe] dowe   66 founde]
sounde

Narracio. In a story of Antyoche is wryton þat whan cryston men
90 besegedon Ierusalem, a fayre ʒong knyte aperud to a preste and sayde
f. 62ᵛ þat he was Seynte George and | ledar of criston men, and comaundud
þat he schulde bere with hym his relikkus and come wit hem to þe
sege. But whan þei comyn to þe wallus off Ierusalem, þe Sarsynus
weron so stronge witinne þat criston men durste not clymbun with
95 here laddures vppe. þan come Seynt George, cladde in whyte and a
rede crosse on hys breste, and ʒode vp on þe laddrus, and bade þe
criston men come afftur hym. And so with þe helpe of Seynte George
þei wonnon þe cite and slowen alle þe Sarsynus þei fownden
þereinne.
100 And þere[fore] prey we to Seynt George þat he wil be oure help at
oure nede and saue þis rewme to þe worchep of God and his modur
Marie and alle þe cumpanye of heuen. A[m]en. *Subscripsit* Addeley.

[31] *De festo sancti Marci euangeliste sermo breuis ad parachianos:*
hoc modo dicendus

Gode cristen men and wommen, suche a day ʒe schal haue Seynt
Markus day, þat was one of þe fowre þat wrytton þe gospelles and
5 preched hem to þe pepul.
þan was þis Marke furste a eʒen man, bot aftur he was folewde of
Seynt Petur and so sewod Seynt Petur longe aftur til he was ful taʒte
in þe beleue. And whan he was ful ilernud of Crystus faythe, þan
Seynte Petur made hym gone and prechon þe pepul Goddes worde.
10 And for he was so holy a man þe pepul wolde algate make hym a
preste, he for grete mekenesse of hymselue he made to kutton off his
one thumbe. Neuerþelesse, whan God wolde haue hit so, Seynte
Petur with grete instaunce makud hym to take þe ordur of preste. þan
was he besy day and nyʒte for to prechon Goddes worde to þe pepul,
15 and alle þat he sayde wyth worde he confermyd hit with gode
ensaumpul and with doinge of miracles.
þus þere be conspiracion of þe Holy Gost he ʒode to þe cite of
Alexandur for to turne þe pepul to þe faythe of Cryste. þan whann he
come into þe cite, at þe forme fote þat he sette inne at þe ʒate his schoe
20 braste and was torne, wherby he wyste welle þat he schulde note gone
frome þenne but þat he schulde take hys ende þare, and so dude. þan
whan he come into þe cite, he saw a man clowtinge pore men schone

100 þerefore] þere   102 Amen] Annen
[31] 1 *Marci*] Marcij   3 Gode] G- *in blue, dec., 2 ll. deep*

þat wheron torne. And þaȝ þis man where a paynym, he was cristened
in his doinge. Wherefore Seynt Marke preyde hym for to amende his
schone þat weron torne. þan þis man, for he saw þat Marke was pore 25
and nedy and of sympul aray, hym þoȝthe þat hit was almus for to
helpon hym, and toke hys schone to hym and began for to schewon
hit. And os he schewod ful helte, be Goddys ordynaunce he wondud
hymselfe in þe hande with his nalle greuoslyche. And so, whate for
sore ache and penaunce þat he hade þereoff, among hys woo he callyd 30
helpe of one Gode. And whan | Seynt Marke herde þat, he þankud f. 63ʳ
Gode. Anone he spytte in þe erþe and makud fen, and with þat fen
anoyntud þe mannus hande in þe name of Ihesu Cryste, and anone
was holle. þan whan þis man saw suche vertu in Seynte Marc, he
prayde hym for to dwelle with hym. þan Marc dwellud wyth þis man 35
and preched hym so þat he folowd hym and alle his howsolde, and
aftur, for grete holynesse þat he saw in hym, he makud þis man a
bischoppe.

þus whan þe m[e]n of þe cite sene how Mark preched þe faythe of
Cryste and despysud here falce goddys, þei toke hym and dydon a 40
roppe abowte his nekke and drew hym on þe stonus, crying infer[e]
and in dispyte of hym: 'Draw we þis bygul to þe bygul-stede.' So
whan þei haddon drawon hym ney to þe dethe, þan þei putton hym
into preson tylle on þe morowhe. þan com þis nyȝte Cryste into
preson to hym and sayde: 'Pes be to þe, Marc, owre ewangelyste, be 45
noȝte [a]gaste, for I am wyth þe.' þan on þe morow þe come aȝeyne
and fetton hym owte of preson and drowe hym tille he were dede. And
whan he felte he schulde dyon, he sayde: '*In manus tuas, domine,
commendo spiritum meum*' and so þerewit ȝaf vp þe gaste. þan aftur
whan þe woldon haue brent hys body for malyce, anone þer come 50
suche a thundur and layte and erþe-quake þat no man durste abydon
bot alle flowen away. þan in þe nyȝte afftur criston men tokon hys
body and byridon hit wit grete worchep, as hit was worthi.

þan felle hit so afftur þat vche contray halowd Seynte Marcus day,
saue one cuntray þat was callud Appullea, þe whyche cuntray was so 55
desesud be hete and be vnkynde droȝte þat alle þe cornes and frytes
faylud hem, þat þei weron neyȝ enfamyed for defaute of corne. Bote
þan come þere a voyce from euen and bade hem halown Seynte
Marcus day as oþur cryston men dydon, and þan schulde þai bene
releued. And whan þai dudon so, God sent to hem alle maner of 60
froytes.

39 men] man   41 infere] in fero   46 agaste] o gaste

Now, gode men and wommen, ȝe haue harde of þis sayntus lyf and
why his day his halowde. þan hit is nedeful to telle ȝow whi ȝe schal
fast his day and gone in procession. *Narracio.* I rede þat in þe cete of
65 Rome on þis day felle suche a qualme and sodeyn deth amonge þe
pepul of þe cite þat whan a man ganed oþur nesed, anone þerwit he
ȝaf up þe goste, and oþur dyed sodenlyche a grete nowmbur. þan þe
poppe Pellagius bade vche man whan he ganed to makon a crosse on
his mowthe, and whan a man herde anoþer nesen, anone he schulde
70 sayne: 'Cryste helpe þe', and so many weron sauid. And also he made
þe pepul faston and gone barfote in processyon, and so pray alle þe
sayntus of heuon for to pray for hem to God þat he of his godenesse
f. 63ᵛ schulde haue mercy of hem, and so dudon. þan come | afftur Seynte
Gregori and makyd hem to done þe same vche ȝere on Seynte Marcus
75 day, boþe faston and gone on processyon, and canonysid hit for to be
done so algate aftur. þan come þere aftur a pope was called Lyberius
and saw how þe froyte b[o]þe of erþe and of trene for tendurnesse of
hymself tokon at þis day offtyme grete harme, whate be þundur and
wyth layȝte, and be unkynde hete, be vnkynde stormys, be whirlyng
80 wynde, by mystes, be mylnedewus, be grete wormus, be long-taylud
flens, and also for þe pepul to sone aftur Astur and reseyuynge of here
howsul turnyd aȝeyne to here synne, hauyng no rewarde to þat hegh
sacurment. þerefore God sende vengeaunce amonge þe pepul more
þat tyme of þe ȝere þan anoþur, off pesteleyns, of werrus, of derþus,
85 of diuerse seknesse. Wherefore þis holy pope, for to putton away
Goddus wrathe from þe pepul, he comaunded alle criston men and
wommen for to halown þis day and fasten, not to sertayne ȝerus, os
lewod men tellon, but algate forthe one, and for to come þat day to þe
chirche and gone one processyone wit þe letanye.
90   Wherefore, gode men, ȝe schul wyton welle þat alle þilk þat done
aȝayne þe constit[u]c[i]ons of Holy Chirche wytinglyche he is acursud
til he come to amendement. And ȝif he dye in þat curs[e] vnschryuon,
he is dampned before God. Herefore, gode men and wommen, I
charge ȝow alle on Holy Chirche behalf þat ȝe faston þat day, bot hit
95 falle on a Sonnenday or in Astur weke, and comyth [þat] day to þe
chirche and here Goddes seruice os criston men awte for to done, and
pray hartefully to Seynt Marc þat he wille pray for ȝow to God for to
put away alle myscheues of body and of sowle and þat ȝe may haue þe
blysse þat he boute ȝow to, þe wyche blysse God brynge ȝow and me,
100 ȝif hit be his wille. Amen.

77 boþe] beþe   91 constitucions] constiticons   92 curse] cursyd   95 þat] *om.*

[32] *De festiuitate apostolorum Philippi and Iacobi sermo breuis*
ad parachianos: hoc modo.

Gode men and wommen, suche a day ʒe schal haue a heʒe feste in
Holy Chirche, Seynt Philippus day and Sent Iacobus day, Cristus
holy apostolus. But for þis day cometh wythine þe tyme of Astur 5
seruise, [ʒ]e schal not faste his evon but comyth to þe chirche os
Goddys awne pepul to worchep God and his holy apostolus.

þan schul ʒe knaw þat þis Philippe was sende be alle þat oþur
apostolus into a cuntray was callud Cythea for to preche Goddys
worde to þe vnbeleuyd pepul. But whan he come þidur and preched 10
aʒeynus he[re] mamentus, preuing þat he were fendus and none
goddys, anone þis mysse-beleuid pepul tokon þis holy apostul and
lade hym into here tempul, and constreyned hym for to done sacrifyce
to here mament, oþur ellus he schulde bene dede. þan as þay weron
besy for to haue done þis seynte dyssese, sodenly a grete dragoun | 15
come oute of þe erþe and sleowʒe þre of þe mysse-leuod men and f. 64ʳ
venymod so þe pepul wit his breþeynge þat þere felle on hem alle
suche a sekenes þat for wo and passione þat þe haddon þai cryed alle
waylinge and wepynge vchone to oþur.

þan sayde Phelyp to hem: 'ʒeff ʒe wyllyn be helud of ʒoure seknes 20
þat greueth ʒow, and also þese men be broʒte aʒeyne to lyue þat bene
dede, castus downe þis mawmentre þat ʒe woldon haue me to
worcheppon and settus þere a crosse leke to þe crosse þat my
mastyr dyud vpon and worcheputh hit.' þan dud þai so gladly, and
fayne for to bene holpon of þere woo þat greuyd hem so sore. And 25
wan þei haddon so done, [anone] ryʒte þei weron alle hole and Seynte
[Philippe] be callynge of Crystus name rerud hem vp aʒeyne to lyue
þe þre men þat weron dede. And whan he hadde done so, he
commaunded þe dragon for to gone into a wyldurnesse þere he
schul neuer greue man ne beste, and so ʒode forthe and was neuer 30
seyne aftur.

þus whan Seyn Phelep hadde preched þe pepul and made hem
stedefaste in fayþe of Ihesu Criste, [he ʒode forthe into a cite
Ieropolym. And for he preched þe fayþe of Ihesu Criste] þat was
done on a crosse, þerefore wykkud men of þat cite tokon hym and 35
dedon hym on a crosse, as Cryste was, and so pynud hym to þe dethe,

[32] 3 Gode] G- *in blue, dec., 3 ll. deep*   6 ʒe] he   11 here] he
15 dragoun] come owte *catchwords bottom f. 63ᵛ*   26 anone] *om.*   and] sayde *add.*
27 Philippe] ione   33–4 he . . . Criste] *om.*

and so ȝode to Cryste his maystur for to dwellon with hym in þe ioy
þat neuer schal haue ende.

Now ȝe schul here of Seynte Iacob, þat was calde amonge þe
40 apostolus Iamus þe lasse for to be knowen be Iamus þe more, þat was
Seyn Ionus broþur þe ewangeliste. But þis Iacob oþur Iamus, þat is
alle one name, was calde Cristus broþur, for he was so leke to Cryst[e]
þat whan þe Iewes tokon oure Lorde Criste, þei cowde notte know þat
one be þat oþur, bot os Iudas betrayud Cryste and so taȝte hem to
45 hym. þis Iamus was so holy from þe tyme þat he was borne alle þe
tyme of hys lyue þat he dranke [no] wyne ne seser no ale, for þere is
none in þat cuntre. And also he hette neuer flesse, ne hys heued was
neuer schauen. He vsud neuer for to be bawmed wit oyle os þe maner
is of þe cuntre for hete of þe sonne. He was neuer bathud. He werud
50 neuer lynnon clothe. He vsud for to knele so myche in his prayeres þat
his kneus werun so þekke of ylle þat þei weron boched os a camel. þis
was þe furste man þat euer songe masse in vestimentes as prestus now
dothe.

þan felle hit so þat þe cite of Ierusalem was enfecte wit þe sinne of
55 þe slaȝte of Cryste þat hit moste nede be distroyed. Wherefore þis
f. 64ᵛ holy man Seynte Iamus was makud | byschop of þat cite Ierusalem
and laffte þere for to prechun þe pepul and turne hem into bettur
leuinge. But for þei weron so cumbrud in synne þat þei haddon no
grace off amendemente, nedely Crystes profecye moste bene fulfyllud
60 and þe cite distroyed. Wherefore men tokon Seynt Iamus and sette
hym on a hey place, preyinge hym for to prechon þe pepulle aȝeynus
Crystus faythe, ffor myche of þe pepul was turnud to þe faythe. þan
Iamus boldely and steffly stode and preched þe faythe of Cryste and
preued be gode opon reson how alle þat leuod not on Criste schulde
65 ben dampned at þe day off dome into þe peynus off helle þat neure
schal haue hende. þan þe maystrus of þe Iewes lawe þrustonud hym
downe ffro on lofte and wit stonus punned hym so þat he was neghe
dede. þan he knelynge on hys kneus prayde to God for to forȝevon
hem his deth. And þerewyth one cursed man of hem wit a walkers
70 staff smote hym on þe heued þat þe brayne wallud owte, and so ȝolde
up þe goste.

þan aftur, what for synne of Crystus deth and ffor þe synne of þis
holy mannus deth, þe cite of Ierusalem, þat was þe strangaste cite of
alle þe worlde and lykly neuer for a bene wonnon, was stroyud so into

---

42 Cryste] crystus (broþur *canc.*)   46 no¹] *om.*   51 nota *in margin with blue
paraph*   59 amendemente] bote *add.*

þe vtturmaste þat vche stone of vche walle was turnud vp-so-downe 75
and neuer one lafte on oþur, ffor so Cryste sayde fourety ȝere before
hit schulde falle. And þe Iewes were dryuen [into] diuerse cuntrayes
and cites and disparpullud so þat sython here kyngdam hath bene
distroyud, and heo weron and ȝitte bene hyndlynges off alle pepulls.

Ȝitte wyl I telle ȝow more of þe distruccone of þe cite off Ierusalem 80
for to schewon ȝow how vengabul God is on hem þat bene leue for to
schedon criston blode as þai weron.

Narracio. þus whan God wolde do vengawnce on þis cite, hit fel so
þat a man of Pylatus þat dud Cryste to dethe come from Ierusalem
towarde Rome, bot be a tempest he was cast vp on þe lande þereas a 85
grete lorde dwellud þat was callud Vaspasianus. þan hade þis
Vaspasianus suche a malady in hys vysage þat oute of his nesethrillus
droppud downe wormus leke waspus. þan sayde Vaspasianus to þis
man: 'Off whate cuntray comyst þou?' þan sayde he: 'From þe cite of
Ierusalem.' þan sayde Vaspasianus: 'I am ful gladde þereoff, ffor os I 90
haue lerud, in þat cuntray ar many gode leches. Wherefore I wotte þat
þou can helle me, and bot ȝif þou do so, for sothe þou schalte be dede.'
þan sayde | he aȝayne: 'I am no leche myselue, but he þat heluth alle f. 65ʳ
seke and rayseth þe dede to liue he may hele þe ȝif he wolle.' 'Who is
þat?' quoth Vaspasianus. 'Sir,' quod he, 'Ihesus off Nazareth þat 95
Iewes hath slayne, in whom, ȝiff þow wilte leuon, þou schalte bene
hole.' þan sayde Vaspasianus: 'I leue wel he may hele me þat rayseth
men from deth to lyue.' Anone wit his worde he was holle as fysche.

þan was Vaspasianus so glade of his hele þat he sende anone to þe
emperoure off Rome and gate leue for to distroyen þe cite of 100
Ierusalem, and so gadurod grete nowmbur off pepul and toke Tytus
hys sone wit hym and ȝode þ[i]dur. þan in mene tyme whil he seguth
þe cite, þe emperoure dyed and he was chosyn emperoure off Rome.
þan went he to Rome and lafte Tytus his sone in hys stede with pepul
inogh for to distroyen þe cite. þan Tytus lay so harde on þe cite and 105
enfamesche hem so þat þei eton here schone and her botus for
hongur, and þe fadur rafte þe mete owte off þe sonus hande, and
tokon hit owte off his mowþe, and þe sone off þe fadur, þe husbonde
off þe wyffe, and þe wyffe off þe husbande.

þan amonge oþur was þere a womman of grete blode þat hadde a 110
ȝunge schylde and for hongur sayde þus to hit: 'My dere sone, I haue
hade myche more peyne for þe þan þou hast hadde for me. Wherefore

hit is more reson þat I bete my hungur on þe þan þat I dye and þou
boþe.' þan toke scheo hur schylde and scloghe hym, and rostud halue
115 and kepud þe toþur halfe rawe. þus os þe flesse rostud, þe safuor of
hit wente into þe strete, and men þat feldon þat sawoure wendon þere
hade bene plenteþ of mete and comþ in for to haue hadde parte of þe
mete. But whan þei comyn in, þis womman wolde haue hydde þis
mete from hem. But þei aӡeynestodun hyr and sayde scheo schulde
120 not, for þei wendon þat hit hadde bene oþur mete þan of a chylde.
þan sayde þe womman: 'Here I haue rostud halfe my chylde for to
eton, and ӡif ӡe wil not leue me—lo, here þat oþur halfe rawe aӡeynus
þe morogh.' þan were þese men so agrysud of þis sythe þat þei ӡode
forthe and lafton þe modur etynge hyr howne chylde.
125   þan encresud hongur so in þis cite and dyudon so thykke pat þei
caston dede bodyes over þe wallus and feldon þe deches so þat þe
sauoure of hem ӡode fer into þe cuntre. And at þe laste nede made
hem þat lyuedon for to ӡeuon vp þe cite. þan come Tytus in wit his
hoste, and rytӡe os Iewes solden Cryste for xxx pans, so þei sowldon
f. 65ᵛ thryty Iewes for one peny and | turnud vp þe cite þat þei laffte not
131 one stone vpon anoþur but distroyud hit into vtturaste.
        þus, gode men, ӡe mowen sene, þer God byde longe, how sore he
smyteth at þe laste and senduth vengaunce vpon alle þat bene lusty for
to schedon criston blode. Suche men God hatuth heghly. Wherefore
135 vche man amende hymself, preing to þeis holy apostolus to bene here
mediatoures betwix hem and God þat þei may haue here verry
repentawnce in herte with schryfte of mowþe, and so wit satisfaccion
off gode dedus comen to þe blysse þat þeise apostolus bene inne.
Amen.

[33] *De inuencione sancte crucis sermo ad parochianos: hoc modo.*

Gode men and wommen, suche a day ӡe sal haue þe Holy Rode Day,
þe whyche day ӡe schal faste his evon no but on deuotione, but comeþ
to þe chirche as criston pepul in þe worchep off hym þat dyud on þe
5 rode for saluacion off mannus kynde.
        þan schal ӡe knowen þat þis day is calde þe feste off þe fyndinge off
þe crosse þat was fowndon on þis wyce: whan Adam, oure forme
fadur, was seke for helde and wolde fayne haue bene dede, he sende
Seth, his sone, to þe angel of paradyse, preing hym for to sende hym

[33]   2 Gode] G- *in blue, dec., 3 ll. deep*

þe oyle off mercy to anoy[n]te his body with whan he was dede. þan 10
answerud þe angel and sayde he my3te in no maner havon hit tul v
mill. and ij c. 3ere were fulfylde: 'But haue þis braunche off þe treo
þat þi fadur syngud wit and sette hit on his graue, and whan hit
beruth froyte, þan schal he haue mercy and none ore.' þan toke Seth
his brawnche and fonde his fadur dede and so sette þis brawnche on 15
his berynesse as þe angel bade, þe whiche growed þere til Salomon
tyme.

So whan Salomon makud his tempul, ffor þis treo was fayre
passinge oþur, he makud to hewon hit downe to þe werke. But for
hit wolde no wayes corde wit þe werke, Salomon made to dygge hit 20
depe into þe erþe, and so was hit hude þare into þe tyme þat
byschoppus of þe tempul lette makon a were in þe same place ffor
to wasschon scheppe ine þat werun offerud vp to þe tempul þereas þe
tre lay. þan whan þis were was makud, þai calde hit on here language
pro[ba]tica piscina, into wyche were vche day an angel come frome 25
hevon downe in worscheppe of þat treo þat lay in þe grownde þeroffe,
and so styrred þe watur | so þat he þat come furste into þe watur f. 66ʳ
afftur þe steringe of þe angel was helud of whatte maner evel þat hym
greuyd, be þe vertu off þat treo.

So þis laste many 3erus til þe tyme þat Cryste was takon for to be 30
done one þe crosse. þan þis treo be Goddys ordenaunce plunged vp
and swam on þe watur. And for þe Iewes haddon none noþur tre redy
to makon þe crosse off, ffor grete haste þei takun þat treo and makud
hit a crosse and so hengud Cryste þereone. And þan þat treo bare þat
dere blessud froyte, Crystus owne body, off þe wyche wallud oyle off 35
mercy to Adam and Eve and to alle her osprynge. But whan Cryste
was dede and takon downe off þe crosse, þe Iewes for envy of hym
tokon þis crosse and too oþur þat þe too þefuus hongud onne eyþur
syde off Cryste and byryed hem depe in þe erþe, for criston men
schulde notte wyton where þei weron. And þay lay þere hud too 40
vnderud wyntur and more tul Seynte Elleyne, þe emperoures modur
Constantyne, fonde hit in þis wyse.

In tyme of þis Constantyne, Maxencius wit stronge hande helde þe
emperoure off Rome. þan Constantyne gadurrude hym power for to
fy3ton wit Maxencius at a grete watur, owre þe whyche watur lay a 45
grete brygge, so þat in þe mydul of þis brygge Maxencius for
disseyte off Constantyne lette makon a trappe, so for to haue
distroyud Constantyne. But þe ny3te before þe batayle, as Constan-

10 anoynte] anoyte   25 *probatica*] prophetica   35 froyte] froyste

tyne lay in his bedde sore adrede off Maxcencius, ffor he was byggar
50 off pepul þan he was, Cryste come to hym wit a syne off þe crosse
schynynge as golde and sayde to hym: 'Tomorne whan þou gost to þe
batayle, take þis syne in þi hande, and be vertu þeroff þou schalt haue
þe victorye.' þan was Constantyne wondur gladde and lete makon a
crosse off treo and bare hit beforne hym to þe batayle. But whan
55 Maxencius sawghe hym neghe þe brygge, he was so ferud in hymself
þat he forȝatte þe trappe þat he had makud, and so os he come
aȝeynus Constantyne, he felle be þe trappe downe into þe watur and
was drownud. þan was alle hys oste wondur fayne and ȝoldon hem wit
fre wille to Constantyne.
60   þan for Constantyne was not folowode, he ȝode to þe pope
Syluestur and was cristoned of hym and also helud off lepur þat he
f. 66ᵛ hade. þan anone be counsayle off | þe pope he sent to hys modur
Elyn, þat was quene off Ierusalem, and p[r]ayde hur for to sechon þe
crosse þat Cryste was done one. þan was þis Eleyne a kyngus dowtur
65 of Englande—þan was he calud Ceolus. And whan Constantyne,
ffadur off þis Constantyne, come into þe londe of Yngland and sawe
Eleyne so fayre, he weddud hur for hur bewte [and] so makud hur
emperes of Rome. But aftur hur husbande dethe scheo hadde þe
kyngdam of Ierusalem to hur dowere, where scheo makud to gederon
70 alle þe Iewes þat myȝton bene funde and sayde hem sothly þat alle
schulde be brente [but] ȝiff þay schewud hyr þe crosse off Cryste.
    þan be counsayle of hem alle þay tokon one man þat þei caldon
Iudas and saydon how þat he wyste whare þe crosse was and how þat
he cowde brynge hur þareto. þan was scheo gladde and putte þis
75 Iudas into harde dystresse tyl he wolde telle hur whare was þe crosse.
þan for þis moste nede telle or ben dede, h[e b]ade sewon hym to þe
hul off Caluarye. And whan he had preyd þere longe, þe erþe quakud
þere þe crosse lay and a smeke as swete os any spycerye com owte off
þe erþe. And whan þe dyggud þare, þay foundon þe crossus. þan for
80 to knowen wyche was Crystes crosse, þei leydon hem vchone aftur
oþur vpon a dede body. But whan Crystus crosse come, anone þe
body þat was dede rosse and þankud God. þan toke Eleyne a party of
þis crosse and sente to Rome to hur sone, and þe remland scheo made
to schryne hit in syluor and lafte hit in Ierusalem wit alle þe worschep
85 þat scheo cowde. þus, gode men, as Holy Chirche makuþ mynde þis
day, þe holy crosse was fowndon. |

    63 prayde] pyayde   67 and] *om.*   71 but] *om.*   76 dede] and *add.* he bade]
    hade   86 Residuum huius istorie post tria folia quere *in bottom margin in red f. 66ᵛ*

þenne as Y rede, Y fynde þat in a cyte þat was called Byretus a f. 70ʳ
cr[i]sten man hyred a hous at a Iew to wonon in. þanne hadde þis man
a rode, þe wyche þat Nichodemus made in worchep and mynde of
Cryste. þen toke he þis rode and sette it in a priuey place in his houce 90
f[ro] syght of þe Iewes and dud it worschep aftyr hys conyng. þan
aftyr it fel so þat þis man stered into anothir hous and toke oute alle
his gode with hym, saue only þe rode þat he forgate, os God wolde he
schulde. þenne com þis Iew and wonyd in þe same hous þat þis
cristen man lafte, and for to make hym dalians he called on of his 95
neghbores to hym ande makyd hym to soupe with hym. So as þei
seton at þe souper and talkyd of þis crysten man þat woned þere
before, þe neghbor lokyd aboute besyde hym, and þan was he ware of
þat rode in a priuey herne. And whan he saw it, anone he begane to
grysbate with þe tethe and rebukyd spytusly þe oþer Iew and bare on 100
hym styfly þat he was a cristen man and hudde þat rode þere to done
it worschep. Ande eure he swore as depe os he myte þat it was notte
so, nor hadde neuer before þat tyme sene it.

Ȝitte went þis other Iew anone to hys neghbores and tolde ham alle
how þat man was a priuey cristen man and how he hadde a rode hud 105
in hys hous. þan com þei alle wode for wrath and bete þis man and
drowen hym and toggyd hym on þe warste maner þat þei cowþen.
And so at þe laste þay sayden infere: 'þis is þe ymage of þat Ihesu þat
oure faderes deden to deth. Wherefore os þei dedyn to hys body, do
we to þis ymage.' þere þei tokyn þis ymage and blyndefelde hym and 110
buffettyd it and beton and bobbyd it, and aftyr beton it with scowreies
and crowned it with þornes, and aftyr dyd it on þe cros and nayled
hand and fotte þerto. And so at þe laste þei made þe strengeste man of
ham to take a spere and with alle hys myȝte þruston it to þe herte. And
anone whanne he dud so, blode and watyr ran oute downe be þe syde. 115
þen were þei alle sore agrysed of þat sythe and sayden: 'Take we a
pycher and fylle we it fulle of þe blode and bere we it into þe tempull
þat lygh ful of seke men of diuerse maledyes, and anoy[n]te we hem
with þis blode. And if þei bene hole, anone crye we: "Cryste, mercy",
and take we folth.' þan þei anoynted þese seke men with þis blode, 120
and þei anone were hole and sownde. þan wenton þeis Iewes to þe
byschoppe of þat cyte and tolden hym þe case how it befelle. And
whan he harde þat, he knelyd downe and thankyd God of hys hye
myrakyl. Ande whanne he hadde folowed þeis Iewes, he toke fy|alus f. 70ᵛ

87 Cauias antea *in top margin in scroll in red f. 70ʳ*   88 cristen] crsten   91 fro] for
97 nota *in margin in red, and* narracio *in later hand*   118 anoynte] anoyte

125 of cristal and of laumbor and of glasse and putte þis blode in ham and
send it aboute to diuers chirches, and of þis blode, os men vnderstand,
þe blode of Hayles com.

As Miletus telleth in hys cronicles, many ȝere aftyr þat Ierusalem
was stroyed, Iewes woldyn a beldyn it aȝeyne. þan os þei ȝode in a
130 morow þidyrwarde, þei fondon many crosys in þe dewe, so þat þei
weryn aferde and turnyd homwarde aȝeyne. þe oþer morow þei
comyn aȝeyne, and þanne were here c[loþ]us ful of crosus of rede
blode. And whanne þei syon þat, þei flowyn hom for fere. Ȝytte þei
wolde notte ben so warnyd bot com aȝeyn þe þrydday, and þan anone
135 sodeynly fyre rose vp owte of þe erþe and brente hem alle to askys, *et
cetera.*

f. 66ᵛ [34] *[Hic incipit aliud sermo], scilicet, dominica prima Quadragesime
ut supra: hoc modo.*

Hortamur vos ne in uacuum graciam Dei recipiatis, ad Corinthios vjº.
Gode men and wommen, þaise wordus þat I haue sayde in latyn bene
5 þus to sayne in englyse: we amonysche ȝow þat ȝe takon note þe grace
off God in vayne. þese bene þe wordus of Seynte Poule, Crystus holy
apostul, þat bene redde in þe pistul of þe day, be þe wyche wordus þis
holy apostul charguth alle Goddus pepul þat þei take hede whatte
grace God senduth hem and þat þei take notte þat grace in veyne.
10   God ȝeffuth grace to man alle tymes. But for a man neduth more
his grace þis tyme þan any oþur, þerfore off his hygh mercy he ȝeueth
f. 67ʳ now þeise dayes more habundawnte | off Lenton þan any oþur tyme,
þe whyche grace he partuth in þre wayus, þat is to sayne, in way off
gracious abydynge, in way off graciows demynge, and in way off
15 graciows amendus makynge. þeis þre wayus Godde senduth his grace
to ȝow now. Wherefore ryȝte os Seynte Poule monyche his disciplus,
ryte so I amonyche ȝow þat ben my childur in God, þat ȝe take not þis
grace of God in veyne.
   Ȝe haue a comyn sawe imonge ȝow and sayne þat Goddus grace is
20 worþe a new fayre. þan takuth hede how myche [worþe] Goddus
grace is: ffor þoff any of ȝow hadde also myche golde as a fayre is
worthe, but he hadde Goddus grace wit hit, hit schulde turne hym
more into schenscheppe þan into worchep. þis ȝe mowne sene be

132 cloþus] crosus
[34] 1 *Hic . . . sermo] canc. with* [cau]ias *and* nota *with red paraph cropped in margin*
3 *Hortamur]* H- *in blue, dec., 3 ll. deep*   20 worþe²] *om.*

verray reson þat Goddus grace is more worthe þan a new feyre. But
ȝitte ȝe schul know ffurre: ffor þoȝ a man hadde neuer so myche 25
ryches and prosperite here, þat comuth alle off Goddus grace, bot ȝiff
he take þat grace welle and plese his God witalle, hit schal turne hym
into dampnacion. But þan for þe pore pleynuth on þe ryche and sayne
þat þei bene vnkynde to God and þai done not os God bydduth hem
done and so ful helde sene a mote in anoþur mannus ee þat cannot 30
sene a be[m]e in here howne, þerefore ȝe schal knowon wel þat hit is a
special grace of God whan he makuth a man ryche and some men
pore. He makuth some ryche þat þe[i] wit here ryches schul sokur þe
pore in here nede and so wit here gode byggon hem hevon, and some
he makuth pore þat here pouerte schal bene here saluacion, ffor God 35
knoweth wel, þof þei were riche, þei wolde forȝeton here God and so
spyllon hemself. þus God ȝefuyth grace boþe to ryche and pore.

Wherefore we amonech ȝow boþe ryche and pore þat ȝe take [not]
þis grace of God in ydul ne in vayne. But he þat is ryche sette not his
herte þervpon but euer be in drede lest he mysse-spende hit, and þank 40
God off hys grace. And he þat is pore gru[c]he he not aȝeynus God ne
deme he not þe ryche man but take hys pouerte in paciens and þank
God off hys grace, for at þe last he schal fynde hit for þe best. But be a
man ryche or be he pore, ȝif he haue grace to se how myche he takuth
off God and how lytul he ȝelduth aȝayne, verray reson will tellon þat 45
he is more worthe dampnacion þan saluacion.

But for God is fful off grace and scheweth his grace to alle his
handy-werke and ffor he knowyth oure frellete, he hath com|passion f. 67ᵛ
of hus and ȝyff us his grace in abydynge off amendemente, þat is: þoȝ
þou trespas sore aȝeynus hym, he wil note smyte anone bot graciously 50
abyduth, ffor he hath myche leuer for to done grace þan vengaunce.
And þat is [for two] cause[s], as Seynte Austene saythe. On his: ȝiff
G[o]d hade takon vengaunce anone, þe worlde had ben endud many a
day agone, and so many one had ben vnborne þat [n]o[w] bene holy
seyntus in heuen. þe oþur cause is: for to schewon how ful he is of his 55
grace and how fayne he wil do off his grace and mercy to alle þat wil
levon evel and do gode. Wherefore he saythe þus be his profyte: *Nolo*
mortem peccatoris sed ut magis conuertatur et viuat. 'I wil not', he saþe,
'þat a synful man be dede, but I wil raþer þat he turne to God and
lyffe.' þus ȝe heruth how gracious God is in abydynge. 60

Whereffore I monas ȝow þat ȝe take not þis grace in vayne. But

---

31 beme] bene   33 þei] þer   38 not] *om.*   41 gruche] gruthe   52 for
two causes] þe cause   53 God] gad   54 now] þou

þenkuth welle how he hath sparud ȝow frome Astur hydurto, þareos
he myȝte be rythe a smyton ȝow wit his swerde off vengaunce vche
day, ffor, as Seynte Anselme sayth, þe leste synne þat a man doth hit
65 vnworcheputh God. þan ȝiff a man dud any þinge þat vnworschepud
his worlely kynge, he were worthi for to takon his deth. Myche more
þan is a man worthy þe deþ þat worcheppud not hym þat his Kynge
off heven and Lorde and Kynge off alle kynges. But rythe os he
passeth alle in dignite, rythe so he passuth alle in grace and in bownte.
70 But þoȝ ȝe felon hym gracious, be noȝte ȝe þe balder for to lyggon in
ȝoure synne, but hyȝeth ȝow for to klansse ȝow þeroff, ffor þoȝ he
byde longe, at þe laste he wil smyte suche þat wil noȝte amende hem,
and whan he smyteth, he smyteth sore.

Narracio. I rede þat þer was a knyte þat hadde no rentus off his
75 owne, bote he hade geton myche gode in werrus. And whan he hadde
alle spende owte, he ȝode and wedde a lady off þe cuntrey þat was
ryche inow. But þoȝ þis knyȝte were pore, ffor he was a semly man of
person, scheo sayde to hym þus: 'I wote welle þou arte a semly man of
body, bot for þou arte pore I may noȝte for schame take þe, bot ȝiff
80 þou haddust oþur myche golde or many rentus. But for þou hast no
golde, os I teche þe, do, and gete þe golde: goo into suche a place þer
many ryche marchawntes cometh and gete þe golde, and þan þou
schalte wedde me.' þan wente he þidur, and so happonud þat þere
f. 68ʳ come a ryche marchaunte þat way, | and he anone toke hym and sclow
85 hym and beryed hym, and bare forthe hys golde and come to þe lady
and sayde: 'Lo, þis some off golde I haue geton off suche a man and
beryed hym þare.' þan seyde þe lady: 'Go aȝeyne þis nyȝte and loke
ȝif þou owthe here.'

þan ȝode he forthe þat nyȝthe and stode be þe dede graue, and at
90 mydnyȝte þere come a lyȝte from hevene downe to þe graue. And þan
þe graue oponud and þe corse sette vp and helde vp hys handus to
God and sayde: 'Lorde þat arte ryȝtwys iuge, þou wreke me vpon þis
man þat hath þus falsly slayne me ffor my gode and for my trew
catelle.' And þerwit com a voyse frome heuen and sayde: þis day
95 thrytty wyntur he schulde haue vengawnce. þan þe cors thankud God
and lay downe aȝayne into his graue.

þan was þis knyȝte sore agaste and ȝode to þis lady and tolde hur
alle, and how þis voyce sayde how þat þat day thrytty wyntir he
schulde haue vengaunce. þan sayde þe lady: 'ȝa,' quothe scheo,
100 'mykul may fallon in xxx wyntur—gow we and be weddud.' So þay

74 Narracio bona *in margin in the long hand*

leuod infere xx wyntur in grete prosperite and in wele. But euer þis
knythe was adrade for þis vengaunce and sayde to þe lady: 'Now
twenty ʒere beth paste, and þe ten wil heye faste. What is þi best
counsayle?' þan sayde scheo: 'We schul make þis castelle als sykur and
also stronge as we may, and þat same day we schal gadur alle oure   105
frendus and stoffon hit with men inow, and so we schul schape welle
inogh', and deden soo.

Whan þe day come, þei gaderud a grete summe of men into þe
castell and setton hem to þe mete and madyn alle þe myrþe þat þei
cowþen. þan was an harper and harpud allegatus at þe mete. But for   110
þer may no wykkud sprytus come þere nyʒe no haue no powste as fer
as þe harpe is harde, þere come a boy owte off þe kychon, a broþell alle
bawded wit gresse, and rubbud hys stryngus wit his bawdy handus.
þan was þis harper wode wrothe and wit his harpe wolde a smyton þis
broþel, but for he flow faste away, þe harper sued hym owte off þe   115
castelle. And whan he come owte off þe castul, þis broþelle vanyschud
away. þan þis harper turnud aʒeyne and segʒh how þis castul sankke
into þe erþe alle on fyre. þus ʒe may se, ʒow God abyde longe, at þe
last he smyteth sore. Wherefore I amonesch ʒow þat ʒe take noʒte his
grace off abydinge in vayne, but bethenkuth ʒow welle off alle ʒowre   120
mysse-dedus and comyth be tyme and schryue ʒow.

For | God ʒyff ʒow also a hygh grace of demynge, ffor þere þar he [is   f. 68ᵛ
i]s trowthe and rythewysnesse, and may not demon bot wit rythewysnesse, and þan schulde þor nere no man schapon vndampnud. For os
Iob saythe: þow we woldyn stryue wit hym, whe may not answere of   125
one godde dede for a þowsande þat he ʒef vs. þus for he sethe þat no
man myʒte scapon his dome vndampnud, þerfore he of hys hye grace
he ʒeveth hys power to a curator for deme mekly alle þat comon to hym
h[au]ynge ferme and stabul [feith in] alle þat he doth, os þus: þere schal
no gode dede be vnquytte ne none evol vnponychud. þerfore ʒyf a   130
curatur ʒif þe þe more penaunce þan þe neduth, þat is more hit schal be
quite and stand þe in grete ioy off encres before God. ʒeff he ʒeffuth
evon, þou arte quit. But ʒiff he ʒeff þe to lytul, þan schalt þou þat haste
to lytul bene ffulfyllud in purcatory. So þat a man schal neuer be
dampnud for no synne þat he is mekly schryuon off and takuth his   135
dome mekely off his schryfte-fadur, ffor alle þing þat is not klansud
here be schryfte and penaunce schal be klansud in purgatory, ffor whan
þou comust to schryfte, þou comest for to be demud off þi schryfte-
fadur. Wherefore God wil note deme þe twye for one þinge.

122 For] ffor *rep. next line*   122–3 is is] as   129 hauynge] honynge   feith in] *om.*

140 þan takuth hede wyche an heyghe grace God ȝevoth ȝow in
demynge, whan he ordeyneth a synful man as þou arte to bene þi
domus-man, for alle his in hegh help to ȝow for to ȝevon boldenesse to
ȝow for to tellon owte alle þat lythe in ȝowre herte and noþinge for to
hyde. For alle þat is now helud in schryfte schal be at þe day of dome
145 knowon to alle þe worlde with myche confusyon, and þan schal he þat
heluth bene demod off God þerfore into þe fyre off helle. þe[r]fore þe
apostul saythe þus: '*Horrendum est incidere in manus Dei omnipotentis*',
þat is to say: hit is horribul and grysly to fallon into Goddus handus.
Wherefore I amonysche ȝow þat ȝe take not þis grace of demynge in
150 veyne, but schryue ȝow clene and leuith noȝte hydde in ȝoure herte.

Narracio. For þus I rede of a womman þat hadde done an horrybul
synne ande myȝte neuer for schame schryue hur þeroff. And ofte whan
scheo come to schryffte, scheo was in purpose to haue bene schryvon,
f. 69ʳ but euer þe fende putte suche a schame in hir herte þat scheo | hadde
155 neuer grace to clanse hur þeroff. þan on a nyȝte os scheo lay in hur
bedde and þowthe myche of þat synne, Ihesus Cryste com to hur and
sayde: 'My dowthtur, why wilte þou noȝte schew me þi herte and
schryuen þe of þat synne þat lythe þerinne?' 'Lorde,' quoth scheo, 'I
may noȝte for schame.' þan sayde Cryste: 'Schew me þi hande', and
160 toke hur hande and put hit into his syde and drow hit owte alle blady,
and sayde: 'Be þou no more aschamud to opon þi herte to me þan I am
to opon my syde to þe.' þan was þis womman agrysud off þe blode and
wolde a wassone hit away but scheo myȝte notte be no way tul scheo
wore schryuen of þat synne. þan whan scheo was schryven, anone þe
165 hande was whyte os þat oþur. þus God dothe grace in esy demynge.

He doth also grace in amendus makynge, wil, for a lytul penaunce
þat a man doþe here, Godde forȝeueth hym þe grete penawnce in
helle and also settuth a man at large for to do his penawnce and notte
in distress, but ȝeueth hym choyse wheþur he wyl do hys penawnce
170 mekely wit gode wylle or none. And ȝif he wil mekly done hys
penawnce, he wil forȝevon hym his gylte and makon hym more chere
to hym þan he dud before and avawncen hym in þe courte off heuen.
And þoȝ he wolde do no penawnce but prudly put hit away, ȝitte into
hyis deth-day he abyduth fro ȝere to ȝere to loke ȝif he wil amende.
175 And ȝef he wil not, þan he wil make byndon hande and fotte and
caston hym into hys preson, þat is into þe payne off helle, and so his
he wille worthy.

144 For] ffor   146 þerfore] þe fore   151 Narracio *in margin in the long hand*
For] ffor   166 makynge] he *add.*

þus, gode men, 3e haue herde how God 3effuth 30w grace in þre
wayes: in graciows abydynge, in gracious demynge, and in gracius
amendus makynge, ffor graciously he abyduth and wil note take 180
vengawnce anone, but euer abyduth amendement; and graciusly he
wil þat a man be demud wit mercy and not to vturmast here; and
gracius[ly] he takuth a mannus amendus, wille for penaunce of a
schorte tyme he for3eveth hym þe penawnce þat euor schal last. And
afftur þat he hath done hys penawnce, he for3eveth hym alle hys gylte 185
and avawnceth hym in þe courte off heuen. For þus muche I presume
of Goddus grace and his mercy, þat þe fende off helle, and he wolde
aske mercy wit a meke herte off Godde, God wolde 3evon hym mercy.
þan myche more he wil 3euon a man mercy þat he sched his herte-
blode fore, and hereoff I wil 3eue 30w ensampul. 190

    Narracio, and make an ende. I rede þere wheron twey chapmen
dwellynge besyde þe cite off Norwyche, off þe whyche one was a gode
lyuer and þat oþur a cursud lyuer. But for þis gode man | dursnot f. 69ᵛ
departe from þat oþur as ofte os he durste, he conseylud hym for to
schryuen hym and amende hym off hys lyuyng. þan þat oþur wolde 195
answere and sayde how hit where tyme inow for to schryuon whan he
schulde dyen. þan hyt fel aftur so þat þis evel man fel sek and lay in
hys deth-bedde. And whan hys felow knew, he cryud on hym faste
and 3arne for to schryvon hym and send afftur hys preste, for he was
bot dede. But þat oþur euer prudly sayde nay: for he wyst wel inow 200
þat God wolde 3ef hym no mercy for hys longe abydynge. þan þis
gode man was wondur sory for hym and ma[d]e [fecche] prestus and
frerus and alle þat he hopud þat wolde haue holpon hym þere [and]
cownseylud hym to gode. But euer he made þe same answere to hem
as he dud to þe gode man, and sayde he wolde not schryuen hym ne 205
none mercy askon.
    þan hadde þis man a lawmp brennynge ny3tus before hys bedde,
and in a bedde besydus hym lay oþur two men to wakon hym. þan
abowte mydny3te þay saw Ihesu Cryste bodely wit blody wondys
standynge before þe seke mannus bedde and sayde to hym þus: 'My 210
son,' quoth he, 'why wyl þou not schryue þe and put þe into my
mercy, þat am redy algatus for to 3eue þe mercy to alle þat wyl mekely
asku[n] mercy?' þan sayde he: 'For I wote wel þat I am vnworthy for
to haue mercy. Wherefore þou wylte 3eue me none.' '3us, sone, for

---

183 graciusly] gracius   amendus] þat *add.*   186 For] ffor   191 Narracio *in*
margin in the long hand   202 made fecche] make   203 and²] *om.*   213 askun]
askum   For] ffor

215 soth, ask hit mekly and þou schalte haue.' And euer he answerud as he
    dud before. þan Cryste toke owte off hys wownde in his syde his
    hande ful of blode and sayde: 'Ʒow fendus schylde, þis schal be redy
    tokun betwyx þe and me in þe day off dome þat I wolde haue ʒevon þe
    mercy and þou woldust notte', and þerwit cast þe blode into his face.
220 And þerwit anone þis seke man cryed and sayde: 'Allas, allas, I am
    dampnud for ay', and so dyed. þan þis oþur men was so aferde off þis
    sythe and off boþe here speche þat hit was longe or þei dud ryson. þan
    at þe laste he rosse up and lyʒte a candul at þe lawmp and com to his
    felow and fonde hym dede, and þe rede blode in hys face and alle þe
225 body as blak as spyche. þan þis man for ferde cryed aftur helpe, and
    when men comyn, he tolde hem þe case and how Cryste dud to hym
    and how he answerud aʒayne.
        Wherefore I amonest ʒow þat ʒe tak not his grace in vayne, but
    schryue ʒow clene of ʒoure synnus and put ʒow fully into hys mercy
230 and into hys grace. And þan wyl he take ʒow into his grace and to hys
    mercy, and bryng ʒow to þe ioy þat euer schal laston, þe whyche ioy
    God graunte ʒow and me. Amen. *In nomine patris et filii et spiritus
    sancti.* Amen. |

f. 70ᵛ   [35] *De sancto Iohanne ante Portam Latinam*

    Suche a day ʒe schul haue Seynte Iones at þe Porte Latyn day, þe
    wyche day ʒe schul *et cetera*.
        Why þis day is called so ʒe schal heron. As þis holy seynte prechud
5   Goddys worde in a cyte þat was callud Ephesy, þe iustyce of þat cite
    see þat Sent Ione turnyd þe pepul faste to Cristes feythe, wherefore he
    wolde han made hym to haue done sacrifice to his falce goddys. And
    for he wolde note, bote rathar lese hys lyfe þan don suche a synne
    before God, þis iustice made to take hym and commanded to put hym
10 into preson, whyl he sent to þe emperoure of Rome to wytte whate he
    schulde do with hym. So whan hys letteres comyn to þe emperoure, in
    þe whyche letteres he called Ion all þat noght was—wyche and traytor
    and trulur and desyver of þe pepul, þan þe emperoure wrote aʒeyun
    to þe iustice and bade sende Ione to Rome, and so he dudde.
15   And whan he was comyn þidir and aposyd of hys doing, and for he
    stode stedefaste in þe lawe of Criste, for grete scorne þe emperoure
    made to clyp away þe herus of Seynt Iones hede, for he hadde a fayre

    [35] 2 Suche] S- *in blue, dec., 2 ll. deep*

heued of fax. þanne whan he was so clypped, alle men lowen hym to scorne ande dede hym desese. þan was he, so forscornyd, lade to a ȝate of þe cyte of Rome, þat was calyd Porte Laton, and þer was a 20 tonne of bras ful of walmyng oyle, þe wyche tonne he was put in and closyd þerin, and a hotte fyre vndyr. And so þei weren ȝerne aboute þat Iohne schuld haue ben brente þerin. But for he was Goddys owne derlyng, he kep hym so þat he felde no peyne. þan for alle men wende þer he hadde ben dede and alle sodon to poudyr, þei vndedon þe 25 tonne and sen Ione also hole and sownde in yche party of hys body and of hys cloþus, as nothyng hadde towchyd hym. Wherefore cristen men makyd þere a chyrche in worchep of God and of Seynt Ione and in memory of þe martyrdam þat he suffered þere.

þenne for þe emperoure sey þat he mythe notte ourecom | Sent Ion f. 71ʳ [for fe]re of no penaunce, he makyd for to exilon hym into an yle þat is 31 called Phatmos. þanne herde Seynt Iones modyr how hir son was sent to Rome for to haue ben done to deth, and for grete sorow and compasion of hym scheo ȝode aftyr hym to Rome. Bot whan scheo harde þat he was sent into exul, scheo turnyd aȝeyne homwarde. And 35 whan scheo com to a cyte was called Vetula[n], þer scheo felle seke and dyed and was byried besyde þe cyte vndir a roche. And whan scheo hadde lyne þer many ȝerus, Sent Iames, hyr odur sone, com þidir and toke vp his modur body, þat smellyd as swete os any spicery, and browte it into þe cite, and beryed it with grete honoure and 40 worchep.

In þe lyf of Seynt Edwarde þe kyng þat lyth at Westmynster, I fynde þat þis holy kyng loued so Seynt Ione þe euangelyste þat he wolde warne no pore man þat he askyd for Seynt Iones sake. þan it fel on a hegh haly-day, as þis kyng ȝode in procession, Seynt Ione cam to 45 hym in lycones of a pylgrym and prayed to ȝevon hym som gode for Seynte Iones loue. þan þe kyng at þat tyme hadde no noþer þing at þat tyme redy, [bot] he toke þe ring of hys fingur and ȝaf to þe pylgryme.

þan sone aftyr too knytes of þis kynges housalde ȝedon to 50 Ierusalem on pylgrymage. And whanne þei com negh þidur, os it happyd ham, þanne þei lafton here company and ȝedon hemself tyl it was nyghte. And whanne it was nyght, it was so darke þat þei myght neyþer sene oþer for darke. Wherefore þei weren alle dyswary of hemself, and os þei stodyn þus alle adredde talkyng infere, þer cam be 55

hem an alderen man with glade chere and semly of persone, with too
chylderen bryngyng too torches beforon hym, þe wyche spake to þeise
men in Englys and sayde: 'Heyle, syres. Why stande ȝe here þis tyme
of þe nyght? and of whatte contre ben ȝe of?' Ȝen sayde þay: 'We
60 standen here for we ben al dyswary of oure way, and we ben
pylgrymes and men of Engelande and woldyn fayne haue herbar for
of oures.' þan sayde þis man to ham: 'How fareth þe kyng of
Engeland?' þan sayde þai þat he ferde wel, os þei hopyd, for he
was a gode man and an holy, os þei vndyrstode. þan sayde þis man to
65 ham: 'Syres, for þe kynges sake commeth now with me and ȝe schal
haue herbar and gode ese', and so lade hem forþe into a fayre place
and makyd hem wel at ese in alle degre.

On þe morow he was redy and browte þis men on hur way, and
sayde þus to ham: 'Greteth wel ȝoure kyng of Engelande on þis
70 token', and betoke ham a ring and badde hem bere to þe kyng: 'And
byd hym bethenk hym wel for whos lof he gaf it away, þat was Seynt
Ion euangelyst, and byd hym makyn hym redy, for within sexe
f. 71ᵛ moneth aftur | ȝe comen hom, he sal be dede and com to me, and
ȝe sal gone hom sounde and saf in alle prosperite.' So whan þeise men
75 comon hom, þei dedon here mesage os þei were bedon and betokyn þe
kyng hys ryng. þan knelud þe kyng adoun on hys kneus and þankyd
God and Seynt Ione. þen whoso lyst to haue þis preued, for soth go to
Westemynstyr, þere he may see þe same.

[36] *De rogacionibus sermo breuis: hoc modo.*

Gode men, þeis þre dayes suyng, Monday, Tuesday and Wednesday,
ȝe schul fastyn and com to chyrche, husbond, wyf and seruande, for
alle we ben syngeres and neduth to haue mercy of God. Wherefore
5 rythe os a man may notte excusyn hym of synne, ryght so Holy
Chyrche ordeyneth þat none schal excuson hym from þeise proces-
siones þat may godely ben þer.

þan he þat withdraweth hym from Holy Chyrche þes dayes he
synguth greuesly before God and alle hys seyntys. Furste he synguth
10 in pride, for he is vnbuxum to God and hys seyntus and to Holy
Chyrche, not doing here commandement. He synguth also in slowth,
þat wotteth hymselfe in synne and wyl not com to Holy Chyrch to
pray to God and hys holy seyntus to ȝeue hym grace and sokor and
remission. He synguth also grettely to absenton hym from Goddys

[36]   2 Gode] G- *in blue, dec., 2 ll. deep*   6 þeise] procession *add.*

seruyce in due tyme. Wherefore rythe os he withdraweth hym 15
wylfully from þe company of Godys pepul þat ben gedered to serue
God in holy tyme, rythe [so] God wyl departe hem from þe company
of heuen and from þe suffrages þat ben done in Holy Chyrch, til he
com to amendement. Wherefore yche man and woman enforce hym
for to com to chyrch þeis dayes and prey deuowtely to holy seyntys of 20
heuen þat þei now helpyn vs in oure nede, os þei woldyn somtyme
haue ben holpyn whanne þei were lyuing here in erþe at here nede.

þan for we alle syngen in þre wayes, þat is, in thowte, in worde and
dede, we schul fasten þeise þre dayes and done oþer penaunce
withineforth with prayer and fastyng and put away þe power of þe 25
fende, for God forȝeuyth man hys gylte and alle þe angelles of heuen
ben makyd gladde and ioyful. þus schul ȝe furste prey to God for
remyssion of ȝoure synnes and sythen to ben holpyn and sokored in
diuorse myscheues and pereles þat falleth namely in þis tyme of þe
ȝere more þan any oþer tyme. For now thunderes ben oftyn herde and 30
þan, os Lincolniencis sayth, fendes þat floteren in þe eyre, for fer of
þat berste of þundyr þat Cryste com to helle-ȝates with and al to-drof
ham, ȝete þe fendes ben so agaste whan þei heryn þondur þat þei
fallyn doun to þe erþe and þan þei goth notte vp aȝeyne tyl þei done
sum wykkyd dede. þan þei reren werres, makyth tempeste | in þe see, f. 72ʳ
drowneth schyppes and men; þei makyth debates betwyssen negh- 36
burres and manslawtes þerewith; þei tendon fyres and brennyn
howses and townes; þei reren wyndes and tempestes and bloweth
down howses, stepulles and trees, and þei makyth womman to oure-
lygge her schylder; þei make men to sclen hemself, hongyn hemself, 40
or drown hemself in wanope, ande suche oþer many cursyd dedys.
þus for to putte away alle suche wykkyd dedys, pereles and
myschefys, Holy Chyrch ordeyneth vche man to faste þese þree
dayes and to gon in processyoun to aske help and sokur of God and
seyntus of heven. 45
Wherefore in processyon bellys ryngyn, baneres bene borne before,
þe cros comyth aftyr, and þe pepul sueth. For ryght as a kyng, whan
he goth to batel, trumpes gone before, banerus bene sprad and cometh
aftyr, þan comyth þe kyng and his oste aftyr, suyng hym, rythe so in
Crystes batel þe belles ben Goddes trumpes ryngyng, þe baneres ben 50
vnfowldyn and opynly borne on heght in þe eyre, þan þe cros in
Cry[s]tes lyknes commeth os kyng of cristen men, and his oste, þat is

17 so] *om.*   35 werres] þ *add.*   52 Crystes] crytes   os] cristen *add. and canc.*
is] þis

cristen pepul, sueth hym. þus he dryueth þe fend oute of hys
lordeschep and reueth hym hys power. And os a tyrande wolde sore
55 drede and he herde þe trumpes of a kyng þat were hys enmye and see
hys baner displayed in þe felde, rythe so þe fende, þe cursyd tyrand of
helle, dreduth hym wondor sore qwan he heruth þe kynges trumpes
of heuen ryngon and crossos and baneres borne abowte. For þis cause,
whan any tempest is, men vseth to ryngon belles and so to dryuen þe
60 fende away.

At þe cyte of Constantyn, as men wenton in procession for a grete
fraye and a dysese þat þe pepul hadde and was in, þei songon þe
letanye. Sodenlyche a chylde was pullyd vp into þe ayre and so in to
heven, and þer angellus tawt hym to syngyn þis song: *Sancte deus,*
65 *sancte, fortis, sancte et immortalis, miserere nobis.* And anone he was
fayre laton doun ayeyne to þe erþe. þan he song þat same song and
anone þei weren holpyn. þan is þis to sayne in Englys: 'Holy God,
holy, strong, holy and neure sal dye, haue mercy on vs.' God wyllyth
þat we ben holy, and he wylleth þat we ben strong to fyght with þe
70 fende, with þe worlde, and with oure owne flesse, and þan wyl he haue
mercy on vs and bryngon vs into þe londe of lyf *et cetera.*

[37] *De ascencione domini sermo utilis*

Gode men, þis day is a hegh day and holy fest in alle Holy Chyrche.
For þis day, os þe feythe of Holy Chyrch beleueth and prechuth,
f. 72ᵛ Criste, Goddys Sone of heuen, veri God and man, stegh vp in|to
5 heuen and syttyth þere on hys Fadir ryghte hande in þe blysse þat
eure schal laston. Wherefore in tokenyng of þis þing, þe paschal, þat is
þe schef lyght in Holy Schyrch þat hath standon fro Astur hydirto
oponly in þe quere, þis day is remevyd away in schewing þat Cryste,
þat is chef lytght of Holy Chyrch and hath þis fourety dayes opynly
10 apered to hys discipulys many wayes and tawthe hem þe fayth, þis day
stay up into heuen and þer schal abyde til þe day of dome.

Botte now ȝe schal heryn þe maner of hys ascensioun. Fro Astur
[Day] to þis day he was notte algate wyth hys disciplus botte apered to
hem diuerse tymes. But þis day he aperud to ham os þei syton at here
15 mete, and þere he ete with hem to schewe þat he was very man in
flesse and blode as þei weren. For som of hem ȝitte þidur werun in
dowte and wend he hadde ben a spryte, þat hath no blode nor flesse.

Wherefore to preue þe sothe and to put hem oute of al maner dowte
he ette with hem in here syghte, and so badde þem gon into þe hylle of
Olyvete. And þer in syght of alle hys dysciplus he blessyd hem and so 20
stey vp into heven, and þer lefte þe steppus of hys fette þruste doun
into þe harde ston, and eure ben sene. þen schul ye know þat þe tre of
olyve burgeneth oyle, and þat betokeneth mercy. Wherefore [Criste]
stegh vp in [þe] hul of Olyvete, schewing opynly þat he is heued of
mercy and is euer redy to ȝef mercy to alle þat askuth it with meke 25
herte. þan in hys vp-stying, þat is kalde ascencion, angelus makyth
suche melody þat no tong may telle, so fayne þei weren of here Lordys
comyng.

He steyed vp swyftely, for os it were in a moment he was fro erþe
into heven. A grete phylosophur Raby Moyses seyth þat hit is as fer 30
fro erthe to heven as an hol man myth lyvon a thowsand ȝere and iche
day gone a thowsand myle. But he þat mette þis way he knew beste
and cowde best tellyn þe myles and þe lengh of ham. þan in hys
ascencion he hadde with hym a grete multitude of sowles, þe wyche
he fette oute of helle from þe fendus bondam. 35

He stey up also wyth hys wondys rede and fresch and blody, and so
os Bede sayth for fyve causus. þe formest is for to verifyen þe feyth of
hys resurrexion, for he ros in very flesse and blode þat dyed on þe
cros. þe secunde: for to schewyn hys wondes to hys Fadyr in helpe of
mankynde. þe þrydde: for to schewen þat men schuldyn sene how 40
mercyful he is to saven. þe fourth: þat [e]le men schuldyn sene how
ryghtfully þei ben dampnyd. þe fyfte: þat he may beren with hym þe
syne of perpetual victory.

He stey also to make a sykurnesse to alle mankynde. For rythe os a
lorde is sykur þat hath algate a sykur avokette and trew beforen a iuge 45
to answere [for] hym, so in sykurnesse [of] alle mankynde we haue
hym oure trewe avokette euremore redy to answere for vs at vche
apechyng þat oure enmy makyth aȝeynus vs. Wherefore Seynte
Barnarde saythe þus: 'A sykur accesse may man | haue to God, f. 73ʳ
where þe Modur scheweth hyr So[n]e [hyr] brestys and hyr pappes, 50
and þe Son scheweth to þe Fadyr hys beton sydes and blody
woundes.' þan how schulde he be put away þat hath suche too
frendes in þe cowrete of heven, and nexte frendes, and moste mon do
with þe kyng?

Also be þe steying of Cryste into heven man hath getyn a grete 55

dignite in heven, for it is a grete dignite for a man to sene hys owne
kyn, þat is hys flesse and hys blode, syttyn at þe rythe hande of þe
Fadyr of heven in hys trone. Wherefore angelys, considering þat
dignite of man now, þei wil notte suffyr man to done hem no
60 worschep os þei dydyn before þe incarnacion, bot þei worschep
men in reuerence of mankynde þat God Ihesu hath in heven
bodyly. Here may a man sene how moche he is holdyn to God, þat
was beforen bonde and þralle and vndirlyng to þe fende of helle, and
now hath made hym of suche fredam and dignite þat angellus schul
65 done hym reuerence ande worschep and seruyse. And þeros angelus
sum tyme kepton þe ȝates of paradyse with brennyng swerdys þat no
sowle myght comyn in, now Criste hath kaste [o]pon þe ȝates and
warneth entre to none þat is stedefaste in þe beleve. For þus sayth
Seynt Austyn: *Aperuisti credentibus regna celorum*, þou hast openyd þe
70 kyngdam of heuen to hem þat leuyth.

ȝe schul also wytyn þat rythe os a kyng of þis worlde hath in hys
courte officeres hyer and lower and som nerrar and more priuyer þan
oþer, rytgh so þe kyng of heuen hath in hys courte angelus, summe
lower and sume hyer and som more pryuey þan somme. Wherefore in
75 steying vp of oure Lorde Ihesu Cryste þe lowe angellus, for a grete
wondur þat þei hadde in Crystes ascencion whan þei seyn hym in
flesche and blode bodyly steyen vp with so grete multitud[e] of
angelus makyng melody and so grete multitud[e] of sowles with
hem, and also for grete wondyr þat þei haddyn whan þei sene fendes
80 of þe ayre flene away for grete drede þat weren wonte with grete pryde
assayle alle soules withoute sparyng, and also alle gode angelus in alle
þe haste þat þei mython þei comyn to `do' Criste seruice and
reuerens, þus for grete wondur þat þeise lower angellys haddyn þei
askyn þe hyer angelus and saydyn þus: 'Whate hys þis þat comyth
85 owte of þe worlde with blody cloþus, as he were kyng of ioy?' [þan
saydyn þe hyer angelus to hem þus: 'þis is þe Lord of all vertu and is
also þe Kyng of ioy.] þus is he þat is wyt of hys modyr, rody in hys
skorgyng, sek in þe cros, strong in helle, lodly in dying, fayre in hys
rysyng, ourecomer of his enemy, and now hys Kyng glorious in
90 heuen.'

þus whan Cryste was steyed into heuen and hys dysciplus stodyn
with his modyr, for grete wondur þat þei haddyn of syght and of
f. 73ᵛ heryng, þei lokyd | vp into heuen, and sodenly too angelus clothyd in

---

67 opon] vpon   77 multitude] multitudo   78 multitude] multitudo
85–7 þan . . . ioy] *om.*

whyte stodyn by hem and sayden: 'Men of Galile, whate stande ȝe þus
lokyng vp to heuen? Ryȝte os ȝe sene Ihesu ȝoure Lorde steyen into 95
heuen, rythe so he schal cum at þe day of dome aȝeyne to demon þe
quyk and þe dede.' Rythe so lyfte up ȝoure hertys to Ihesu Cryste þat
now syttyth in heuen at hys Fadir ryght hand redy to ȝevyn mercy to
alle þat asken it with meke herte, so þat ȝe mown haue none
excusacion bot þat ȝe mon ben sauyd, and ȝe wyllen. For þow a 100
man and a womman ben neure so synful, and þei wyl askyn mercy
with meke herte, he wil ȝeuen hym mercy and takyn hym to hym.

þan for to schewyn þe grete godenesse of hym and how grete
compasion he hath of mankynde, I telle ȝow þis ensaumpul: It was
sum tyme, os we redyn in þe lyf of Seynte Karpe, how a mys-beleued 105
man turnyd a cristen man oute of hys fayth to hys mysbeleue.
Wharefore þis holy man Karpe was so wroth þat he fel into a grete
sekenesse, and whan he schulde haue prayed for hur amendement, he
prayed bysily day and nyght to God þat he moste sene hem haue
bodyly veniauns. þan os he prayed þus at mydnyght, sodenly þe 110
houce þat he was inne clef on too, and he sawe an hoged howuen
brennyng so spytusly þat wondur was to sene. þan lokyd he vp to
heuen and saw Ihesus with grete multitud[e] of angelus syttyng in hys
trone. And þan he lokyd aȝeyun and þan he sawe þeis too men
stondyng before þis owen, quakyng and tremelyng for grete fere and 115
drede, and nedderes and brenny[n]g wormys comyng oute of þe ovene
to drawen þese men in wyt hem into þe ovene, and oþer fendys comyn
and holpyn to puttyn on with.

þan was þis Carpe so fayne of þeise mennus venieauns þat he lafte
þe fayre syght of oure Lorde Ihesu Criste and of hys angellus and 120
lokyd alle to þeise mennus vengeauns and was wrothe þat þei taried to
be putte in here penaunce, þat he sette to hande hymselfe and halpe
whatte he myghe. And whan þei weryn in þis fyre, þan lokyd he vp to
Criste and sey hym for grete compassion þat he hadde of þeis men
rysyn up from hys trone, and cam doun to þeise men and toke hem 125
oute of heyre peyne and sayde þus to Karpe: 'Stresche forth þine
hande and fyghte aȝeynus me. I am ȝitte redy, and nede were, to dyon
eftonsones for mankynde.' Be þis ensaumpul ȝe mowen wel knowyn
how redy God hys to alle þat wil askyn hym mercy and deseruyth to
haue mercy. He is worthy to haue mercy þat is sory for his trespase 130
and is in ful wylle to amendon hym, *et cetera.*

---

113 multitude] multitudo   116 brennyng] brennyg

[38] *De vigilia Pentecostes sermo*

Gode cristyn creatures, on Saturday nexte comyng, os ȝe knowen

f. 74ʳ welle, wil be Whytson Even, | þe wyche day ȝe schul alle faston and
comyn to chyrch to sene and heren þe seruice þat schal be sayde in
5   Holy Chyrch þat day. Ȝe schal alle make ȝow redy and clene in sowle
þat ȝe may be redy þat day to reseyue þe Holy Goste þat þe Fadir of
heuen sendeth among mankynde.

Wherefore I charge ȝow, if þer be any man or womman þat is fallyn
in any grevous synne, þat ȝe comyn to me and clanse ȝow þerof or
10 Sonday comme, and I wil be redy to help in alle þat lythe in me wyth
gode wylle. For takuth in sertaynn, rythe os a man of ȝow wil note go
into a place þeras is stynkyng careyn, bote he stoppe hys nese and hye
hym þennes, ryght so þe Holy Goste fleght fro þe soule þat is
combred wyth dedly synne and alle angelus wyth, stoppyng þer
15 nese. For myche more fouler dedly synne stynkyth in þe nese of God
and of angelus þan doth any careyne in oure neses. And ryght os þe
Holy Goste fleth fro hem þat be[n] combered in dedly synne, ryght so
he hyeth to hem þat ben in clene lyf and in charite to God and to man,
and haue mercy in herte and compassion of hem þat ben in myschef
20 and dysese. To suche þe Holy Gost commyth, suche he visiteth,
suche he loueth, wyth suche he hath lyste and lykyng to abyde, and
techeth hem and comforteth hem in alle here nede.

But at þe seruice of þat fest he is more preysed þan anoþer tyme,
for at þe fest alle Holy Chyrche spekyth of hym and specialy calleth to
25 hym to haue helpe and grace and parte of þe dole þat he makyth þan
to alle hem þat ben abul to reseyve his ȝeftys. But ȝe schal undirstande
þat þe Holy Gost makyth hys dole oþer wayes þan men don. For þei
doluth vche man, more and lesse, yle[c]he myche. But þc Holy Gost
deluth to vche man þat is spedeful to ham and ȝeuyn som more,
30 somme lasse, somme of one ȝefte and somme of anoþer.

Somme a ȝeuyth grace of wysdom and makyth hem clerkys and wyse
in holy scripture, and ȝefeth hem so grete sauoure and lykyng þerine,
þat þei ben lusty to prechyn and techen þe vertu and þe grace þat þei
felon þerine. Bote for þei ben wyse, þei done it in tyme and to suche þat
35 þei hopyn þat wollyn beren it away wyt hem. For somme settyn noght
be Goddys worde but haddyn lere heren a tale of rybbaudy þan it.
Wherefore to suche Goddys worde schal not ben preched.

Somme he ȝaf grace of vndirstandyng, þat not only vndyrstandyn here owne [langage but also oþur] langage of frenche or romayne wythoute any travayle o[f] leryng it. þis is a grete ȝefte of God þat iche 40 man kan vndyrstande oþur in spekyng. For fyve letteres makyth vche worde of alle þe langages þat ben vndyr heven vn|dyrstondyn, and f. 74ᵛ wythoute one of þeise fyve letteres þer may no man know whate anoþer spekyth, and þeise ben þe letteres: A, E, I, O, V.

And somme he ȝeveth grace of counsel, somme to 'ȝeue' counsel, 45 and somme to don aftyr counsel. Somme he enspireth wythinne-forthe, þat he scheweth hem and makyth hem to know before whate wyl fallyn aftyr and ȝeueth hem dyscrecion to deme þe gode fro þe ele and þe bettur be þe worse. Wherefore þei ben so wyse and ware in counseling þat vche man is lusty to here hem speke and to haue 50 counsel of hem. Somme he ȝeueth grace to do aftyr counsel þat Criste ȝaf hymself, consaylyng a man þat wol ben perfyte to leve all þat he hath and gon to relygion and þer ben ladde and gouerned be hys wardeynes counsel and not be hys owne. þis counseyl comyth of God, and wel is hym þat may performe itte. 55

Some he ȝeueth grace of strenche, boþe in body and in sowle, to bere mekely and in gladde schere grete bodyly harmys and diuerse sekenesse and losse of godde and catell and of frenschep. He hath a special ȝefte of þe Holy Goste þat may beren suche burþenus wyth esy herte, þankyng God þereof. 60

He ȝeueth also grace of diuerse sciens in lernyng of diuerse craftys, and somme to lerne one and somme anoþer, so þat vche man [hath] be ȝefte of þe Holy Gost grace to lerne a sciens be þe wyche he may geton hys lyflode in trewth.

Somme he ȝeuith grace in pyte and fylleth here herte so wyth pyte 65 and compassion of alle þat ben in desese and in myschef þat þei ȝevyn hem of þere gode and helpyn hem in here nede and seruyth hem in þat þei may done as þagh þei haddon Criste in presens before hem, and haue suche herte of mercy þat þei ben eure redy to forȝevyn alle þat trespase to ham. 70

Somme he ȝeueth grace to drede God so þat þei haue eure in herte [þe] hegh vengeans þat Cryste schal ȝeu to þilk þat ben euyl at þe day of dome and þe horybul peynus of helle þat neure schal haue ende, whereþorogh þei ben adrade day and nyght to done anythyng amys and ben eure bysy to done eure wel, also wel in priuete in sygh of God 75

39 langage . . . oþur] om.   40 of] or   62 hath] om.   72 þe¹] om.   hegh] in add.

and angelus os in opyn place in syght of men. þan he þat hath þis
ȝyfte [h]e is my[che] holdyn to thank þe Holy Gost, for þis is a special
ȝyfte of hym and fewe ben þat þis ȝefte haue.

þeis bene þe seuen ȝyftis of þe Holy Goste. þese þe Holy Goste
80 departeth among mankynde, and ȝy[ff]e somme more and somme
lasse so þat none may bene excused bot he hath somwhatte of þese
ȝeftus. And þese þe Holy Goste assyneth to vche man in tyme of hys
cristening. Wherfore þe byschopp whan he confermeth chyldryn þat
ben follod, [h]e rehers[yth] þeis ȝeftys, praying þe Holy Goste to
85 confermyn hem aftur in here lyving þat be assyned to ham in here
cristening.

f. 75ʳ   þan to styr ȝoure deuocion þe more to þis holy | sacrament, I telle
ȝow þis ensaumpul in þe lyf of Seynt Remys þat was a holy byschop
and turnyd Lewys þe kyng of Fraunce to cristen fayth. And whan þe
90 kyng com to be folowod, at þe font-halowyng was grete prese of
pepul, þat þe byschoppes clerke þe wyche bare hys crismatory myght
not be no way bryngyn it to þe byschep. þan whan þe font was
halowod to þe vyntyng wyth creme and myuth not com þertoo, he
lyfte vp hys hande to God, preyng hym devoutely of help. þan
95 þerwyth anone þer com fleying fro heven in syght of alle þe pepul a
colvyr as whyte os mylke, beryng in hyr bill a fial ful of creme to þe
byschop. And whan he opynned þat fyal, þer com oute so sote a smel
þat alle þe pepul was gretly wondred þerof and was gretly comforted
þerby, and last so til alle þe seruis was don. Hereby ȝe may know wel,
100 þaw þe prest say þe wordys, þe Holy Gost wyrcheth þe sacrament and
doth þe vertu of þe wordys be halowing of þat þe prest sayth in
hering.

ȝe schul now knele down and pray þe Holy Goste to make ȝow
clenc in body and sowle so þat ȝe mon ben redy to reseyue þe grace of
105 his ȝyftys in clannes, þat God may be plesed.

[39] *De die Pentecostes sermo*

[G]ode men, ȝe knoweth wel þat þis day is callyd Wyt Sonday for
encheson þat þe Holy Goste as þis day broght wytte and wysdam into
alle Crystes dysciplus, and so be here prechyng aftur into alle Crystys
5 pepul. þan schul ȝe knowen þat many haue wytte bot no wysdom. For
many haue wytte to speke wel and teche wel and wysly, but al to few

77 he is myche] be his myght   80 ȝyffe] ȝytte   84 he rehersyth] be rehersyd
[39] 2 Gode] Sode (S- *in blue, dec., 2 ll. deep*)

haue wysdom to do wel. [For þer ben] many wyse techeres, bot, more harme is, al to fewe gode doeres and lyueres. For many travayle bysylych to haue wytte and conyng, bot few travelyth to haue knowing of gode lyving. þus wytte of sleght is makyd myche of, but wysdam of holynesse is noght sette by. For he þat hath [wytte to gete goode he is holdyn a wyse man, but he þat hath] wysdam to forsake goode and bene pore for Goddys sake he is holdyn a fole. Nerþeles, be a man nere so ryche, at þe laste he schal be pore. For noght he bringyth into þis worlde and noght he schal bere oute wyth hym. But þe Holy Gost he bryngyth wyth hym boþe wytte of wyse prechyng and wysdam of gode levyng. For he þat levyth wel he techeth wel, for a gode ensaumpul is a gode doctrine. þis grace os þis day was ȝeven to Crystes disciplus, for þei taght wel and lyved wel, so þat be here gode techyng and gode ensaumpul of lyving þe faythe of Holy Chyrche is spradde alle aboute þe worlde.

þan how þei comyn to þis grace ȝe schal heren. Whan oure Lorde Ihesu Cryste was steyed into heuen, hys disciplus weren in grete care and mornyng and sorowful at here hertys, for þei haddyn loste here | maystir þat þei loued so myche, and haddyn for his loue lafte alle here gode and here frenschep and sued hym pore in hope þat þei schulde han ben gretly holpyn by hym. And þan were þei alle mased and þratte of þe Iewes to ben takyn and kaste into preson and aftyr done to deth. þis made here herte sore and colde and dursnot gon opynly among þe pepul opynly, bot in hulkyng to gete hem mete of somme priuey frendys þat þei haddyn. But ȝit as Criste badde hem in hys ascencioun, þei ȝodyn into þe cyte of Ierusalem, and þere in a houce of stage þei seton infere, preying to God wyth one herte and one spryte for help, socor and comforde in here grete desese. þan os þei weryn in here preyeres, sodenly a grete sownde was made in þe firmament and lyk a grete berste of þondyr, and þerwyth anone þe Holy Gost com amonges hem and lyght on yschone of hem in lyknes of tonges of fyre, os it were þe lem of lyght fyre schapet lek tonges, brennyng not smertyng, warmyng notte harmyng, lyghtyng not frytyng, and fyllyd hem so full of gostly wytte and [wysdam] þat anone, þereos beforyn þei weren bot wery ydiotos and lewed men and ryght noght cowþen of clergy, sodenly þe weren þe wysest and best clerkys in alle þe worlde and spokyn alle maner language vndyr son. And þeras beforen here hertys weron colde and sore for fer of persecucion and of deth þat þei durste not gon, þan soddenly þe

7 For þer ben] *om.*   11–12 wytte . . . hath] *om.*   40 wysdom] *om.*

Holy Gost so schaffet her hertys wyth fyre of love þat anone þei ʒodon and preched Goddys wordys, sparing for no drede of deth ne oþer penaunce bot were fayne and redy to take deth for Cristis loue.

50 þan were þer in Ierusalem, os God wolde, þat day men of alle nacion vnder heuen and werin comyn togydyr into þe tempul for fere of þat berste þat þei hardon in þe hayre and demyd what it myth ben. þan os þei weryn þere, þe apostelys comen into þe tempul and boldely preched þe feyth of Cryste. þan were þeis men gretely astonied and merueleyde þat vchon of hem harde hem speke hys owne langage. þan

55 saydon somme of hem: 'þeise men haue dronkyn so myche of muste—þat is new wyne—þat þei ben alle dronkyn, and so þei mameleth [þ]ey wytte nere whate.' þan answered Seynte Petur for alle hys felowes: 'Syres and bretheren, we beth note dronkyn os ʒe weneth. For it is not ʒitte vndren of þe day and, os ʒe wytteth wel, it is

60 not lawful neyþer to eton nor drynkyn before vndir. But þis was profecyed be þe profyte Ioel how þat þe Holy Gost schulde ben holde

f. 76ʳ oute so plentevously on Goddys pepul þat þei schulde spekyn | wyth alle tonges and prophecion, þat is to say, to prechen of þe ioy þat is to cum to alle þat beleuyn in Criste.' þen myche of þat pepul þat herdyn

65 þeis wordys turnyd to Criste, and whan þei comyn into here cuntre, þei toldyn oþer of þe grete wondres and þe myracles þat þei hadden seyvne and so turnyd many oþer to Cristes feyth, so þat wythine a schorte tyme of ʒerus þe fayth was sprade alle þe worlde.

Now to wytyn why þat þe Holy Gost com in lyknes of tonges rather

70 þan any oþer membur of mannus body, and why to ham syttyng infere rather þan standyng. þan to þe forme, why he com in lyknes of tongys, þis was þe cause: for a tong is þe best membur of a man whyl it is wel rewlyd ande þe werste whan it is oute of rewle. For as Seynt Iamys sayth: 'A tong is fyred wyth þe fyre of helle', and may neure be

75 schastysed wyl þat fyre brenneth hur. And for þe tong moste nedys speke þe wordys of þe feyth, þerfore þe Holy Goste com in tongys of fyre. For ryght os blessed fyre ourecomyth and dryueth away þe fyre of leyte, righ[t]e so þe fyre of tonge[s] of þe Holy Gost schulde dryuen away and ourecomyn þe fyre of helle þat reyneth þat tyme and ʒet

80 doth in mannus tong, and for encheson þat þe apastolus and alle oþer prechorus aftur hem schuldyn spekyn brennyng wordys, þat is, neyþer for loue ne for hate ne drede of deth sparon to tellyn þe pepul here vyse and here synne þat reyneth wythin hem, and seyn

57 þey] ney   78 of ʳ] helle *add. and canc.*   righte] righe   tonges] tonge
82 loue] ne for drede *add.*

boldely þat whosoeure wil not leue hys synne and amendyn hym bot contyneth to hys deth-day he schal wythoute remedy go to þe fyre of 85 helle, and he þat wil leuyn hys synne and amende hym, þagh he hadde syngyd neuer so greuoslyche beforen, he schal go to þe blessed fyre of hevn, þat is, þe precious loue of God þat brennyth among angelus and alle holy seyntus.

Also he com in brennyng tongys, for hit is þe kynde of fyre to make 90 low þat thing þat is hyegh; and warme þat is colde; ande make harde þat is nesche; and mak nesche þat is harde. So þe Holy Gost makyth hye hertys and proude, be þe grace þat he ȝeveth, to be lowe and meke; and hem þat lyggeth colde in envye he maketh hem warme in love and scharite; and hertus þat ben harde [i]n gedering of gode and 95 holdyng he makyth þem nesse and liberal to dele þe pore for Goddys sake and to do many werkys of scharite; and nesche in flesly lustus he makud harde wyth doing of penawnce and streytenesse of lyving. þus is þe Holy Goste besy in alle wayes to makyn salue to alle maner synne and to helyn þe sowle of alle maner sores. 100

þe othyr skyl is: why þe Holy Gost com to | þe postelys syttyng f. 76ᵛ infere rather þan standyng? For syttyng infere betokneth meknesse of herte in vnite of pes and reste, þe wyche a man most nedes haue þat wil be visitud of þe Holy Gost, for to suche he cometh and to none oþer. For ryght os drye brondys, whyl þei lygge togydyr at þe fyre 105 wythoute stering, þei brennyn fayre and lyght, ryght so, whil men ben togydyr wythoute sowrenes and m[i]scheues of malys, vchon loweth oþer and vchone is fayne of oþer, and alle makyth and susteyneth gode tonges. But as sone as þe brandes ben caste in twynne be discencioun and discorde, anone þan þe fyre of lowe quenchyth, and smoke of 110 malys and envye rysyth betwene partyes and greuyth so þe yee of þe herte þat it may haue no grace to sene reson. For þenne is [þe] wykkyd gost redy and boyleth þat herte so in venome of envye þat it may haue no reste nyth nor day but eure þ[e]n[ke]th and stodyeth how he may be wrokyn of hys enmye. And þus is a man browght into plithe to be 115 lorne body and sowle, bot þe Holy Goste sokur and helpe—and alle hys longe on wykkyd tonges. Wherefore þe Holy Gost com in tongys of fyre to brennyn oute of cursyd tonges here malys, and so anoynten hem wyth swetnes of hys grace þat þei schulde leue malys and speke of godenesse, and leue wordys of envye and debate and to speke 120 wordes of pes and reste.

90 in] into   95 in] and   107 mischeues] muscheues   112 þe] *om.*
114 þenketh] þan goth   118 tonges] of *add.*

Whe[r]fore, gode men, ȝe schul so prey þis Holy Goste þat he ȝeve ȝow grace so to tempur ȝoure tonges þat ȝe mon eure spek gode and lyven wele, and þat he fede ȝoure hertys so wyth þoghtys of mekenes
125 þat ȝe may eure ben worthy to be vysyte of hym, as Seynt Gregory was whan he expowned þe profecye of Esechyel þe prophette. þis holy pope Seynt Gregory, whan he expowned þis prophesie, he toke to hym Petur hys dekyn to wryton os he expownot, and makyd to drawen a rydel betwyx hem þat Petur schulde not sene how he dede in
130 his stodying. þan os Gregory satte in hys chayer stodying and holdyng vp hys handys to hewnen, anone com þe Holy Gost leke a colver whyte os mylke wyth fette and bylle of brennyng golde, and lyght on hys ryght schuldyr and put hur bille into Gregorye mowth a whyle. And whan scheo wythdrowe it, þan Gregor bad Petur wryte.
135 Eftesones whan he began to stodyon, þe Holy Gost put hys byl aȝeyne to hys mouthe, and so alle þe tyme tyl he hadde makyd a ende. But for encheson þat he expowned þat harde prophesye so clerkelyk, Petur hadde grete merveyle þerof and thoght þereof to wytton how þat he dydde, and so priuely in þe rydel he made an hole and seyg all
140 how þe Holy Gost fede hym wyth holy þoghtys. And [þe Holy Gost]
f. 77ʳ warned hym how þat Petyr | aspyed on hym. þan Gregor blamed Petur þerfore and chargyd hym heyghly þat he schulde neure diskoure hym whyl þat he were on lyue, ne dyd not. But whan he was dede and heretykys woldyn han brent alle þat þis holy man hadde
145 made, þan [Petur] ȝeynstode hem and tolde opynly how he seygh þe Holy [Gost] fede hym wil he expowned þe prophecye, and so sauid hys bokys vnbrente, *et cetera.*

[40] *De festo sancte trinitatis sermo vtilis*

Gode cristyn pepul, os ȝe knaw wel, þis is called Trinite Sonday and is a heygh principal feste in Holy Chyrch. For þereas oþer tymes of þe ȝere Holy Chyrch makyth solempnite of oþur festes þat ben halowed in
5 worchep of þe Son, os is Cristmas and Astur Day and þe Ascencion Day, and in vorchep of þe Holy Goste Whyt Sonday and þe weke aftyr, but now þis day is halogh in hegh reuerens of þe þre personis in Trinite, Fadir an Son and Holy Gost. Wherefore, os I hope, ȝe ben comyn þis day to chyrche for to do reuerens and worchep to þis Holy Trinite.

122 Wherfore] whefore   124 so] þat *add.*   140 þe Holy Gost²] *om.*
144 man] made and *add.*   145 Petur] *om.*   146 Gost] *om.*
   [40]   2 Gode] G- *in blue, dec., 2 ll. deep*

Ʒete for to styre ʒ[o]wre deuocion þus to þe Trenite, ʒe schul 10
knowyn why, how and what was þe cause þat þis fest was ordeyned.
þis fest was fonde for þre skylles: for þe Trinite fyrste fyndyng, for
heretykkys hye confondyng, and for þe Trinite worscheppyng.
Furst it was ordeyned for þe forme Trinite fyndyng, and þat was,
[os] a grete clerk Ion Be[l]et telleth, þat þe forme Trinite was fondon in 15
man, þat was Adam oure forme-fadyr, as þus: Adam was formyd of þe
erþe, on person, and Eve of Adam, þe secunde persone, and of þem
boþe com a man, þat was þe þrydde person. þis Trinite was þus
foundon in man be worchyng of þe hegh Trinite of heuen. Wherefore,
for þat man schulde haue mynde of þe Trinite, Holy Chyrche 20
ordeyneth þat in weddyng of man and womman þe masse of þe Trinite
is songyn, and at þe deth of a man þre tretus schul be rongyn at his knyl
in worchep of þe Trinite, and, for a womman was þe secunde in þe
Trinite, too tretus schul be ronge. þan for þat Holy Chyrche ordeyneth
suche worchep to a man in mynde of þe Trinite, a man is miche holdon 25
to don honure and reuerens to þe Holy Trinite in heven.
þe secunde skyl why þis fest was ordeynid is in confondyng of
heretekys and to distroyen þe falce opynions þat þei heldyn aʒeynus
þe Holy Trinite, os Lollerdes doth now. For rythe os heretykys in þe
begynny[n]g of þe fayth weryn abowten wyth here smethe wordys 30
[and] plesyng and falce opynyons to ha distroyed þe feythe of þe
Trinite, ryght so now þis Lollardes wyth here smethe wordys and
plesyng to þe pepul bene abowtyn to drawen þe pepul fro þe fayth of
Holy | Chyrche þat holy popys, byschoppes and dotteres taghton and f. 77ᵛ
hath ben holdyn and vsyd eure into þis tyme. Wherefore ryght os 35
heretykys in þe begynnyng of Holy Chyrch pursued holy popes,
martyres and confessoures to þe deth, ryght so now þeys Lolleres
pursueth men of Holy Chyrche and ben abowtyn in alle þat þei may to
vndon hem, if þei myght haue here purpose forth. And so in þat þei
scheweth opynly þat þei be not Goddys servauntes, for þei ben fer 40
oute of charite, and he þat is oute of scharite he is fer from God. God
byd hys servauntes do gode to here enmyes and pray for hem, and
suffyr desese and persecucion mekely and quite not here hele dedus
by no way. But þogh God suffyr Holy Schyrch to ben pursued be
suche mys-beleuid men, eure at þe laste and at nede he ordeyneth 45
suche helpe þat [sc]he hath here grounde forth and here enmyes ben
confounden.

10 ʒowre] ʒewre   15 os] *om.*   Belet] beket   30 begynnyng] begynnyg
31 and¹] *om.*   46 sche] he

þus felle it in tyme of a emperoure of Rome þat hatte Attyla and
was made be counseyle of heretykys, as Ion Be[l]et telleth, to pursuen
50 cristen pepul and distroyen Holy Chyrch. Wherefore alle þe bokys þat
he mythe fynden of Holy Chirch feyth he made to brenne. But þan, os
God wolde, þer was a gode holy man and a grete clerk was called
Alpynyus, þat in mayntenyng of þe fayth made þe story of þe Trinite
and of Seynt Stevne and broght hem to þe pope Alexander to han ben
55 songyn in Holy Chyrche. But þis pope be consel of other grete clerkys
toke þe story of Seynte Steven and refused þe story of þe Trinite and
sayde þat Holy Schirche schulde syng no more of þe Trinite þan it
dyd of þe vnite. But aftyr it fel so þat, for þe malys of þe heretykus þat
rysen so thyk, þat Seynt Gregor þe holy dottvr soght vp hys story of
60 þe Trenite and ordeynyd þis fest to ben halowed in Holy Chyrch and
þe story to ben songyn in confusion of heretykys þat berkuth aȝeyne
þe Trenite. So by halowing of þis fest and be seruys þat is done in
Holy Chyrch þe fayth of þe Trinite is worscheped and loued in alle
cristyn pepul.
65 þe þridde skyl why þis fest was foundyn: for þe hey Trinite
worschepyng and for to know how and what maner a man sal beleuyn
in þe Trinite. For as Holy Chyrche techeth, he þat beleueth wel in þe
Trinite he schal be saued, and he þat beleuyth not he schal be
da[m]pned. þan is it nedeful to vche man to lerne how he schal haue
70 þis beleue. þan schul ȝe knowen wel þat perfyte love to God makyth a
man to comm to beleue, for [he] þat loue[th] he makyth none
aposynges nor questions. Why? For loue hath no lake. þereas he
has no love, he wil make questions and aposayles of suche materes, þat
neure avayleth. For feyth hath no meret where mannus wytte ȝyveth
f. 78ʳ experiment. þan is it gode to vche | man to make love to be mediatour
76 to þe Holy Gost, þat is loue, praying hym so to lyghten hym wythinne
þat he may haue grace to sene how he schulde beleue. Herfore was þis
day sette nexte to Wyt Sonday, hopyng þat þe Holy Gost wil ben redy
to vche man þat wyl calle to hym, and namly in lernyng of þe fayth.
80 But ȝette for many wyttes ben latte and heve to levyn þat þei mow
note sene ne heryn, bot if þei be broght in be grete ensaumpul,
þerfore, þogh þis ensaumpul be not alle commendabul, ȝitte for þe
more parte it may so lython his wytte so þat he may þe sonnar cum to
beleve. þan [þe] ensaumpul is þis: take hede on watyr and one hyse
85 [and] one snowe, how þei ben vchon diuerse in substawnce and ȝit þei

49 Belet] beket   54 and broght] *rep.*   69 dampned] dapned   71 he¹] *om.*
loueth] loue   72 he] is *add. and canc.*   84 þe] *om.*   85 and¹] in

ben bot on watyr. Wherefore be þe watyr ȝe may vndirstande þe
Fadyr, be þe yse þe Son, and be þe snow þe Holy Gost. For watyr is
an element þat hath grete myth and strench and is abouen heven, as
maystyr Alexander sayth, in maner of yse lik to cristal and doth
worchep to heven. And anone it is vndir erþe and þe erþe groundeth 90
þervpon—so Dauid in þe sauter seyth. It is also all abowte þe worlde
and in alle þing, for harde ston and yron sumtyme swetteth watyr.
Wherefore be þis watyr ȝe mon vndirstande þe Fadir þat is so grete of
myght and of strenth þat he gouerneth alle þing, he beryth alle þing,
and alle þing is at hys wille and commaundement. Be þe yse, þat is 95
watyr conielyd, harde and brygel, ȝe mon vndyrstond þe Son Ihesu
Criste þat is veri God and toke þe substaunce and þe freylete of
mankynde whan he was conseyved of þe Holy Gost in þe virgyne
Marie and borne of hure, very God and man, and aftyr sufryd
passioun and deth on þe cros and was beryed and ros from deth to 100
lyve and aftyr stey vp into heven and schal com aȝeyne to deme þe
quik and þe dede on þe day of dome. Be þe snow ȝe may vndirstande
þe Holy Goste. For ryght os snowe comyth of watyr and of yse on
heyght in þe heyre, but how no man can telle, so cometh þe Holy
Goste of þe Fadyr and of þe Sone, bot how we mow not despitoun bot 105
saddely belevyn. þus is þe Fadyr ful of myth, and of hym comyth þe
Sone, and so of þe Fadir and of þe Son comyth þe Holy Gost.

þis Trinite was knowyn in þe folwynge of Ihesu Criste, for, os þe
gospel telleth, whan oure Lorde Ihesu Criste was baptised in þe fl[o]m
of Iordayne and alle þe pepul negh of cuntre was folwod þer wyth 110
hym and weren in here preyeres, and Ihesus praying for hem, þan
heven opned and an hoged lyght com fro heven. þan þe Holy Gost in
lyknesse of a coluyr lyght vpon Crystes heved in syght of alle þe
pepul, and þan þe Fadur of heven spak | þus to Criste and sayde: f. 78ᵛ
'þou arte my leue Sone, þe wyche lykyth me wel.' þus was þe [H]oly 115
Trinite. þan þe Fadur was herde spekyn in hys person, þe Holy Gost
was seyon in hys person, and þe Sone was þere bodyly in hys person,
and ȝitte þeise þree persons ben bot one God. Wherefore it is nedeful
to vche cristyn man and womman to prayen to God bysily to ȝeve hem
grace of vndirstandyng and of perfyte beleue in þe Trenite. 120

I rede þat þe modur of Seynt Edmunde of Pownteney aperud to
hym stodying and layde in hys hande þree [r]ingys, ichone wythinne
oþer, and in þe forme wryton þe Fadyr, in þe othur þe Sone, and in

þe þrydde þe Holy Gost, and sayde to hym: 'My dere Son, to suche
125 fygures take hede and lerne what þou myght.' Whereby we may haue
ensaumpul to be bysy to lerne þe beleue of þe Holy Trinite and know
wel þat, ryght os a ring is rounde wythoute begynnyng and wythoute
endyng, [ryght so is þe Fadyr, so is þe Son, so is þe Holy Gost
wythoute begynnyng and wythoute endyng], þre persones in one
130 Godhed. But for to stody how þis may ben it is bot a foly, for mannus
wytte may neure comprehende it.

I rede of a grete maystur of diuinite þat stodied bysyly to han
broght into one boke why God wolde ben leevot on God in þree
persones. þan on a day os he walkyd be þe see-syde deplyche stodying
135 in þis mater, he was ware of a f[a]yre schylde syttyng on þe see-sonde
an hadde made a lytel pytte in þe sonde. And wyth hys hande wyth a
lytel schelle he clawte of þe see-watyr and powred in þe pytte. þan
þoght þis maystyr þat he was a fole to do soo and spake to hym and
sayde: 'Sone, whereaboute arte þou?' þan sayde he: 'Syr, I am abowte
140 to heldyn alle þe watyr in þe see into þis putte.' þan sayde þe maystur:
'Leue of, sone, for schal neure þou done.' 'Syr,' quoth he aȝeyne, 'as
sone schal I do þis os þou schalt done þat þou arte abowte.' And whan
he hadde sayde so, he vanesched away. þan þe maystur beþoght hym
how it was notte Goddys wylle þat he was abowth and lafte hys study
145 and þankyd God þat so fayre warnyd hym. þis ensaumpul I haue
sayde to ȝow os God hath enspyrid me, wyllyng ȝow to haue ful beleve
in þe Holy Trinite.

[41] *De festo corporis Cristi sermo*

Gode men, [ȝe] know wel þat þis is a heygh fest and a solemp in alle
Holy Chyrch and is kalled þe fest of Corpus Christi, þat is, þe feste of
Cry[s]tes body þe wyche is vche day offered in Holy Chyrch in þe
5 auter to þe heygh Fadir of heuen in remission of synne to alle þat
levyn here in perfite charite and in grete sokor and relese of [he]re
peyne þat ben in purkatory.

þan schal ȝe know þat þis fest was foundyn be a pope was called
9 Vrbane þe ferþe, þe wyche hadde grete deuocioun in þis sacurment,
f. 79ʳ consyderyng þe | grete and þe heygh helpe þat God ȝaf to alle þe

128–9 ryght . . . endyng] *om.*   132 nota *in margin with blue paraph*   135 fayre]
fyre
[41] 2 Gode] G- *in blue, dec., 2 ll. deep*   ȝe] *om.*   3 Corpus] corporus
4 Crystes] crytes   6 here²] oure

pepul be vertu of hys sacurment. Wherefore he ordeyned þis fest to be
haloghed þe þrusday nex aftyr þe fest of þe Trinite. For ryght os vche
cristen man þat wil ben savyd mote nedys haue perfyte feyth in þe
Holy Trinite, rythe so he mote haue ful feyth in þe sacrament of
Cristes body þat is makyd on þe auter be vertu of þe holy wordys þat 15
þe prest sayth þer and be worchyng of þe Holy Gost. þan for þis holy
pope þoght to draw Goddys pepul wyth þe bettyr wylle to come to
chyrch þis day, he graunteth alle þat ben worthy, þat is, very contrite
and schryuen of hure synnes and ben in chyrch at boþe evensonges of
þis fest and at masse and at mateynys, for vche of þeise a hundred 20
dayes of pardon, and for vche oþer oure of þis day fourety dayes of
pardon, and for vche day of þe vtas a hundred dayes of pardon, to
dyron for here mede for euremore.

þan schul ȝe know wel þat oure Lorde Ihesu Criste on Schyre
þrusday at nythe, whan he hadde sowped and wyst how he schulde on 25
þe morowgh suffyr deth and so passon oute of þis worlde to hys
Fadur, he ordeynyd a perpetual memory of hys passyon to abydon
wyth hys pepul. þus he tok bredde and wyne and makyd hys owne
flesse and blode and ȝaf it to hys dysciplus and badde hem eten it and
drink it in mynde of hym, and so ȝaf hem and alle oþur prestys power 30
and dignite to make his owne body of bredde and wyne on þe auter, so
þat vche prest hath of Cristes ȝefte power to mak þis sacrament, be he
gode lyver or euel lyver. For þat sacrament is so heygh and holy in
hymselfe þat þer may no gode man amende it ner none euel man
apeyre it. But þat prest þat is a gode lyver and doth hys office 35
worthyly he schal be wel þat eure he was bore, for [he] schal haue of
Goddys ȝyfte here in erþe þat he ȝaf neuer angel in heven, þat is, to
make Goddys body. Wherefore he schal haue suche a worchep in
heven among angelus þat no tong can telle ne herte þenke. And he þat
is an euel lyuer and wot hymself in dedly synne and is [in] no purposse 40
to amende hym he may be sykur to haue a perpetual confusion and
schame of fendys in helle and ben vndir hem in eurelastyng peyne.

þan schal ȝe know wel þat Criste lafte þus þis sacrament to ben
vsed euremore in Holy Schyrch for foure skyllys nedeful to alle
Goddys pepul. Furste for mannus grete helpyng; for Cristes passyon 45
myngyng; for grete loue schewing; and for grete mede geting.

Furste for mannus grete helpyng boþe in lyfe and in deth. Furste in
lyving, for as Seynt August sayth: | 'Also ofte os a man or a womman f. 79ᵛ

31 to make] *rep.*   36 he³] *om.*   40 in²] *om.*   44 nota *in margin with blue paraph*

comyth to þe chyrch to here masse, God ȝeueth hym seven ȝeftes, and
50 ben þese: þat day hym schal wante no bodyly fode; ydul spech þat day
is forȝeven hym; ydul lyght othes ben forȝen hym; he sal not þat day
leson hys sytgh; [he sal not þat day dye no sodeyn deth]; he schal not
eldon whyl he is at masse; and þe gode angel telleth vche pase þat he
goth to þe chyrch [i]n grete worchep to hym before God.' þis helpe he
55 hath in lyving.

In dying a cristyn man sendeth aftyr þe preste to com to hym wyth
Goddys body for too causes nedeful at hys endyng. On is to sen þe
sacrament of Goddys body and reseyve it, knowlachyng þat he
beleuyth stedefastly þat it is þe same flesse and blode þat Criste
60 toke in oure Lady *Sancta* Marie and was borne of hyre, very God and
man, and aftur suffryd deth on þe cros and was beried and ros fro deth
to lyve and now sytte at hys Fadyr rythe hand in heven and schal com
aȝeyne to deme quike and dede. And so wyth þis perfyte beleve he
armyth hym and makyth hym strong and myghty to stonde aȝeynus
65 þe fendys þat wyllyn assayle hys sowle anone whan it passeth from þe
body in alle wyse þat þei conen to sayen if þei mowen bryngyn hym
oute of þe byleue. þan schal þe sacrament þat he reseyueth makyn
hym so myghty þat he schal ourecom hym and settyn hem at noght.

þat othur skyl is to askyn mercy of Criste and remyssion of hys
70 synnes, havyng ful beleue þat Criste is eure redy to forȝeu alle þat
askyn mercy wyth trewe herte. þis was schewed be ensaumpul whan
he hengyd on þe crosse betwene too thefes þat weron men of cursyd
lyuing and þerfore weren dampned to be dede. þan one of hem askyd
Criste mercy with meke herte and repentyng, and at þe forme prayer
75 anone Criste ȝaf hym mercy and morewyth graunted hym to come to
paradyse þat same day. þat oþer þef wolde aske no mercy for a
prowde herte þat he hadde, and þerfore he was dampned. þan as
Criste þat day schedde hys blode on þe cros in help of mankynde, so
ȝete vche day in þe masse he schedeth hys blode in hegh mede to alle
80 hem þat þis sacrament leveth, for wythoute þis beleue þer may no
man ben sauid.

Wherefore I telle þe ensaumpul þat I rede in þe lyve of Seynt Odo
þat was byschop of Caunterbury. þis bischop hadde wyth hym of hys
clerkys þat beleuyd not perfytly in þe sacrament of þe auter and
85 sayden þay mygh not belevyn þat Criste schadde hys blode in þe
masse. þan was þis byschop sory for here myssebeleve and prayde

52 he¹ ... deth] *om.*   54 in] and   60 *Sancta*] stancta   82 nota *in margin with red paraph*

God ȝerne for here amendement. And so on a day os he was at hys masse, whanne he hadde made þe fraccion as þe maner | is, he saw þe f. 80ʳ blode droppyn downe fro þe oste faste into þe schalys. þan he made a syne to hem þat myssebeleuyd to come and sene. And whanne þei 90 seyon hys fyngris blody and þe blode [rennyng] of Cristes body into þe chalys, þei weron so agryson þat for grete fere þei cried and sayde: 'Oo þou blessed man þat hast þis grace þus to handelon Cristes body, we beleuyth now fully þat þis is veri Goddys body and þat hys blode þat droppeth þere into þe chalys is hys blode. But now pray to hym 95 þat þou hast þere in þi handes þat he sende no vengeans vpon vs for oure mysbeleue.' And so þe sacrament turned into hys forme of bred as it was before, and þei weren gode men and perfyte in þe beleue alle way aftur.

þe secunde cause þat þe sacrament is vsed in þe auter is to make 100 man be ofte seing to han mynde on Cristes passyon in his herte and so to be armode euer aȝeyne þe fende. For Seynt Austyn seyth: 'þe mynde of Cristes passion is þe best defence aȝeyns alle temptacions of þe fende.' Herefore ben rodes sette on heyght in chyrches, for a man to sene it anonesoeuer he comyth into þe chyrch and so be syght þerof 105 he hath mynde of Cristes passion. And so crosses and oþer ymages ben necessary in chyrches, whatte-euer þeis Loleres seyne, for if þei had not ben profettabul, gode holy faderes wolde a dystroyed hem oute of chyrches many ȝeres agone. But ryth os a man doth worchep to hys kyngys seel, note for loue of þe seel bot for reuerrens of þe kyng 110 þat howeth itte, rythe so, for þe rode is þe kynges seel of heuen and oþer ymages of seyntus þat ben wyth hym, þerfore men worchepyth ymagys. For os Ion Belet seyth: 'Ymages and peyntoures ben lewed mennus bokys', and sayth þat þer ben many thowsand of þe pepul þat cowde not ymagyn in here herte how Criste was don on þe rode bot os 115 þei lernyn it in sytght of ymages and poyntowres.

þus to make men to haue bettyr mynde of Cristes passion I telle ȝow þis ensaumpul. þer was a cristyn man of Yngland and ȝode into hethynnesse to sene wondres of þe lande, and hyred a Sarseyne to ben hys gyde. And so þei comyn into a fayre wode, bote alle was stylle and 120 no burde steryng. þan sayde þe cristen man: 'I mervayle þat þer is no noyse of byrdes in þis fayre wode.' þan answered þis Saresyne and sayde: 'þis is þe weke þat ȝoure grete prophette dyed ine. Wherfore on Sonday þat laste was, þat ȝe calle Palme Sonday, alle þe bryddes of

---

91 rennyng] *om.*   101 seing] is to make man *add.*   117 Nota bene *in margin in the long hand*

125 þis wode weren dede for mornyng, and alle þis weke schal ben. But on Sonday þat next comyth, þat ȝe calle Astur Day, þei schal quikyn aȝayne, and þan schul þei alle þe ȝere aftyr fyllyn þis wode wyth

f. 80ᵛ melody of swete song. Wherefore loke | vp into þe treys and see!' And þan sagh he vche tree ful of bryddes lyggyng vpryght dede and here

130 wenges spradde os þei hadde ben straute on þe crosse. Syne swyche byrdes haue mynde of Cristus passyon, myche more schulde a man þat was boght be hys passyon.

þe þridde cause why þe sacrament is vsid in þe auter is for loue, þat men schal be sythe þerof þhenkyn how þe Fadyr of heuen hadde

135 bot on Sone þat he louyd passyng oure alle þhyng, and ȝytte to by man owte of þe fendus þraldam he sende hym into þis worlde and wyth hys owne herte blode wrote hys schartur of fredam and makyd hym free euer but he forfeted hys scartyr. So whyl þat he louith God, he keputh hys schartyr, for God askuth no more of a man bot

140 loue. Wherefore he saythe þus to hym: 'Sone, yef me þine herte, and þat is inogh to me.'

þan take hede and ensaumpul of syr Auberte þat was erle of Venes, þat louid þe sacrament of þe auter and dyd to hit þe reuerens þat he cowde. But whan he schulde dyen, he mythe not resyue hyt for drede

145 of vp-castyng. þan makyd he to clanse hys syde and hyl it wyth a clene cloþe of sandel and ley þeron Goddys body, and sayde þus to hym: 'Lorde, þou knowest wel þat I love þe and wolde fayne reseyue þe, and I durste, wyth my mowth. Bot for I may not, I ley þe on þat place þat is nexte to myn herte, and so I schew þe myn herte and my loue.'

150 And þerwyth in syght of alle men hys syde openyd and þe oste glode into hys body. And þan þe syde closyd aȝeyne hol os it was beforyn, and so sone aftyr he ȝaf vp þe gost. þus loue ȝe þe sacrament of Goddys body in ȝoure lyve and so he wyl sokur ȝow in ȝoure deth.

þe f[e]r[þ]e cause why þis sacrament is vsyd is for grete mede

155 geting to vche man and womman þat perfytly leveþ þerine. þagh he haue þe lykenes of bred and þe taste also, ȝytte he mote perfyttly leuen þat it is very Cristes body þe wyche he toke in þe virgine Marye and aftyr dyed on þe crosse and rose from deth to lyue and now is in heven and schal comyn to deme þe quik and þe dede. þan he þat reseyuith

160 hit and beleuith he geteth hym grete merette, for he geteth hym þe kyngdam of heven. And he þat leueth not þus and reseyuit hytte he takyth hys dampnacion in þe peyne þat eure schal laston.

þan for to schapyn ȝoure beleve þe bettyr I telle þis ensaumpul. I

150 oste] openyd and *add.*   154 ferþe] furste

rede þat in Seynte Gregory tyme was a womman þat hatte Lasyna and
made brede þat þe pope song wyth and hoselled þe pepul. þan on a 165
day whan þis pope hoseled þe pepul, he cam to þis womman Lasyna
and | sayde: 'Take here Goddys body', and þan scheo smylyd. But f. 81ʳ
whan Seynt Gregory saw hyr smyle, he wythdrow hys hande and
leyde þe ost on þe auter and turnyd to þis womman and sayde:
'Lasina, why smylest þou whan þou schuldyst haue takyn Goddys 170
body?' þan sayde scheo: 'For þou callest Goddys body þat I made
wyth myne owne handes.' þan was Gregory sory for hyr mysbeleue
and badde þe pepul pray to God to schew so hys miracul þat þe
womman mythe ben holpyn owte of hyr mysbeleve. And whan þei
haddyn prayed, Gregory ȝode to þe auter and fonde þe ost turnyd into 175
raw flesse bledyng, þe whyche he toke and schewed þis womman. þan
scheo cryed and sayde: 'Lorde, now I leve þat þou arte Criste, Goddys
Sone of heven, in forme of bredde.' þan badde Gregory þe pepul pray
eftesones þat it most turnyn aȝeyn into lyknes of bredde, and so
dydde. þanne wyth þe same oste he hosellod þe woman. þerfore 180
takyth hede what I haue sayde to ȝow and worcheputh Goddys body
wyth alle ȝoure mythe and louith it wyth alle ȝoure herte and beleuyth
saddely þerine, os I haue sayde to ȝow. And þan wyl he love ȝow and
bring ȝow to þe blysse wythowtyn ende.

I rede þat in Deveneschyre besyde Axoburgge dwellyd an holy 185
vicar and hadde in hys paryche a seke woman þat lay alle at þe deth
half a myle fro hym in a towne, þe wyche womman at mydnyght send
aftur þis vicar to come and done hyr hyre rythyns. þan þis vikar wyth
alle þe haste þat he myth he ros and ȝode to þe chyrch and tok
Goddus body in a box of yver and put it in hys spayer—for þat tyme 190
men vsyd syrkotys wyth spayeres. And so he ȝode towarde hyrwarde
and wente ouer a medow þat was þe nexte way. þan os he went on hys
way, or he wyste, þe box schoggod oute of hys bosom and fel doun on
þe erþe, and in þe fallyng þe box opynyd and þe oste trendyl oute on
þe grene. þan he went forþe and wyst notte þerof. 195

þan whan [he] hadde schryven þis woman, he askyd hyr if scheo
wolde ben hoseled, and scheo sayde ȝe. þan putte he hys hand in hys
bosom and sowthe þe box. And whan he fond it notte, he was hogedly
aferde and sayde to þe woman: 'Dame, I schal gon aftyr Goddys body
and heye me aȝeyne alle þat I may', ande ȝode aȝeyne, wepyng sore for 200
negligens. And he com be a wythyn-tre and made þerof a ȝerde and
dede hymself nakyd and bete hymself wyth þe ȝerde þat þe blode ran

185 nota *in margin with red paraph*   196 he¹] *om.*

downe be hys sydes, and seyde to hymselfe: 'þou foule thef þat hast
lost þi creature—þou schalte abye!' And whan he hadde betyn
205 hymself soo, þan he caste on hys cloþus and wente forth.

And þan wente he forthe and was ware of a pyler of fyre laste fro þe
f. 81ᵛ erþe | into heven. þan was he agaste, bot aftyr he blessyd hym and
3ode nerre it. þan see he alle þe bestys of þe [medowe] alle aboute þat
pyler in compas. So whan he com to þis pyler, it schone as brythe os
210 þe sonne. And þan was he ware of Goddys body lyggyng in þe grasse
and þe pyler of fyre from it vp into heven. þan fel he downe on hys
knees and askud mercy wyth alle hys herte, wepyng sore for hys
neglygens. But whan he hadde makyd hys prayeres, he ros vp and
lokyd aboute and see alle þe bestes knelyng on alle here foure kneus
215 and worschepyd Goddys body, saue one blake horse he knelyd bot on
hys on knee. þan sayde þis gode man to hym: 'If þou be any beste þat
may spekyn, I bydde þe in þe vertu of þis body þat here lyght þat þou
speke and telle me why þou knelyst bot on on knee, whyl alle þeis oþer
knelyn on boþe þere kneus.' þan answered he and sayde: 'I am a fende
220 of helle and wolde not knele on nere neþer knee my wylles, bot I am
made to do so a3eyne my wylle. For it is wrytyn þat vche knee of
heven and erþe and helle schal bowe to hym.' þan sayde he: 'Why arte
þou leke a horse?' He answered and seyde: 'I goo þus lyk an horce to
make men to stelle me, and at þat toune such a day on man was
225 hangyd for me, and at þat toun anoþer, and at þe þrydde anoþer.' þan
sayde þis vicar: 'I commawnde þe in þe vertu of þis body þat here is
þat þou goo into wildernesse þere no man cometh and be þere til
domysday.' And so anone he vanyschode away. And þe vikar wyth alle
þe reuerrens þat he cowth he toke vp þe oste and putte it in þe box,
230 and so 3ode a3eyne to þe woman and hoselod hyre þerwyth, and so
3ode hom þankynge God wyth alle hys herte for þe schewing of þis
mirakul.

[42] *De festiuitate sancti Barnabe apostoli*

Suche a day 3e schal haue þe feste of Seynte Barnabe apostly. Bot for
he was not on of þe noumbur of þe twelve apostolus, þerfore hys [day]
is note haloghed bot in diuerse places. Bot in eureiche place it is
5 womman holy and plowes for Goddes loue.

þis man was an holy man, for whan he herde Criste prechen, he

208 medowe] *om.*
[42] 2 Suche] S- *in blue, dec., 2 ll. deep* 3 day] *om.*